RAVE MASTER™

12

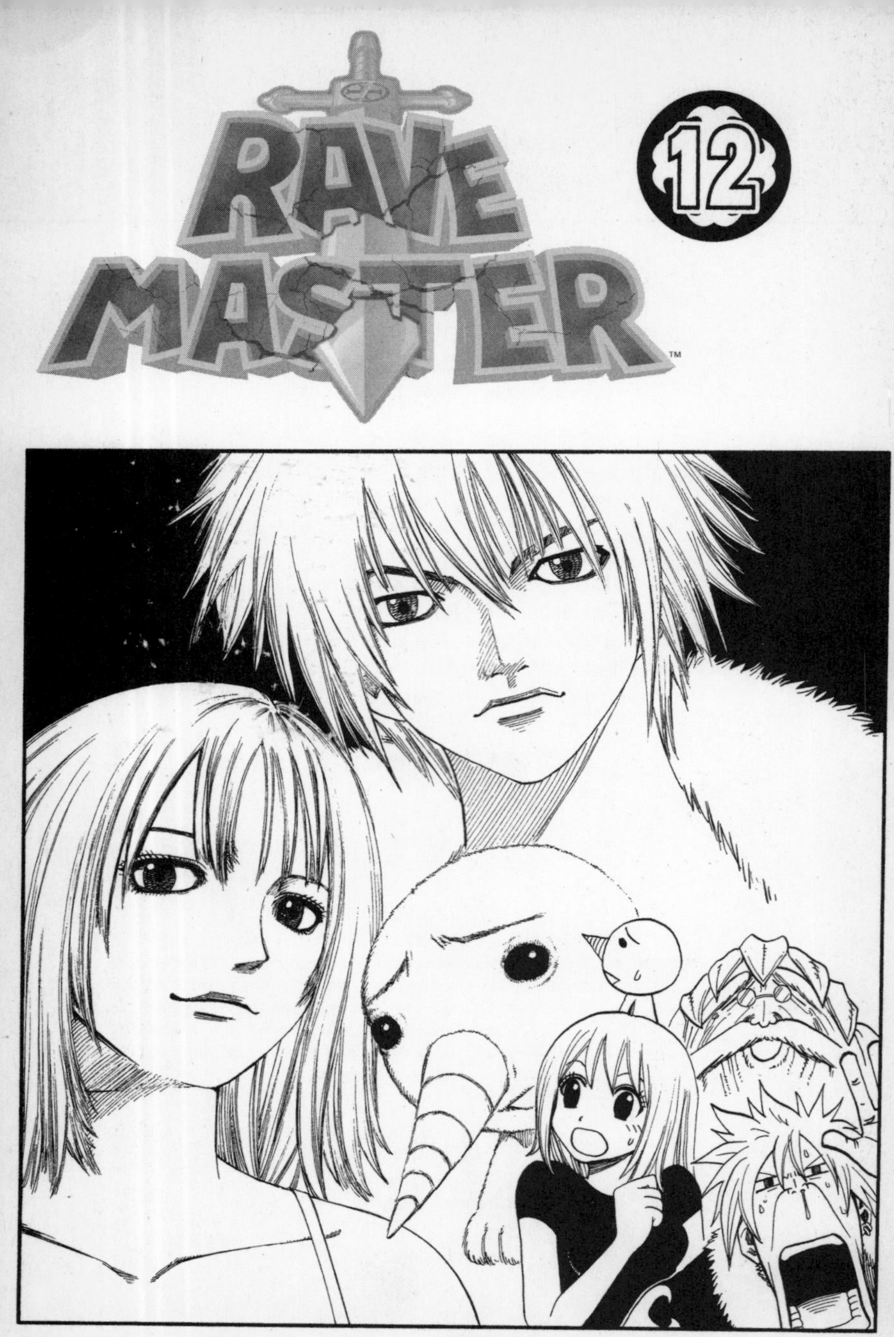

Rave Master Vol. 12
created by Hiro Mashima

Translation - Jeremiah Bourque
English Adaptation - Jake Forbes
Retouch and Lettering - Eric Pineda
Production Artist - Louis Csontos
Cover Design - Raymond Makowski

Editor - Jake Forbes
Digital Imaging Manager - Chris Buford
Pre-Press Manager - Antonio DePietro
Production Managers - Jennifer Miller and Mutsumi Miyazaki
Art Director - Matt Alford
Managing Editor - Jill Freshney
VP of Production - Ron Klamert
Editor-in-Chief - Mike Kiley
President and C.O.O. - John Parker
Publisher and C.E.O. - Stuart Levy

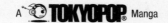

A 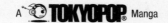 Manga

TOKYOPOP Inc.
5900 Wilshire Blvd. Suite 2000
Los Angeles, CA 90036

E-mail: info@TOKYOPOP.com
Come visit us online at www.TOKYOPOP.com

ISBN: 1-59182-522-9

First TOKYOPOP printing: December 2004
10 9 8 7 6 5 4 3 2 1
Printed in the USA

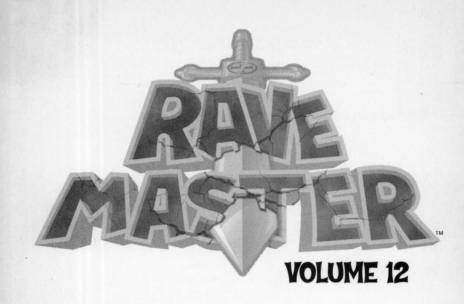

VOLUME 12

Story and Art by

HIRO MASHIMA

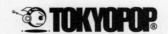

HAMBURG // LONDON // LOS ANGELES // TOKYO

THE STORY SO FAR...

After passing through the Death Storm, Haru and his companions made it to **Symphonia**, only to find the once great capital a **wasteland**. Using Elie as a compass, they made it to a sacred spot where a map of the world appeared. The map showed them the location of the two remaining Rave Stones, but also five dark lights, representing the five **True Dark Brings**. Before they could set out again, Haru's team was confronted by the **Dark Bring Master**-the Blond Demon who escaped from Mega Unit. After a display of power that put Haru to shame, the Dark Bring Master left our heroes to pursue his own stones of power. But it was out of the frying pan and into the fire as no sooner did he leave than the **Oracion Six**, Demon Card's top generals, returned! And this time, they're not leaving until Elie is **DEAD**.

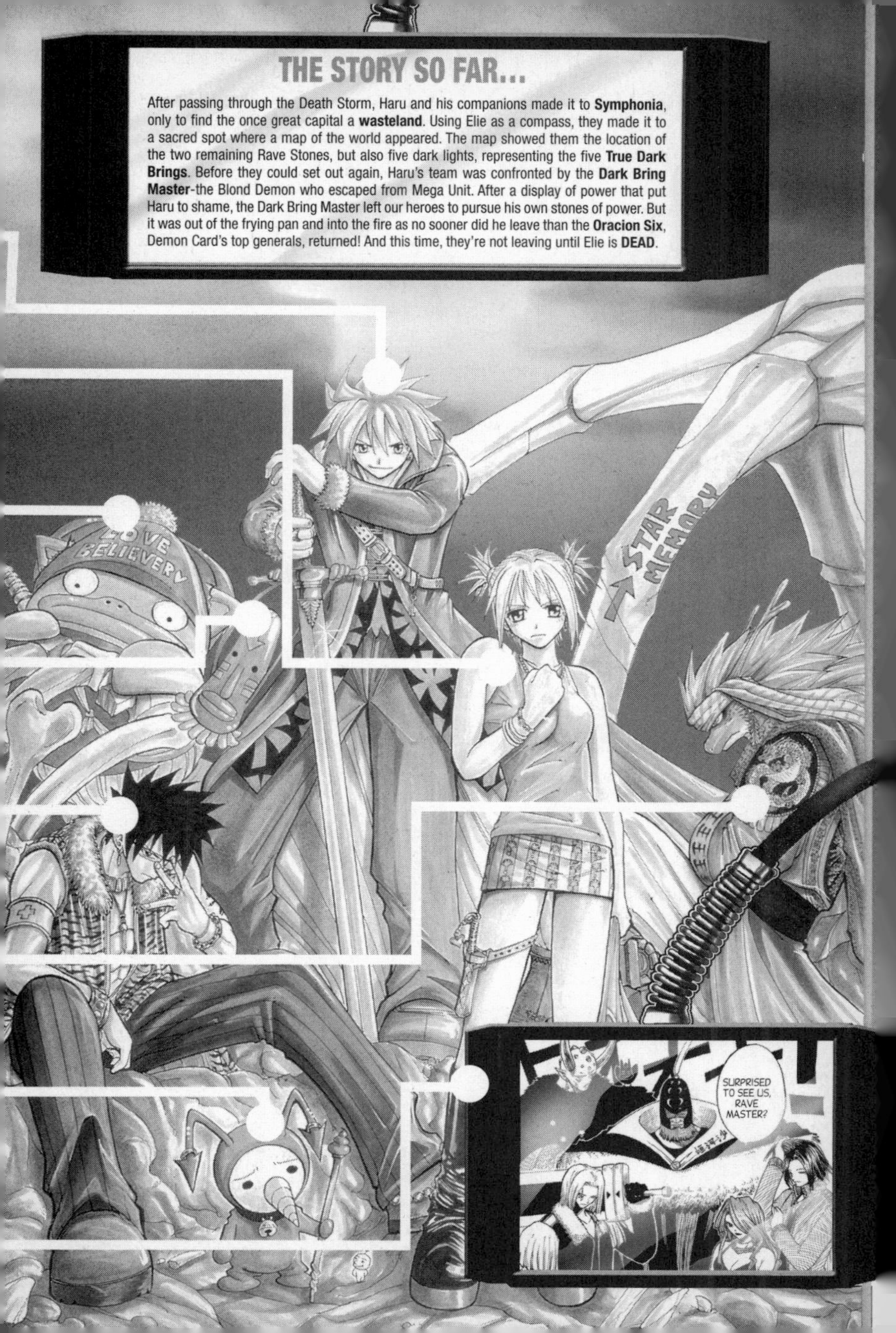
LOVE BELIEVER
STAR MEMORY
SURPRISED TO SEE US, RAVE MASTER?

THE RAVE MASTER CREW

HARU GLORY

A small-town boy turned savior of the world. As the **Rave Master** (the only one capable of using the holy weapon RAVE), Haru set forth to find the missing Rave Stones and defeat Demon Card. He fights with the **Ten Powers Sword,** a weapon that takes on different forms at his command. With Demon Card seemingly out of the way, Haru now seeks the remaining two Rave Stones in order to open the way to Star Memory.

ELIE

The girl without memories. Elie joined Haru on his quest when he promised to help her find out about her past. She's cute, spunky and loves gambling and shopping in equal measures. Locked inside of her is the power of **Etherion.**

RUBY

A "penguin-type" sentenoid, Ruby loves rare and unusual items. After Haru saved him from Pumpkin Doryu's gang, Ruby agreed to sponsor Haru's team in their search for the ultimate rare treasures: the Rave Stones!

GRIFFON KATO (GRIFF)

Griff is a loyal friend, even if he is a bit of a coward. His rubbery body can stretch and change shape as needed. Griff's two greatest pleasures in life are mapmaking and peeping on Elie.

MUSICA

A **"Silverclaimer"** (an alchemist who can shape silver at will) and a former street punk who made good. He joined Haru for the adventure, but now that Demon Card is defeated, does he have any reason to stick around?

LET

A member of the Dragon Race, he was formerly a member of the Demon Card's Five Palace Guardians. He was so impressed by Haru's fighting skills and pureness of heart that he made a truce with the Rave Master. After passing his Dragon Trial, he gained a human body, but his blood is still Dragon Race.

PLUE

The **Rave Bearer,** Plue is the faithful companion to the Rave Master. In addition to being Haru's guide, Plue also has powers of his own. When he's not getting Haru into or out of trouble, Plue can be found enjoying a sucker, his favorite treat.

THE ORACION SIX

Demon Card's six generals. Haru defeated Shuda after finding the Rave of Wisdom. The other five generals were presumed dead after King destroyed Demon Card Headquarters.

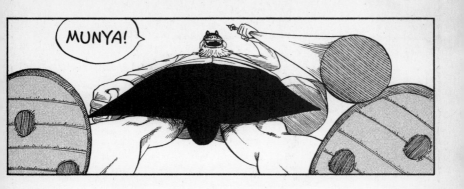

MUNYA!

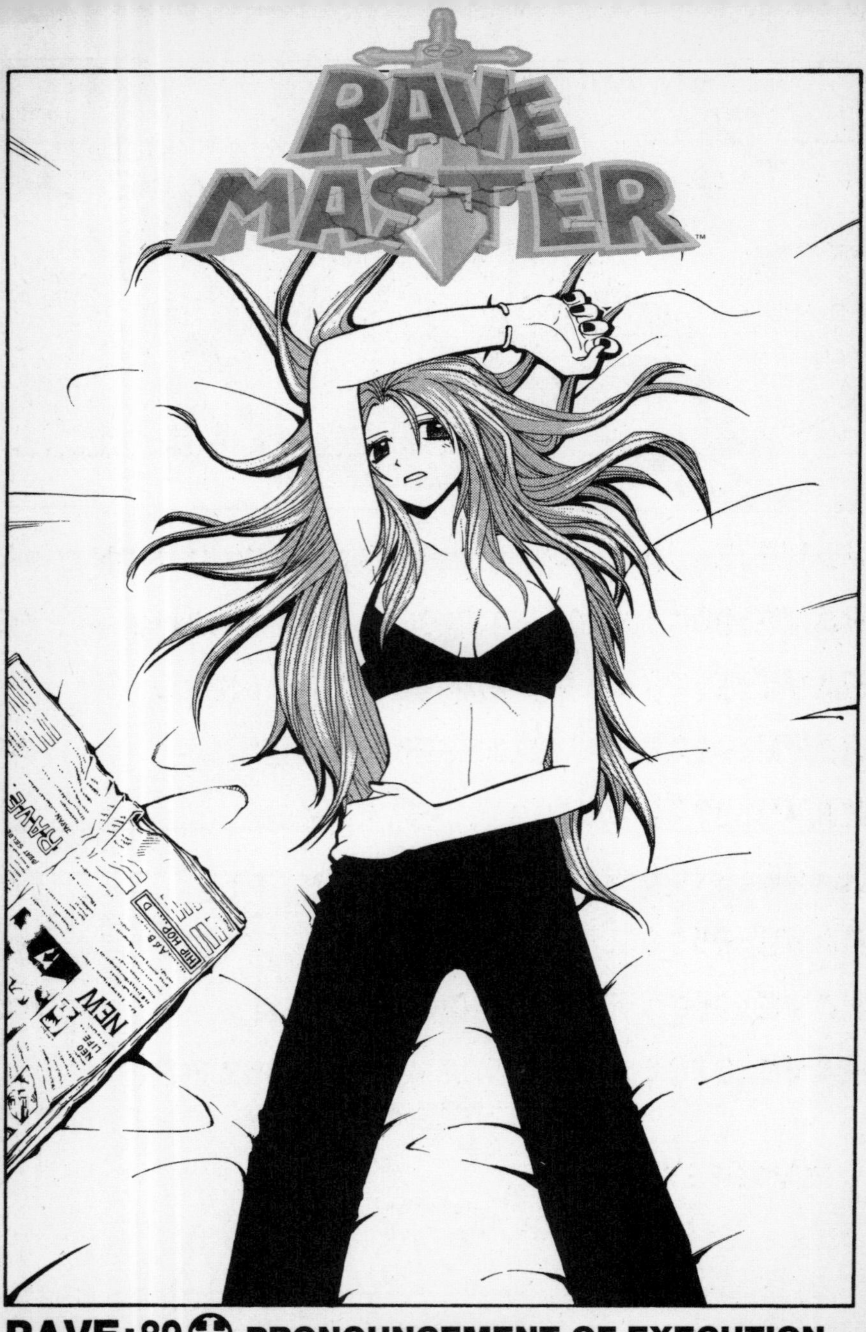
RAVE MASTER

RAVE: 89 ✠ PRONOUNCEMENT OF EXECUTION

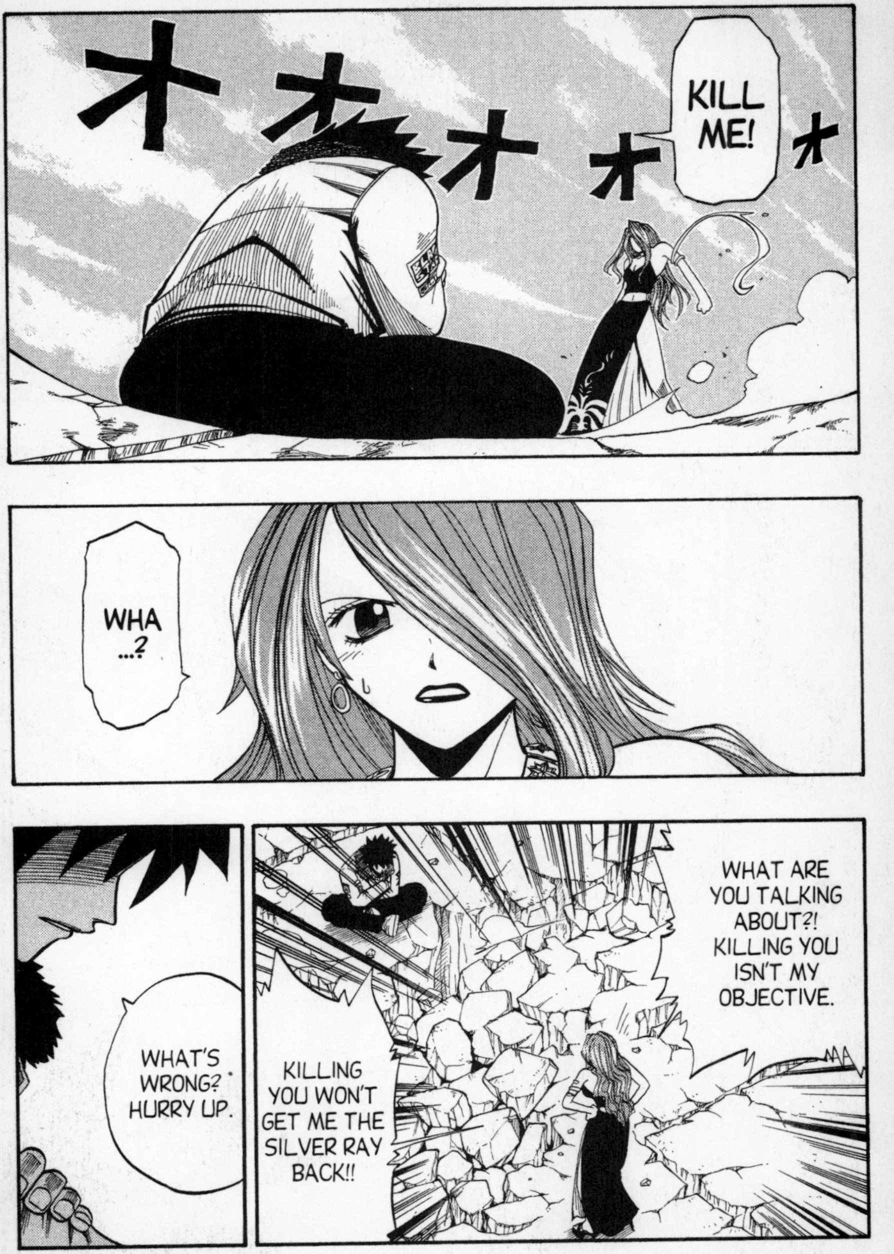
オオオオオ
KILL ME!
WHA ...?
WHAT ARE YOU TALKING ABOUT?! KILLING YOU ISN'T MY OBJECTIVE.
KILLING YOU WON'T GET ME THE SILVER RAY BACK!!
WHAT'S WRONG? HURRY UP.

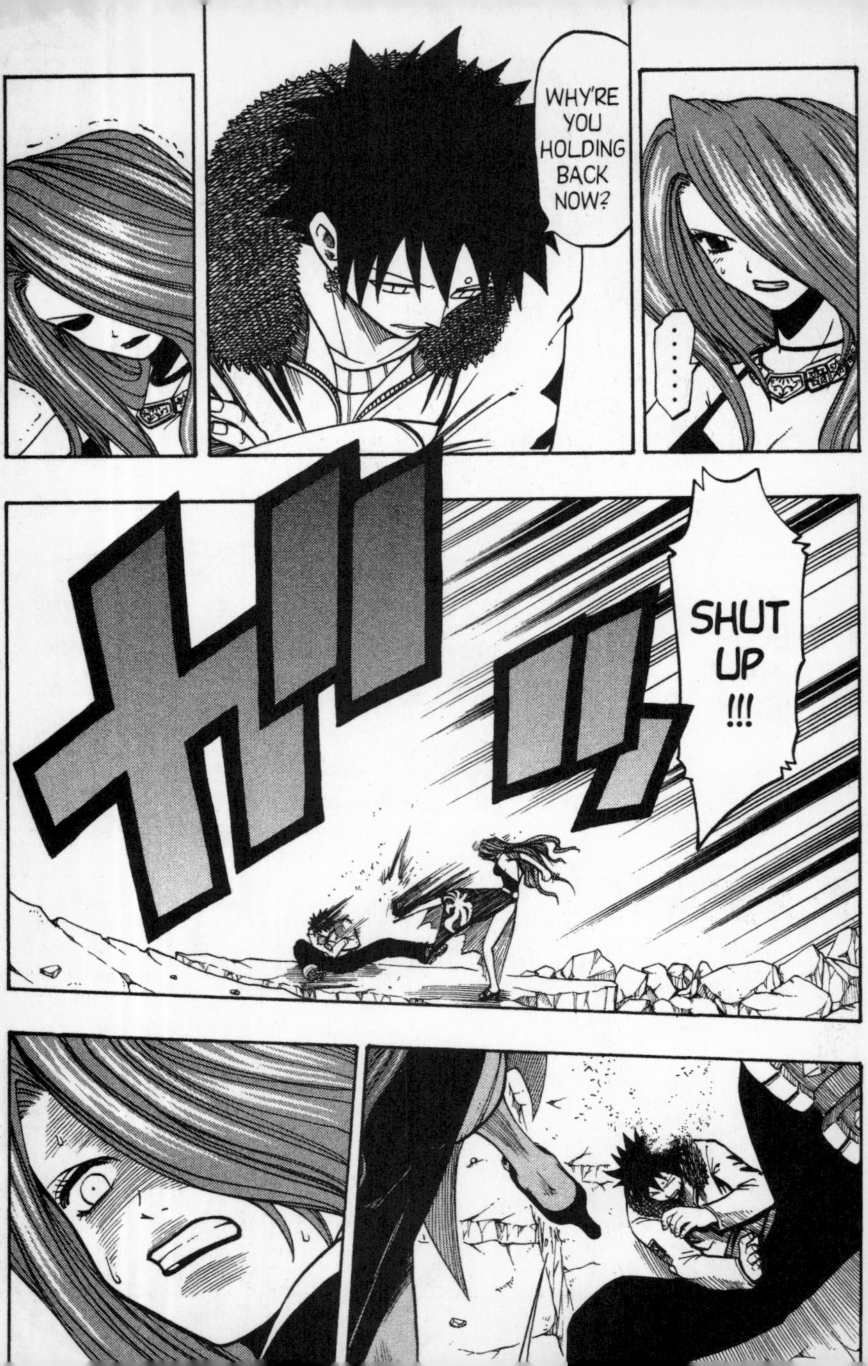
......
WHY'RE YOU HOLDING BACK NOW?
SHUT UP !!!

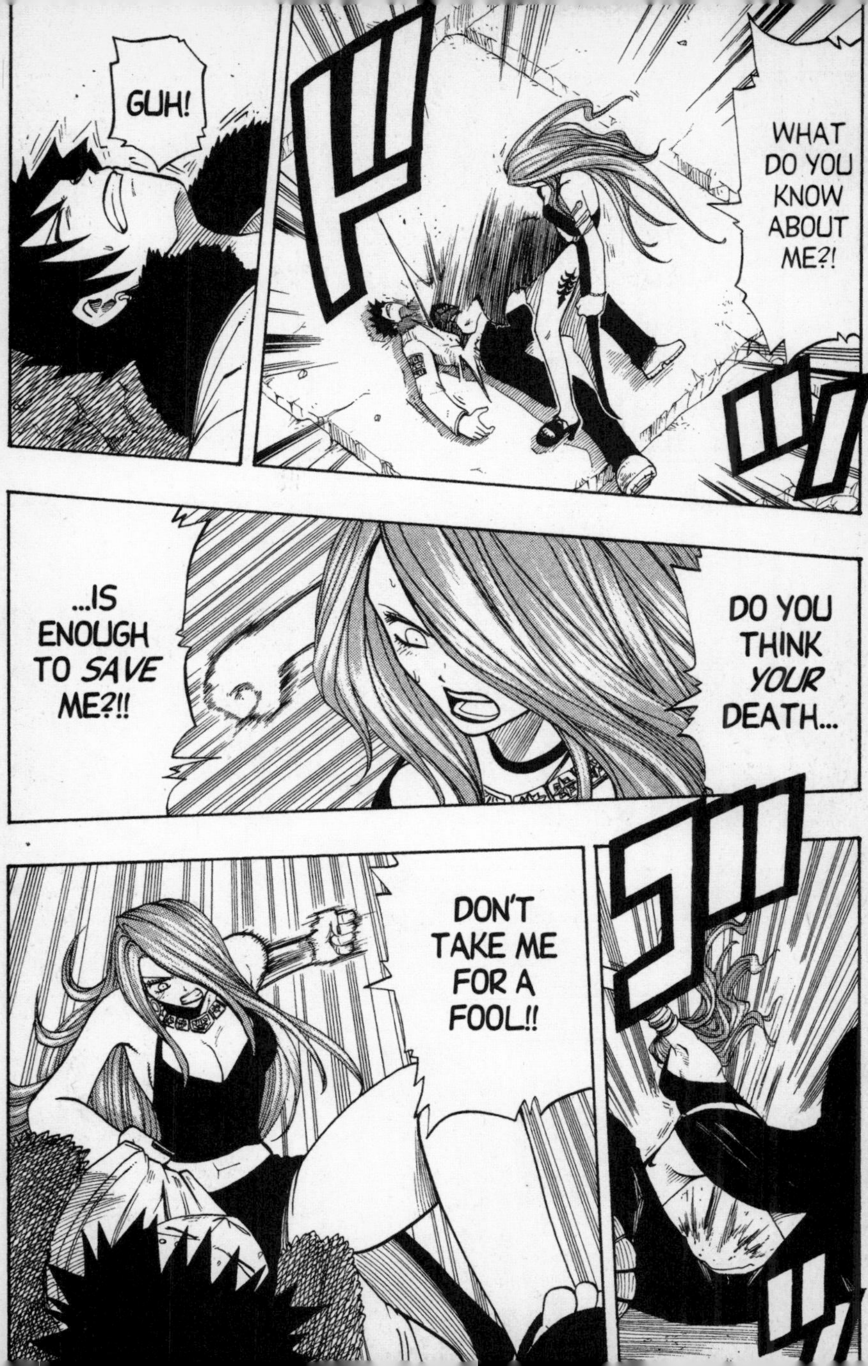
WHAT DO YOU KNOW ABOUT ME?!
GUH!
DO YOU THINK YOUR DEATH...
...IS ENOUGH TO SAVE ME?!!
DON'T TAKE ME FOR A FOOL!!

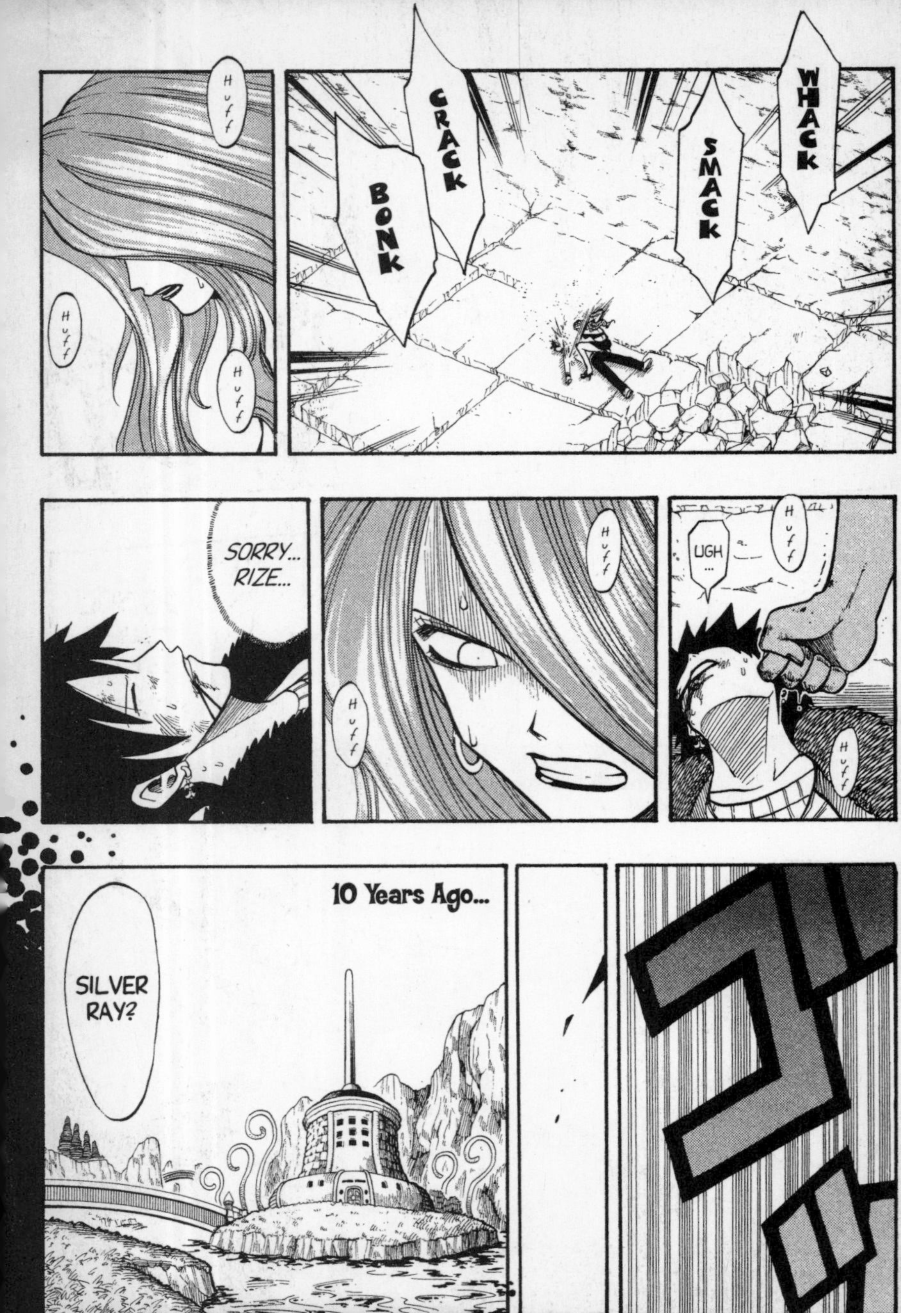
WHACK
SMACK
CRACK
BONK
Huff
Huff
Huff
Huff
UGH...
Huff
Huff
Huff
SORRY... RIZE...
10 Years Ago...
SILVER RAY?

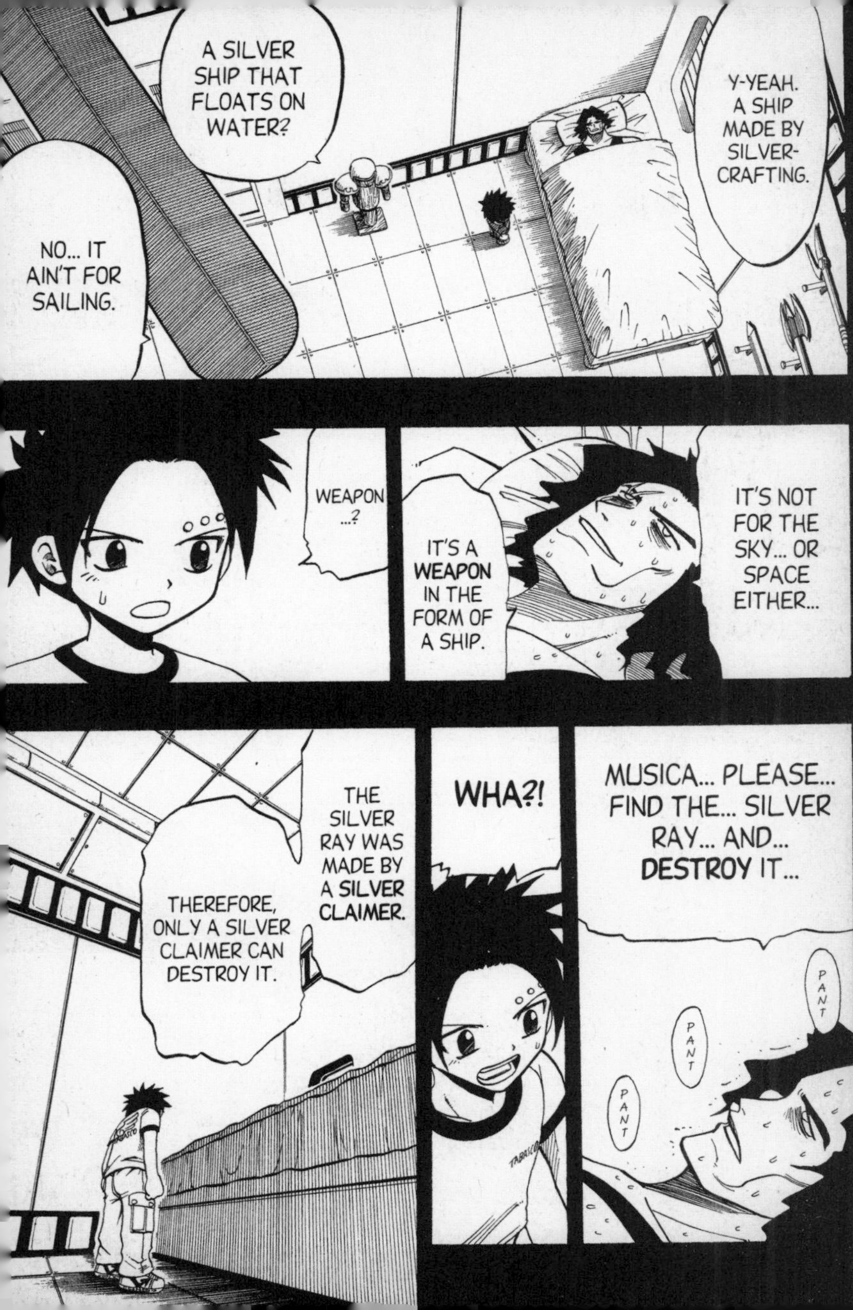
Y-YEAH. A SHIP MADE BY SILVER-CRAFTING.
A SILVER SHIP THAT FLOATS ON WATER?
NO... IT AIN'T FOR SAILING.
IT'S NOT FOR THE SKY... OR SPACE EITHER...
IT'S A WEAPON IN THE FORM OF A SHIP.
WEAPON ...?
MUSICA... PLEASE... FIND THE... SILVER RAY... AND... DESTROY IT...
PANT
PANT
PANT
WHA?!
THE SILVER RAY WAS MADE BY A SILVER CLAIMER.
THEREFORE, ONLY A SILVER CLAIMER CAN DESTROY IT.

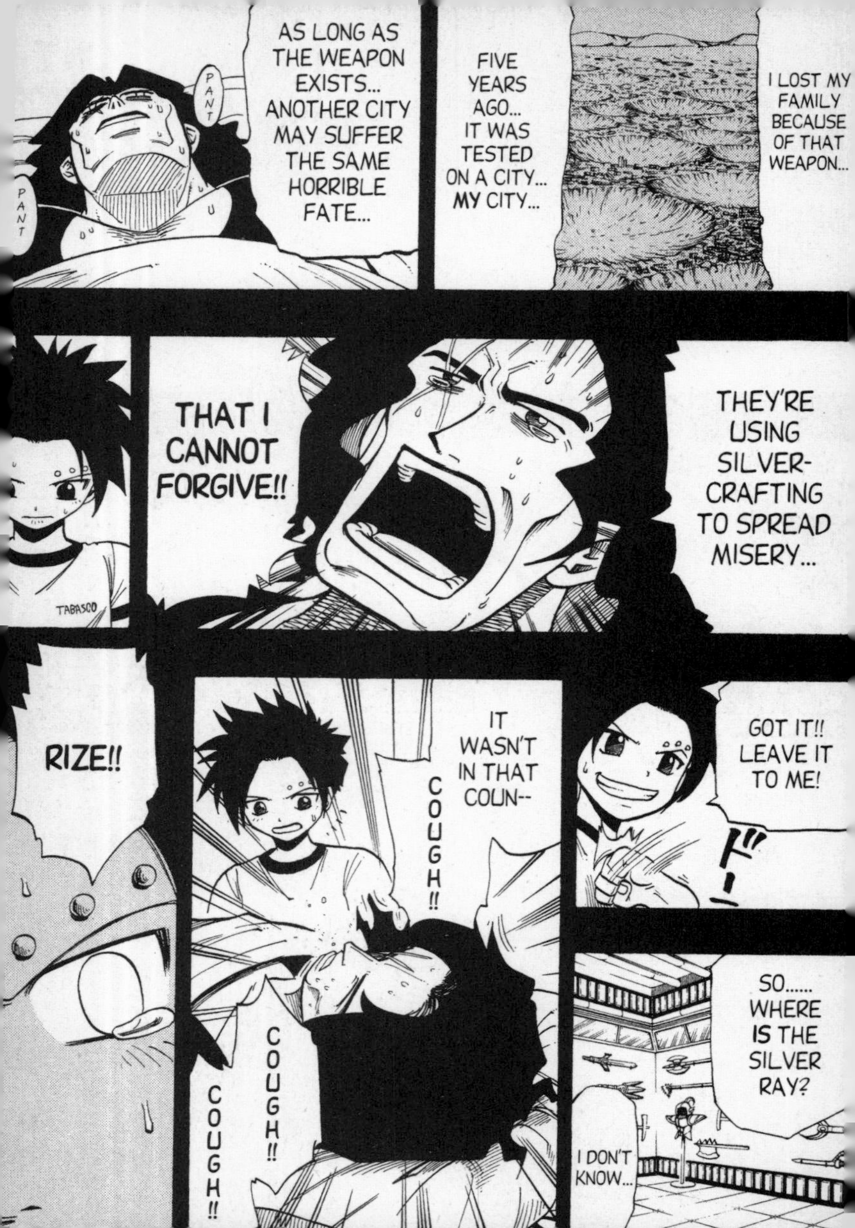
I LOST MY FAMILY BECAUSE OF THAT WEAPON...
FIVE YEARS AGO... IT WAS TESTED ON A CITY... MY CITY...
AS LONG AS THE WEAPON EXISTS... ANOTHER CITY MAY SUFFER THE SAME HORRIBLE FATE...
PANT
PANT
THEY'RE USING SILVER-CRAFTING TO SPREAD MISERY...
THAT I CANNOT FORGIVE!!
TABASCO
GOT IT!! LEAVE IT TO ME!
SO...... WHERE IS THE SILVER RAY?
I DON'T KNOW...
IT WASN'T IN THAT COUN--
COUGH!!
COUGH!!
COUGH!!
RIZE!!

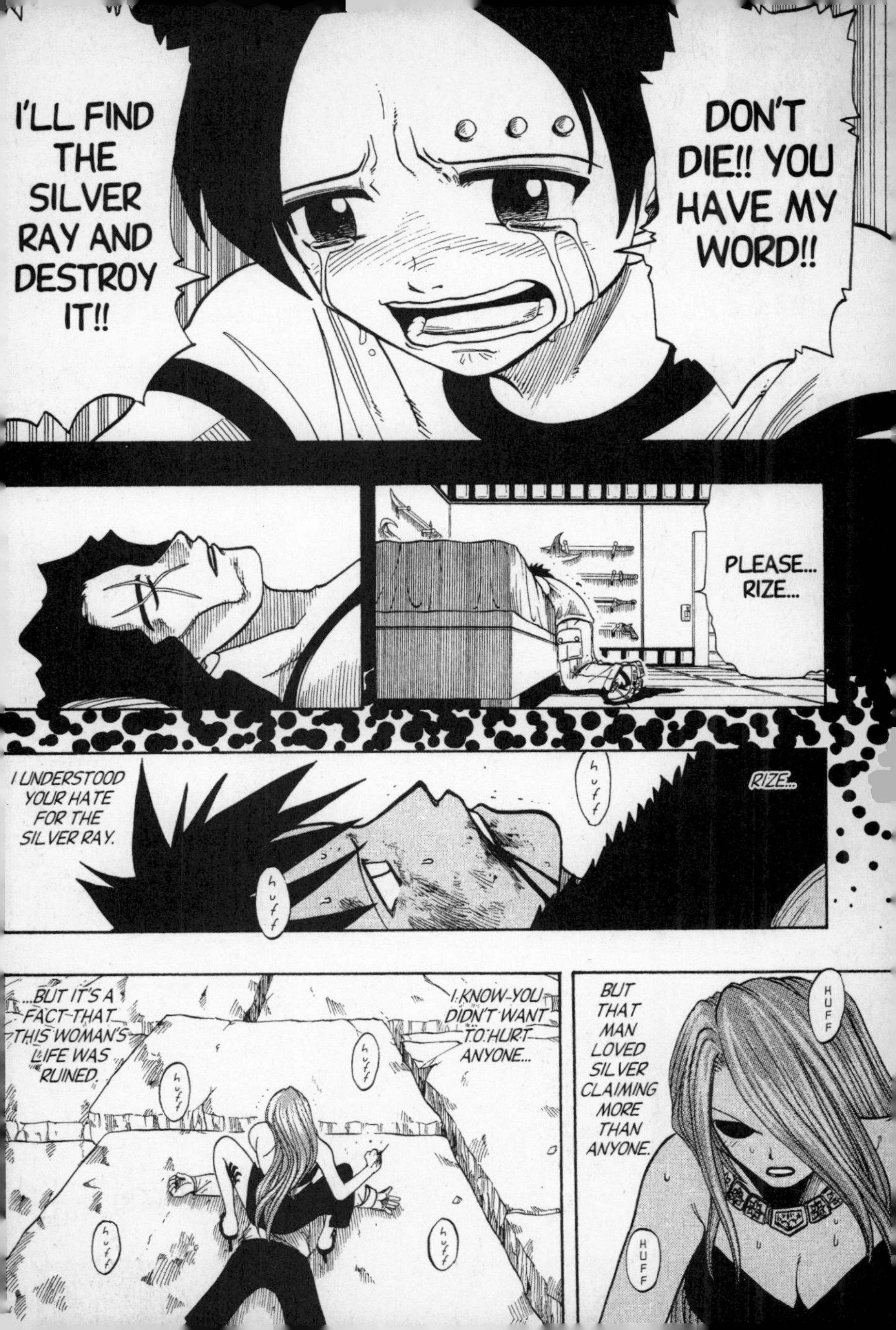
DON'T DIE!! YOU HAVE MY WORD!!
I'LL FIND THE SILVER RAY AND DESTROY IT!!
PLEASE... RIZE...
RIZE...
huff
huff
I UNDERSTOOD YOUR HATE FOR THE SILVER RAY.
HUFF
BUT THAT MAN LOVED SILVER CLAIMING MORE THAN ANYONE.
HUFF
I KNOW YOU DIDN'T WANT TO HURT ANYONE...
...BUT IT'S A FACT THAT THIS WOMAN'S LIFE WAS RUINED.
huff
huff
huff
huff

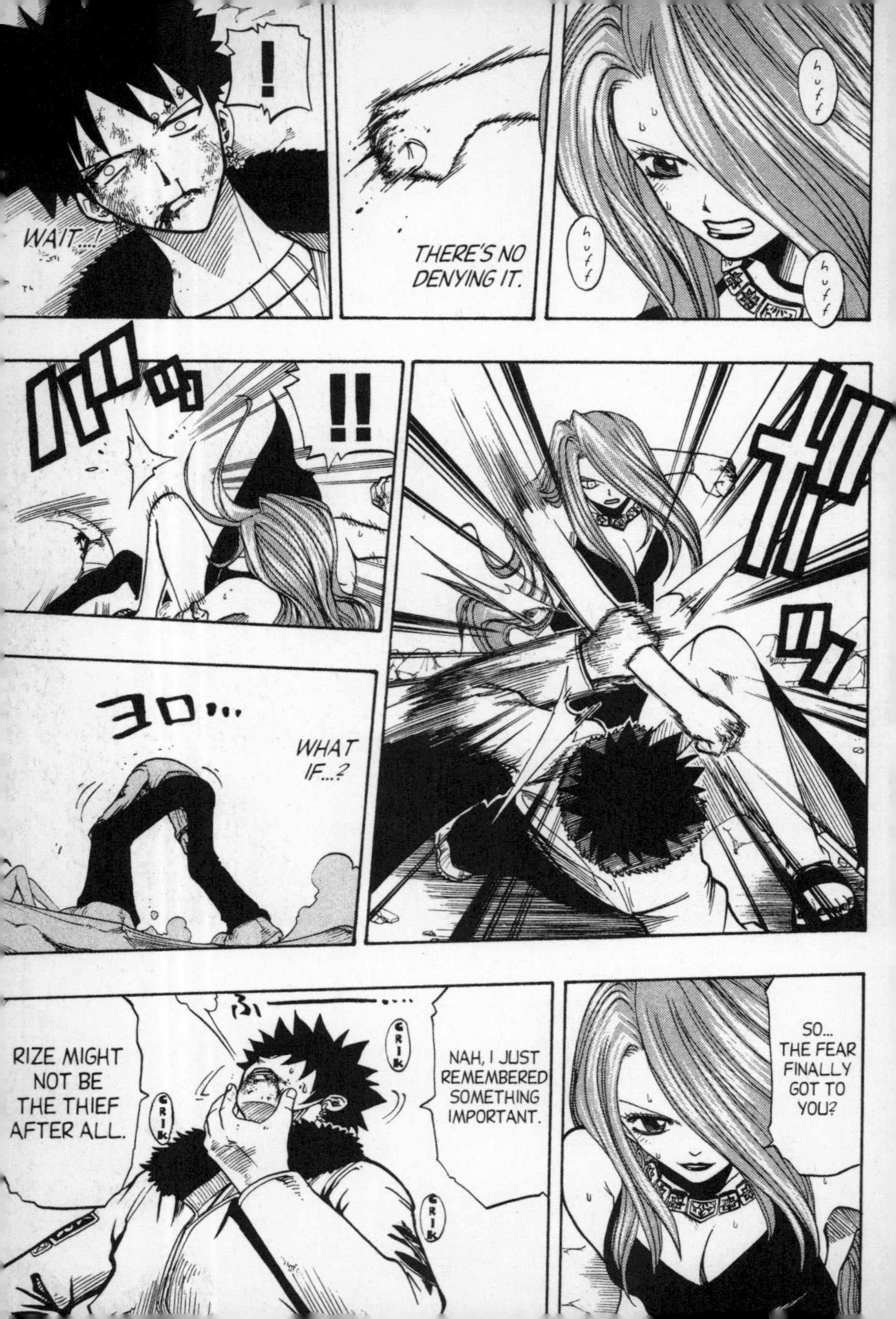
huff
huff
huff
THERE'S NO DENYING IT.
!
WAIT...!
ガッ
ハッ
!!
ヨロ...
WHAT IF...?
SO... THE FEAR FINALLY GOT TO YOU?
CRIK
NAH, I JUST REMEMBERED SOMETHING IMPORTANT.
ふ——....
CRIK
CRIK
RIZE MIGHT NOT BE THE THIEF AFTER ALL.

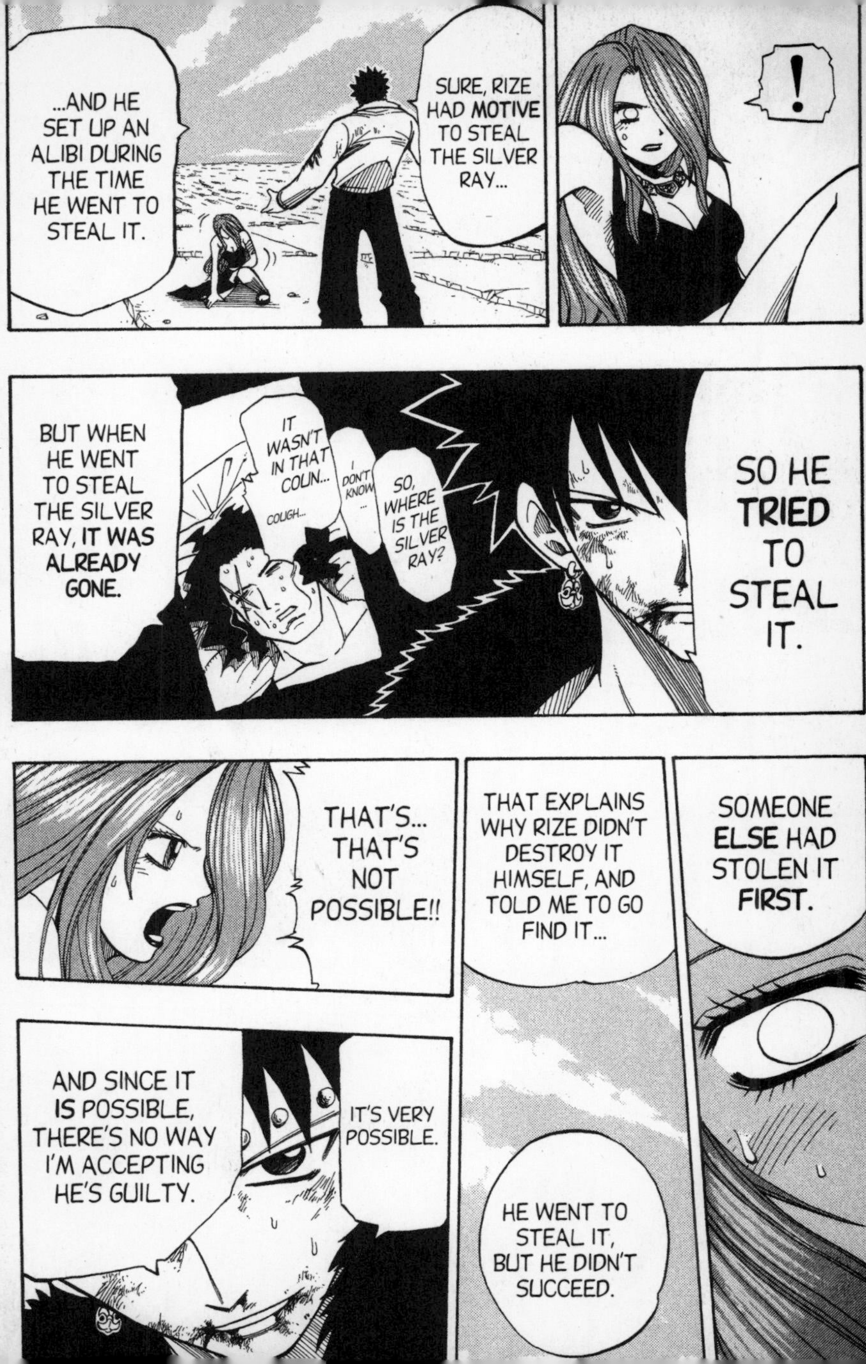
!
SURE, RIZE HAD MOTIVE TO STEAL THE SILVER RAY...
...AND HE SET UP AN ALIBI DURING THE TIME HE WENT TO STEAL IT.
SO HE TRIED TO STEAL IT.
SO, WHERE IS THE SILVER RAY?
I DON'T KNOW...
IT WASN'T IN THAT COUN...
COUGH...
BUT WHEN HE WENT TO STEAL THE SILVER RAY, IT WAS ALREADY GONE.
SOMEONE ELSE HAD STOLEN IT FIRST.
THAT EXPLAINS WHY RIZE DIDN'T DESTROY IT HIMSELF, AND TOLD ME TO GO FIND IT...
HE WENT TO STEAL IT, BUT HE DIDN'T SUCCEED.
THAT'S... THAT'S NOT POSSIBLE!!
IT'S VERY POSSIBLE.
AND SINCE IT IS POSSIBLE, THERE'S NO WAY I'M ACCEPTING HE'S GUILTY.

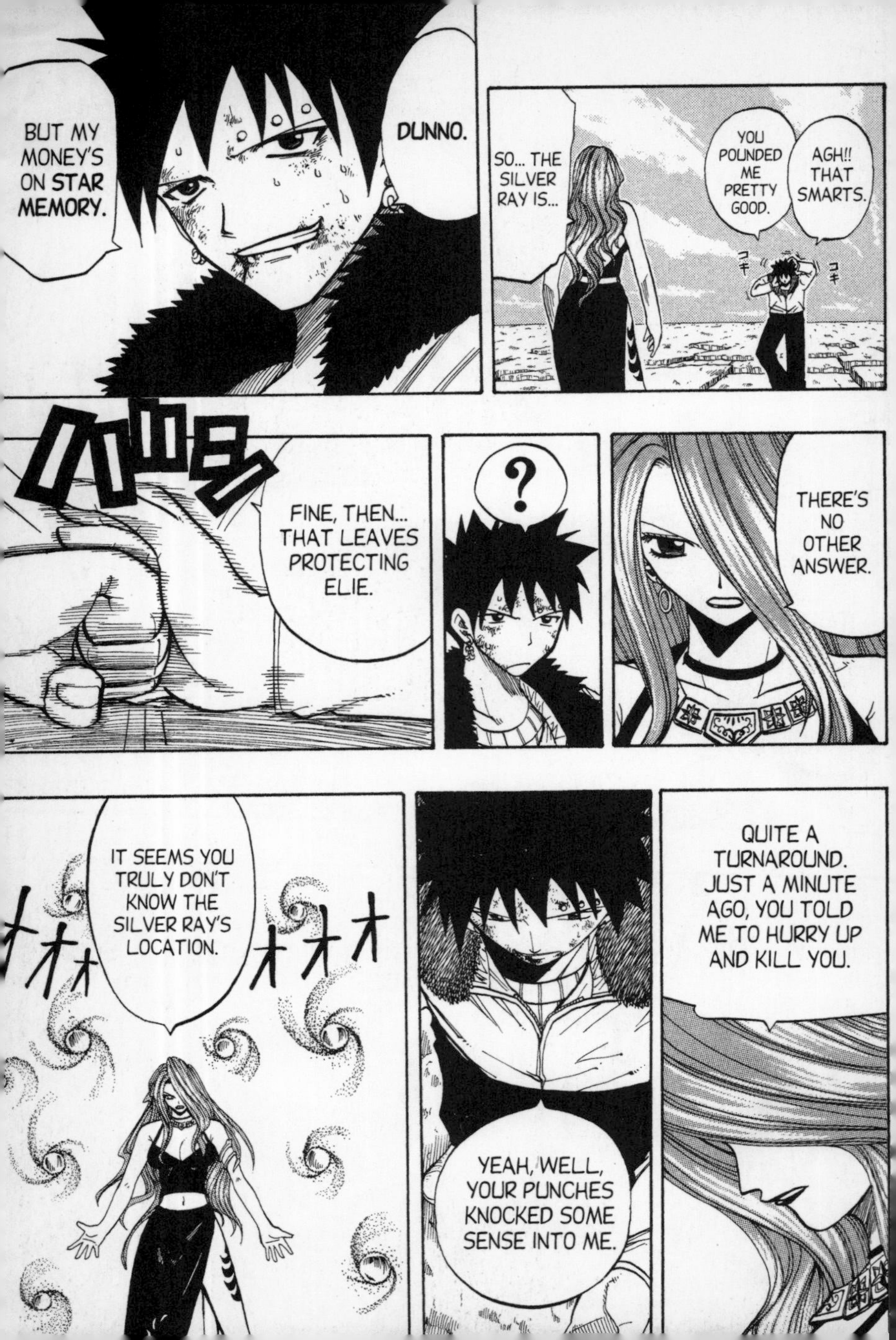
AGH!! THAT SMARTS.
YOU POUNDED ME PRETTY GOOD.
コキ
コキ
SO... THE SILVER RAY IS...
DUNNO.
BUT MY MONEY'S ON STAR MEMORY.
THERE'S NO OTHER ANSWER.
?
FINE, THEN... THAT LEAVES PROTECTING ELIE.
QUITE A TURNAROUND. JUST A MINUTE AGO, YOU TOLD ME TO HURRY UP AND KILL YOU.
YEAH, WELL, YOUR PUNCHES KNOCKED SOME SENSE INTO ME.
オオオ
IT SEEMS YOU TRULY DON'T KNOW THE SILVER RAY'S LOCATION.
オオオ

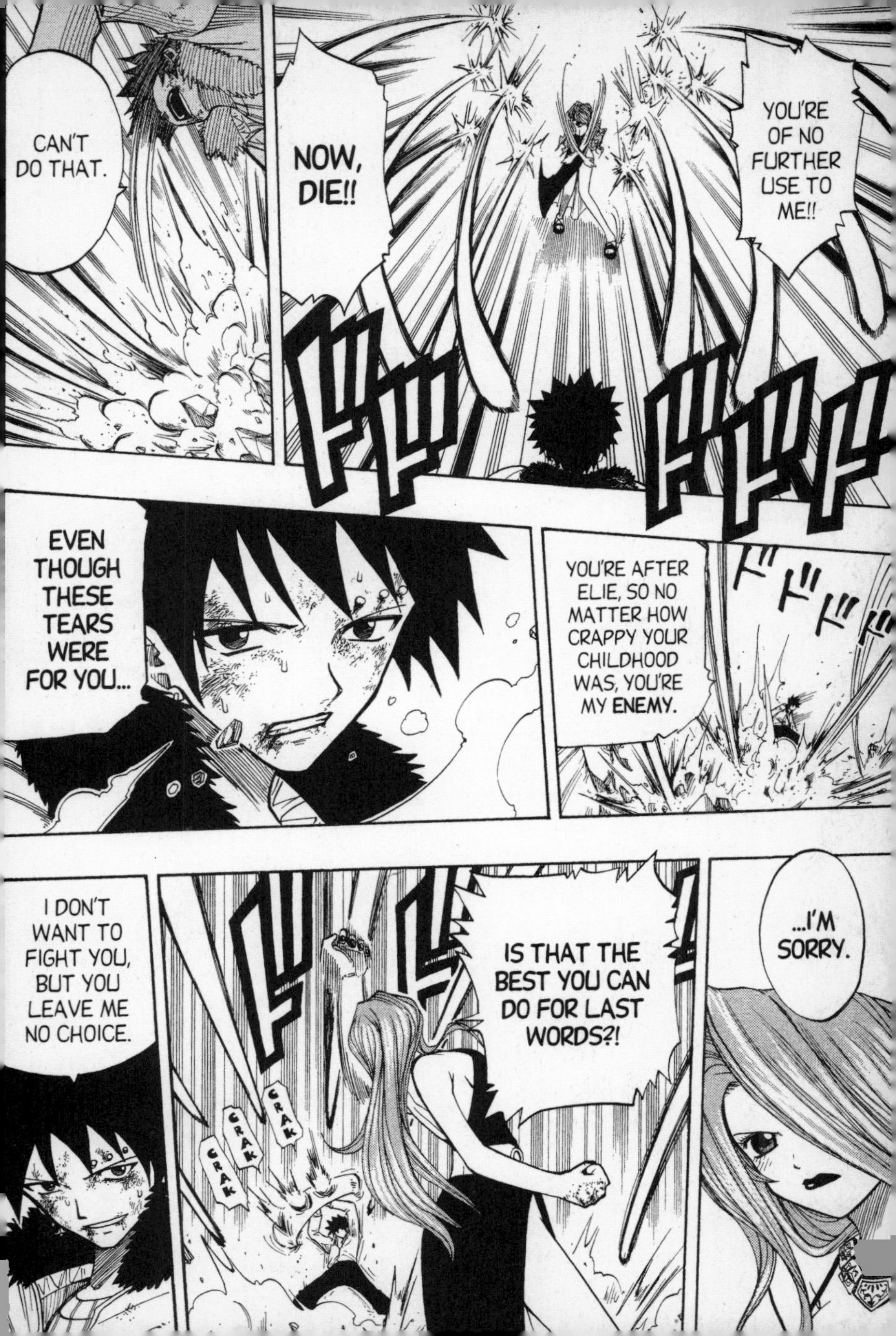
YOU'RE OF NO FURTHER USE TO ME!!
NOW, DIE!!
CAN'T DO THAT.
YOU'RE AFTER ELIE, SO NO MATTER HOW CRAPPY YOUR CHILDHOOD WAS, YOU'RE MY ENEMY.
EVEN THOUGH THESE TEARS WERE FOR YOU...
...I'M SORRY.
IS THAT THE BEST YOU CAN DO FOR LAST WORDS?!
CRAK
CRAK
CRAK
I DON'T WANT TO FIGHT YOU, BUT YOU LEAVE ME NO CHOICE.

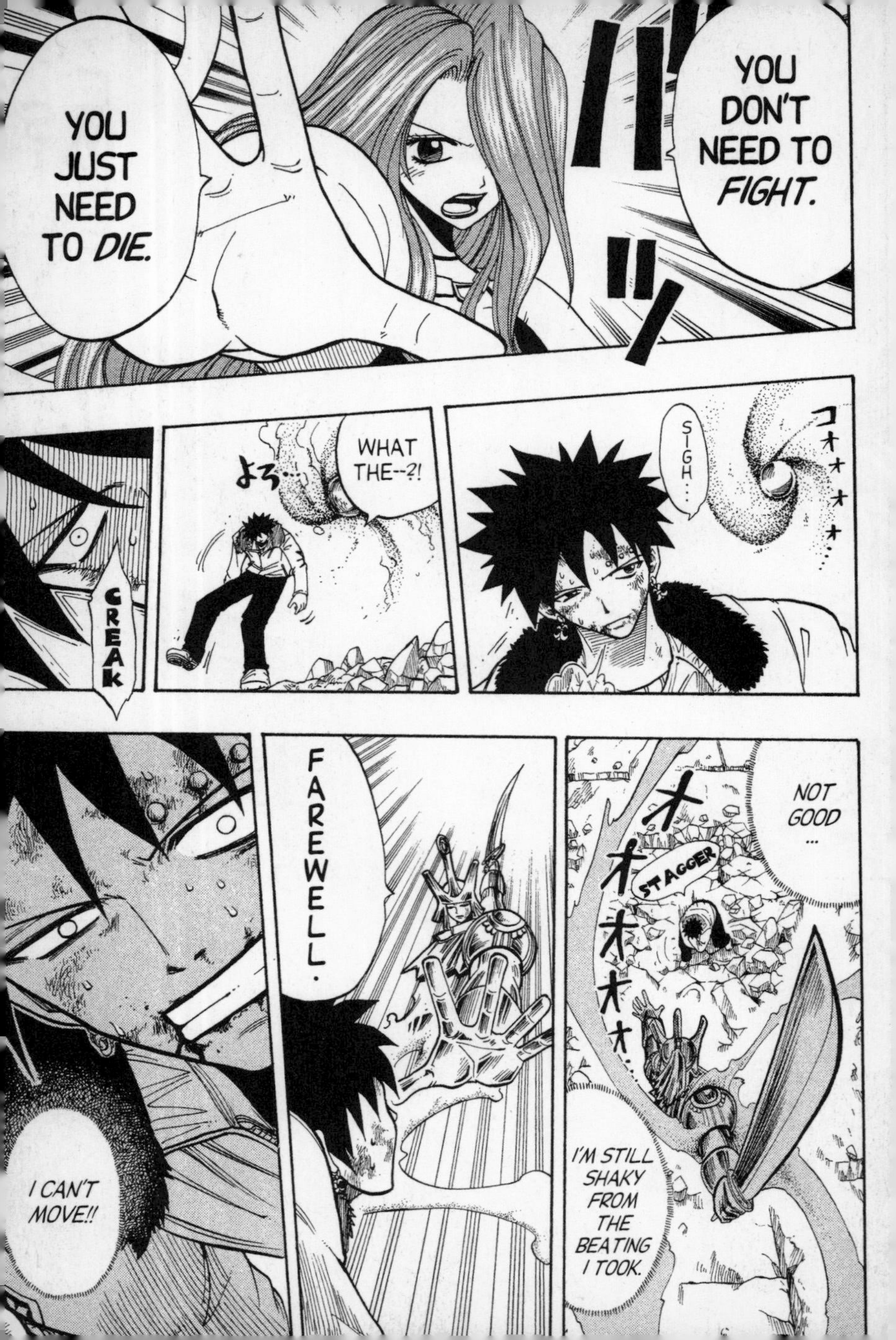
YOU DON'T NEED TO *FIGHT*.
YOU JUST NEED TO *DIE*.
コォォォォ…
SIGH…
よろ…!
WHAT THE--?!
CREAK
NOT GOOD…
STAGGER
I'M STILL SHAKY FROM THE BEATING I TOOK.
FAREWELL.
I CAN'T MOVE!!

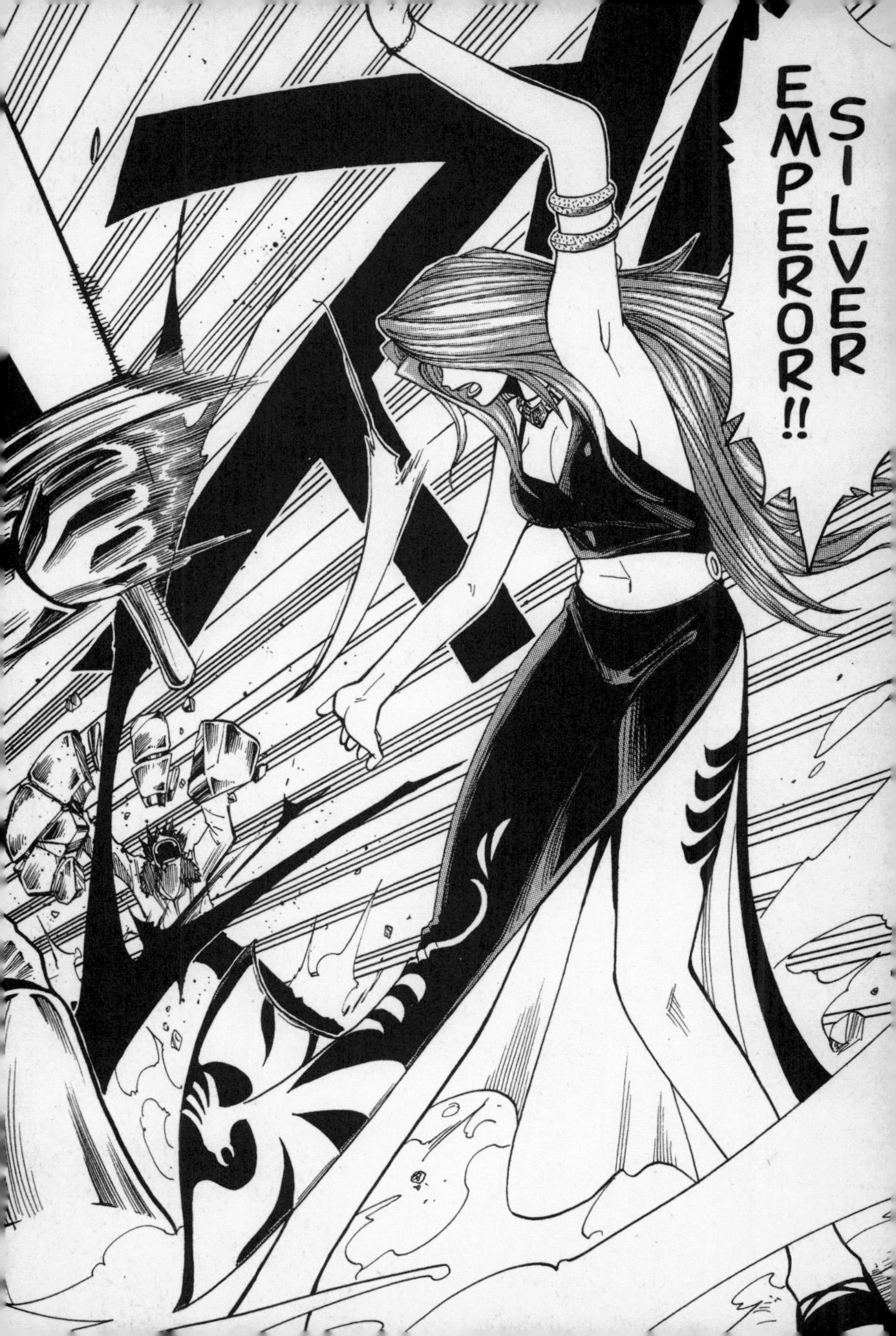
SILVER EMPEROR!!

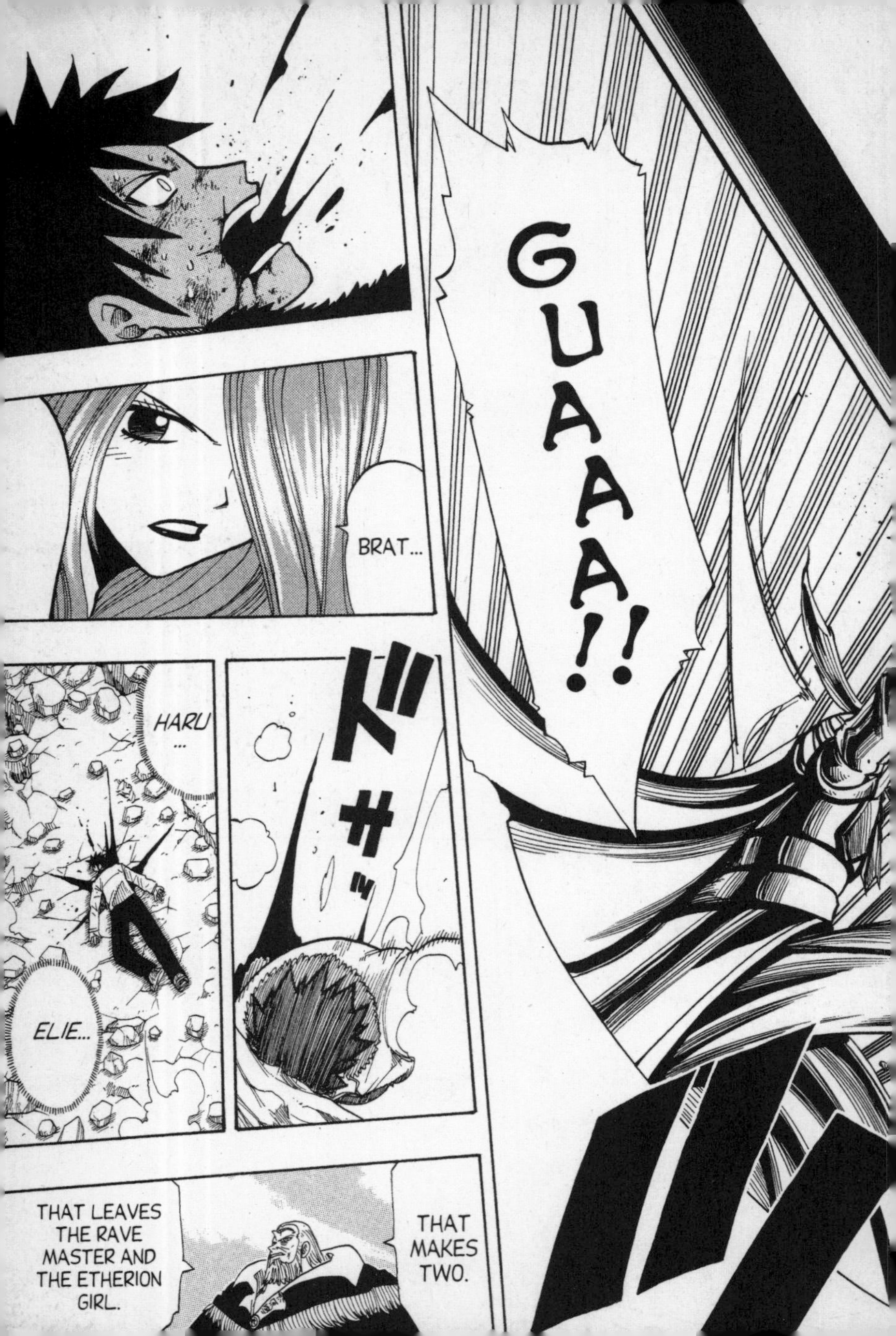
GUAAA!!
BRAT...
ドザッ
HARU...
ELIE...
THAT MAKES TWO.
THAT LEAVES THE RAVE MASTER AND THE ETHERION GIRL.

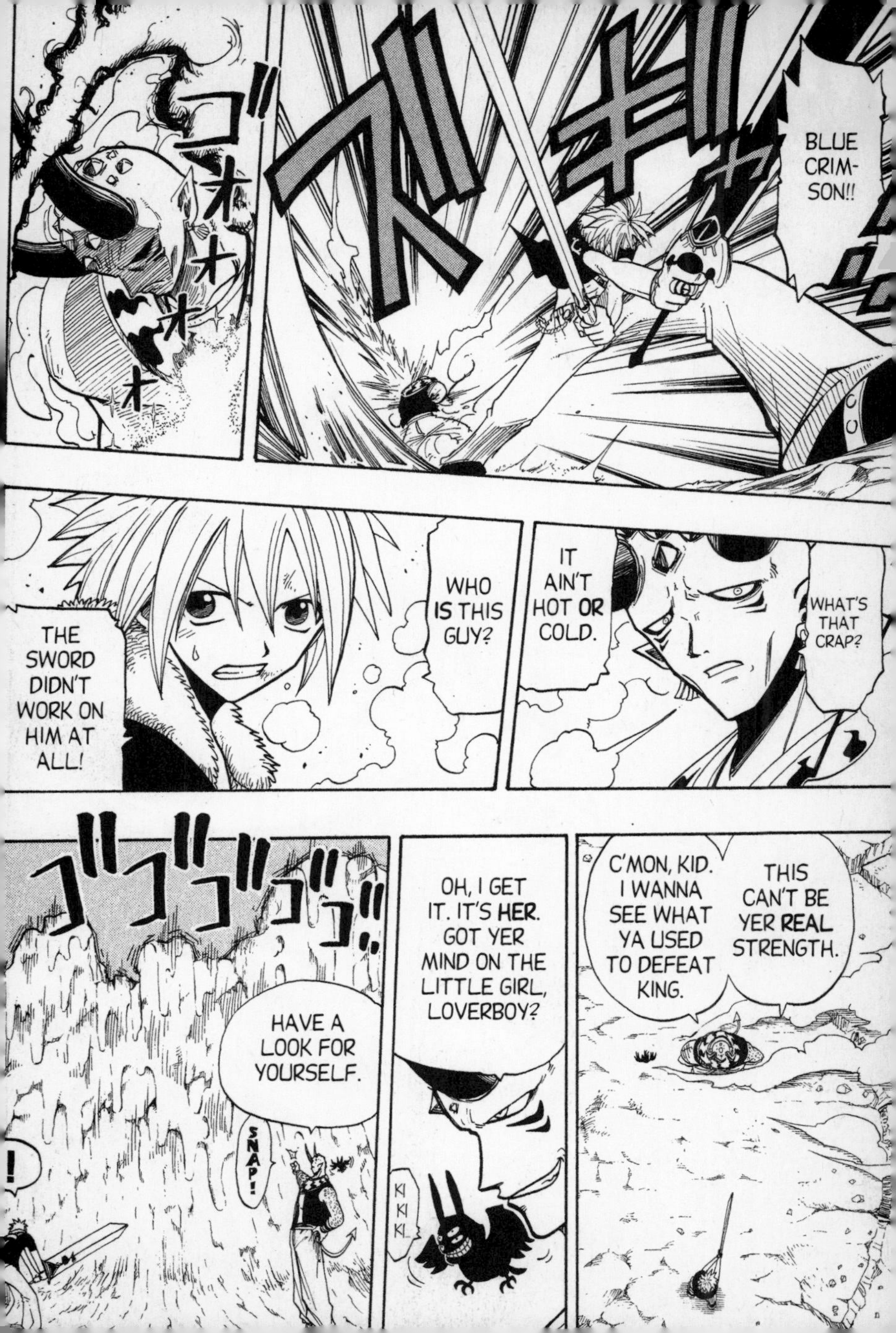
BLUE CRIM-SON!!
WHAT'S THAT CRAP?
IT AIN'T HOT **OR** COLD.
WHO **IS** THIS GUY?
THE SWORD DIDN'T WORK ON HIM AT ALL!
THIS CAN'T BE YER **REAL** STRENGTH.
C'MON, KID. I WANNA SEE WHAT YA USED TO DEFEAT KING.
OH, I GET IT. IT'S **HER**. GOT YER MIND ON THE LITTLE GIRL, LOVERBOY?
KI KI KI...
HAVE A LOOK FOR YOURSELF.
SNAP!
!

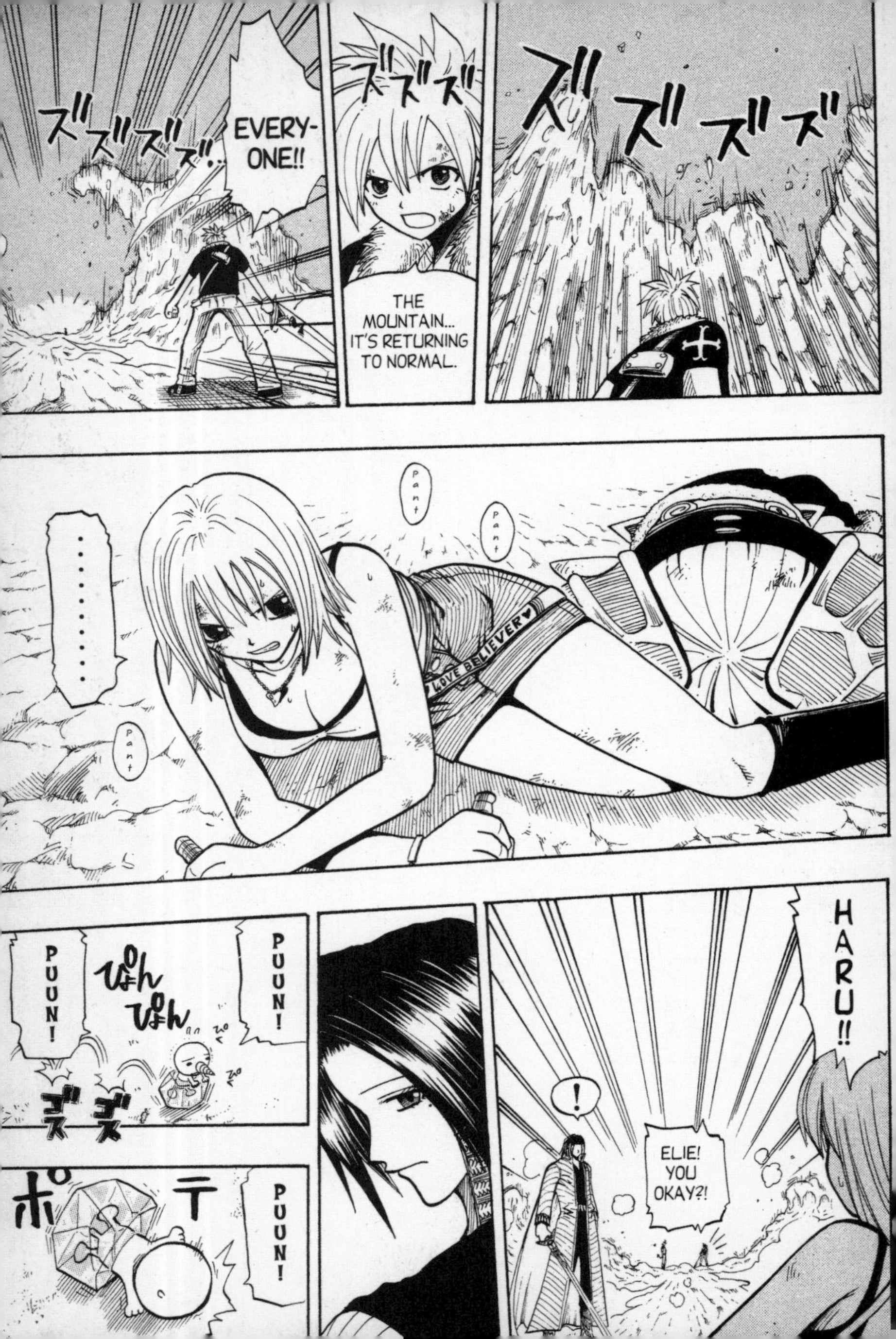
ズズズズ
ズズズ
THE MOUNTAIN... IT'S RETURNING TO NORMAL.
EVERY-ONE!!
ズズズズ!!...
Pant
Pant
Pant
......
HARU!!
!
ELIE! YOU OKAY?!
PUUN!
ぴょん ぴょん
PUUN!
PUUN!
ポテ

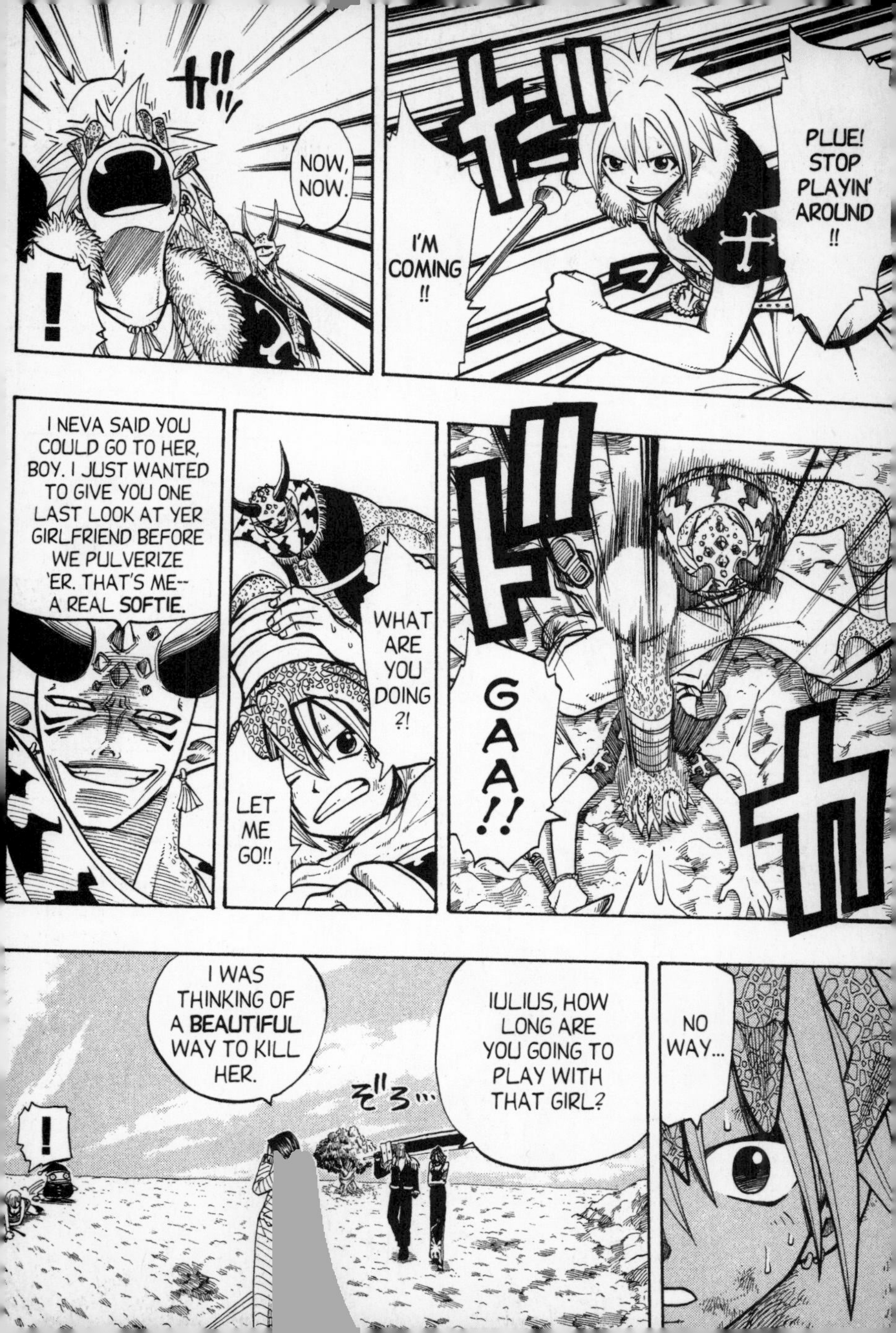
PLUE! STOP PLAYIN' AROUND !!
I'M COMING !!
NOW, NOW.
!
GAA!!
WHAT ARE YOU DOING ?!
LET ME GO!!
I NEVA SAID YOU COULD GO TO HER, BOY. I JUST WANTED TO GIVE YOU ONE LAST LOOK AT YER GIRLFRIEND BEFORE WE PULVERIZE 'ER. THAT'S ME-- A REAL **SOFTIE**.
NO WAY...
IULIUS, HOW LONG ARE YOU GOING TO PLAY WITH THAT GIRL?
I WAS THINKING OF A **BEAUTIFUL** WAY TO KILL HER.
!

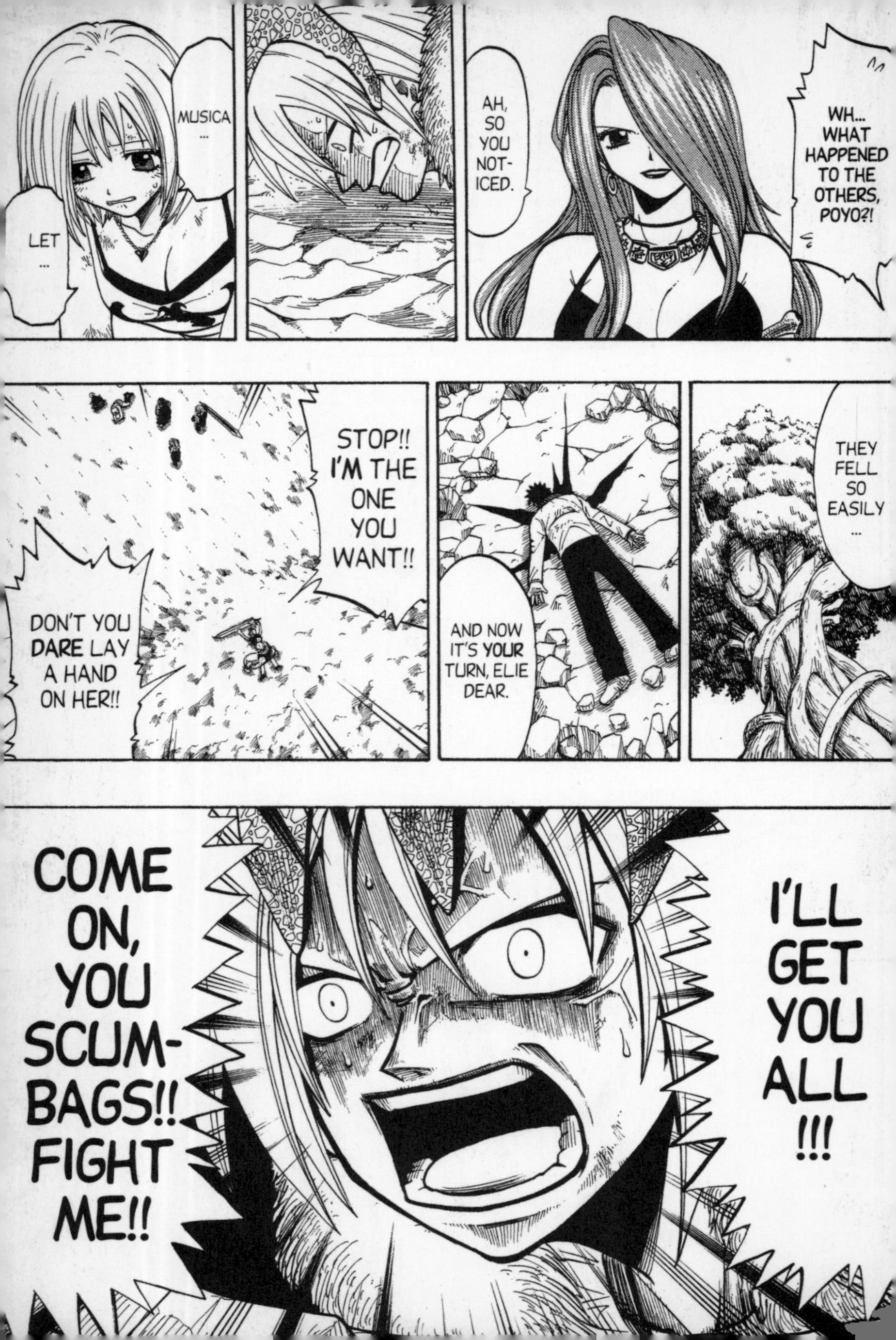
WH... WHAT HAPPENED TO THE OTHERS, POYO?!
AH, SO YOU NOTICED.
MUSICA ...
LET ...
THEY FELL SO EASILY ...
AND NOW IT'S YOUR TURN, ELIE DEAR.
STOP!! I'M THE ONE YOU WANT!!
DON'T YOU DARE LAY A HAND ON HER!!
I'LL GET YOU ALL!!!
COME ON, YOU SCUMBAGS!! FIGHT ME!!

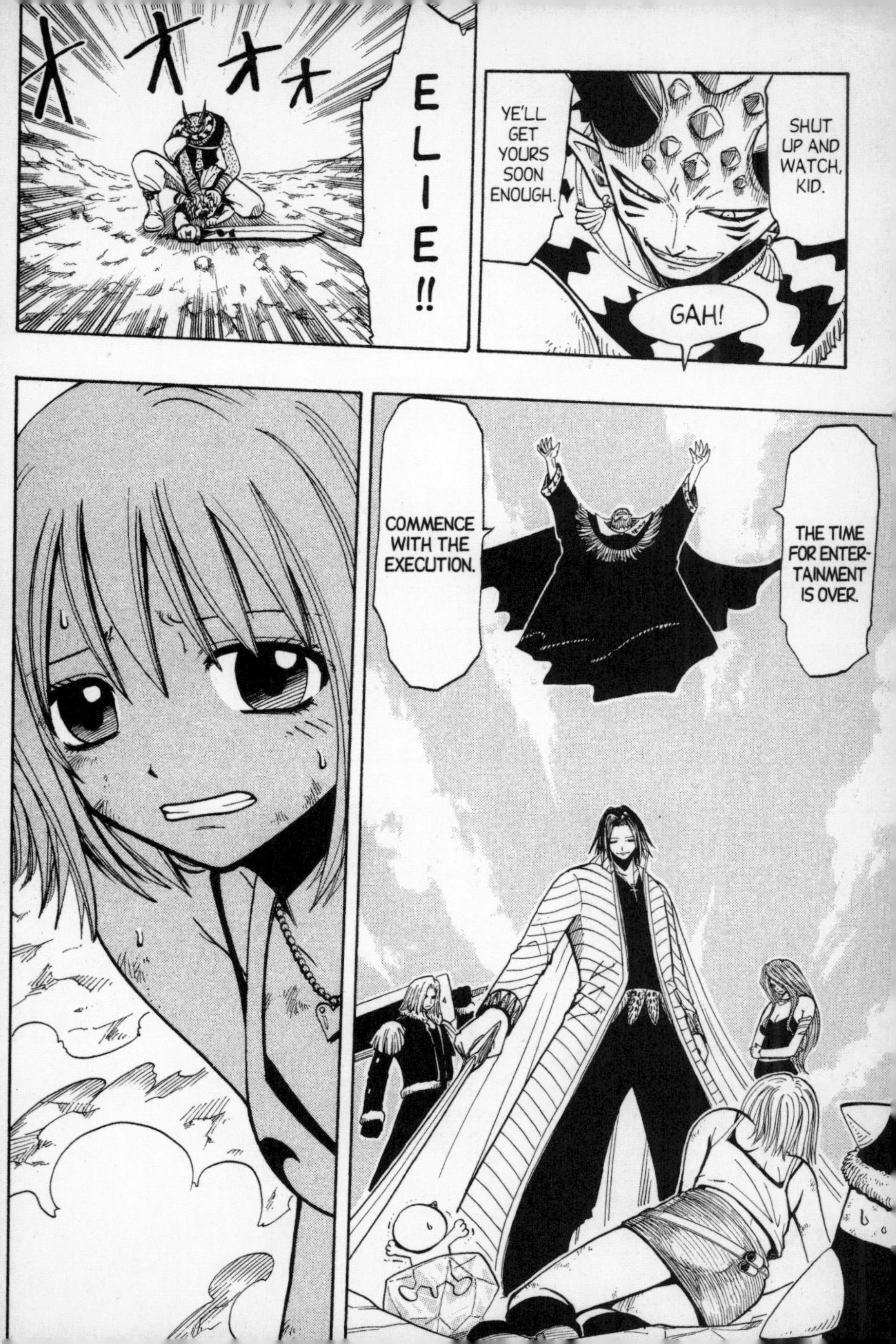
SHUT UP AND WATCH, KID.
YE'LL GET YOURS SOON ENOUGH.
GAH!
オオオォ
ELIE!!
THE TIME FOR ENTER-TAINMENT IS OVER.
COMMENCE WITH THE EXECUTION.

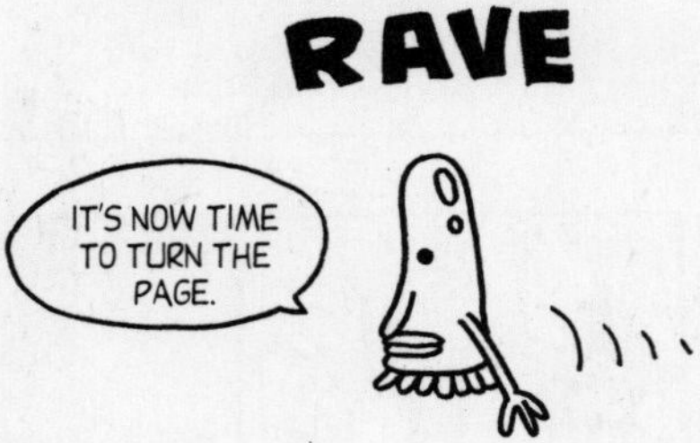

RAVE

IT'S NOW TIME
TO TURN THE
PAGE.

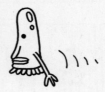

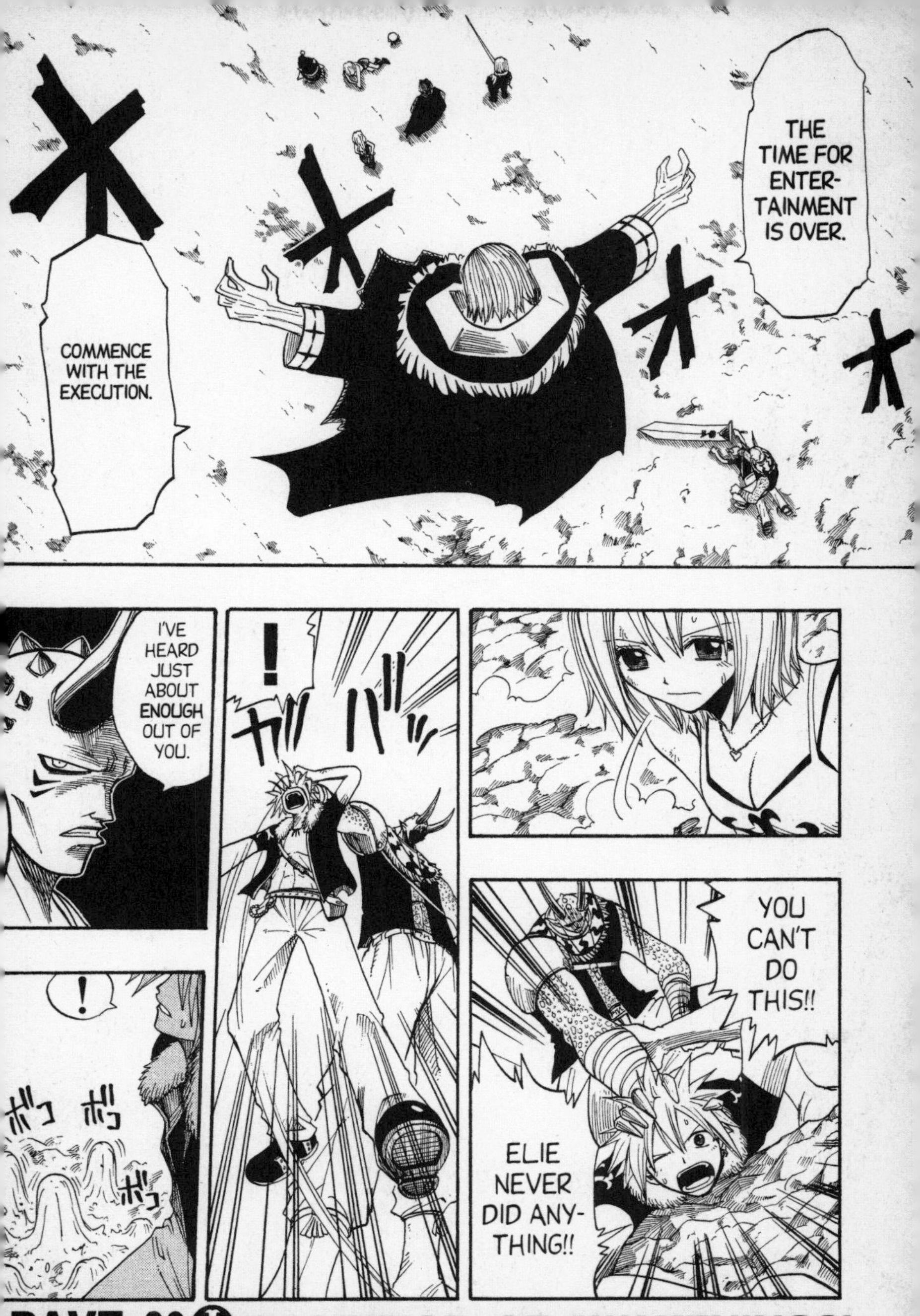
THE TIME FOR ENTER-TAINMENT IS OVER.
COMMENCE WITH THE EXECUTION.
YOU CAN'T DO THIS!!
ELIE NEVER DID ANY-THING!!
!
ガバ
I'VE HEARD JUST ABOUT ENOUGH OUT OF YOU.
!
ボコ ボコ
ボコ

RAVE:90 ✠ SACRIFICE, OR AWAKENING?!

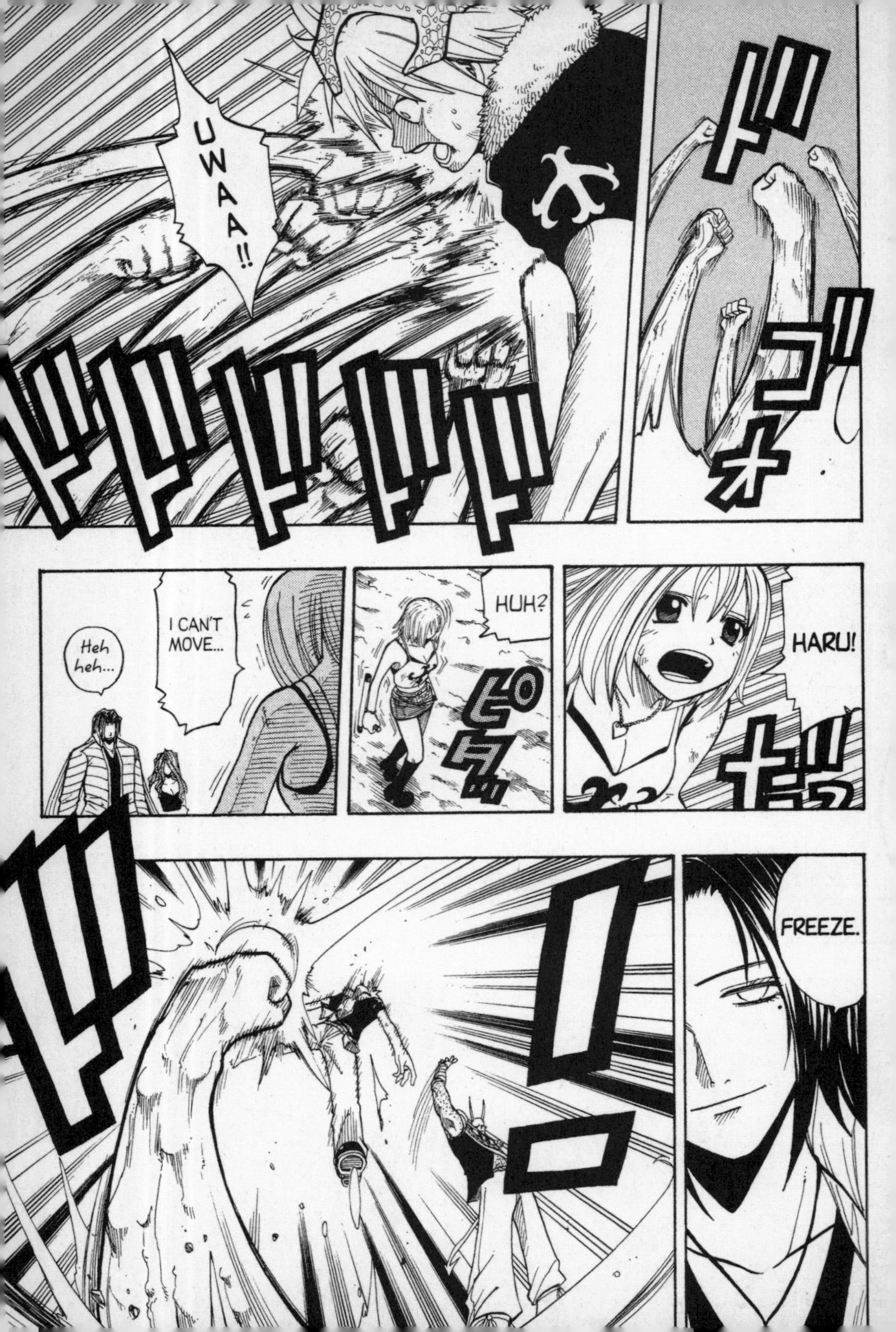
UWAA!!
HARU!
HUH?
I CAN'T MOVE...
Heh heh...
FREEZE.

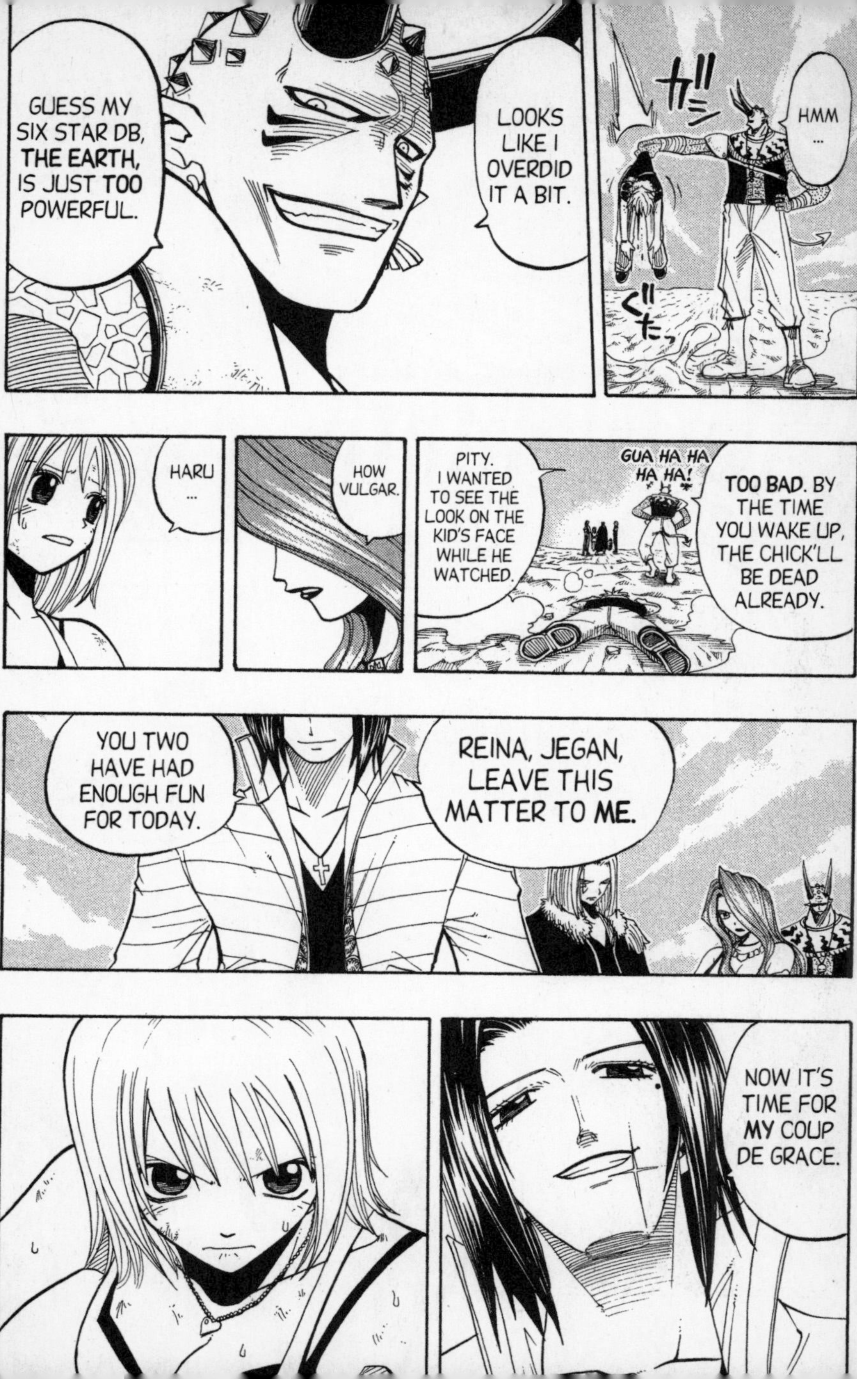
HMM ...
LOOKS LIKE I OVERDID IT A BIT.
GUESS MY SIX STAR DB, THE EARTH, IS JUST TOO POWERFUL.
TOO BAD. BY THE TIME YOU WAKE UP, THE CHICK'LL BE DEAD ALREADY.
GUA HA HA HA HA!
PITY. I WANTED TO SEE THE LOOK ON THE KID'S FACE WHILE HE WATCHED.
HOW VULGAR.
HARU ...
REINA, JEGAN, LEAVE THIS MATTER TO ME.
YOU TWO HAVE HAD ENOUGH FUN FOR TODAY.
NOW IT'S TIME FOR MY COUP DE GRACE.

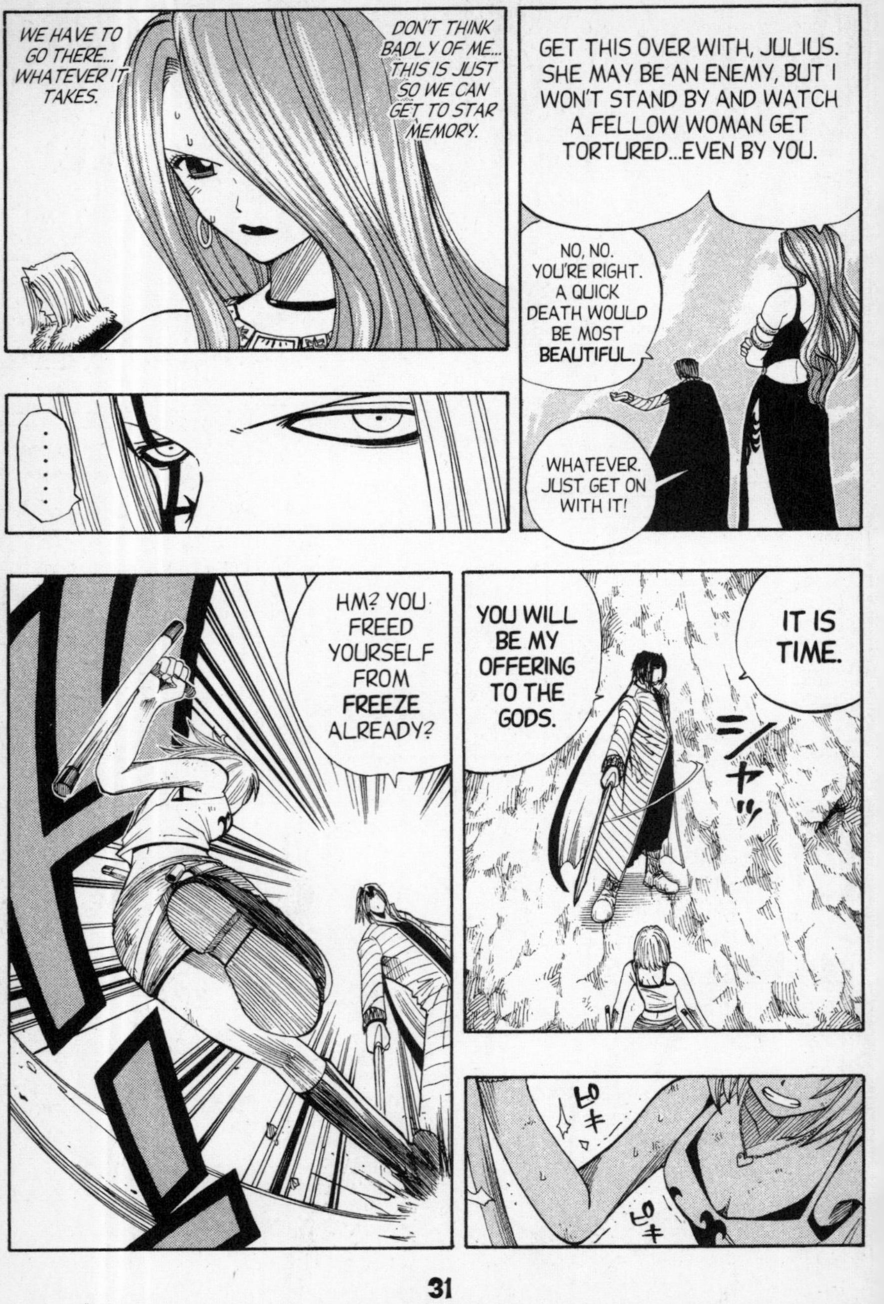
GET THIS OVER WITH, JULIUS. SHE MAY BE AN ENEMY, BUT I WON'T STAND BY AND WATCH A FELLOW WOMAN GET TORTURED...EVEN BY YOU.
NO, NO. YOU'RE RIGHT. A QUICK DEATH WOULD BE MOST **BEAUTIFUL.**
WHATEVER. JUST GET ON WITH IT!
DON'T THINK BADLY OF ME... THIS IS JUST SO WE CAN GET TO STAR MEMORY.
WE HAVE TO GO THERE... WHATEVER IT TAKES.
......
IT IS TIME.
YOU WILL BE MY OFFERING TO THE GODS.
ニヤッ
ピキ
ピキ
HM? YOU FREED YOURSELF FROM **FREEZE** ALREADY?

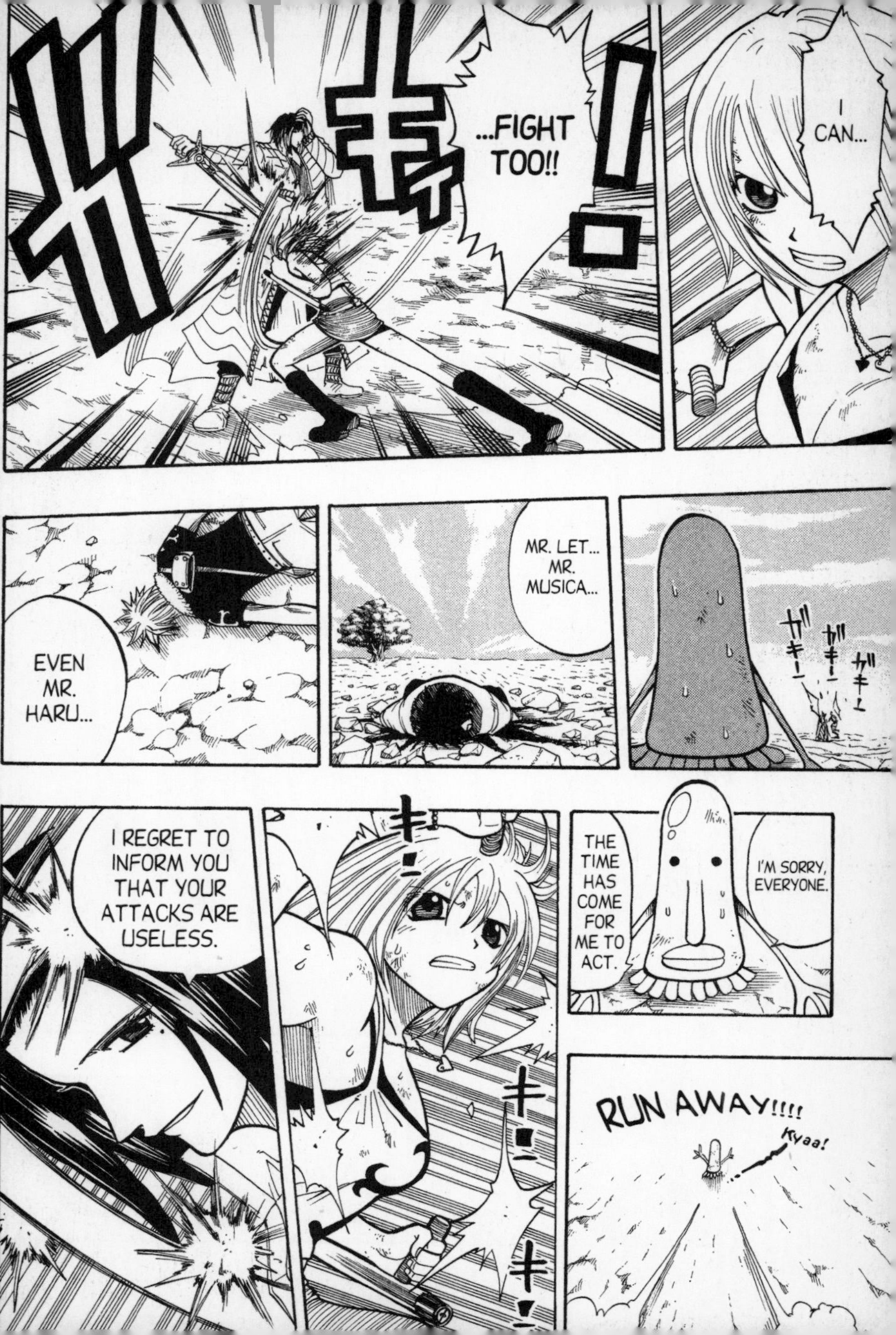
I CAN...
...FIGHT TOO!!
MR. LET... MR. MUSICA...
EVEN MR. HARU...
I'M SORRY, EVERYONE.
THE TIME HAS COME FOR ME TO ACT.
RUN AWAY!!!!
Kyaa!
I REGRET TO INFORM YOU THAT YOUR ATTACKS ARE USELESS.

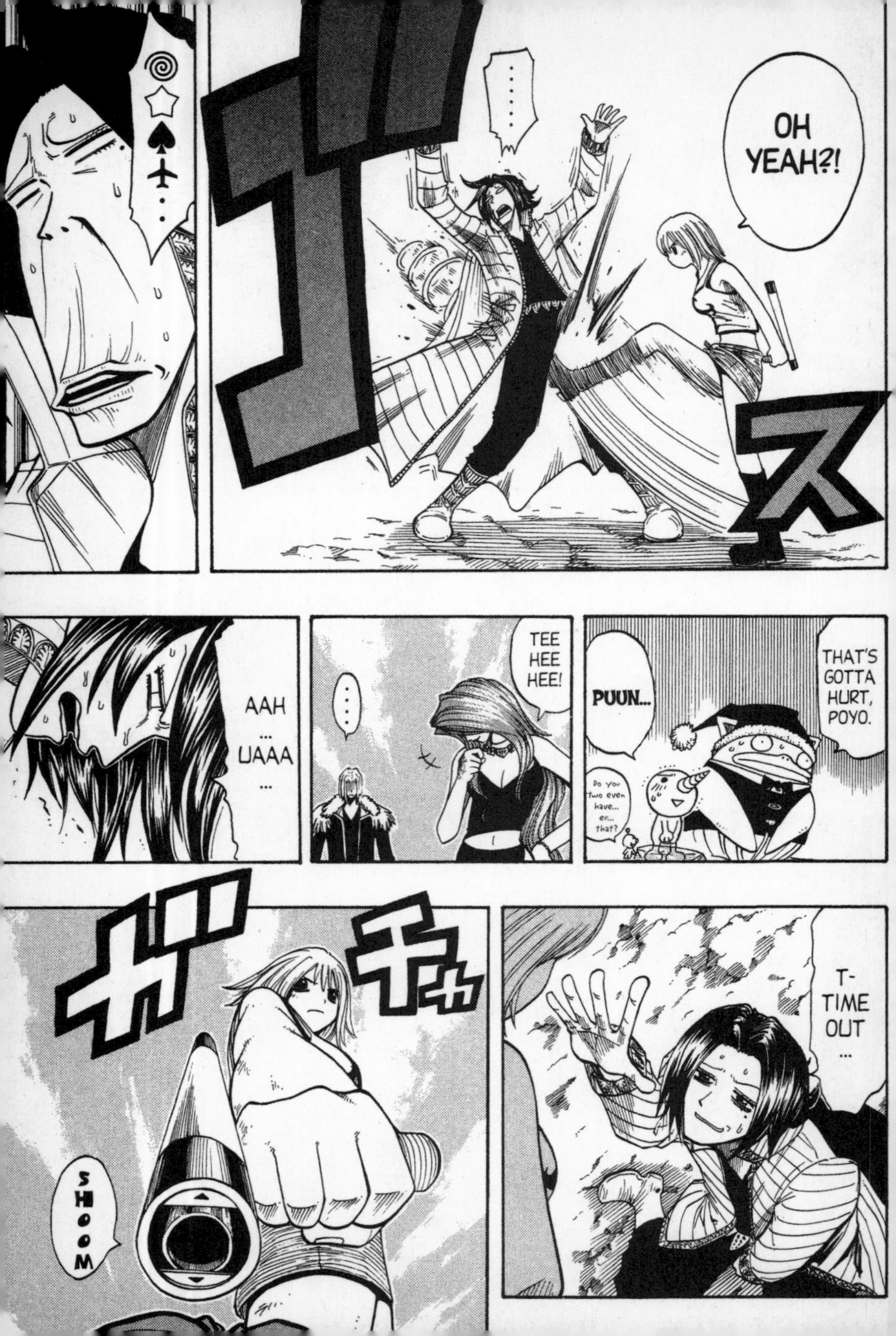
OH YEAH?!
......
THAT'S GOTTA HURT, POYO.
PUUN...
Do you two even have... er... that?
TEE HEE HEE!
......
AAH ... UAAA ...
T- TIME OUT ...
SHOOM

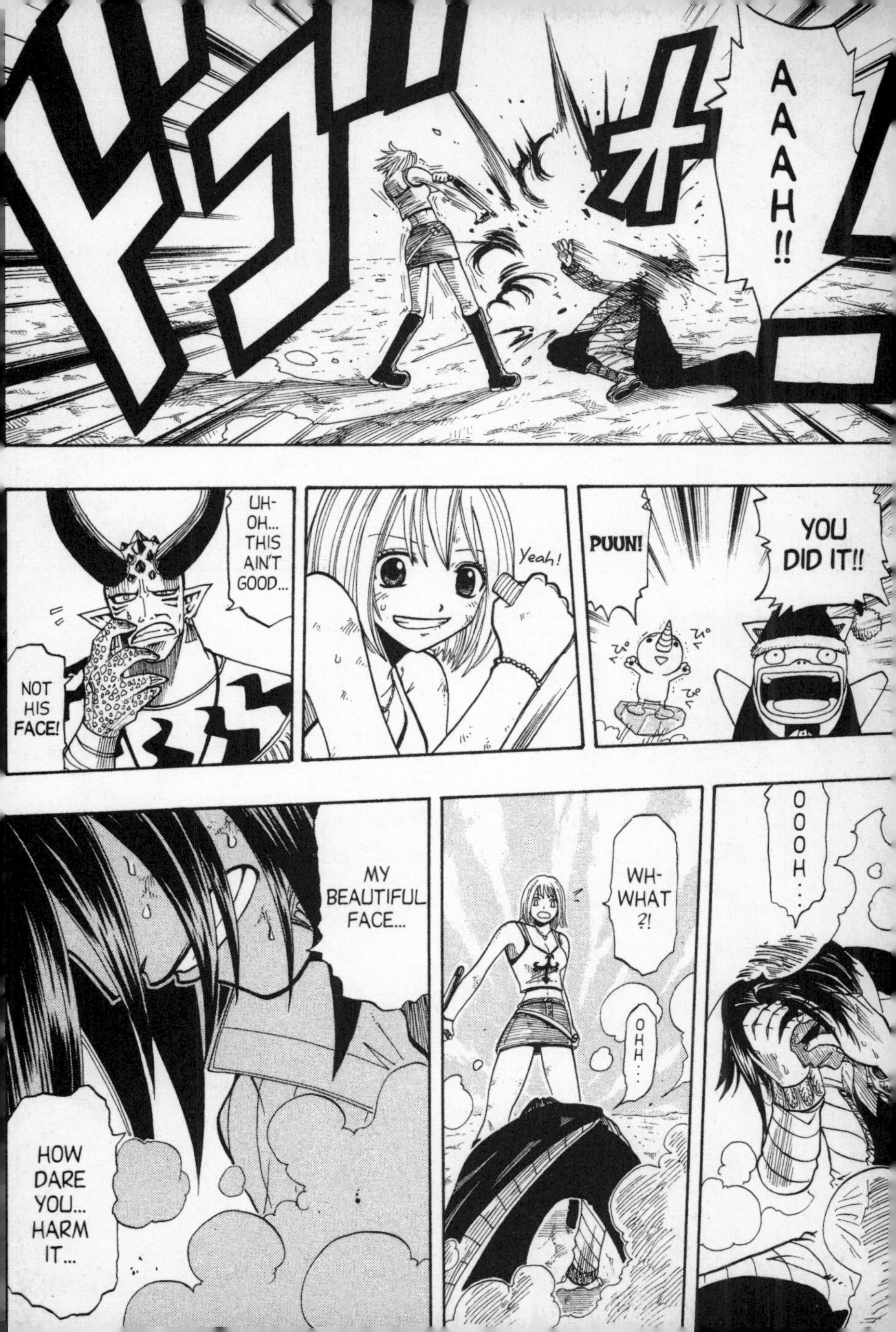
AAAAH!!
YOU DID IT!!
PUUN!
Yeah!
UH-OH... THIS AIN'T GOOD...
NOT HIS FACE!
OOOOH...
WH-WHAT?!
OHH...
MY BEAUTIFUL FACE...
HOW DARE YOU... HARM IT...

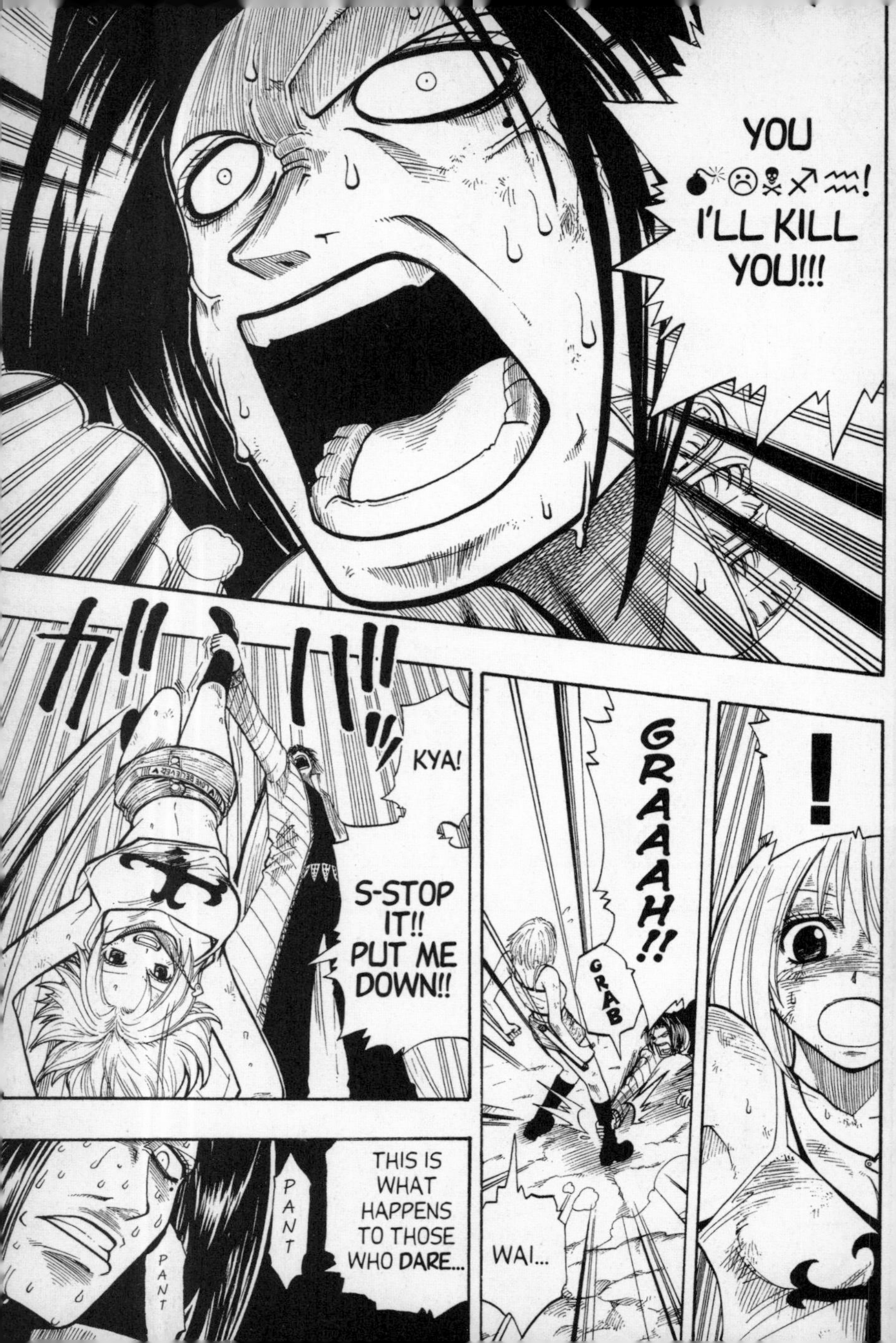
YOU
I'LL KILL YOU!!!
!
GRAAAAH!!
GRAB
WAI...
ガッ
KYA!
S-STOP IT!! PUT ME DOWN!!
THIS IS WHAT HAPPENS TO THOSE WHO DARE...
PANT
PANT

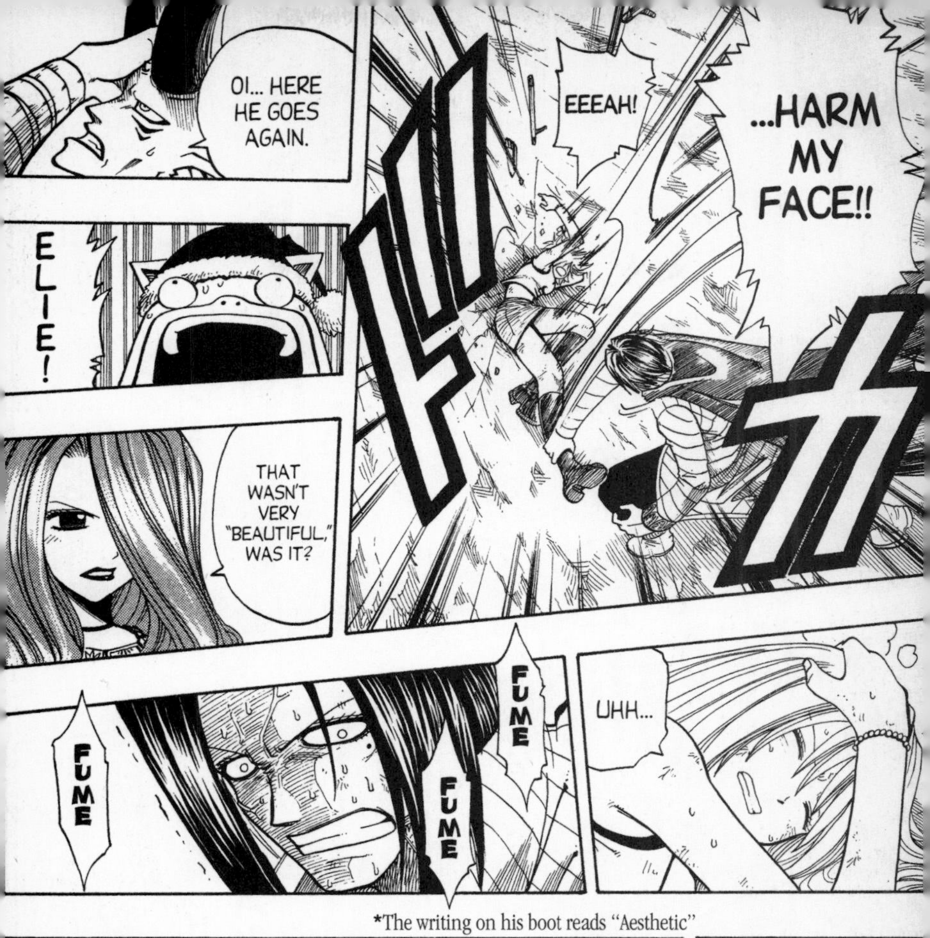
...HARM MY FACE!!
EEEAH!
OI... HERE HE GOES AGAIN.
ELIE!
THAT WASN'T VERY "BEAUTIFUL," WAS IT?
UHH...
FUME
FUME
FUME

*The writing on his boot reads "Aesthetic"

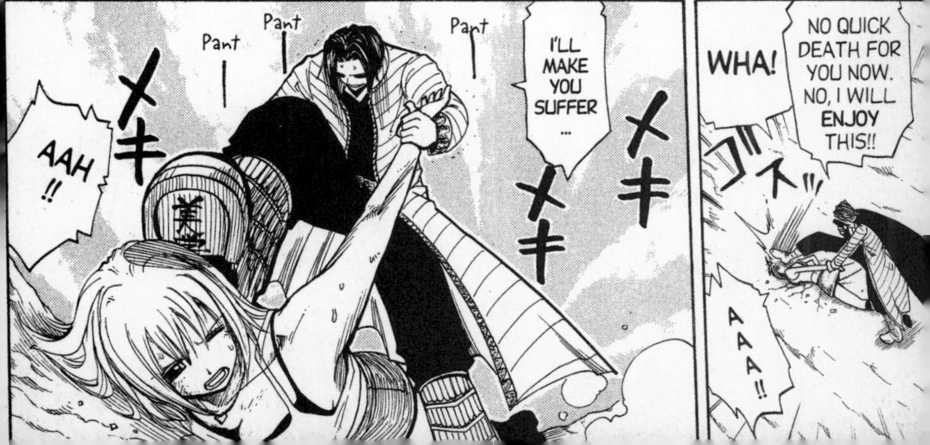
NO QUICK DEATH FOR YOU NOW. NO, I WILL ENJOY THIS!!
WHA!
AAA!!
I'LL MAKE YOU SUFFER ...
メキ
メキ
Pant
Pant
Pant
メキ
AAH!!

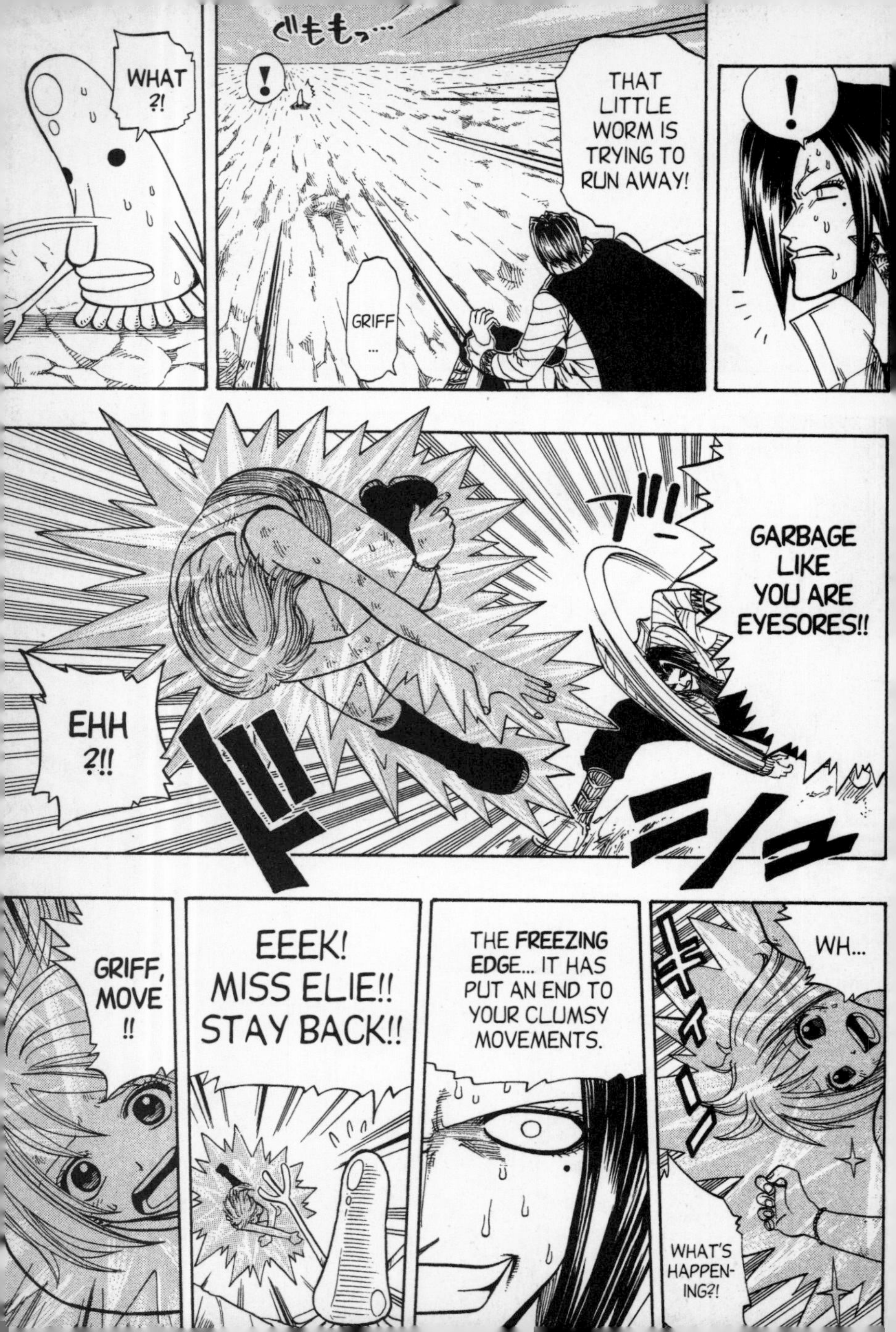
!
!
THAT LITTLE WORM IS TRYING TO RUN AWAY!
GRIFF ...
WHAT ?!
GARBAGE LIKE YOU ARE EYESORES!!
EHH ?!!
WH...
WHAT'S HAPPEN-ING?!
THE FREEZING EDGE... IT HAS PUT AN END TO YOUR CLUMSY MOVEMENTS.
EEEK! MISS ELIE!! STAY BACK!!
GRIFF, MOVE !!

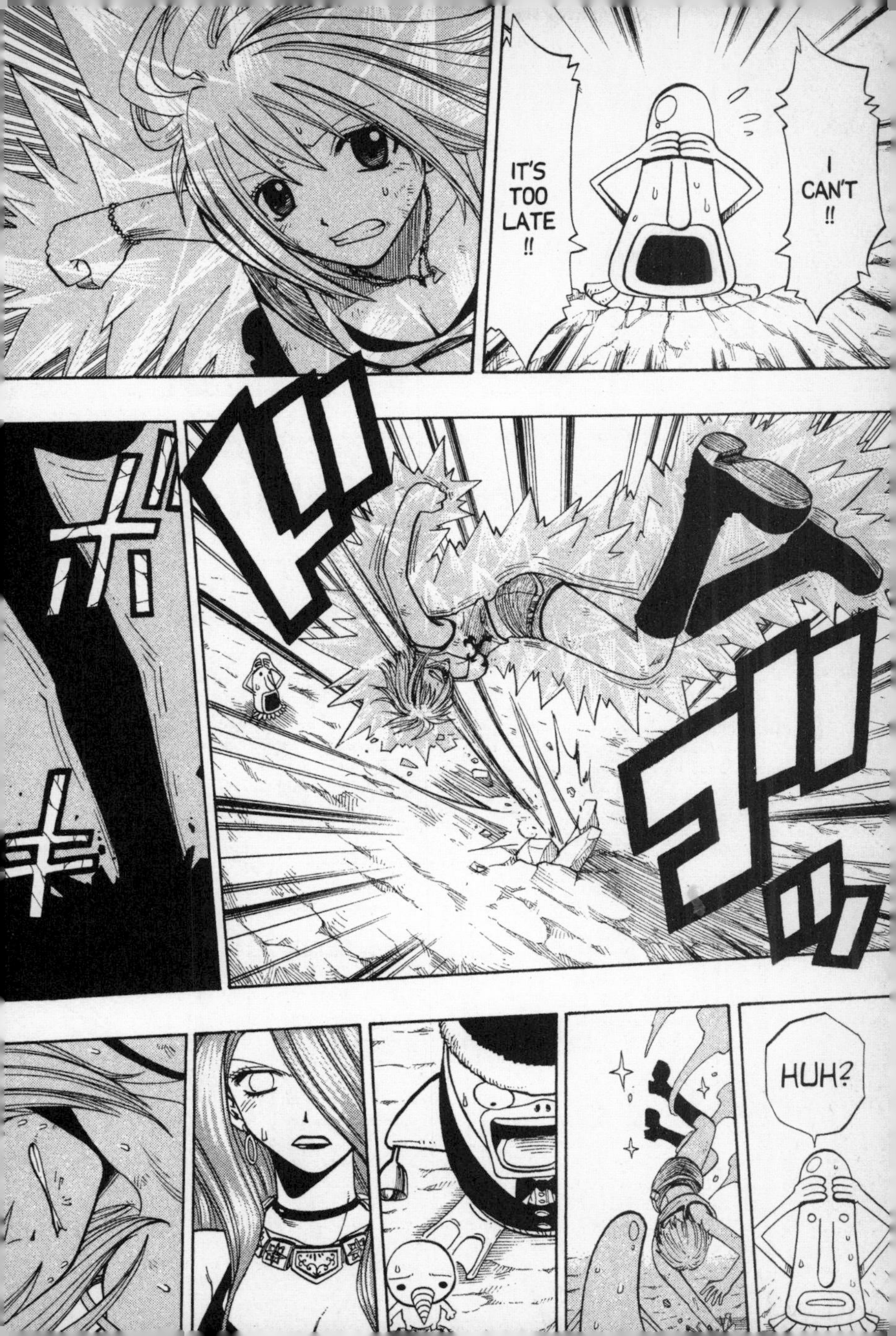
I CAN'T !!
IT'S TOO LATE !!
HUH?

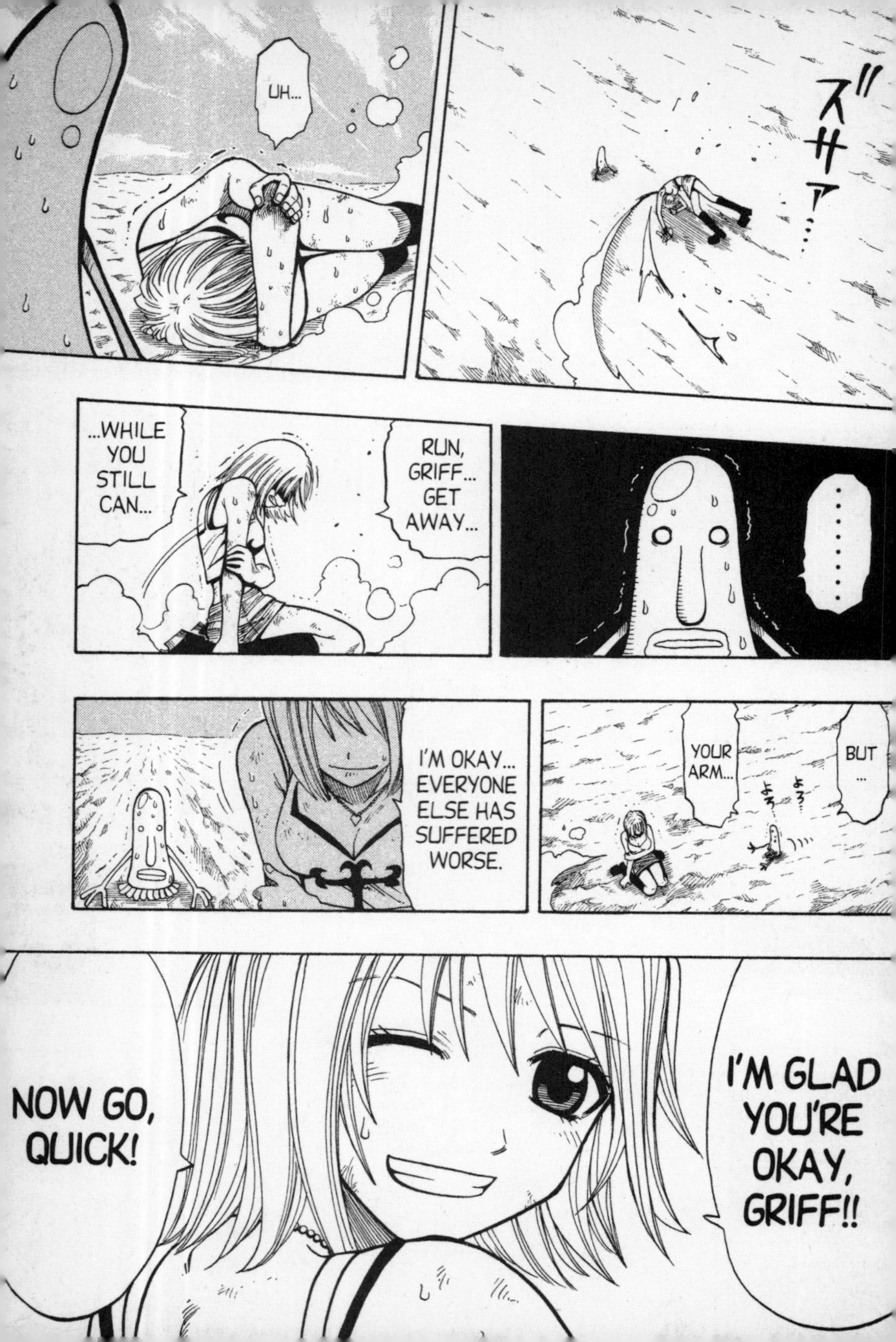

ズサァ…
UH...
......
RUN, GRIFF... GET AWAY...
...WHILE YOU STILL CAN...
BUT ...
YOUR ARM...
I'M OKAY... EVERYONE ELSE HAS SUFFERED WORSE.
I'M GLAD YOU'RE OKAY, GRIFF!!
NOW GO, QUICK!

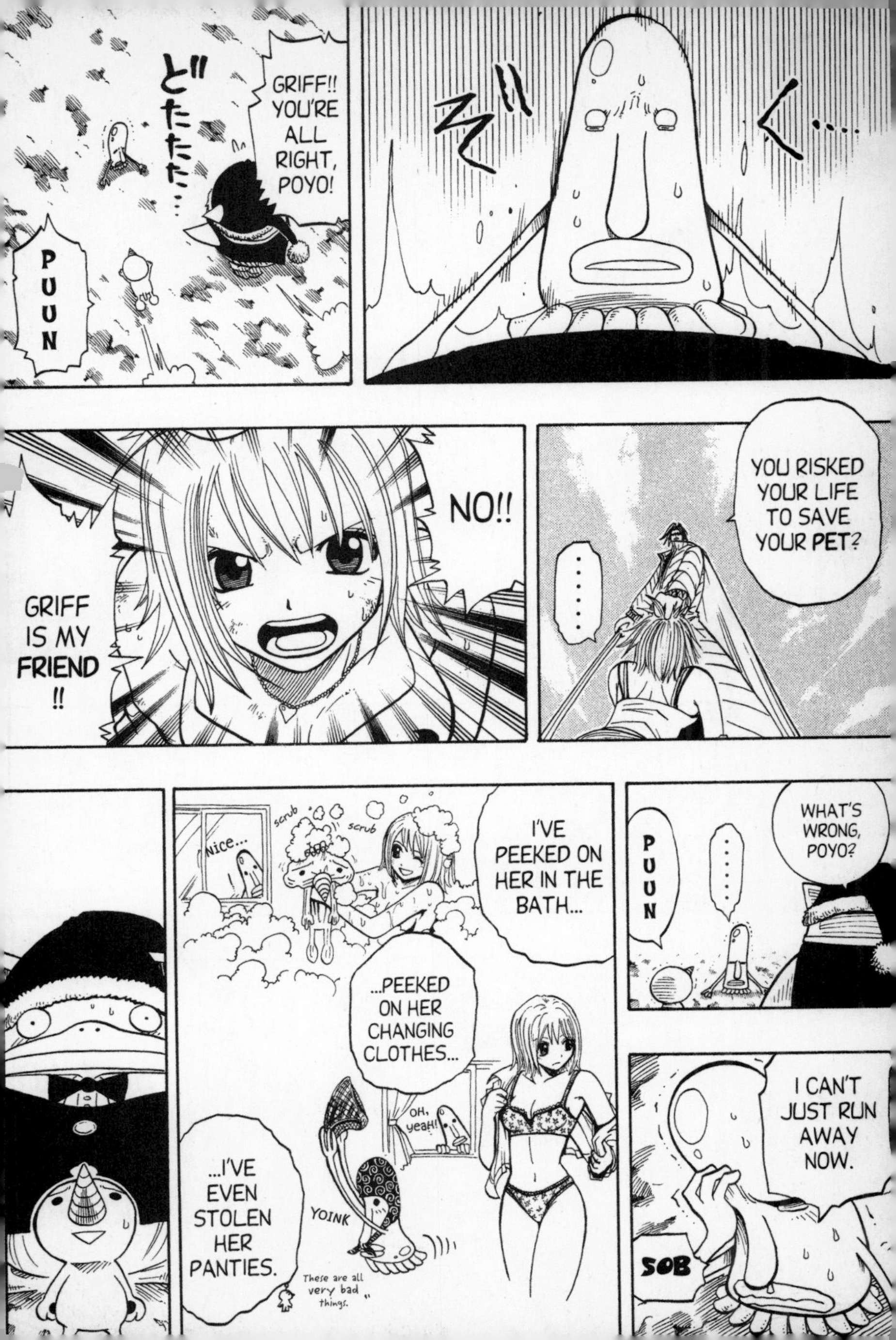
ぞ
く…
GRIFF!! YOU'RE ALL RIGHT, POYO!
どたたた…
PUUN
YOU RISKED YOUR LIFE TO SAVE YOUR PET?
……
NO!!
GRIFF IS MY FRIEND !!
WHAT'S WRONG, POYO?
……
PUUN
I CAN'T JUST RUN AWAY NOW.
SOB
I'VE PEEKED ON HER IN THE BATH...
scrub
scrub
Nice...
...PEEKED ON HER CHANGING CLOTHES...
OH, yeah!
YOINK
...I'VE EVEN STOLEN HER PANTIES.
These are all very bad things.

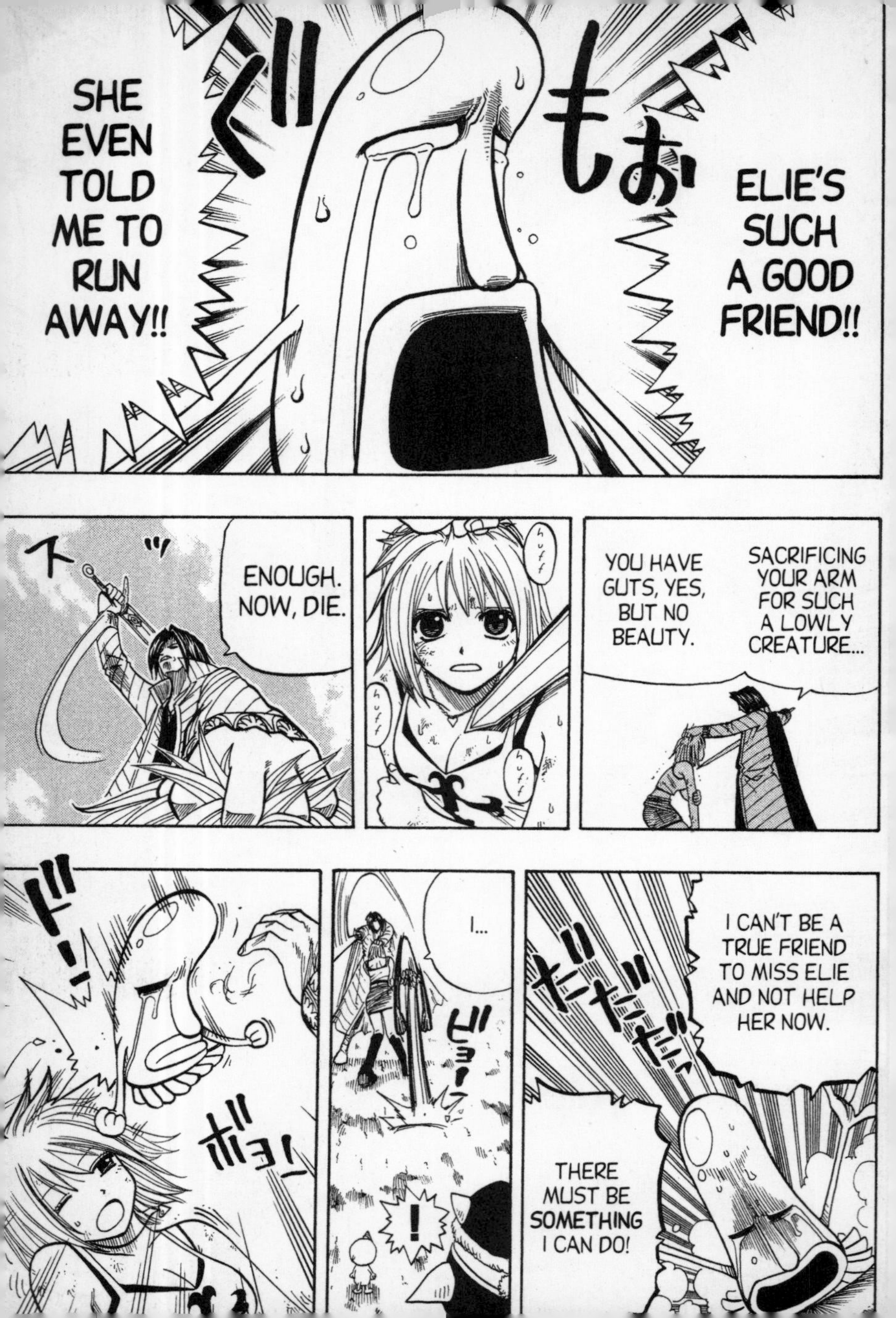
ELIE'S SUCH A GOOD FRIEND!!
もぉ
SHE EVEN TOLD ME TO RUN AWAY!!
SACRIFICING YOUR ARM FOR SUCH A LOWLY CREATURE...
YOU HAVE GUTS, YES, BUT NO BEAUTY.
huff
huff
huff
ENOUGH. NOW, DIE.
I CAN'T BE A TRUE FRIEND TO MISS ELIE AND NOT HELP HER NOW.
THERE MUST BE SOMETHING I CAN DO!
I...
!
ド!!

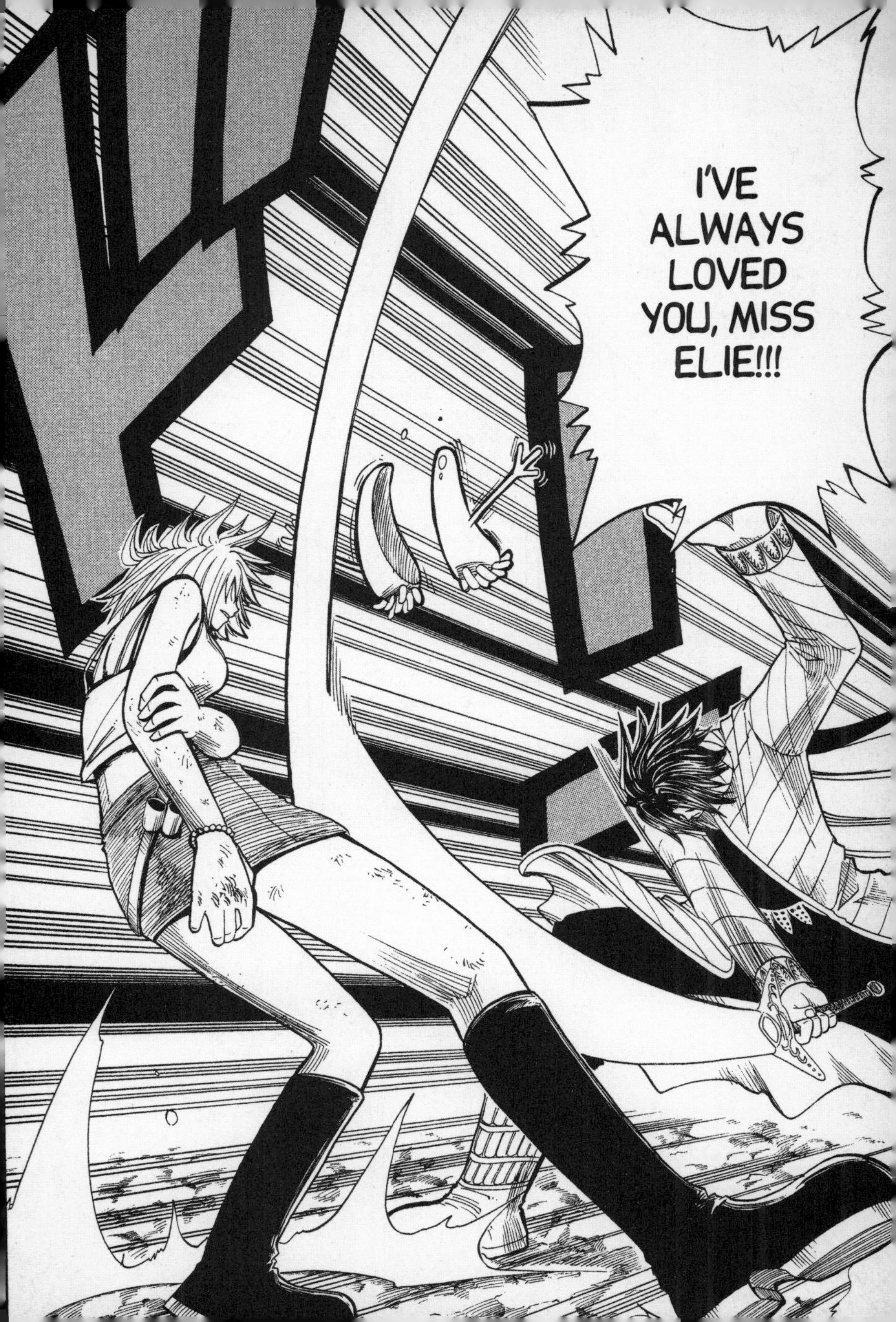
I'VE ALWAYS LOVED YOU, MISS ELIE!!!

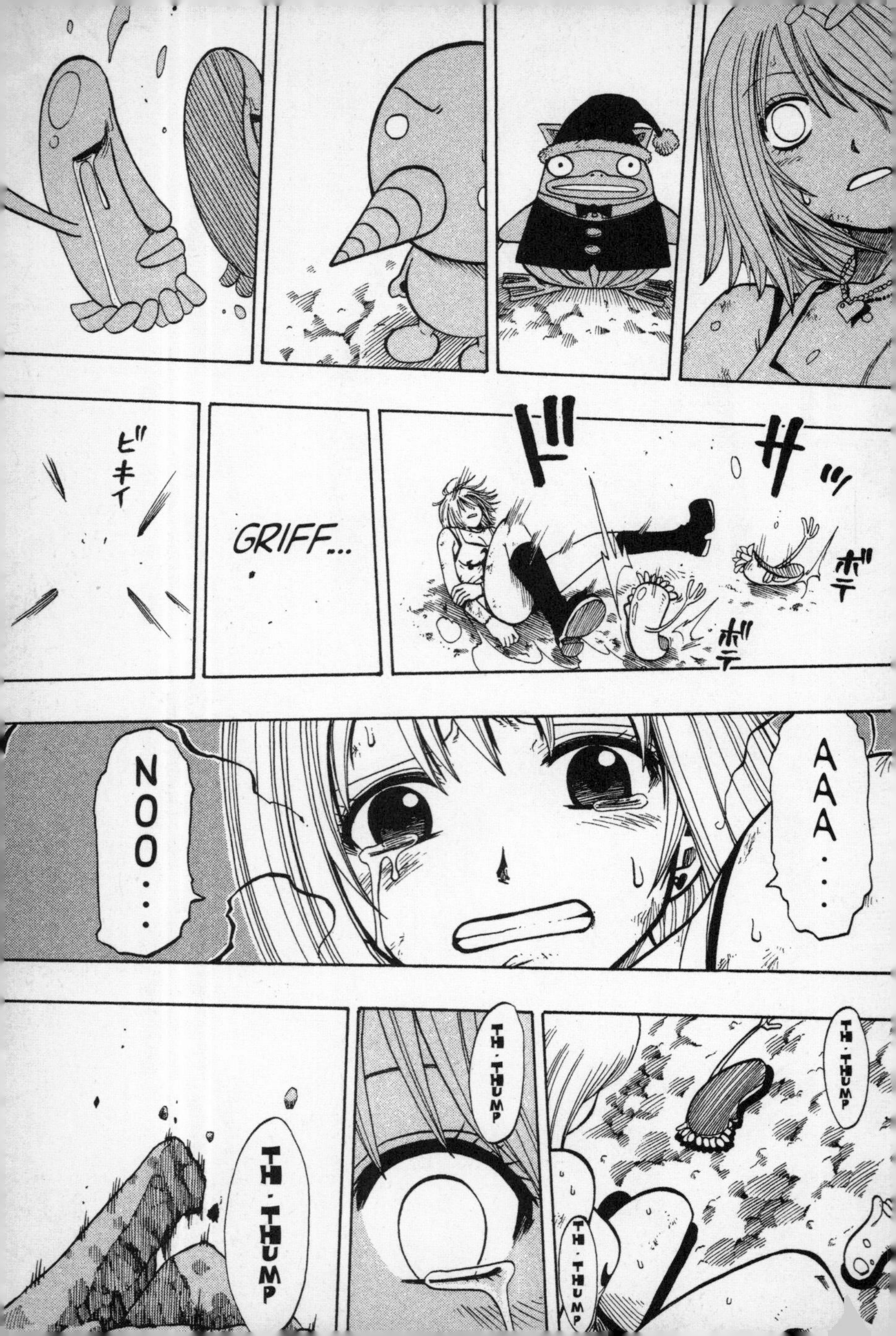

ザッ
ド
ボテ
ボテ
GRIFF...
ビキイ
AAA...
NOO...
TH-THUMP
TH-THUMP
TH-THUMP
TH-THUMP

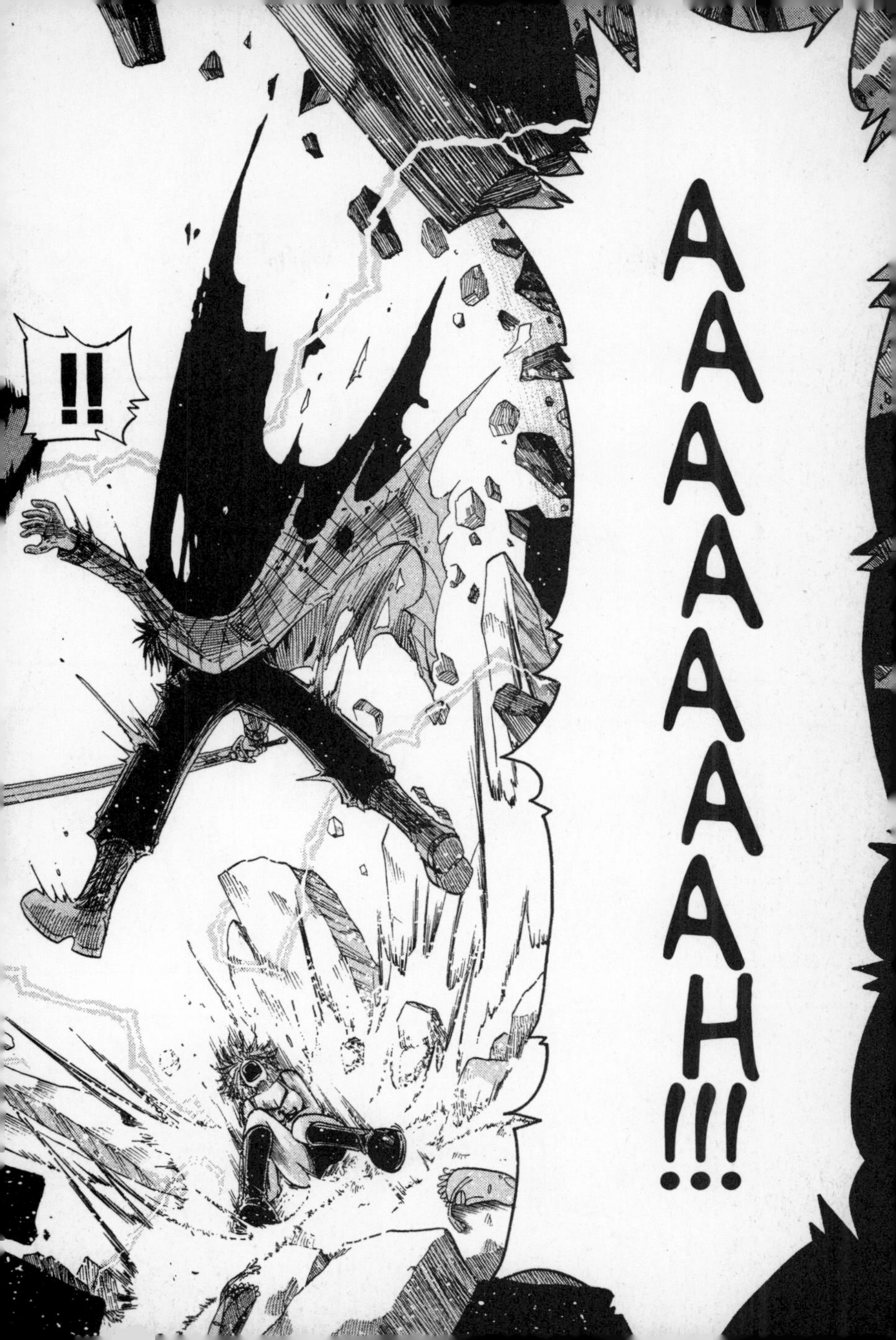
AAAAAAAH!!!
!!

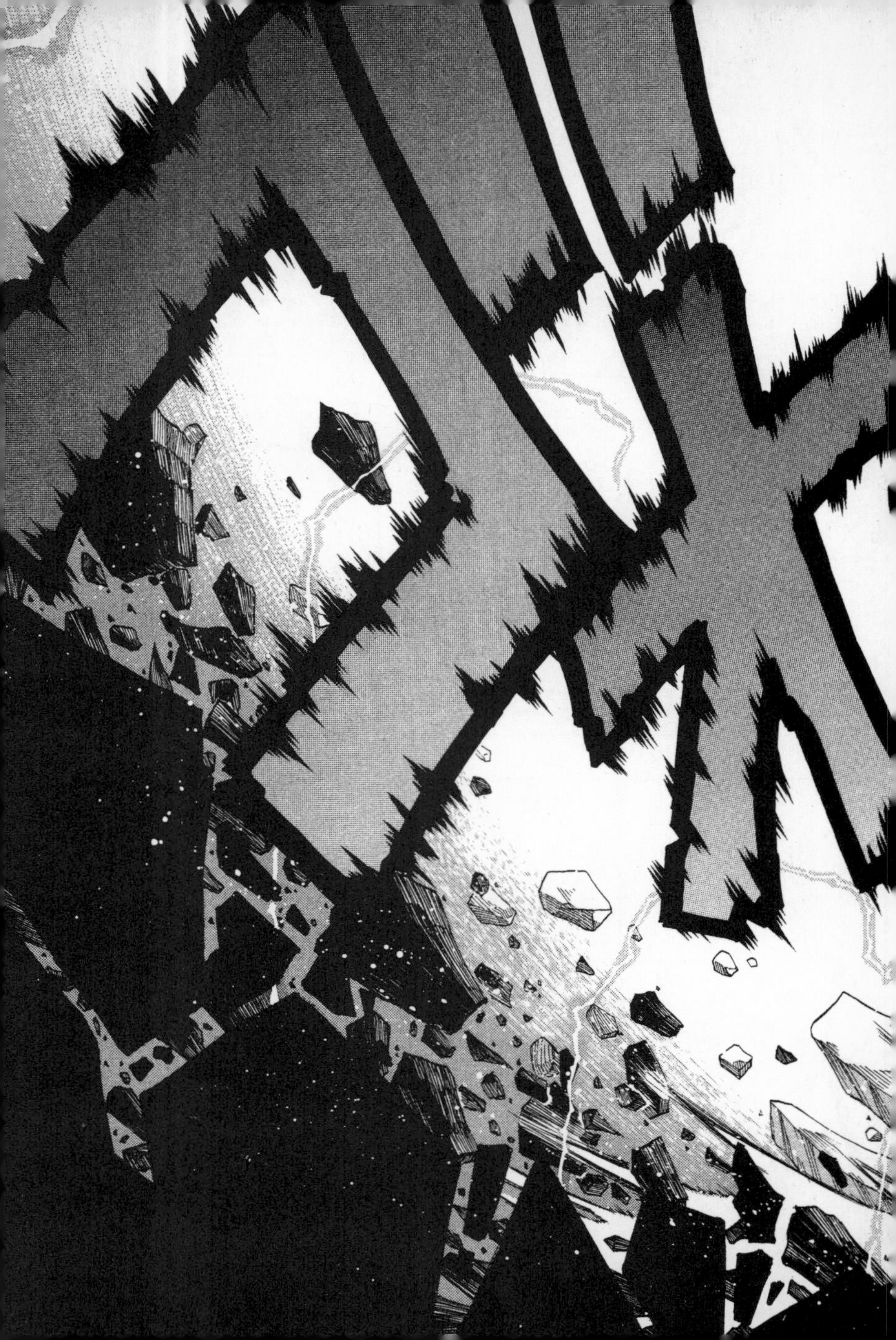

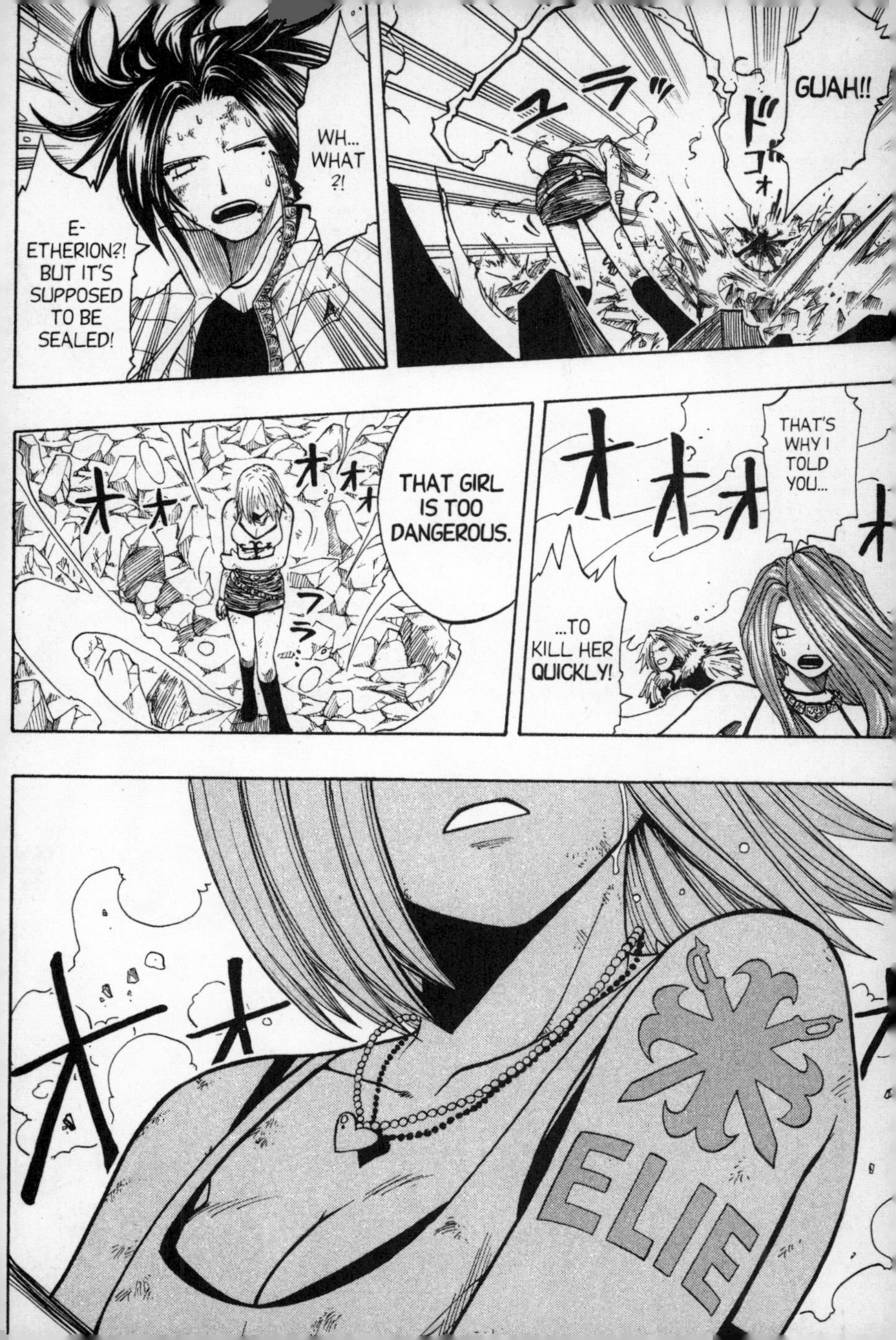
ドゴォ
GUAH!!
WH... WHAT ?!
E- ETHERION?! BUT IT'S SUPPOSED TO BE SEALED!
オオオオ
THAT'S WHY I TOLD YOU...
...TO KILL HER QUICKLY!
オオ
THAT GIRL IS TOO DANGEROUS.
フラ
オオ
ELIE

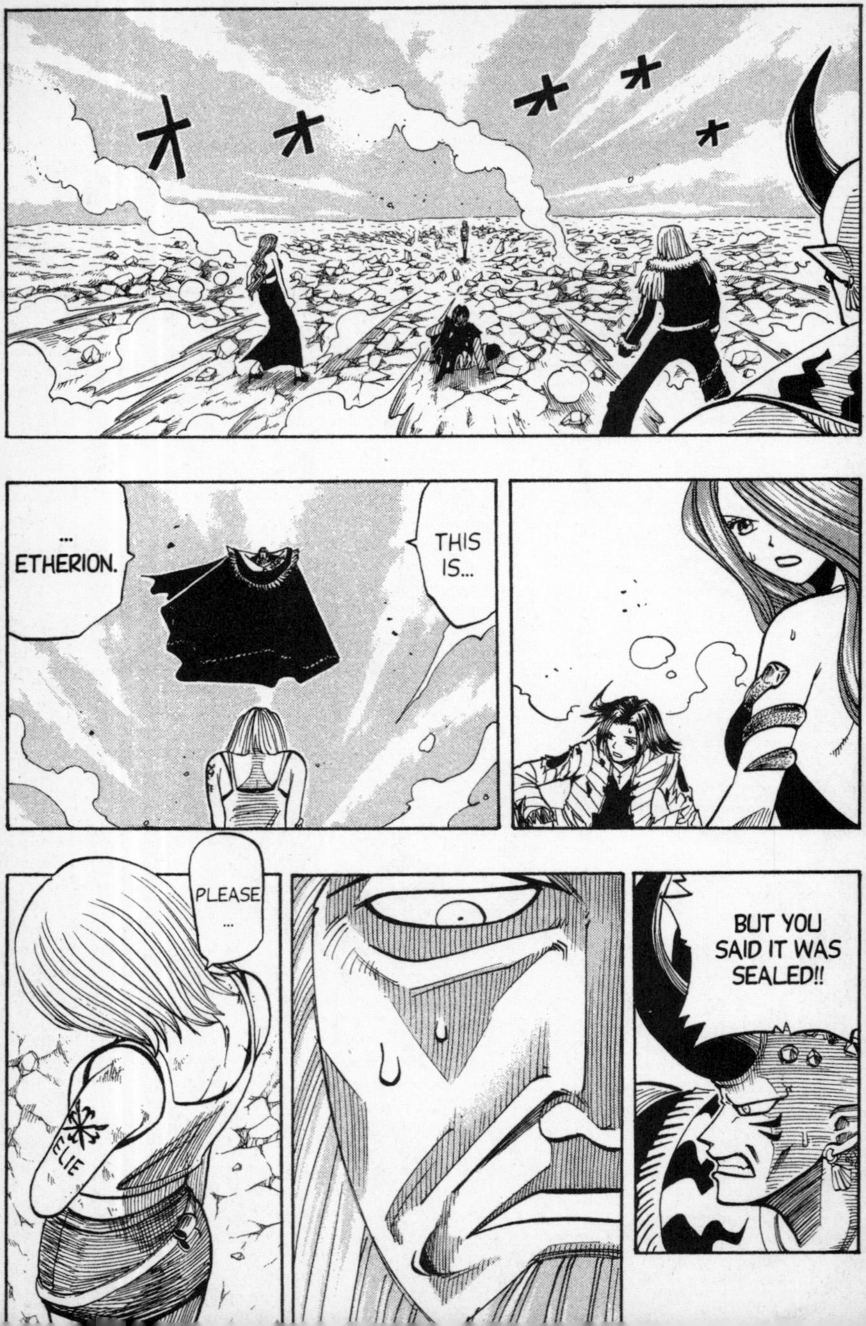
オオオオオ
THIS IS...
...ETHERION.
BUT YOU SAID IT WAS SEALED!!
PLEASE ...
ELIE

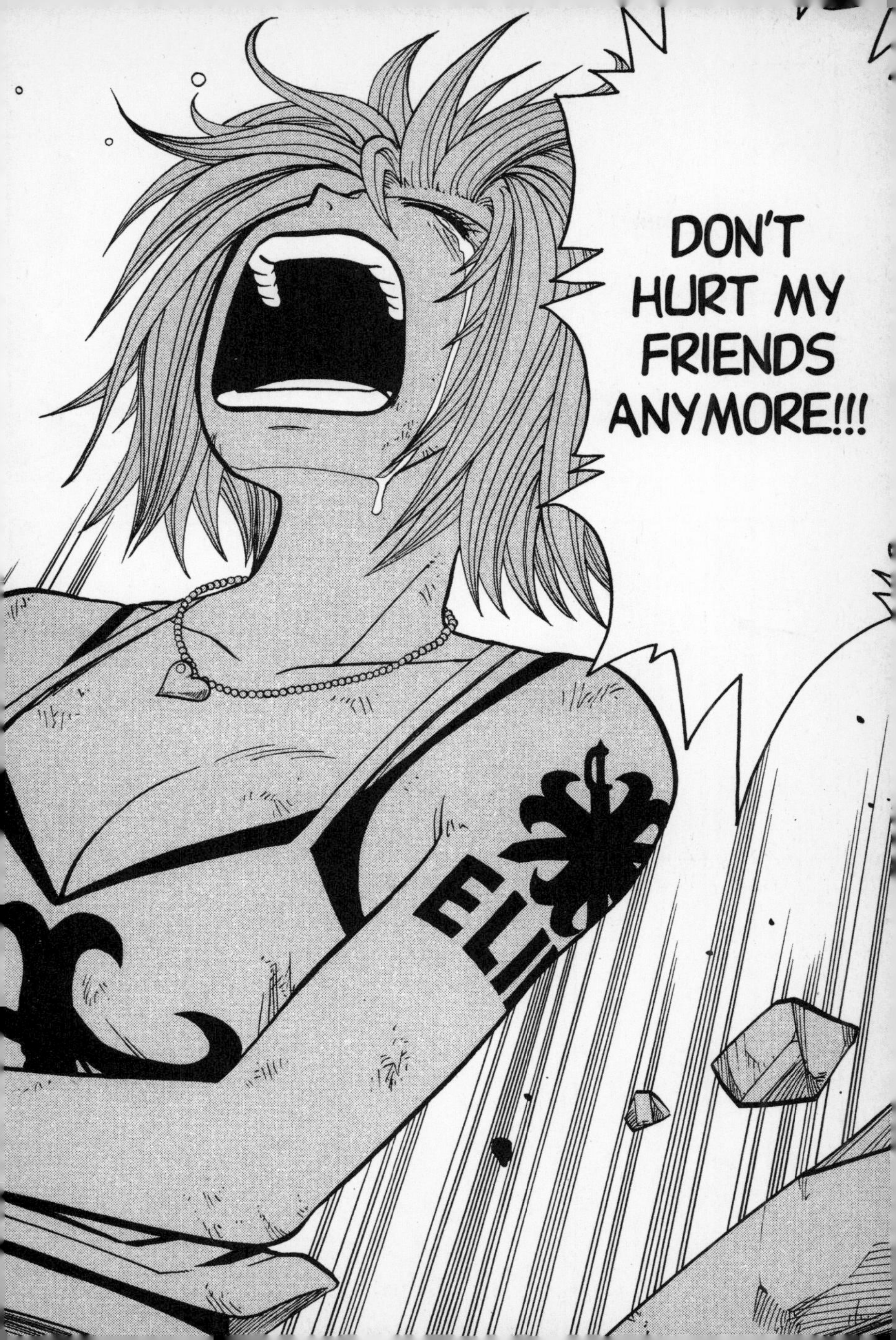
DON'T HURT MY FRIENDS ANYMORE!!!
ELI

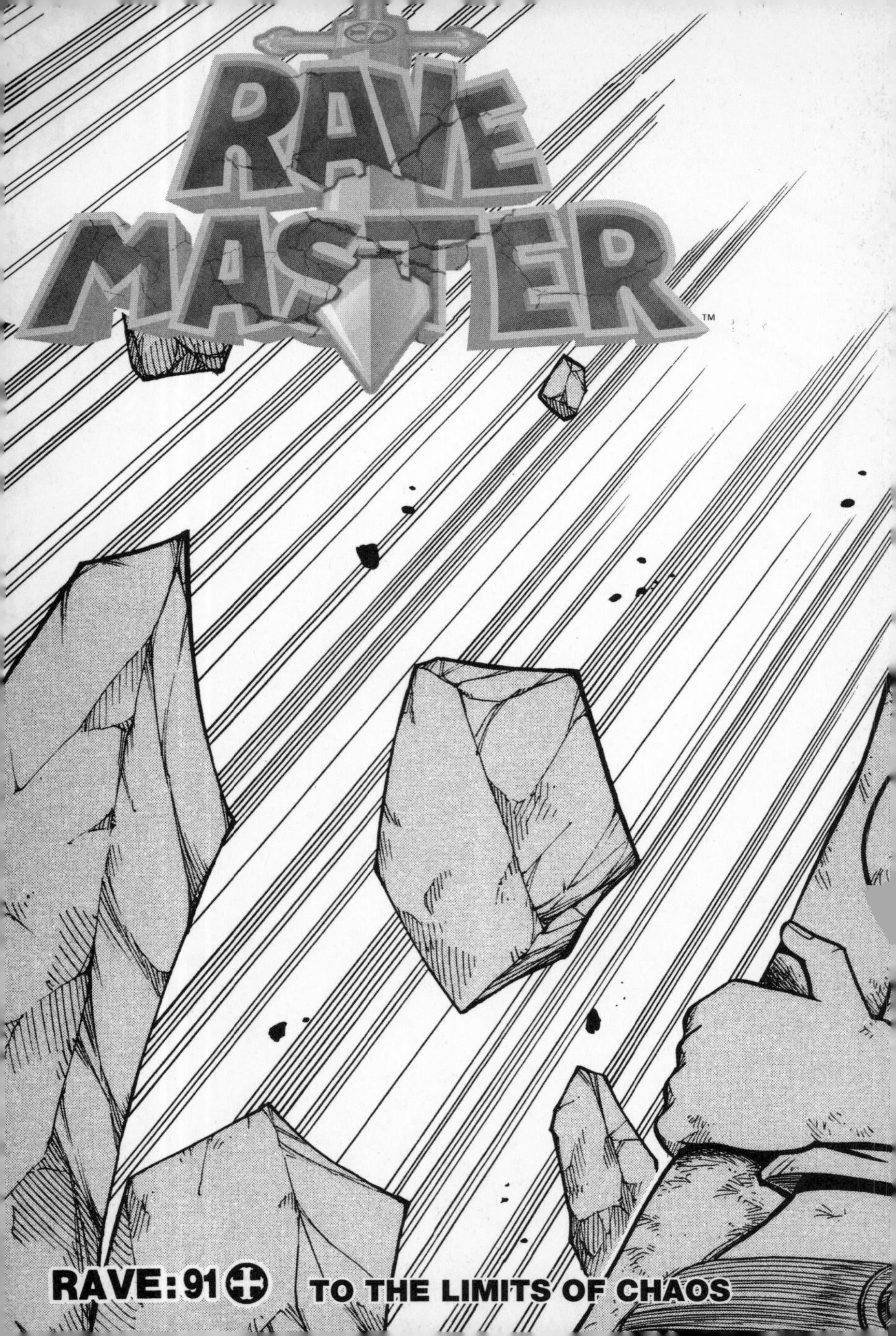
RAVE MASTER™
RAVE:91 TO THE LIMITS OF CHAOS

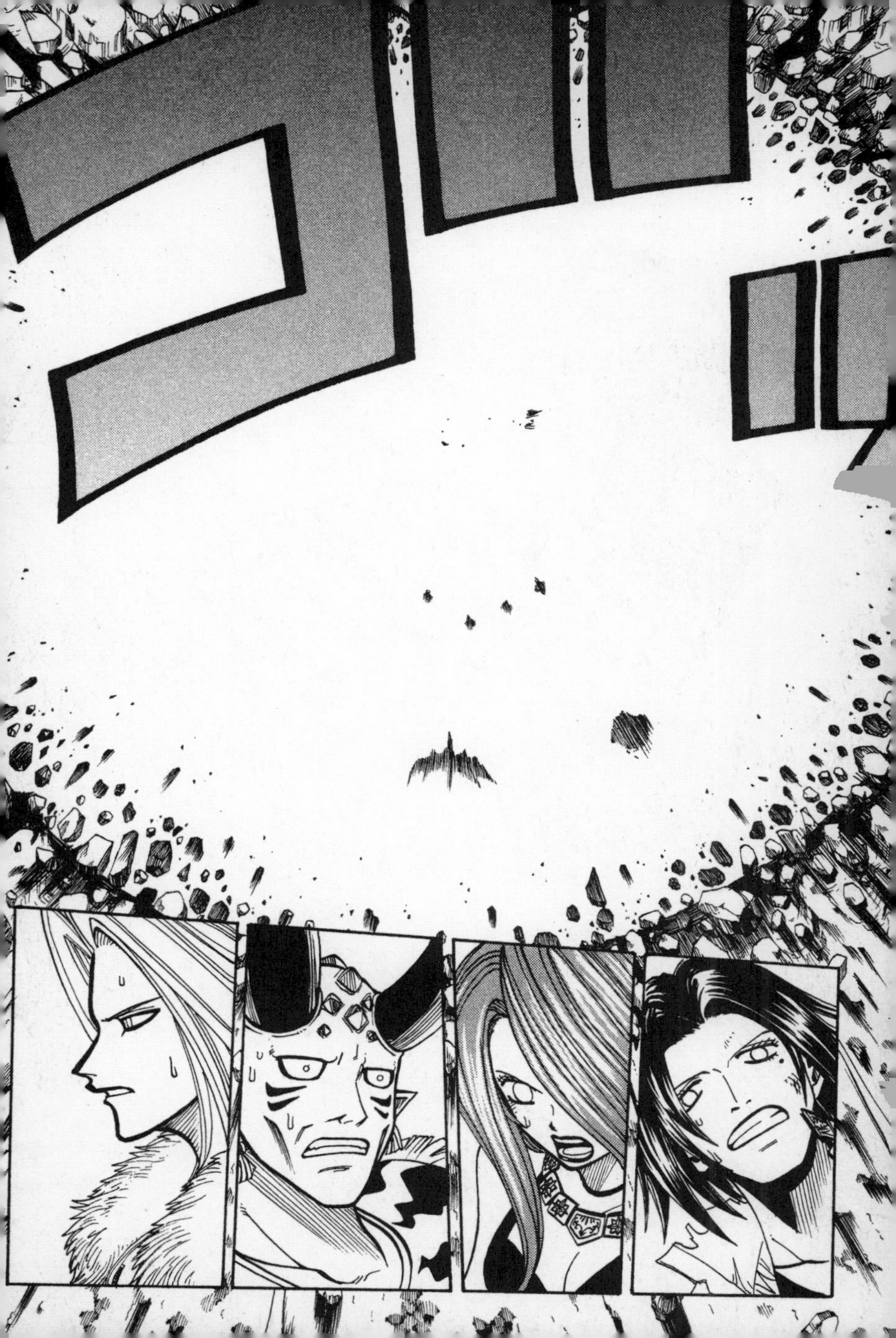

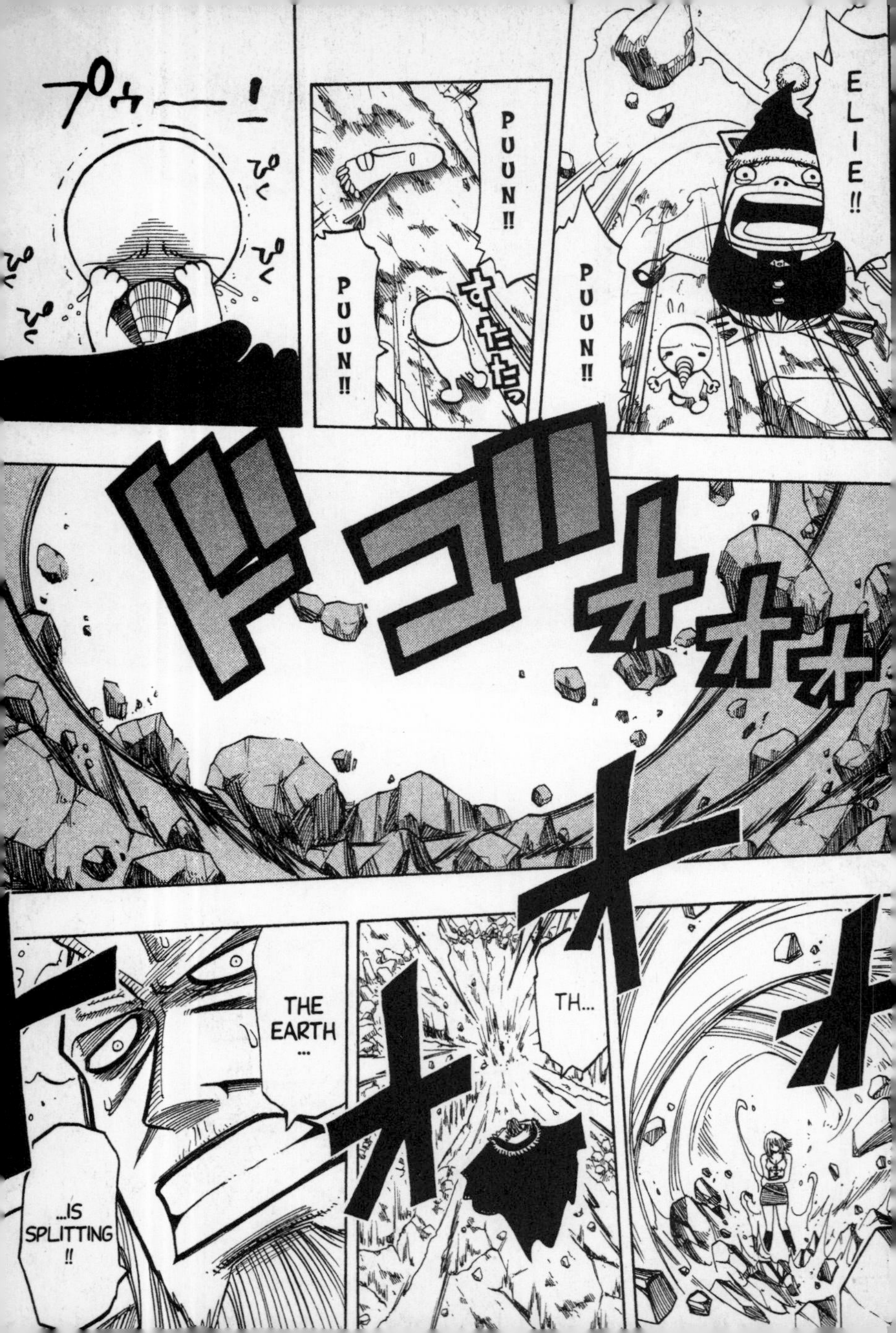

ELIE!!
PUUN!!
PUUN!!
PUUN!!
すたたっ
ぴく
ぴく
ぴく
ぴく
ドゴォォォォ
TH...
THE EARTH ...
...IS SPLITTING !!

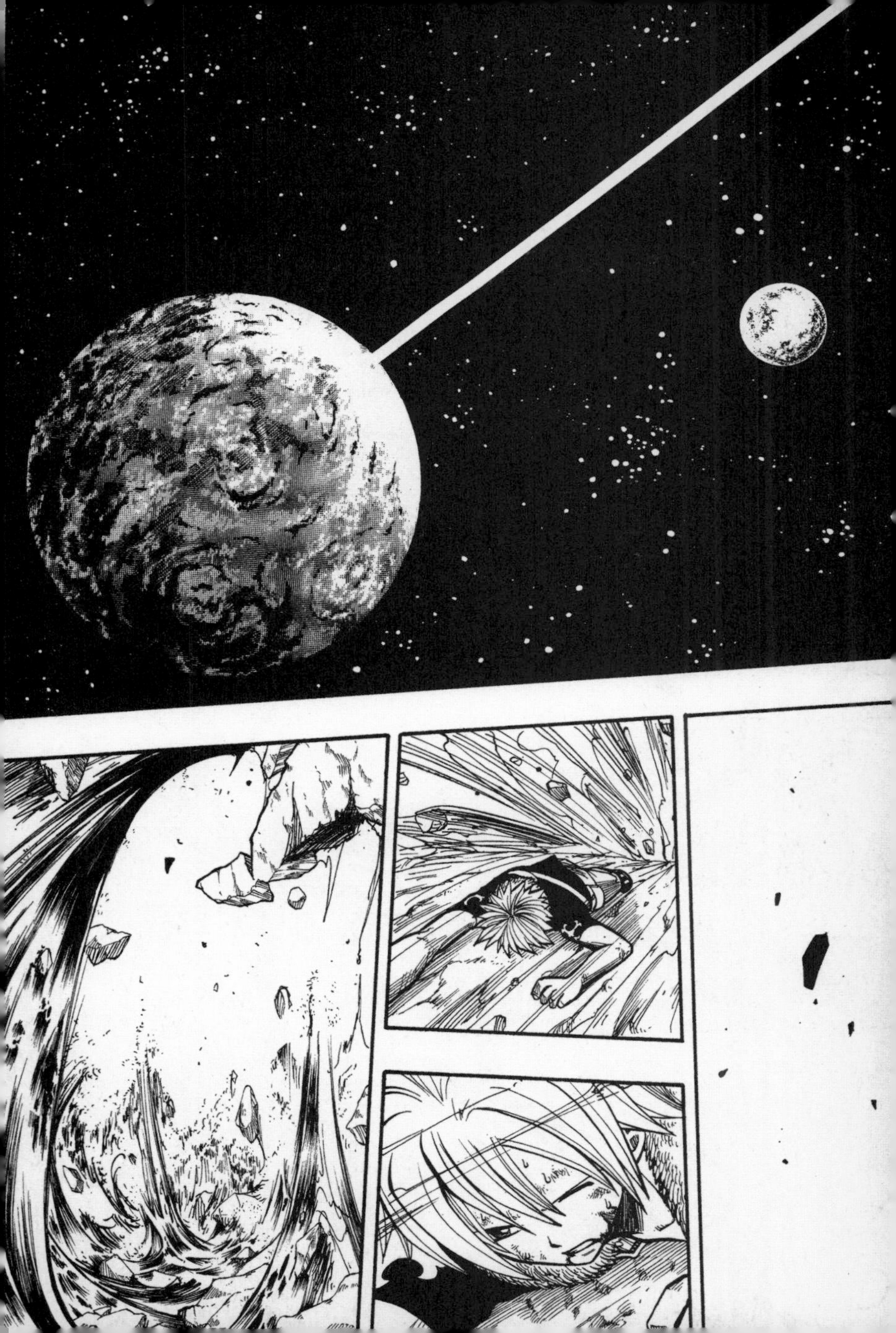

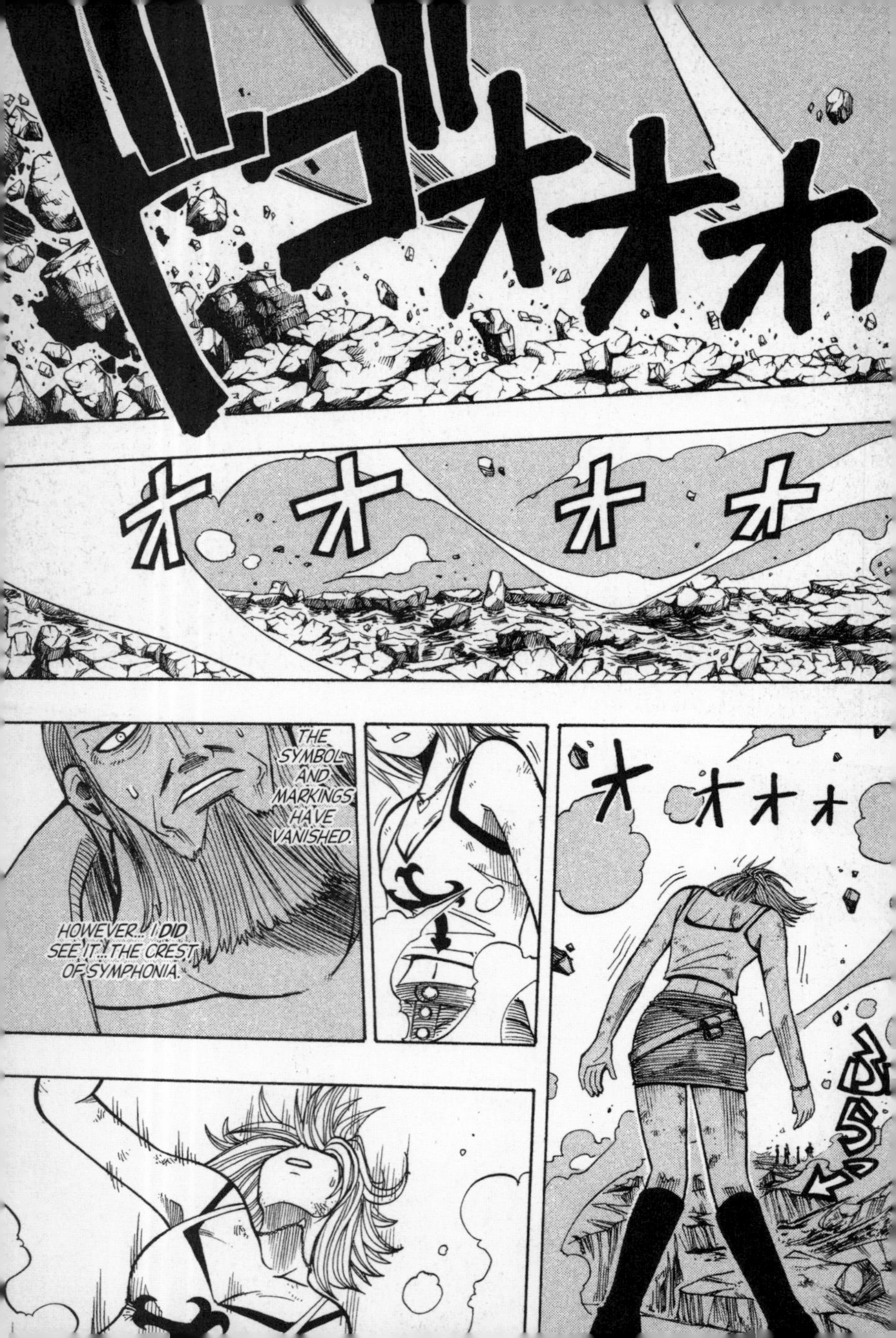

ドゴオオオ
オオオオ
オオオオ
THE SYMBOL AND MARKINGS HAVE VANISHED.
HOWEVER... I DID SEE IT... THE CREST OF SYMPHONIA.

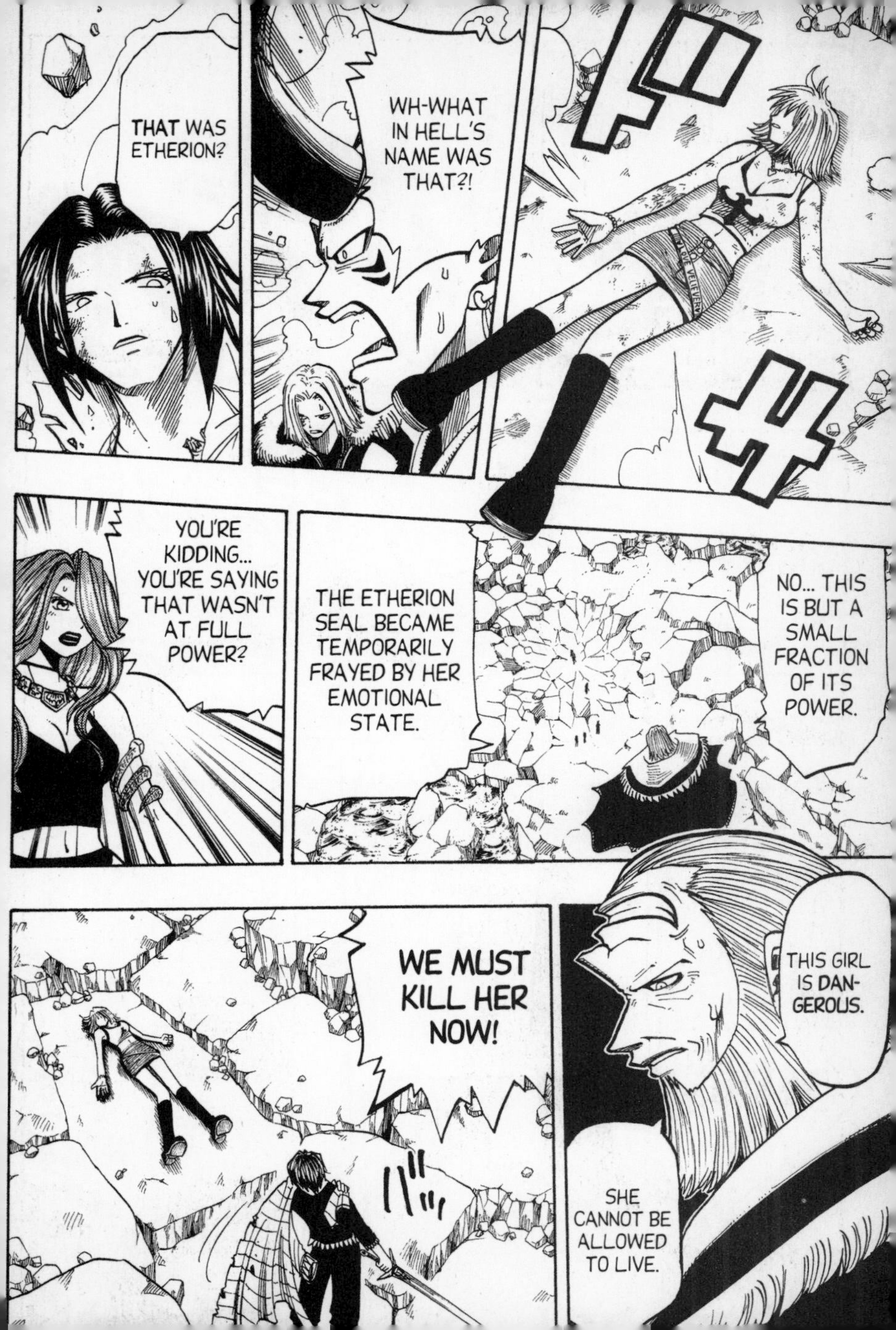
WH-WHAT IN HELL'S NAME WAS THAT?!
THAT WAS ETHERION?
NO... THIS IS BUT A SMALL FRACTION OF ITS POWER.
THE ETHERION SEAL BECAME TEMPORARILY FRAYED BY HER EMOTIONAL STATE.
YOU'RE KIDDING... YOU'RE SAYING THAT WASN'T AT FULL POWER?
THIS GIRL IS DANGEROUS.
SHE CANNOT BE ALLOWED TO LIVE.
WE MUST KILL HER NOW!

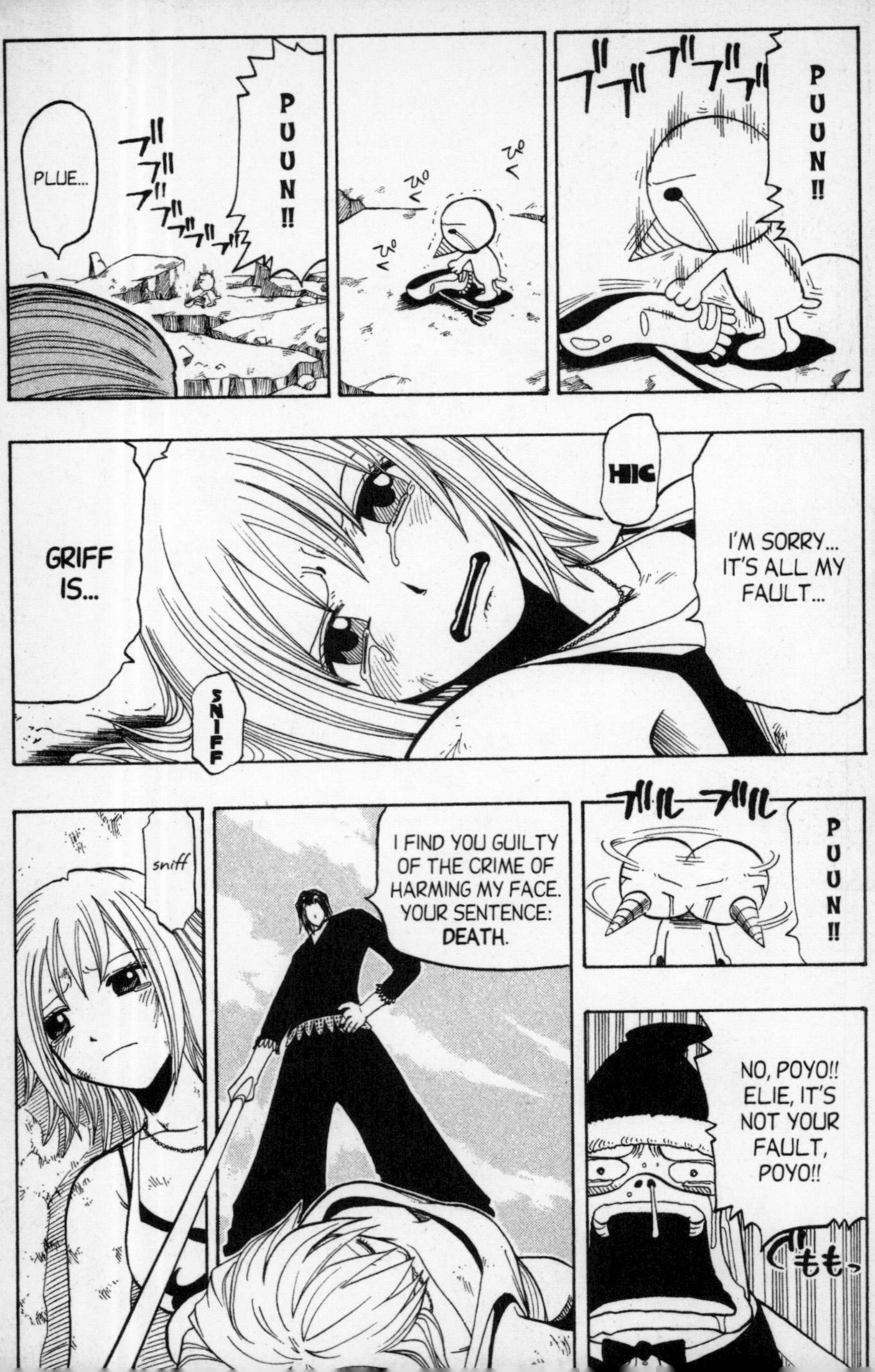
PUUN!!
PUUN!!
PLUE...
HIC
I'M SORRY... IT'S ALL MY FAULT...
GRIFF IS...
SNIFF
ブルブル
PUUN!!
NO, POYO!! ELIE, IT'S NOT YOUR FAULT, POYO!!
I FIND YOU GUILTY OF THE CRIME OF HARMING MY FACE. YOUR SENTENCE: DEATH.
sniff

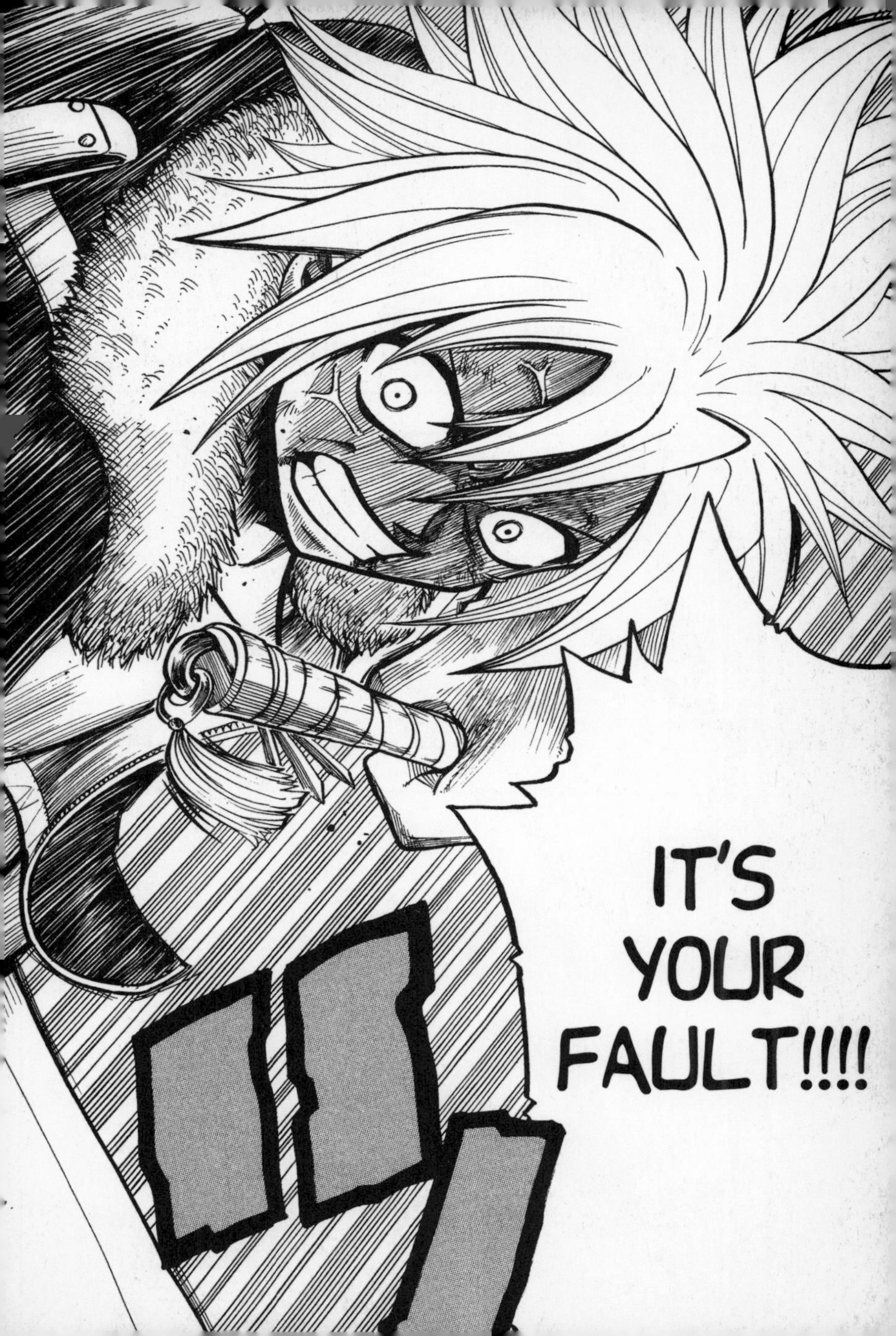
IT'S YOUR FAULT!!!!

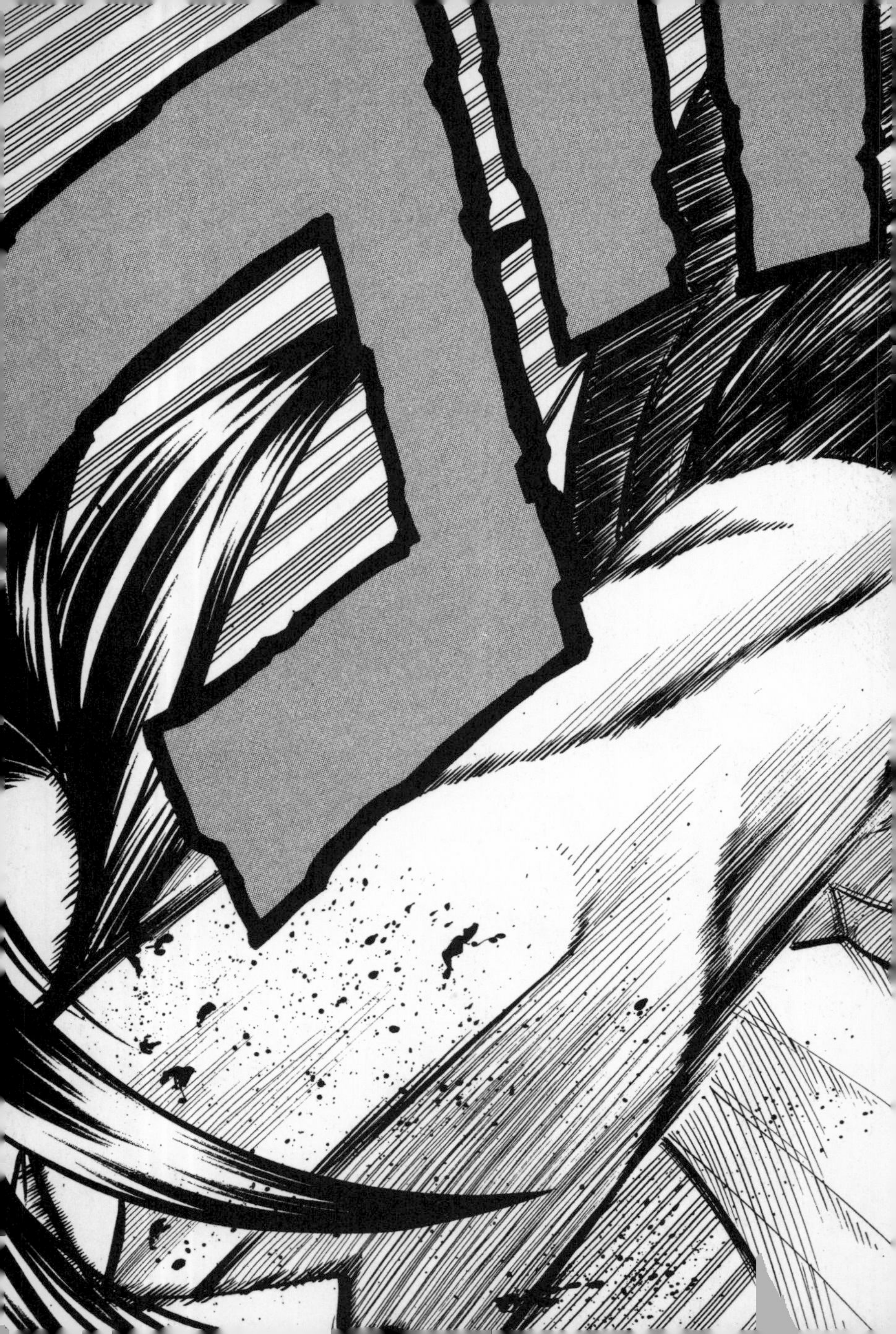

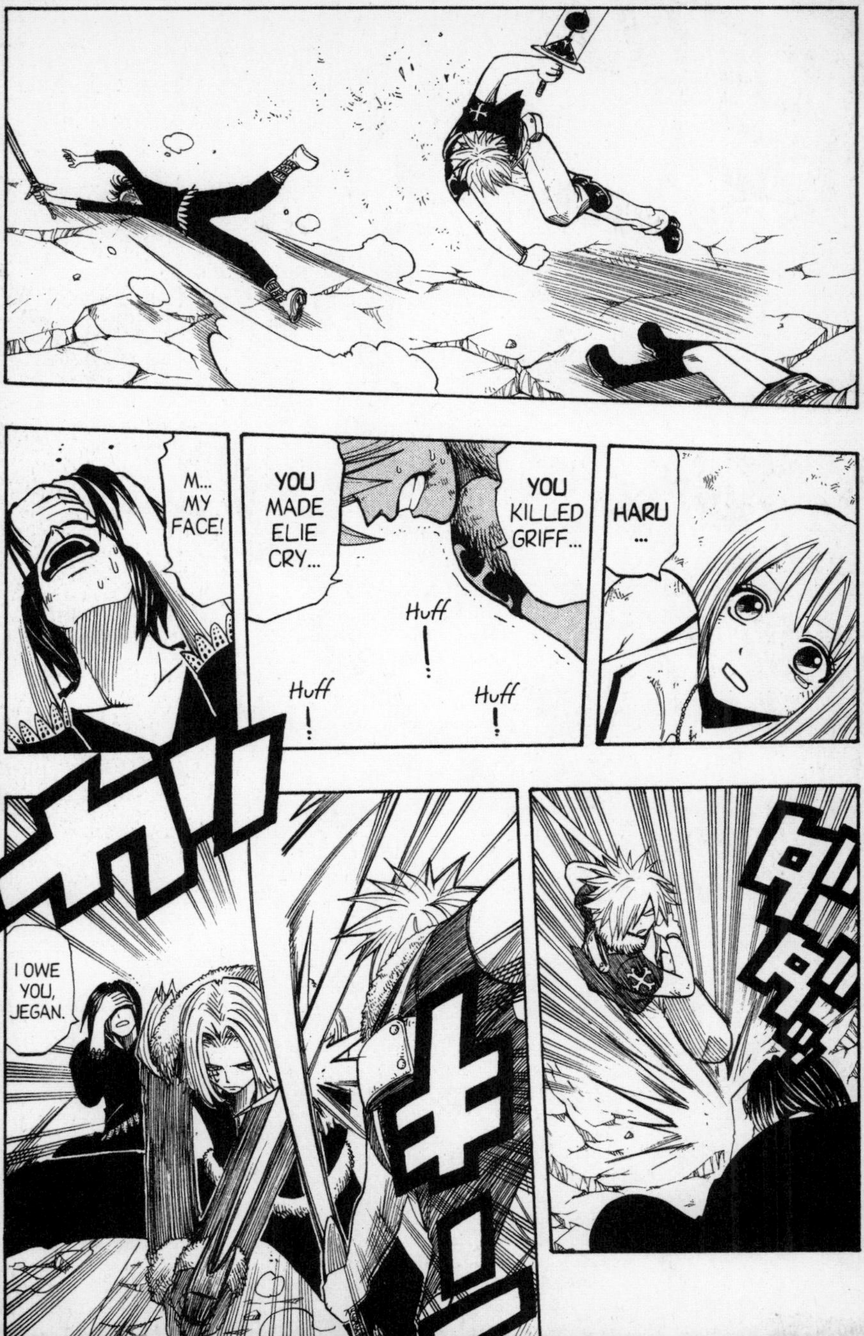
HARU ...
YOU KILLED GRIFF...
YOU MADE ELIE CRY...
Huff
Huff
Huff
M... MY FACE!
I OWE YOU, JEGAN.

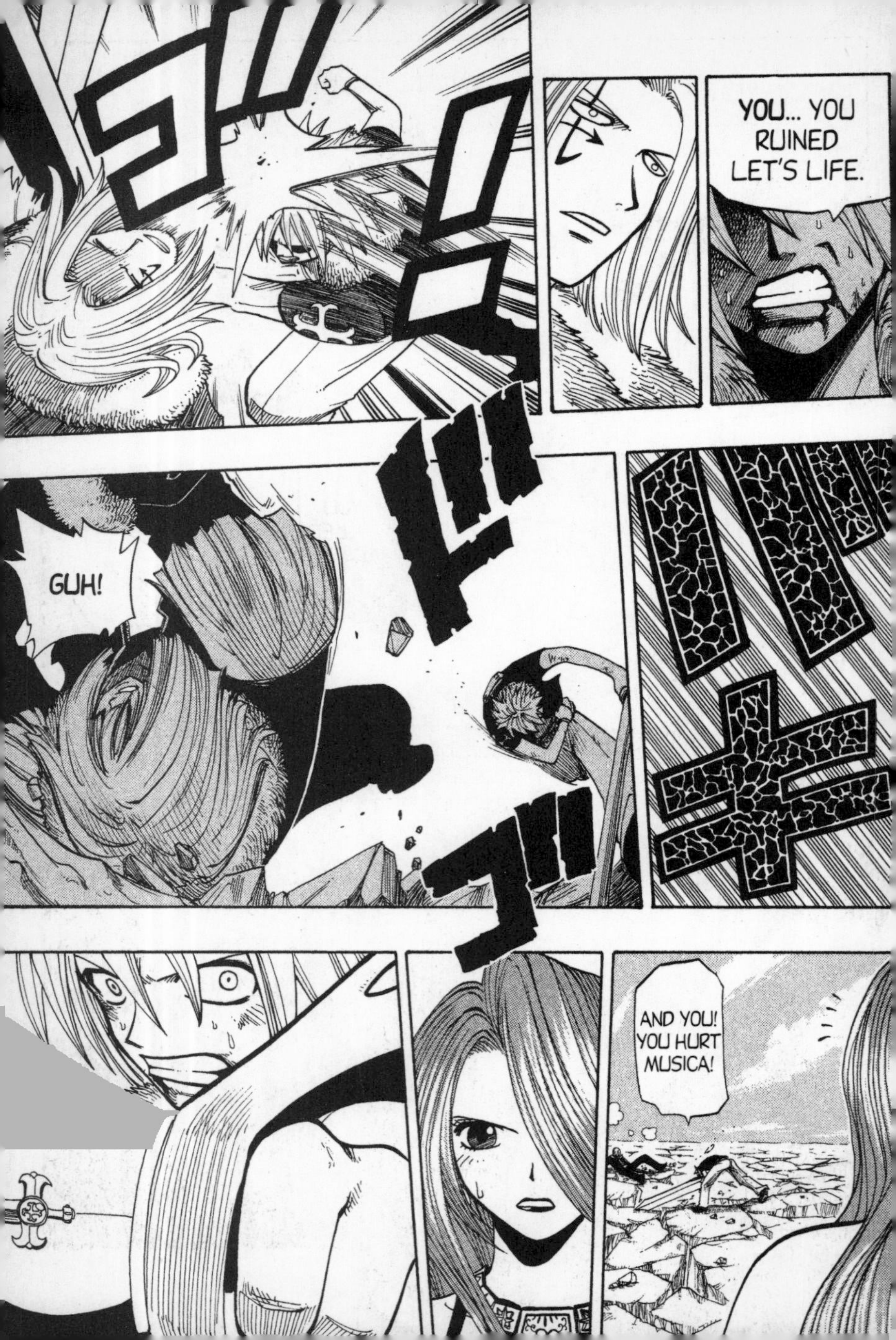
YOU... YOU RUINED LET'S LIFE.
GUH!
AND YOU! YOU HURT MUSICA!

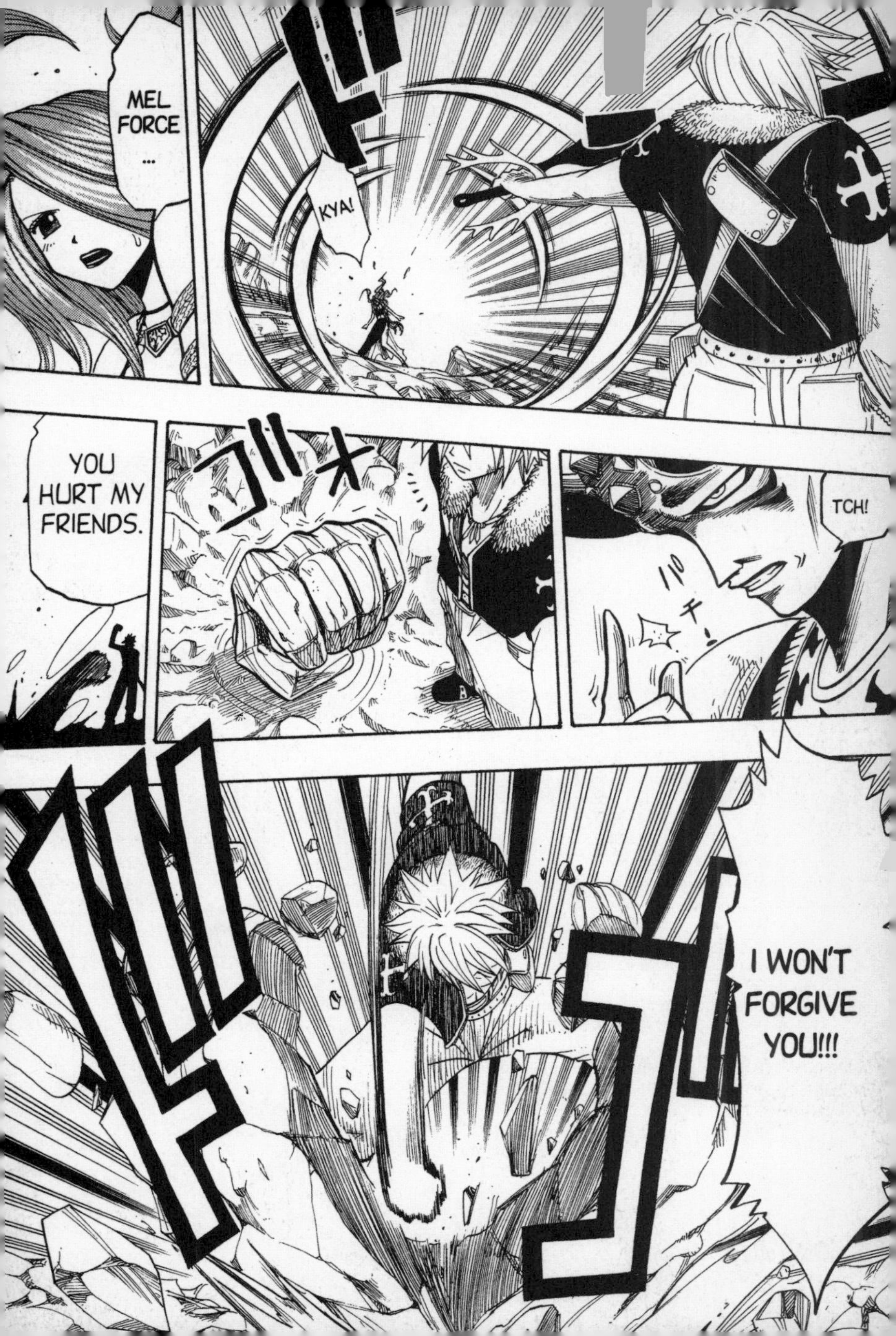
KYA!
MEL FORCE ...
TCH!
YOU HURT MY FRIENDS.
I WON'T FORGIVE YOU!!!

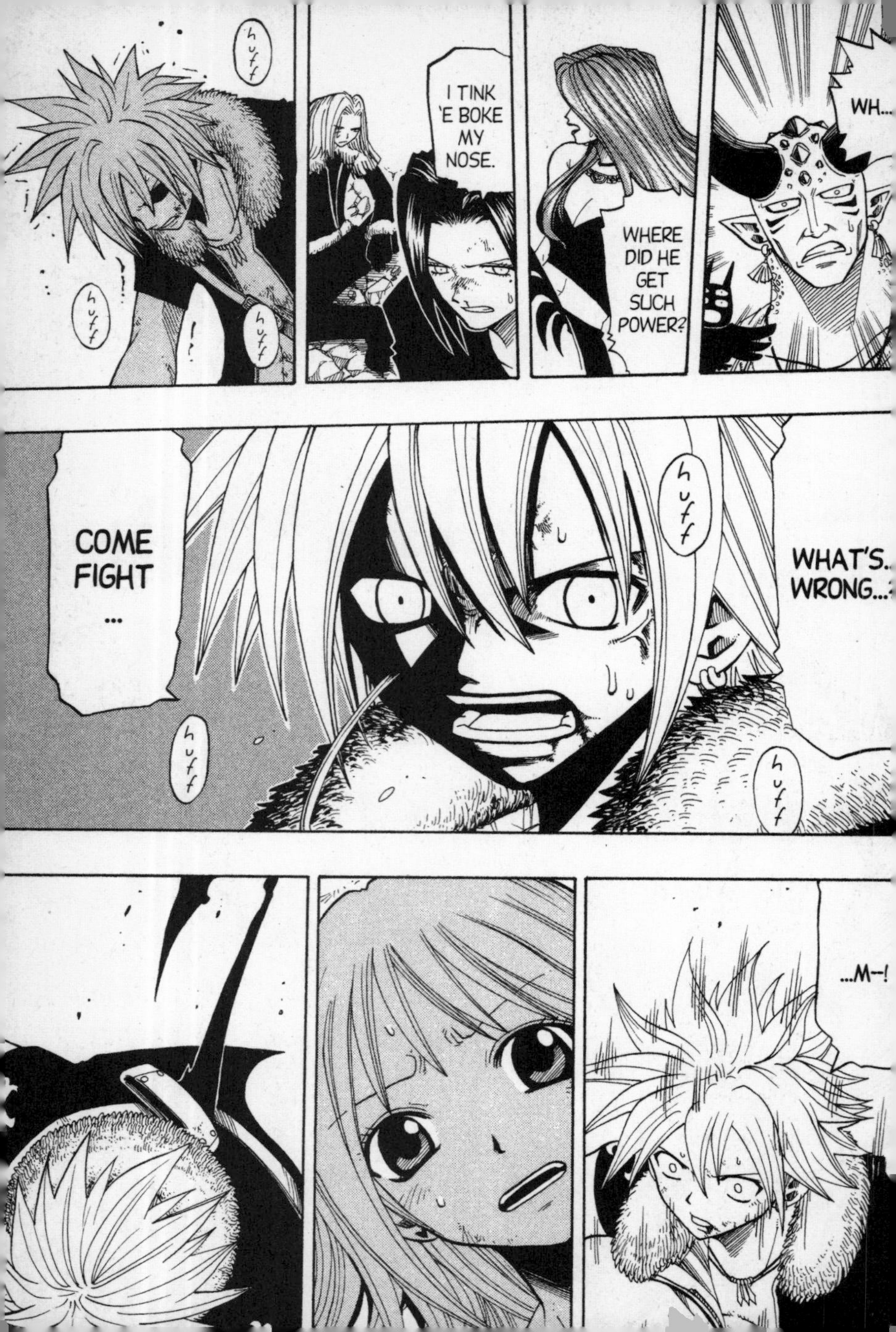
WH...
WHERE DID HE GET SUCH POWER?
I TINK 'E BOKE MY NOSE.
huff
huff
huff
huff
WHAT'S... WRONG...?
huff
COME FIGHT ...
huff
...M--!

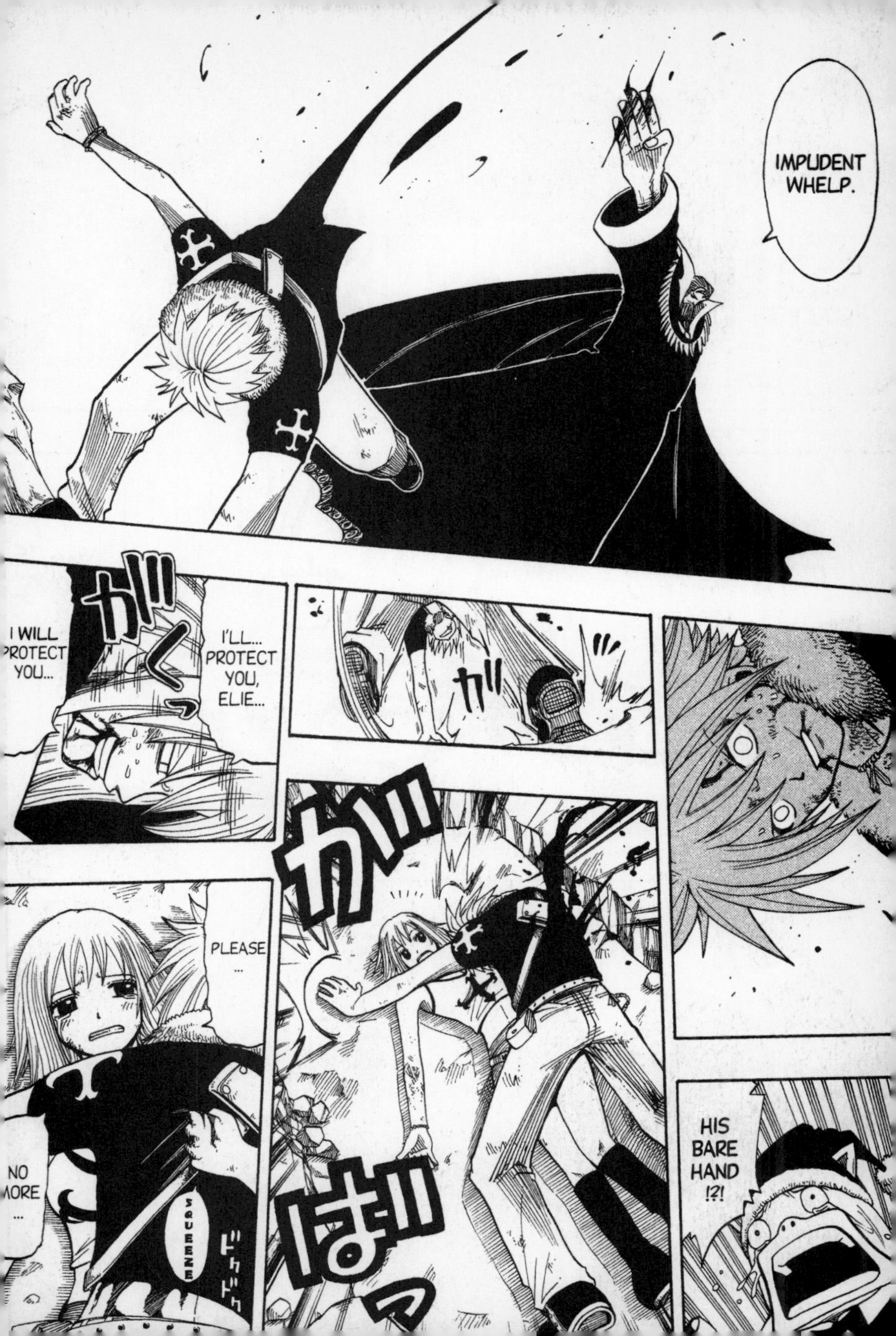
IMPUDENT WHELP.
ガッ
I'LL... PROTECT YOU, ELIE...
がくっ
I WILL PROTECT YOU...
HIS BARE HAND !?!
がっ
ばっ
PLEASE ...
NO MORE ...
SQUEEZE
ドクドク

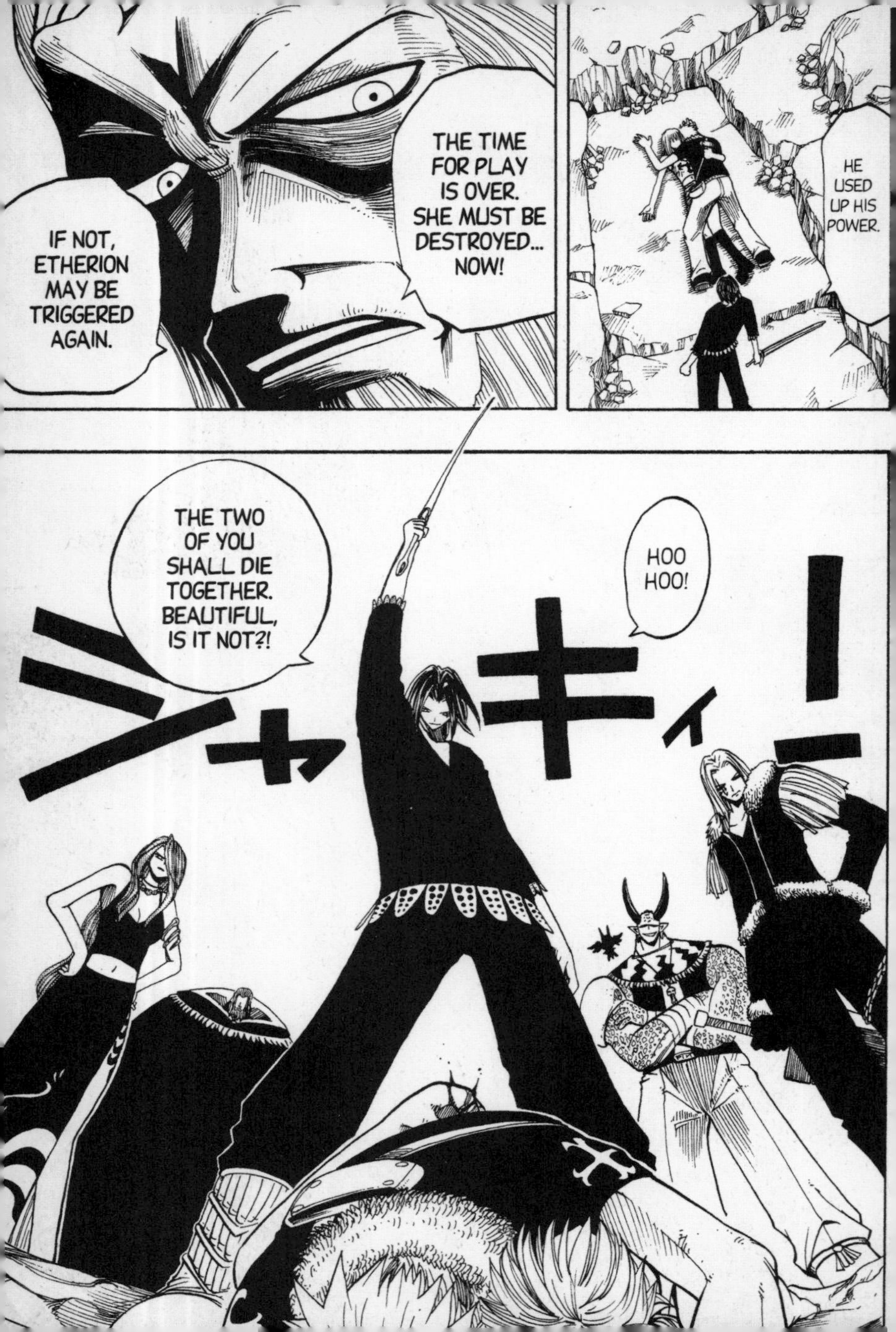
HE USED UP HIS POWER.
THE TIME FOR PLAY IS OVER. SHE MUST BE DESTROYED... NOW!
IF NOT, ETHERION MAY BE TRIGGERED AGAIN.
HOO HOO!
THE TWO OF YOU SHALL DIE TOGETHER. BEAUTIFUL, IS IT NOT?!
シャキィーン

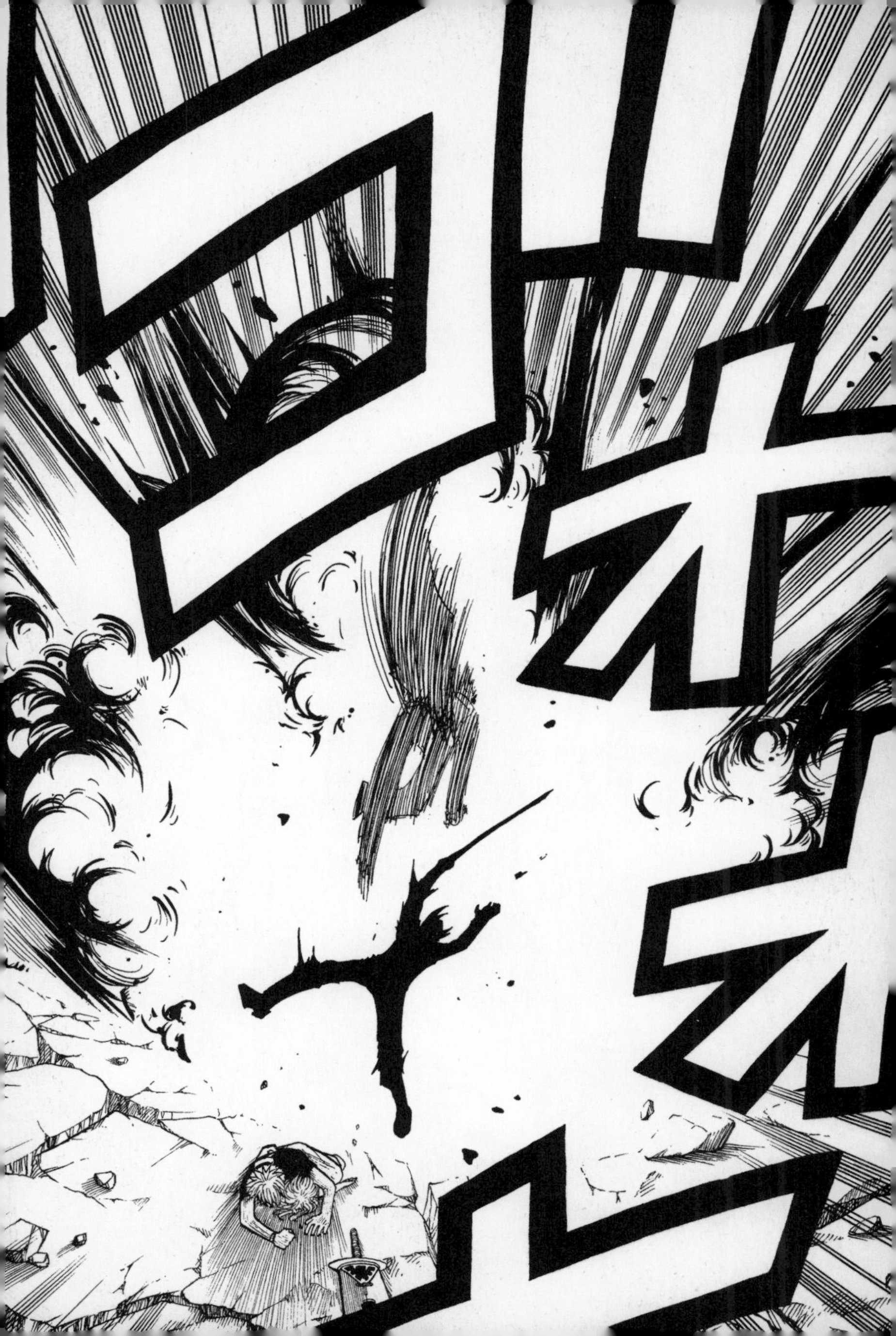

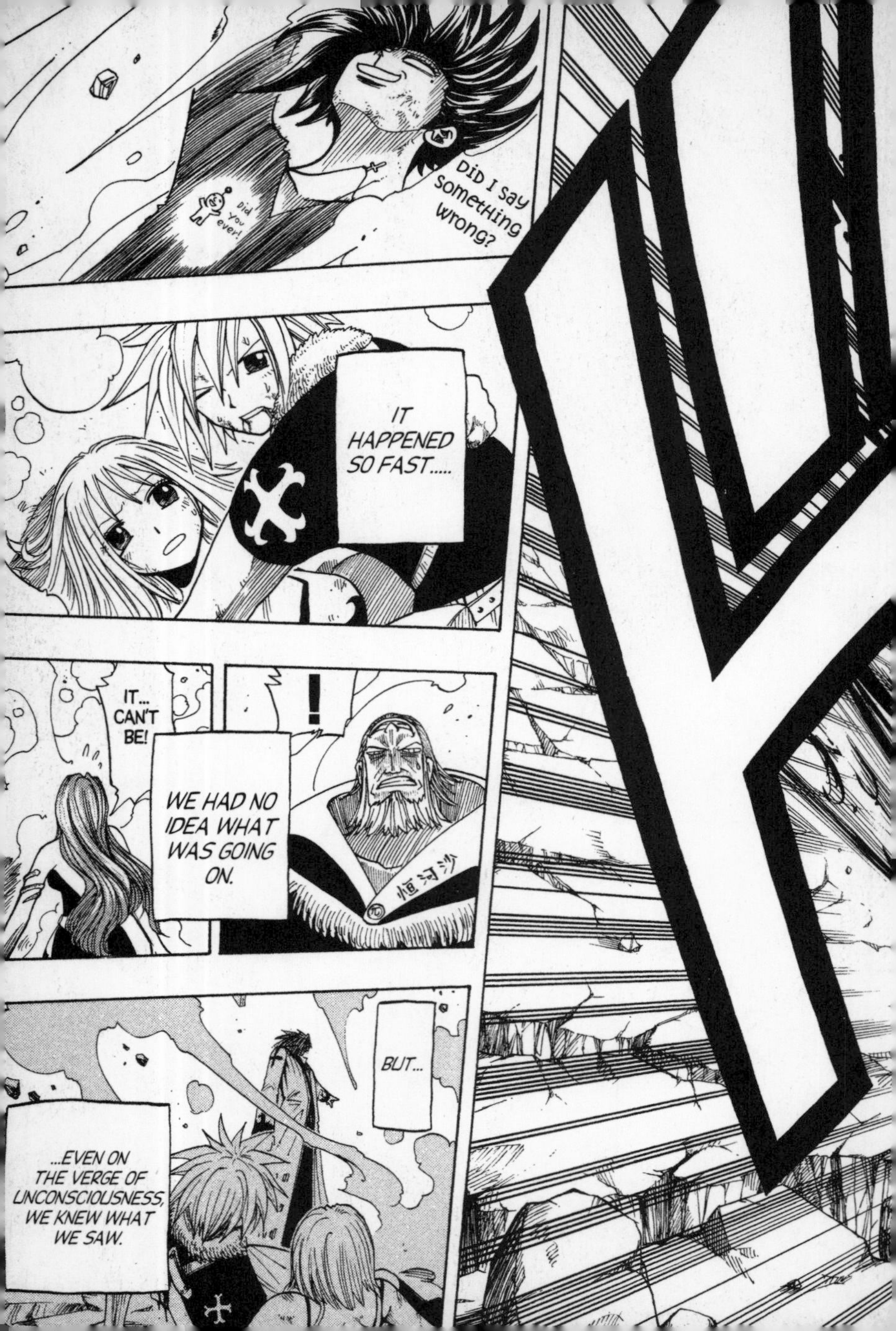
DID I SAY SOMETHING WRONG?
Did you ever!
IT HAPPENED SO FAST.....
!
WE HAD NO IDEA WHAT WAS GOING ON.
恒河沙
IT... CAN'T BE!
BUT...
...EVEN ON THE VERGE OF UNCONSCIOUSNESS, WE KNEW WHAT WE SAW.

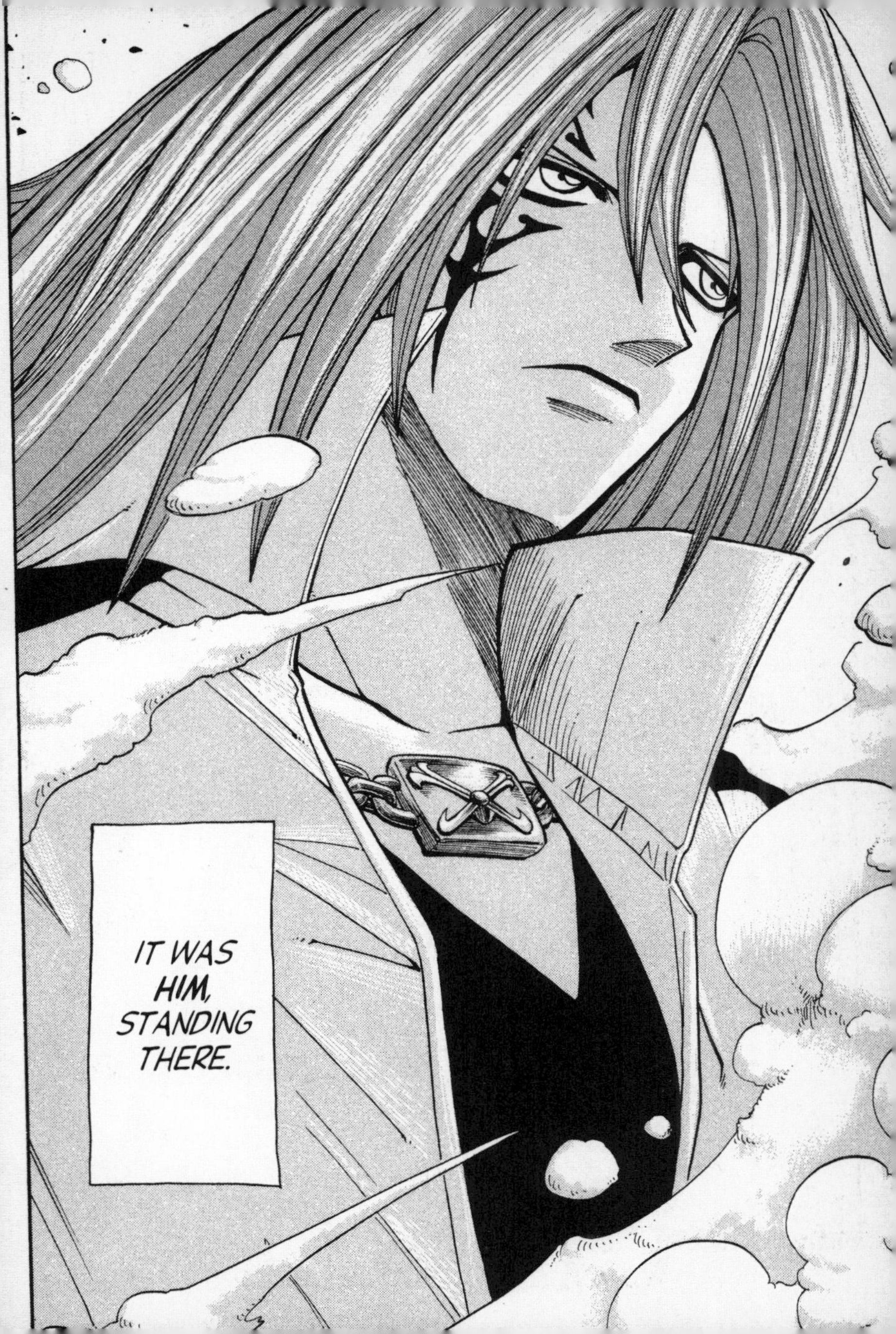
IT WAS HIM, STANDING THERE.

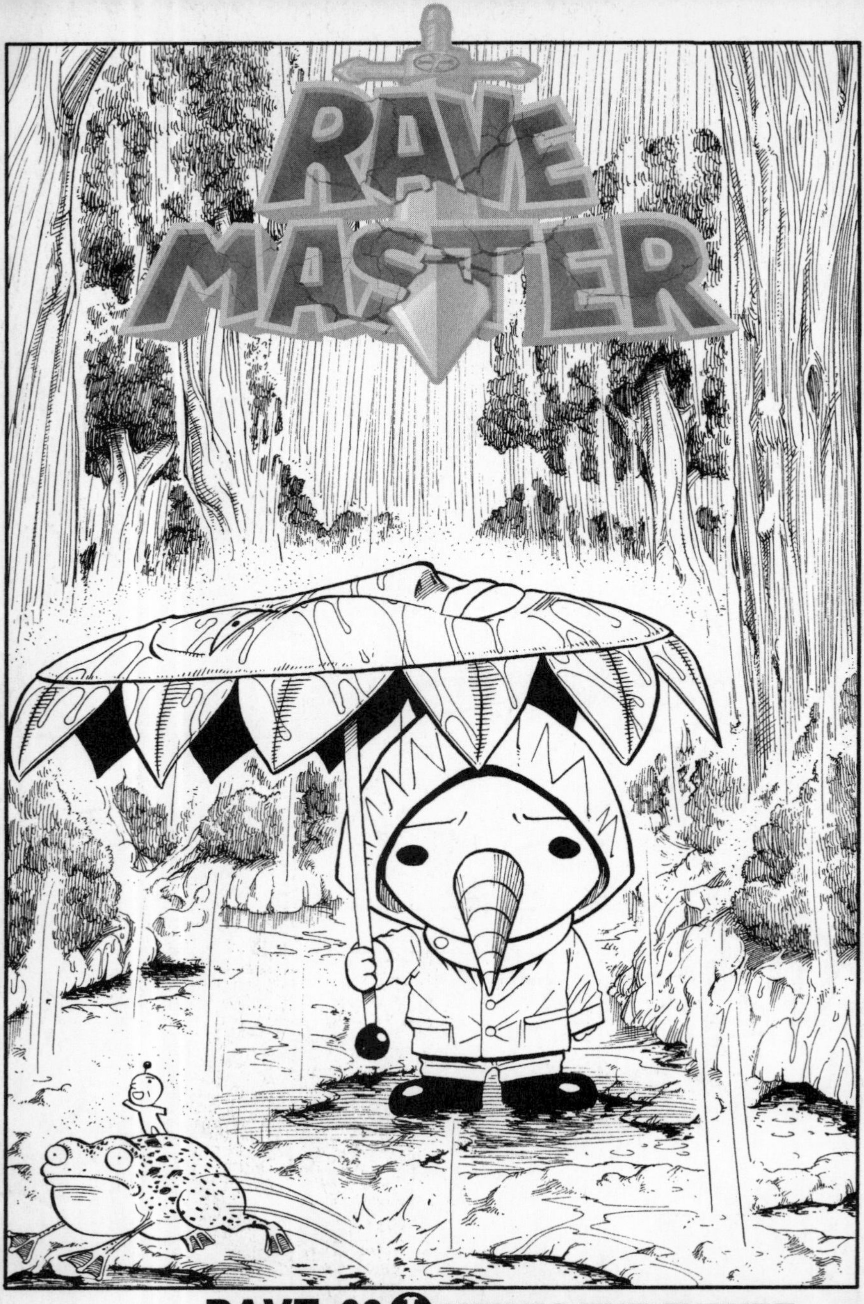
RAVE MASTER

RAVE: 92 ✠ KEY TO THE FUTURE

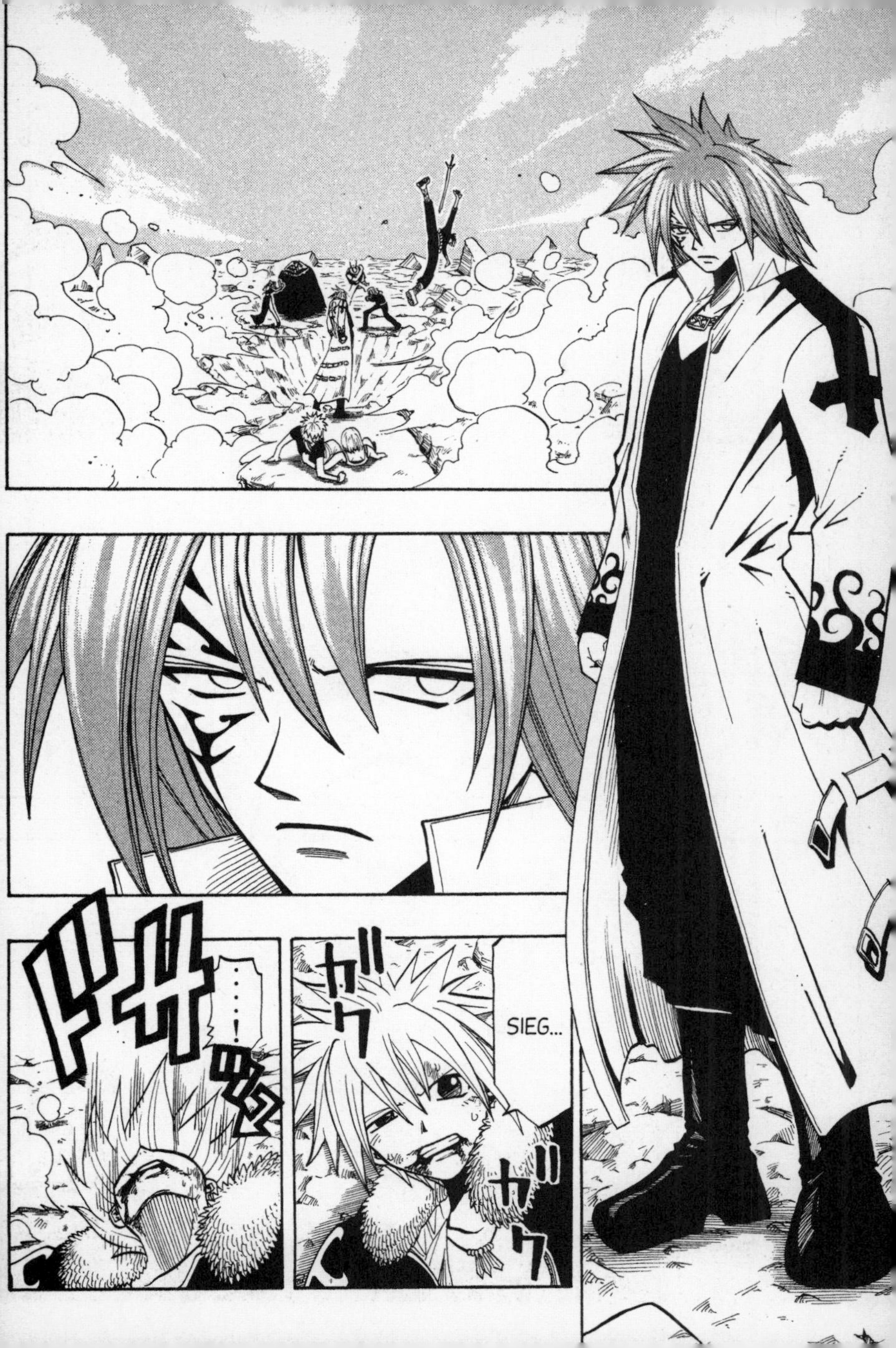
SIEG...
ガク
ガク
ドキ
....!

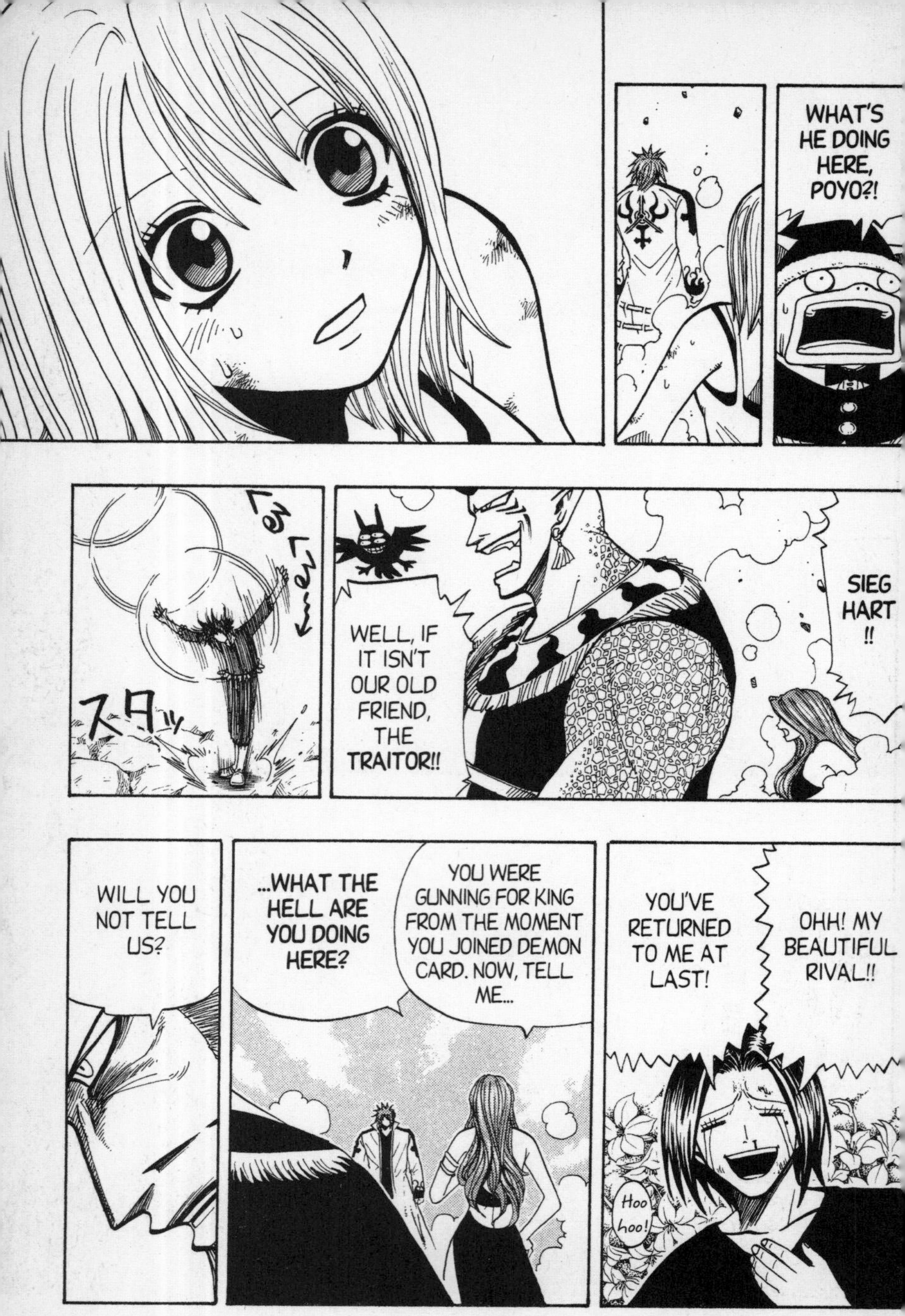
WHAT'S HE DOING HERE, POYO?!
SIEG HART !!
WELL, IF IT ISN'T OUR OLD FRIEND, THE TRAITOR!!
くるくる
スタッ
OHH! MY BEAUTIFUL RIVAL!!
YOU'VE RETURNED TO ME AT LAST!
Hoo hoo!
YOU WERE GUNNING FOR KING FROM THE MOMENT YOU JOINED DEMON CARD. NOW, TELL ME...
...WHAT THE HELL ARE YOU DOING HERE?
WILL YOU NOT TELL US?

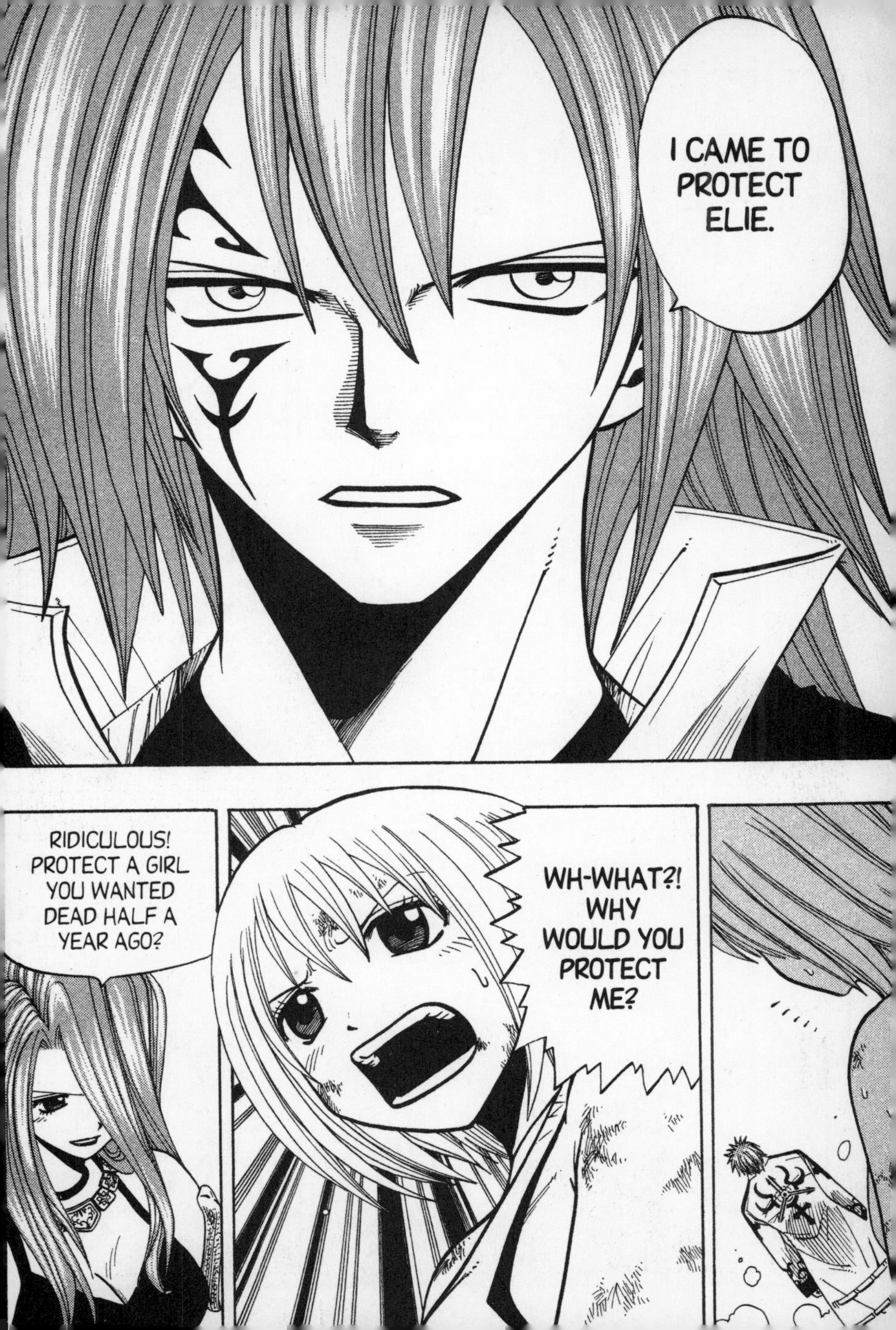
I CAME TO PROTECT ELIE.
WH-WHAT?! WHY WOULD YOU PROTECT ME?
RIDICULOUS! PROTECT A GIRL YOU WANTED DEAD HALF A YEAR AGO?

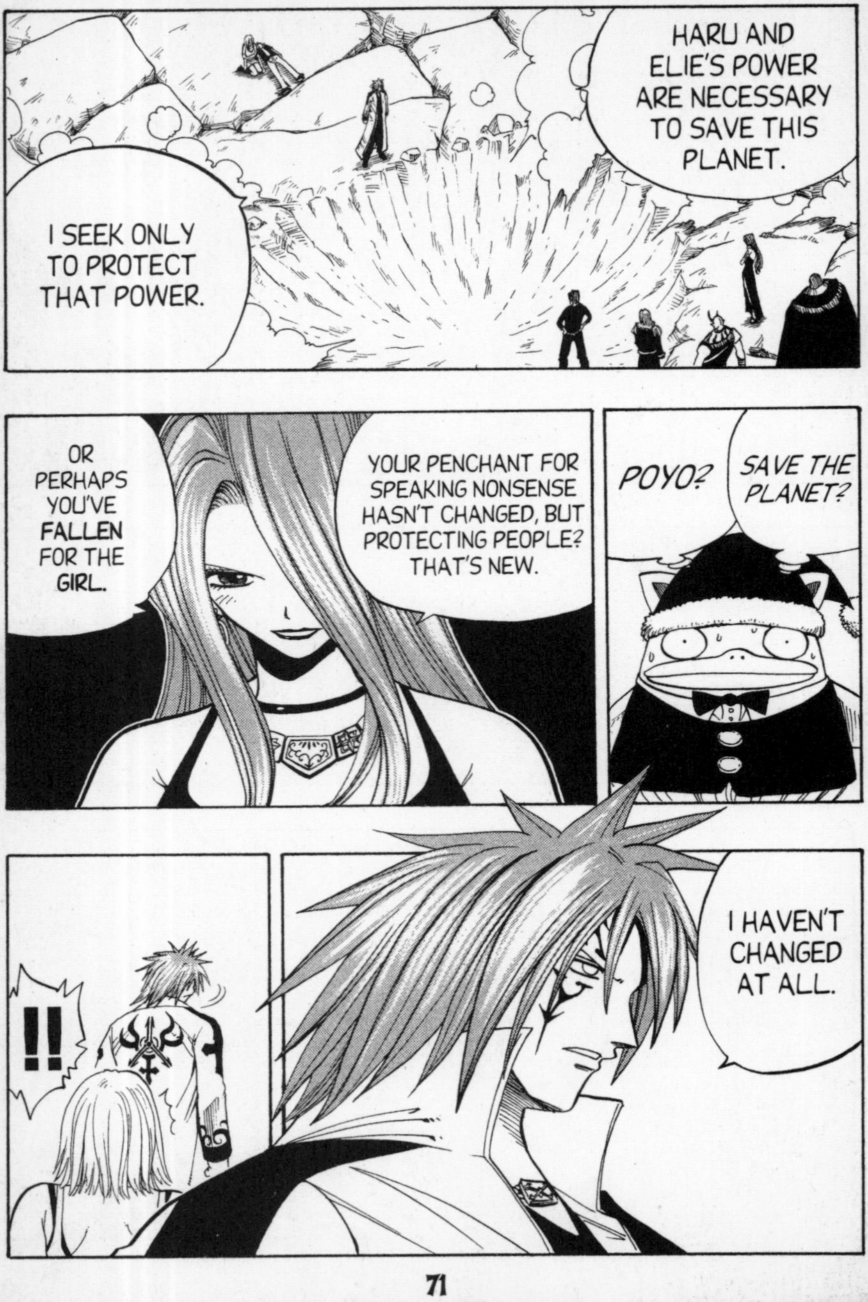
HARU AND ELIE'S POWER ARE NECESSARY TO SAVE THIS PLANET.
I SEEK ONLY TO PROTECT THAT POWER.
SAVE THE PLANET?
POYO?
YOUR PENCHANT FOR SPEAKING NONSENSE HASN'T CHANGED, BUT PROTECTING PEOPLE? THAT'S NEW.
OR PERHAPS YOU'VE FALLEN FOR THE GIRL.
I HAVEN'T CHANGED AT ALL.
!!

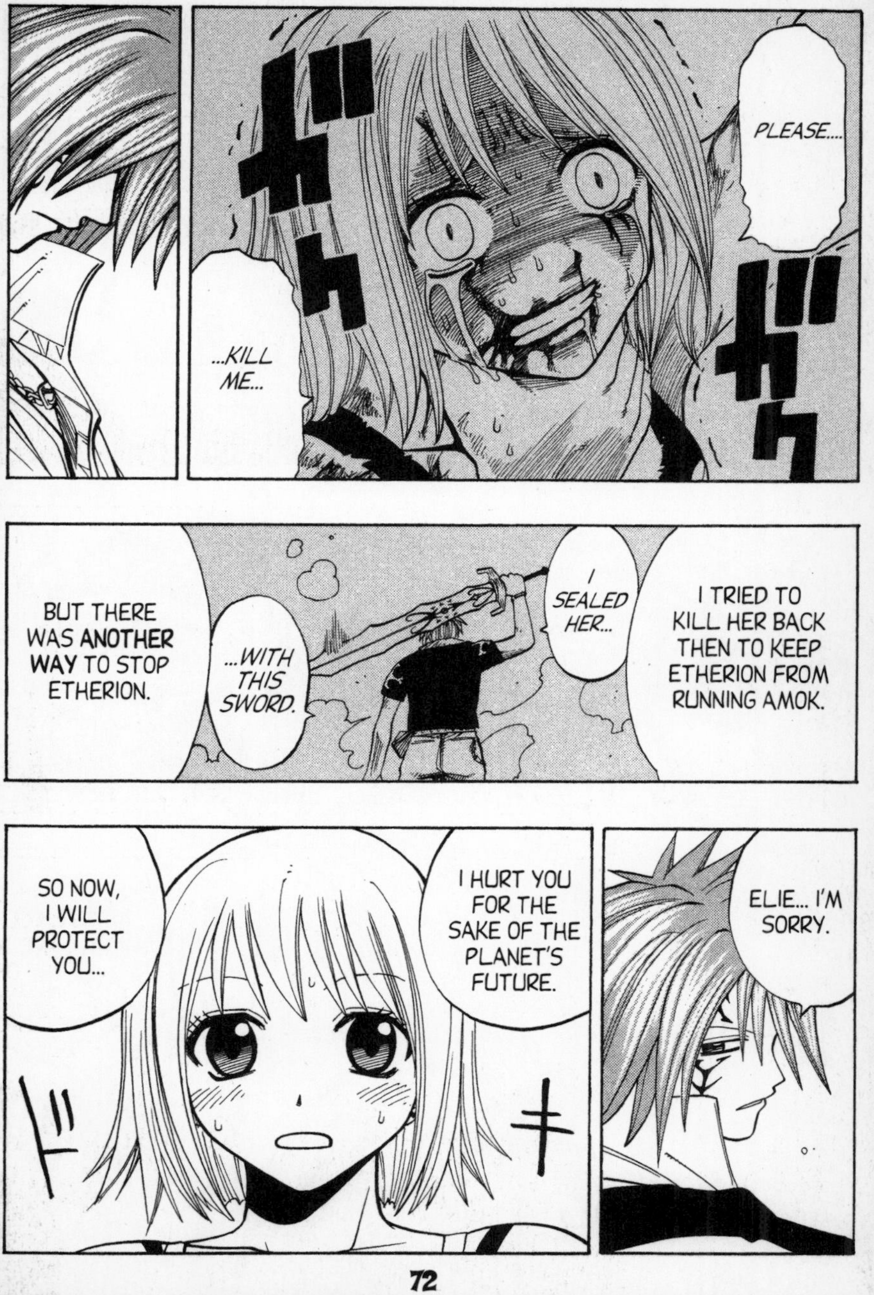

PLEASE....
...KILL ME...
I TRIED TO KILL HER BACK THEN TO KEEP ETHERION FROM RUNNING AMOK.
I SEALED HER...
...WITH THIS SWORD.
BUT THERE WAS **ANOTHER WAY** TO STOP ETHERION.
ELIE... I'M SORRY.
I HURT YOU FOR THE SAKE OF THE PLANET'S FUTURE.
SO NOW, I WILL PROTECT YOU...

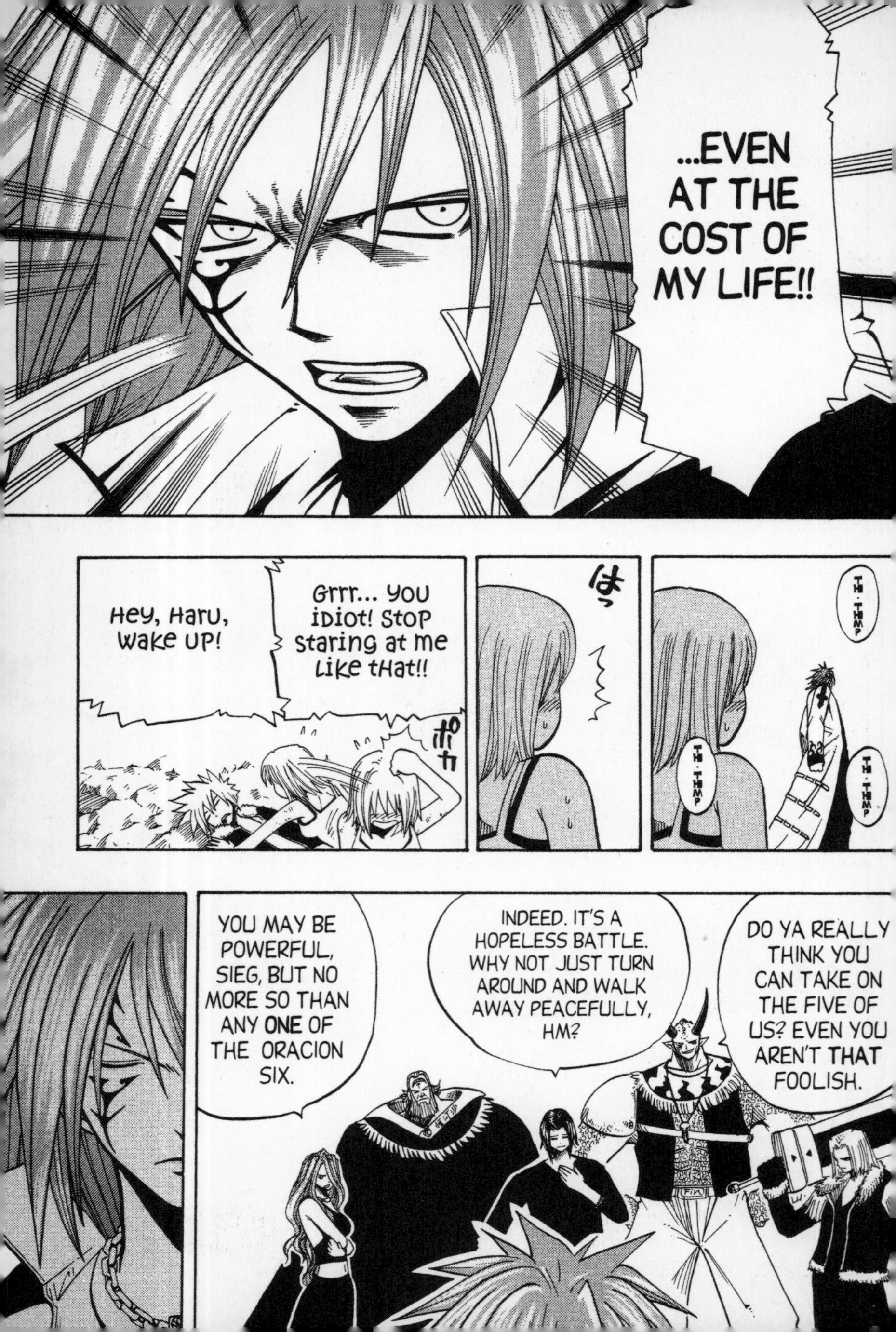

...EVEN AT THE COST OF MY LIFE!!
TH-THMP
TH-THMP
TH-THMP
はっ
Grrr... you idiot! Stop staring at me like that!!
Hey, Haru, wake up!
ポカ
DO YA REALLY THINK YOU CAN TAKE ON THE FIVE OF US? EVEN YOU AREN'T THAT FOOLISH.
INDEED. IT'S A HOPELESS BATTLE. WHY NOT JUST TURN AROUND AND WALK AWAY PEACEFULLY, HM?
YOU MAY BE POWERFUL, SIEG, BUT NO MORE SO THAN ANY ONE OF THE ORACION SIX.

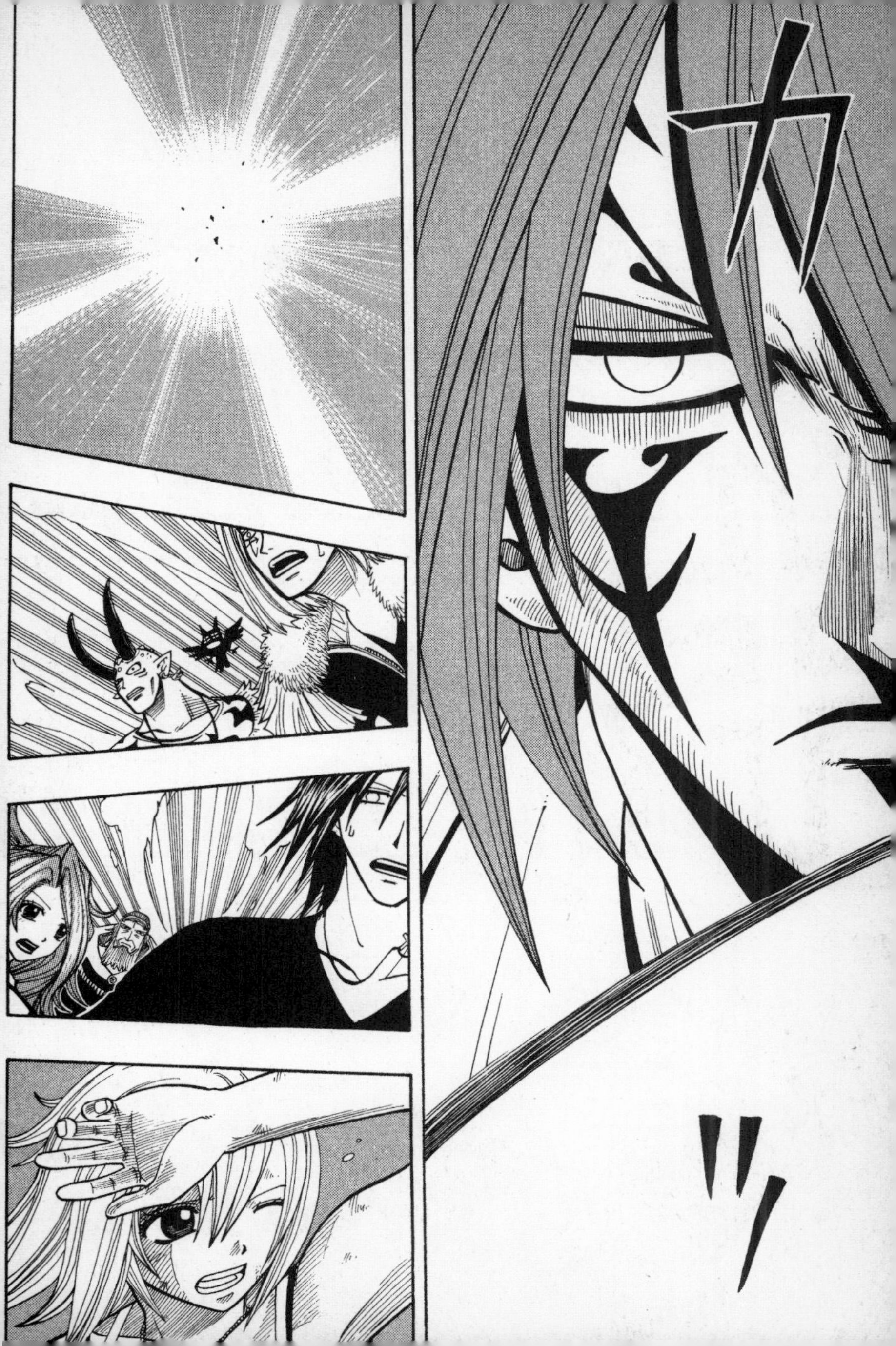
カッ

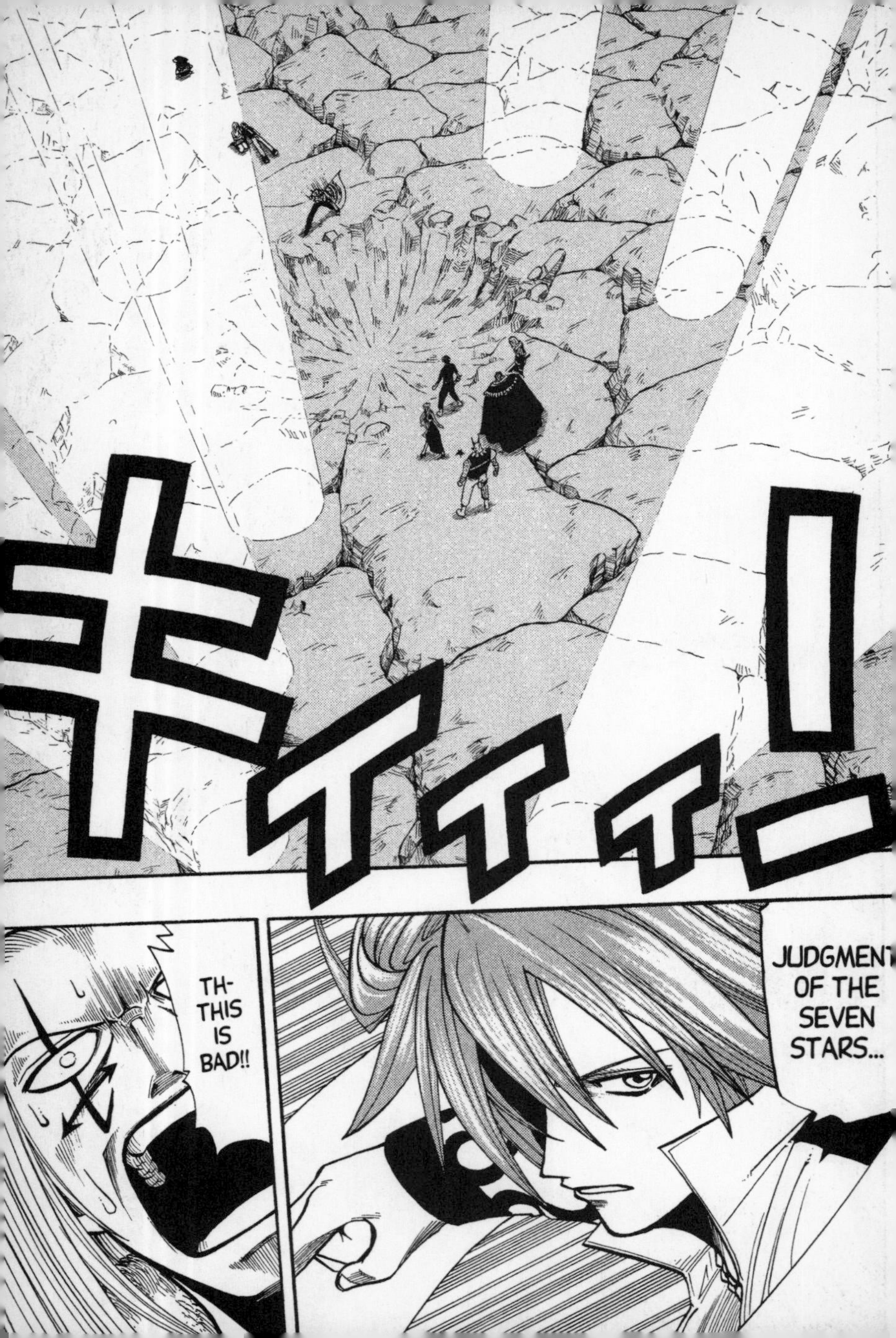
KIIIIN!
JUDGMENT OF THE SEVEN STARS...
TH-THIS IS BAD!!

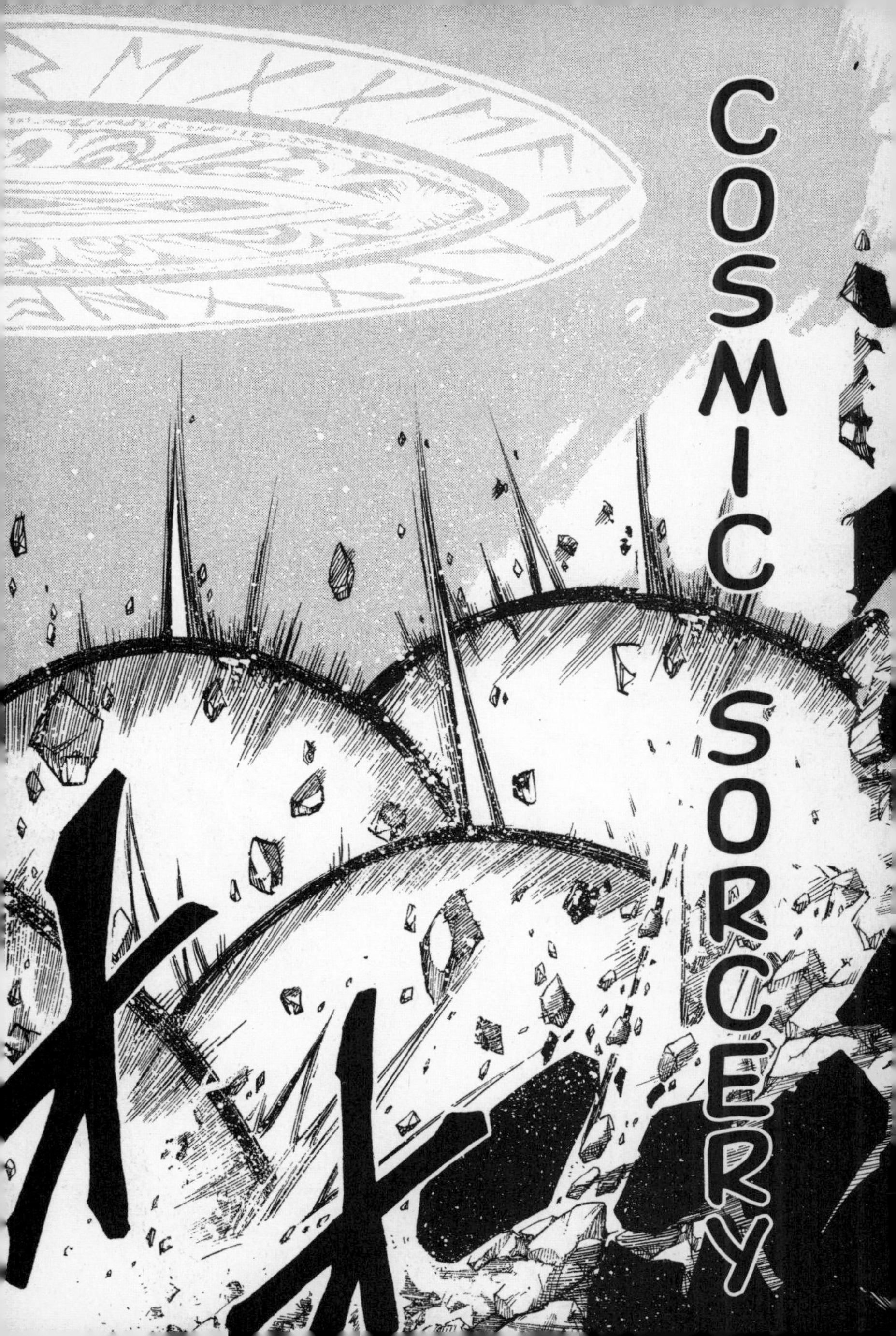
COSMIC SORCERY

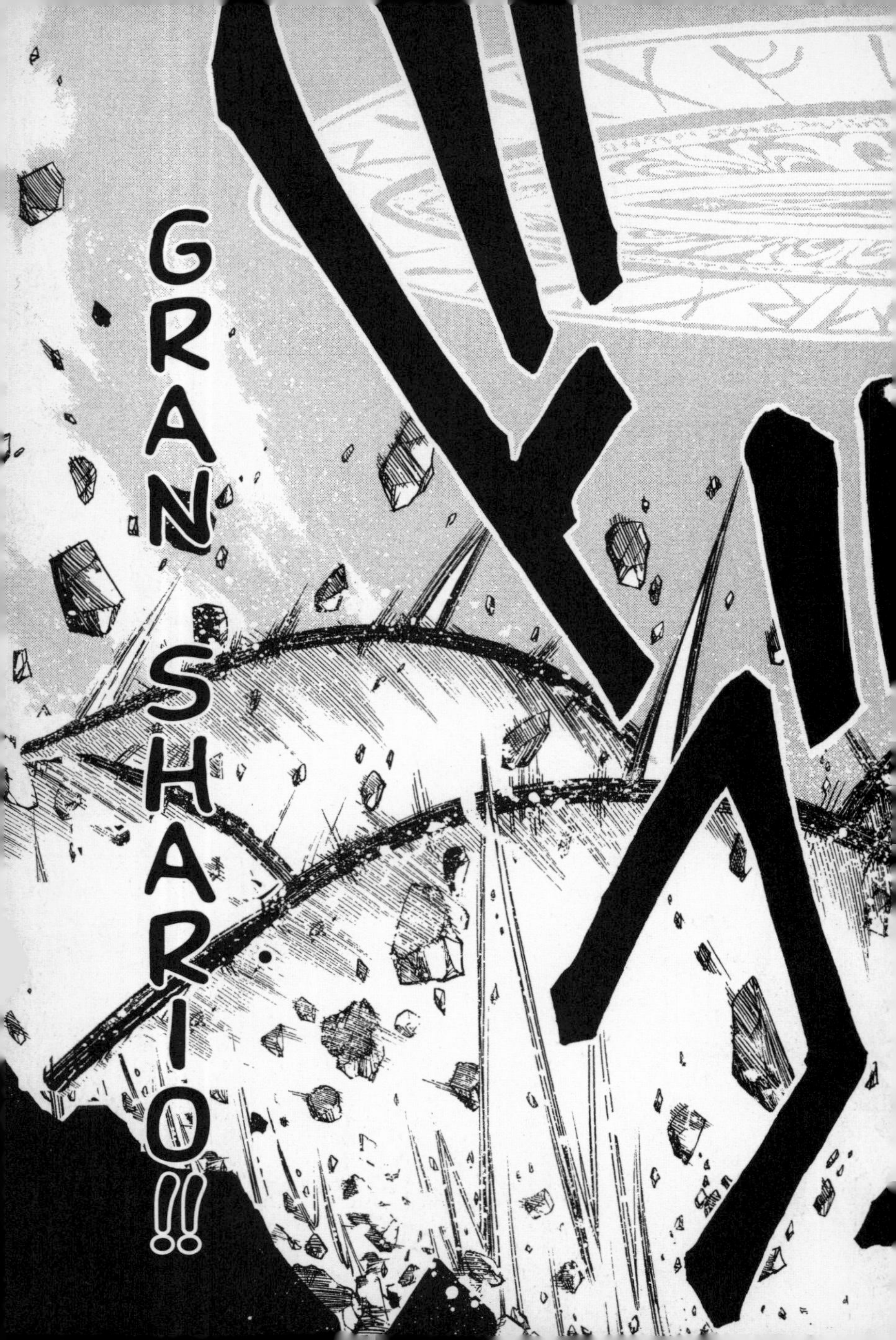
GRAN SHARIO!!

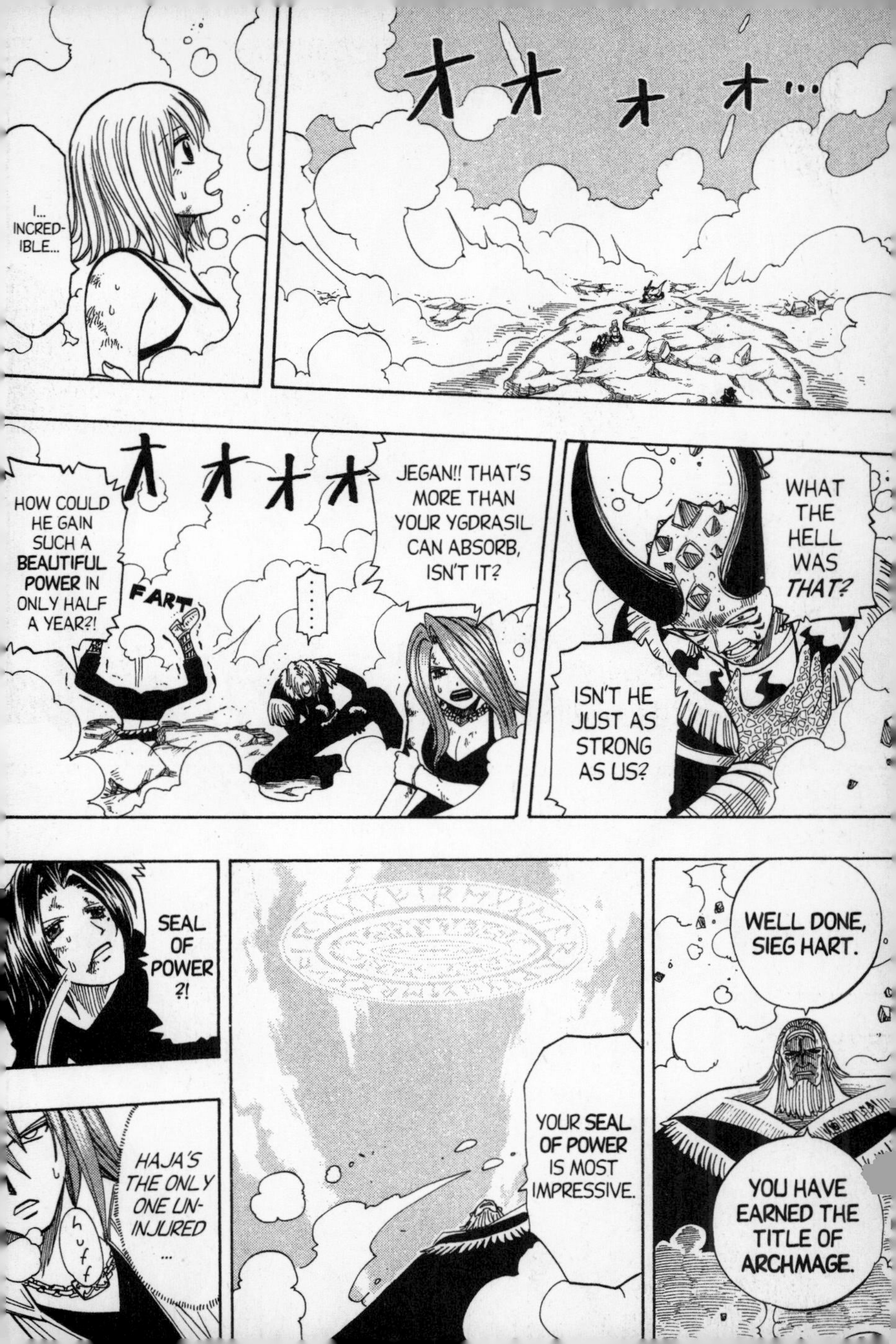

オオォォ…
I... INCREDIBLE...
WHAT THE HELL WAS THAT?
ISN'T HE JUST AS STRONG AS US?
JEGAN!! THAT'S MORE THAN YOUR YGDRASIL CAN ABSORB, ISN'T IT?
......
オオオオ
HOW COULD HE GAIN SUCH A BEAUTIFUL POWER IN ONLY HALF A YEAR?!
FART
WELL DONE, SIEG HART.
YOU HAVE EARNED THE TITLE OF ARCHMAGE.
YOUR SEAL OF POWER IS MOST IMPRESSIVE.
SEAL OF POWER?!
HAJA'S THE ONLY ONE UN-INJURED...
huff

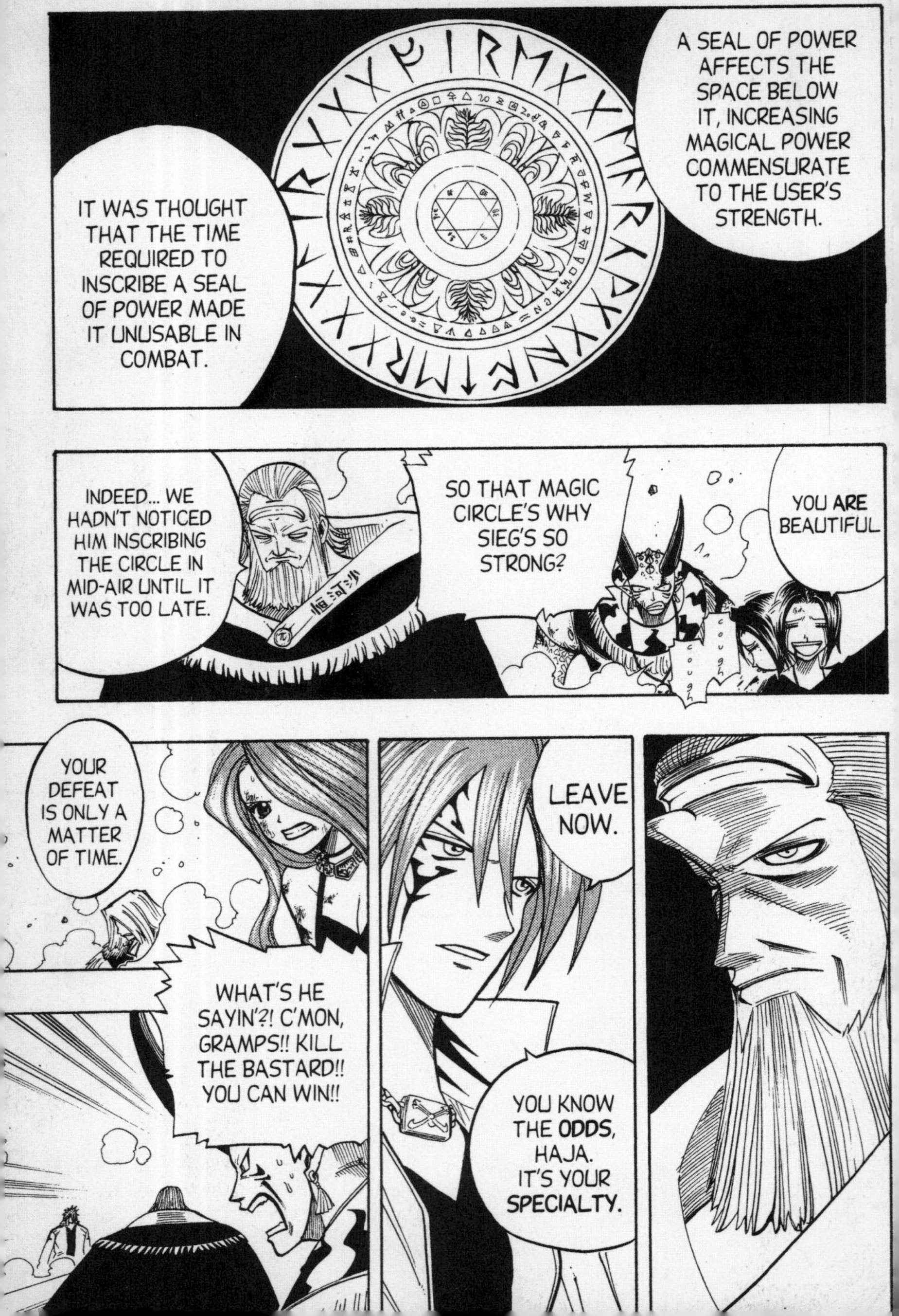
A SEAL OF POWER AFFECTS THE SPACE BELOW IT, INCREASING MAGICAL POWER COMMENSURATE TO THE USER'S STRENGTH.
IT WAS THOUGHT THAT THE TIME REQUIRED TO INSCRIBE A SEAL OF POWER MADE IT UNUSABLE IN COMBAT.
YOU **ARE** BEAUTIFUL
SO THAT MAGIC CIRCLE'S WHY SIEG'S SO STRONG?
cough cough
INDEED... WE HADN'T NOTICED HIM INSCRIBING THE CIRCLE IN MID-AIR UNTIL IT WAS TOO LATE.
LEAVE NOW.
YOU KNOW THE **ODDS**, HAJA. IT'S YOUR **SPECIALTY**.
YOUR DEFEAT IS ONLY A MATTER OF TIME.
WHAT'S HE SAYIN'?! C'MON, GRAMPS!! KILL THE BASTARD!! YOU CAN WIN!!

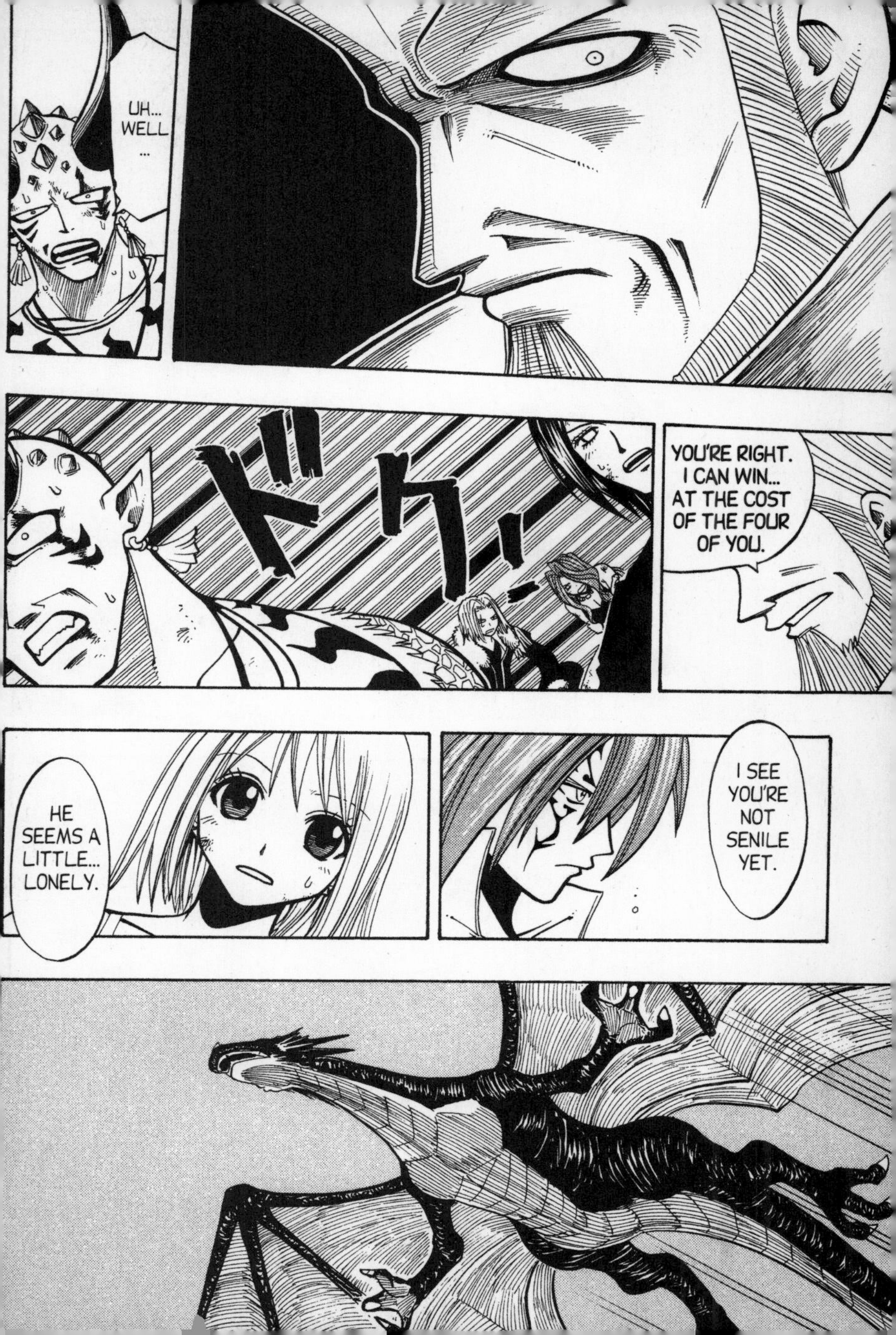
UH... WELL ...
YOU'RE RIGHT. I CAN WIN... AT THE COST OF THE FOUR OF YOU.
ドク
I SEE YOU'RE NOT SENILE YET.
HE SEEMS A LITTLE... LONELY.

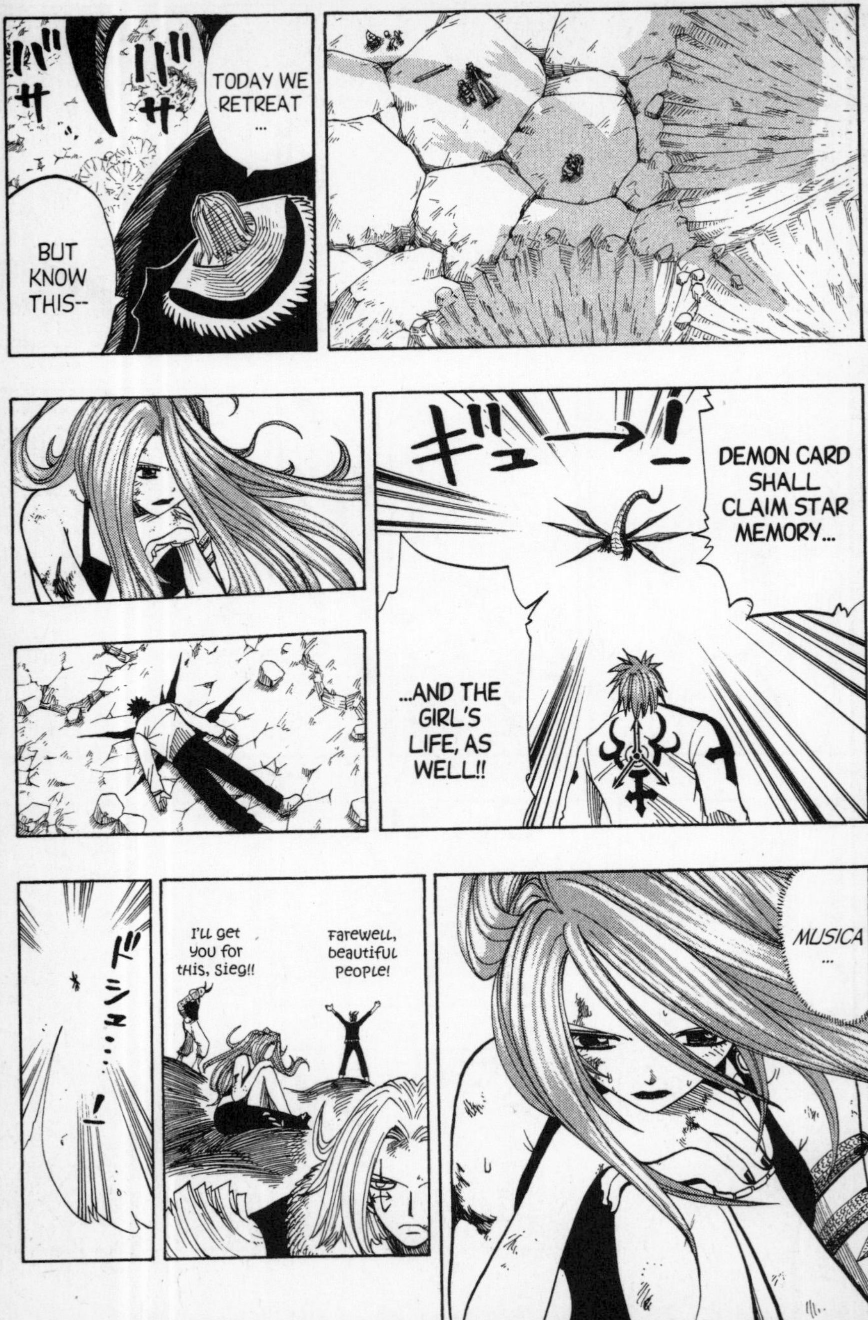

バサ
TODAY WE RETREAT ...
バサ
BUT KNOW THIS--
ギュー!
DEMON CARD SHALL CLAIM STAR MEMORY...
...AND THE GIRL'S LIFE, AS WELL!!
MUSICA ...
Farewell, beautiful people!
I'll get you for this, Sieg!!
ドシュ…!

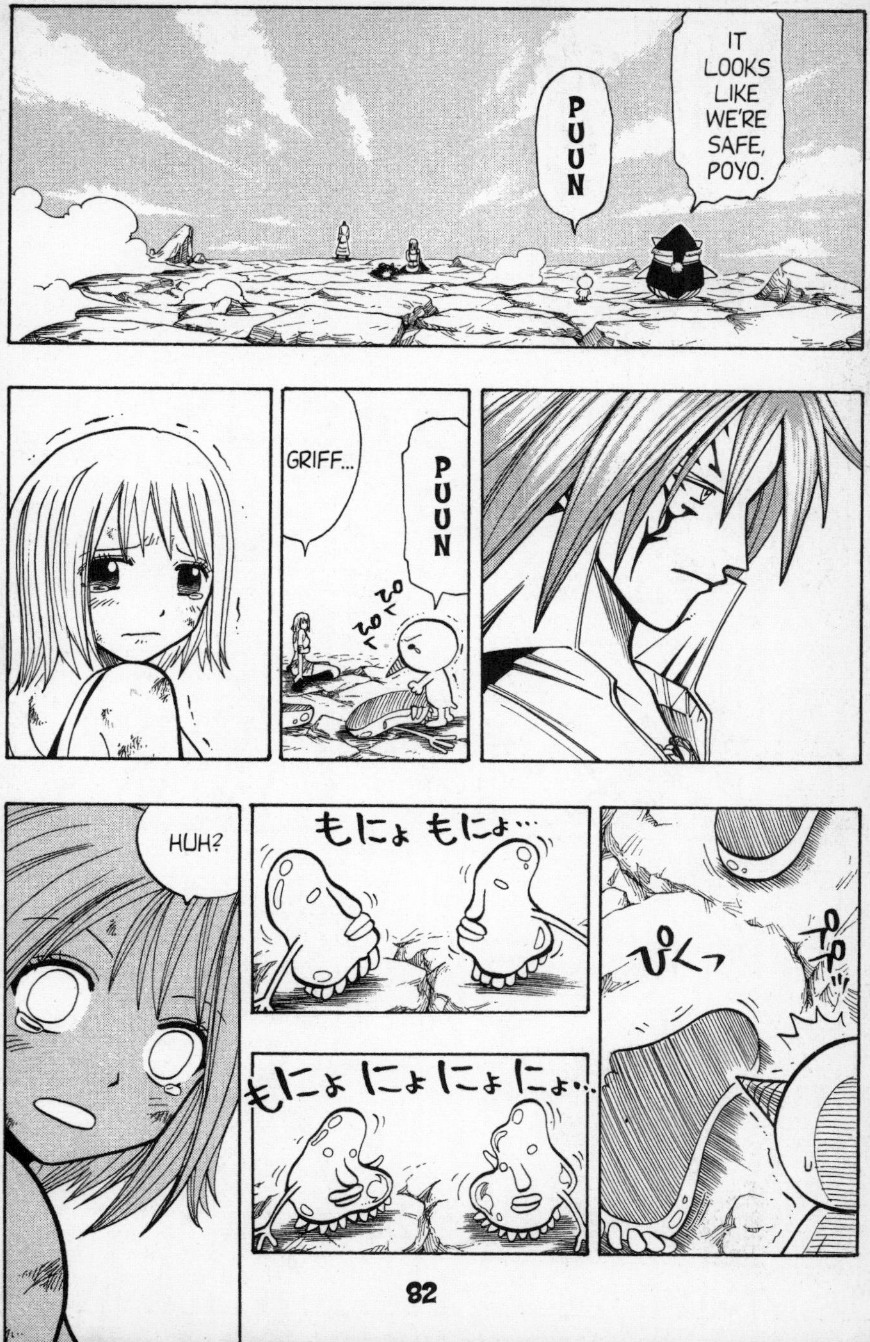
IT LOOKS LIKE WE'RE SAFE, POYO.
PUUN
PUUN
ぴくぴく
GRIFF...
ぴくっ
ピクッ
もにょ もにょ…
もにょ にょ にょ にょ…
HUH?

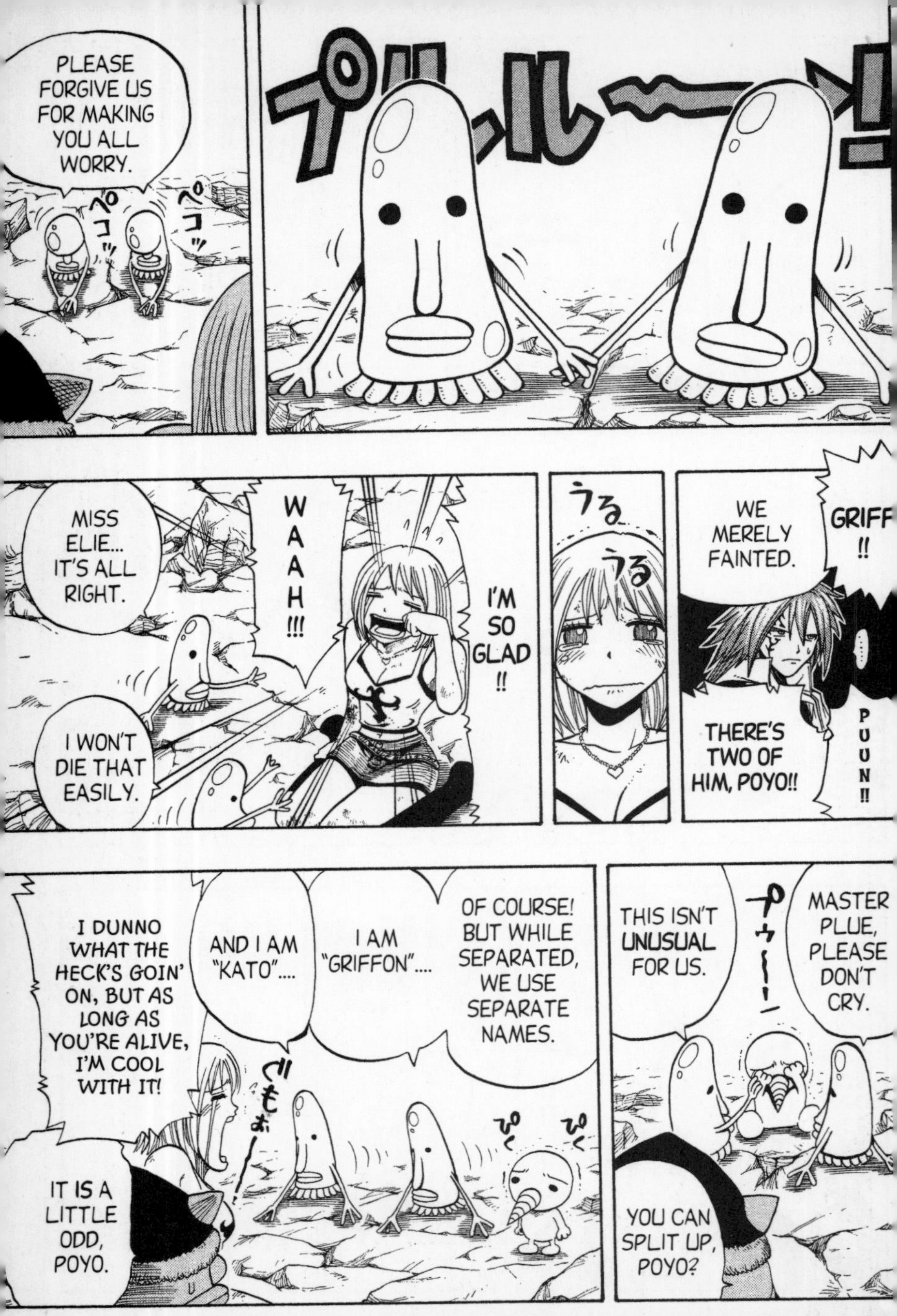
PLEASE FORGIVE US FOR MAKING YOU ALL WORRY.
ペコッ
ペコッ
GRIFF!!
WE MERELY FAINTED.
...
PUUN!!
THERE'S TWO OF HIM, POYO!!
うる
うる
WAAAH!!!
I'M SO GLAD!!
MISS ELIE... IT'S ALL RIGHT.
I WON'T DIE THAT EASILY.
MASTER PLUE, PLEASE DON'T CRY.
プゥ〜!
THIS ISN'T UNUSUAL FOR US.
YOU CAN SPLIT UP, POYO?
OF COURSE! BUT WHILE SEPARATED, WE USE SEPARATE NAMES.
I AM "GRIFFON"....
AND I AM "KATO"....
ぴく
ぴく
でもぉ〜!
I DUNNO WHAT THE HECK'S GOIN' ON, BUT AS LONG AS YOU'RE ALIVE, I'M COOL WITH IT!
IT IS A LITTLE ODD, POYO.

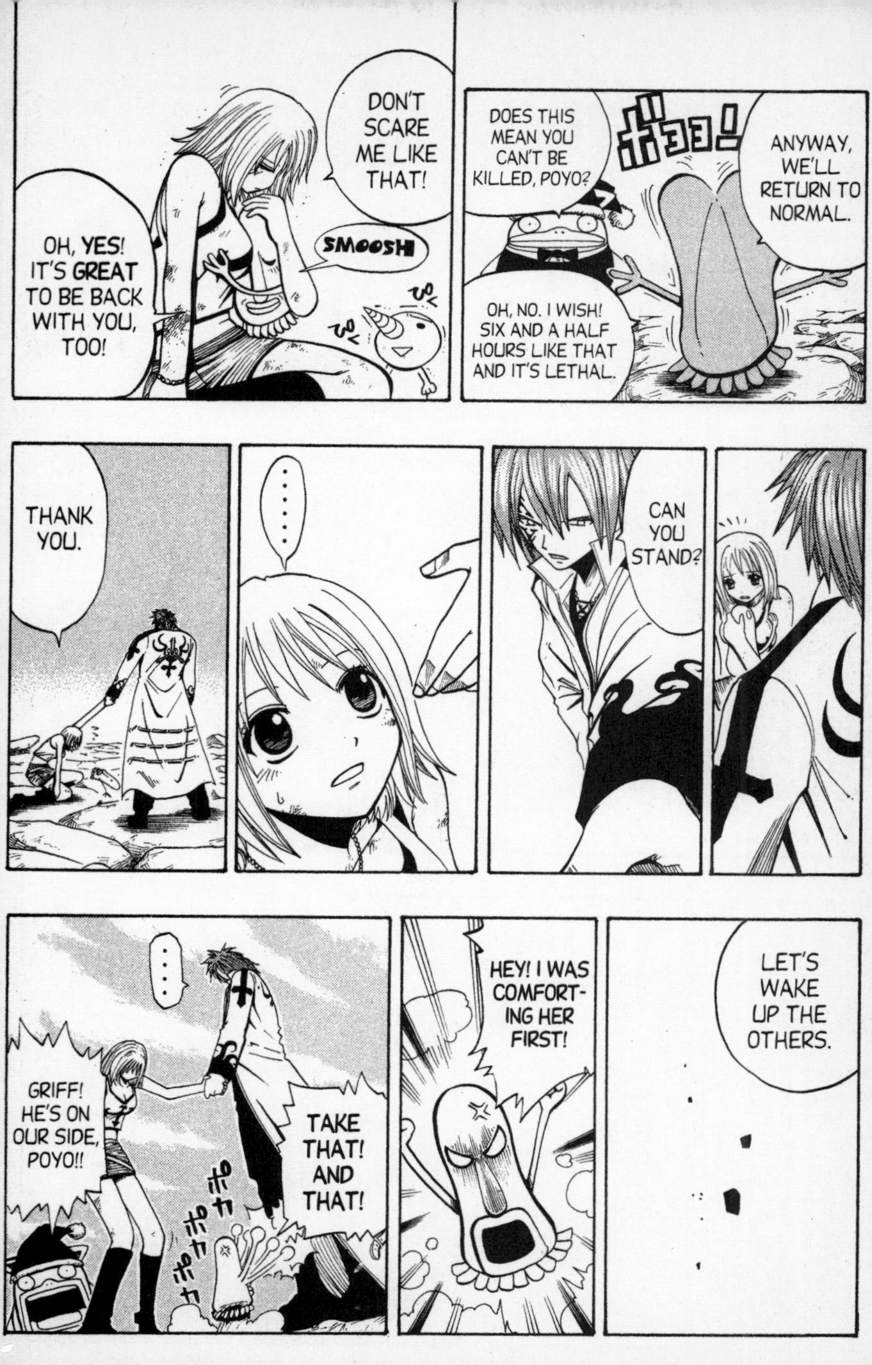
ANYWAY, WE'LL RETURN TO NORMAL.
DOES THIS MEAN YOU CAN'T BE KILLED, POYO?
OH, NO. I WISH! SIX AND A HALF HOURS LIKE THAT AND IT'S LETHAL.
DON'T SCARE ME LIKE THAT!
SMOOSH
OH, YES! IT'S GREAT TO BE BACK WITH YOU, TOO!
CAN YOU STAND?
......
THANK YOU.
LET'S WAKE UP THE OTHERS.
HEY! I WAS COMFORTING HER FIRST!
TAKE THAT! AND THAT!
....
GRIFF! HE'S ON OUR SIDE, POYO!!
ポカ ポカ ポカ ポカ

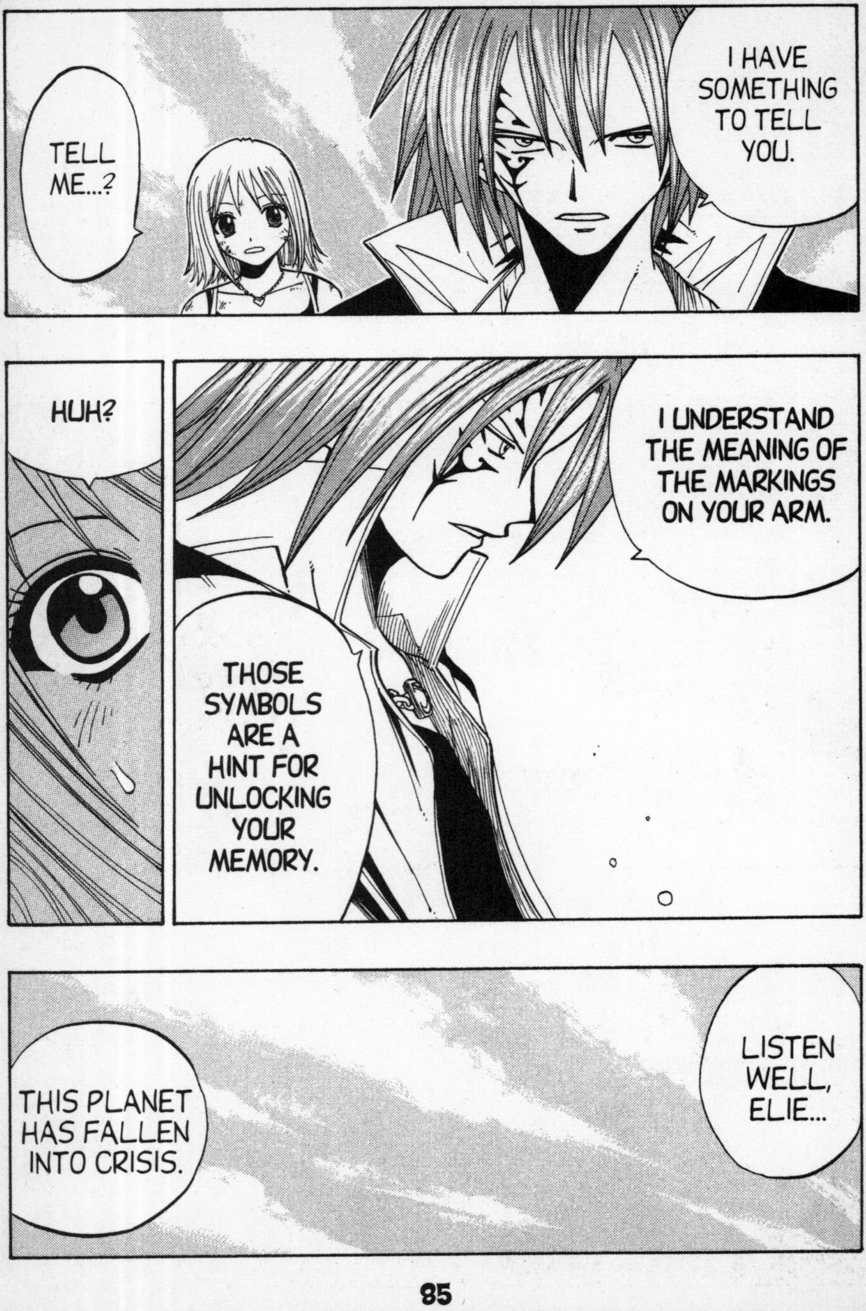
I HAVE SOMETHING TO TELL YOU.
TELL ME...?
I UNDERSTAND THE MEANING OF THE MARKINGS ON YOUR ARM.
THOSE SYMBOLS ARE A HINT FOR UNLOCKING YOUR MEMORY.
HUH?
LISTEN WELL, ELIE...
THIS PLANET HAS FALLEN INTO CRISIS.

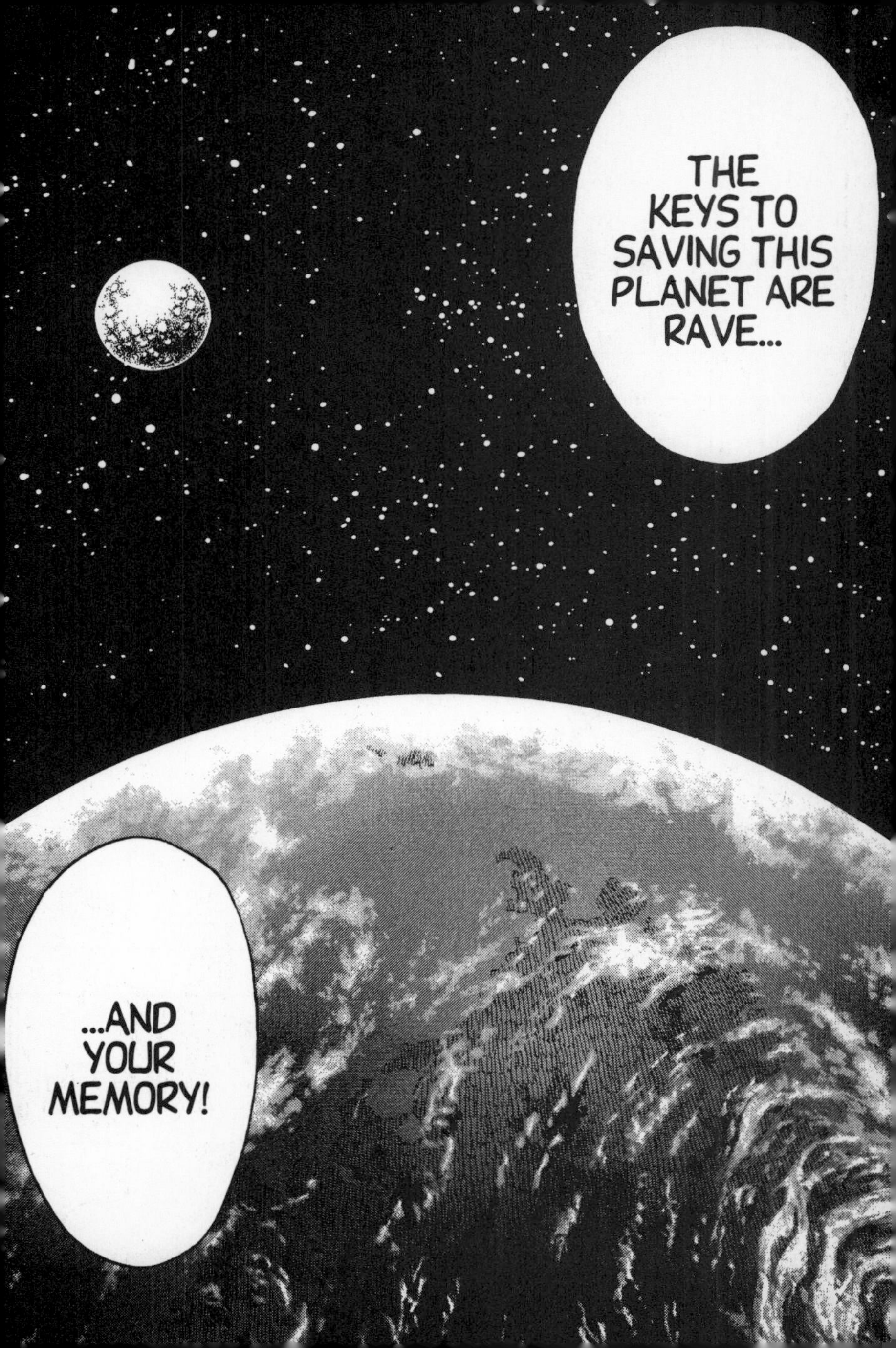
THE KEYS TO SAVING THIS PLANET ARE RAVE...
...AND YOUR MEMORY!

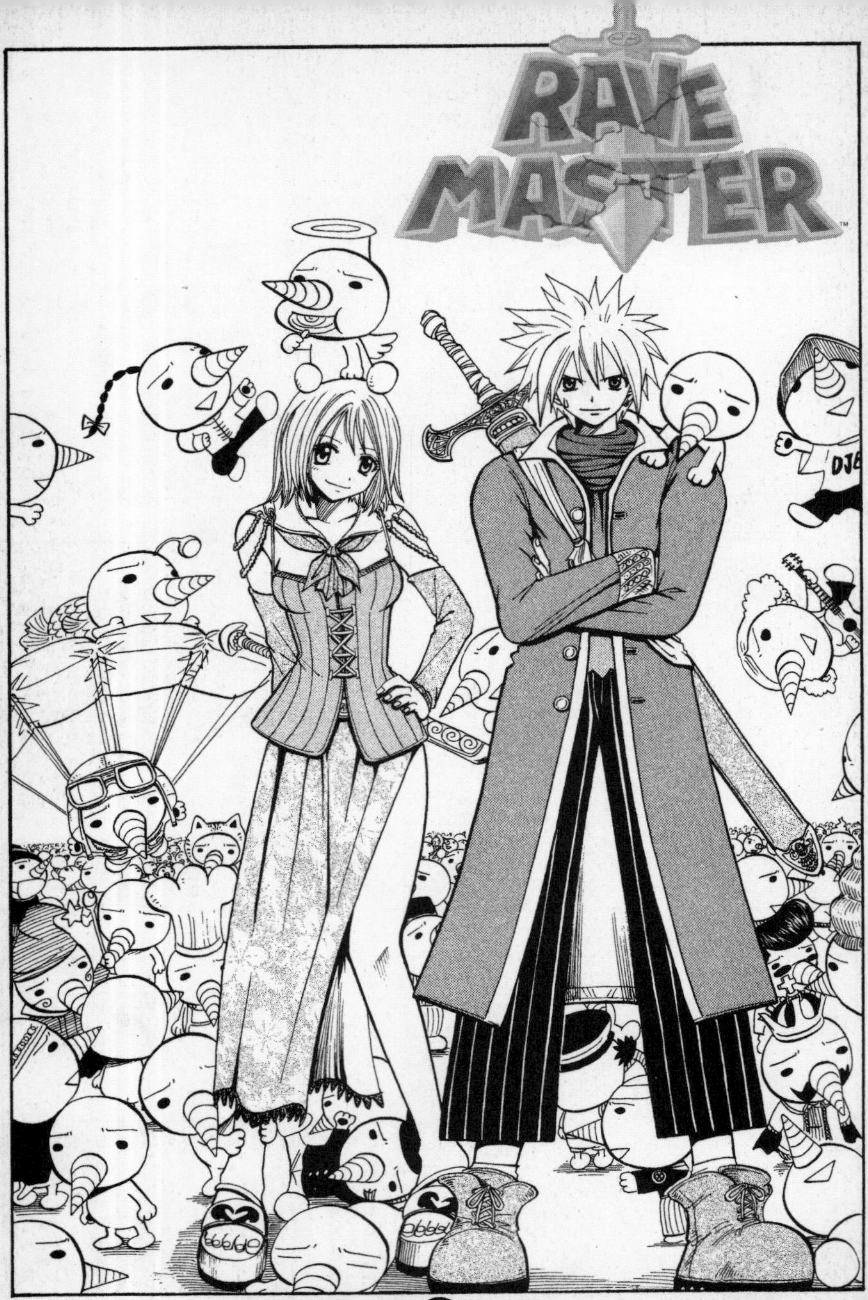
RAVE MASTER™

RAVE:93 ✠ DARK ASCENSION

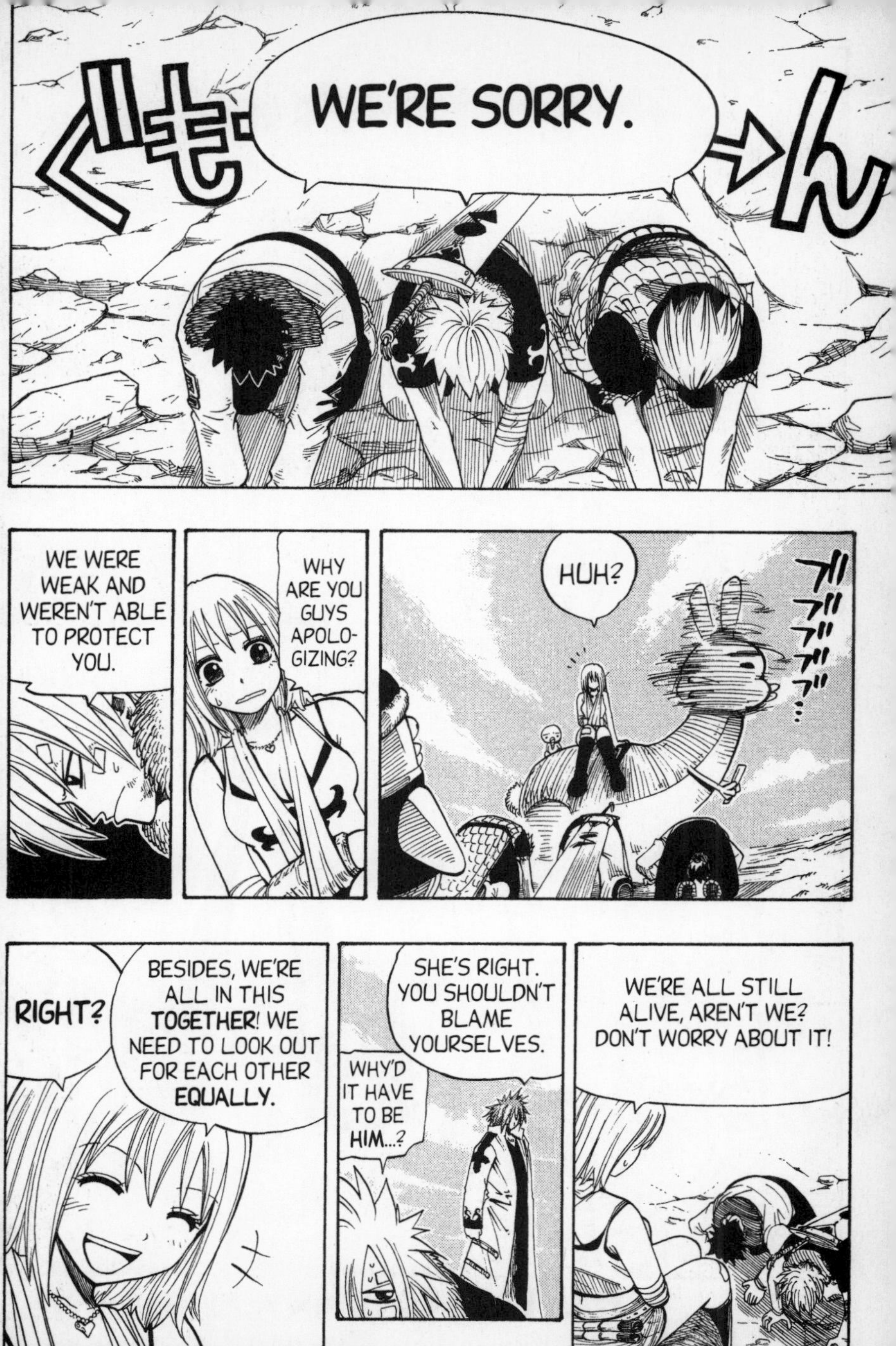
WE'RE SORRY.
HUH?
WHY ARE YOU GUYS APOLOGIZING?
WE WERE WEAK AND WEREN'T ABLE TO PROTECT YOU.
WE'RE ALL STILL ALIVE, AREN'T WE? DON'T WORRY ABOUT IT!
SHE'S RIGHT. YOU SHOULDN'T BLAME YOURSELVES.
WHY'D IT HAVE TO BE HIM...?
BESIDES, WE'RE ALL IN THIS TOGETHER! WE NEED TO LOOK OUT FOR EACH OTHER EQUALLY.
RIGHT?

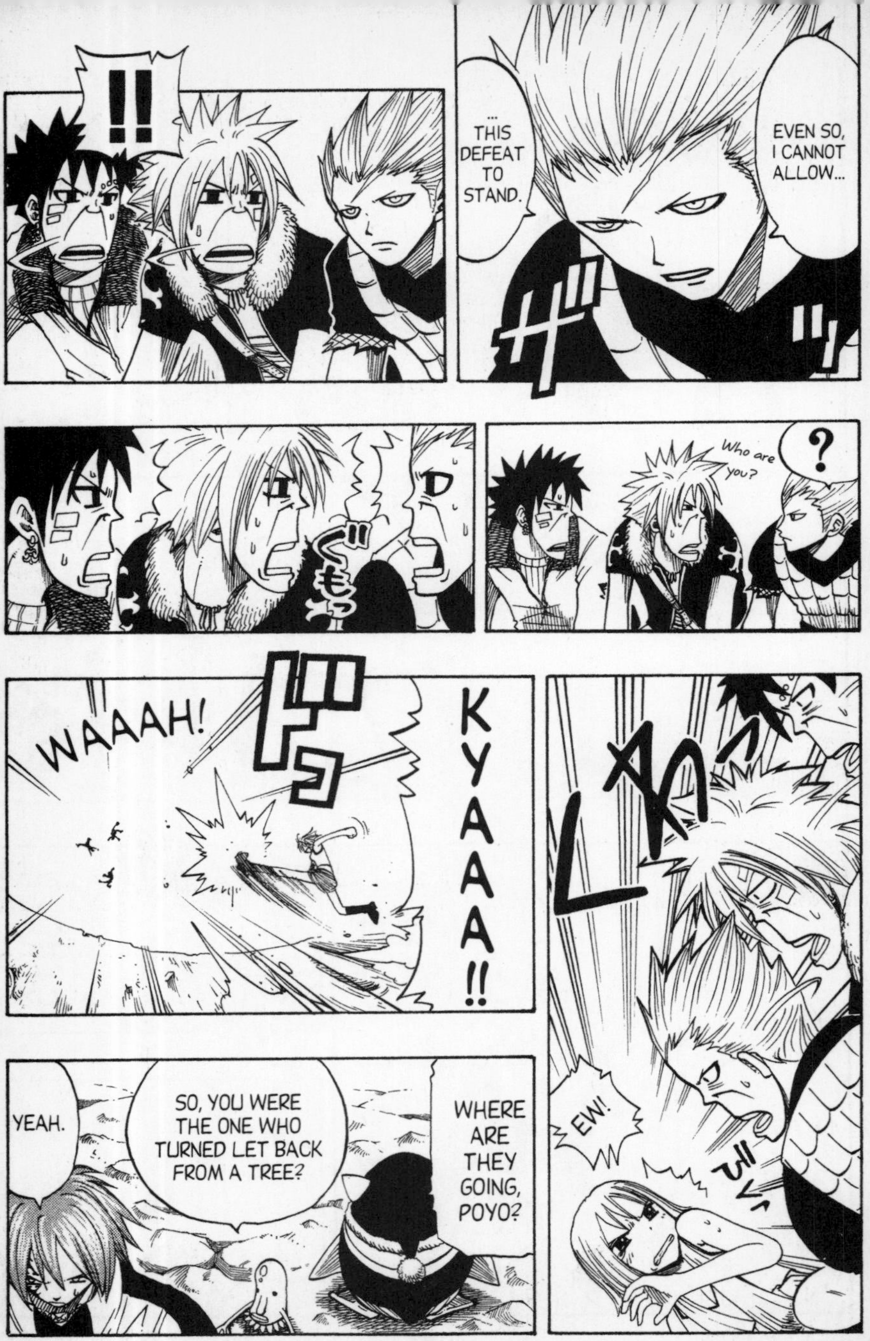
EVEN SO, I CANNOT ALLOW...
... THIS DEFEAT TO STAND.
!!
?
Who are you?
EW!
KYAAAA!!
WAAAH!
WHERE ARE THEY GOING, POYO?
SO, YOU WERE THE ONE WHO TURNED LET BACK FROM A TREE?
YEAH.

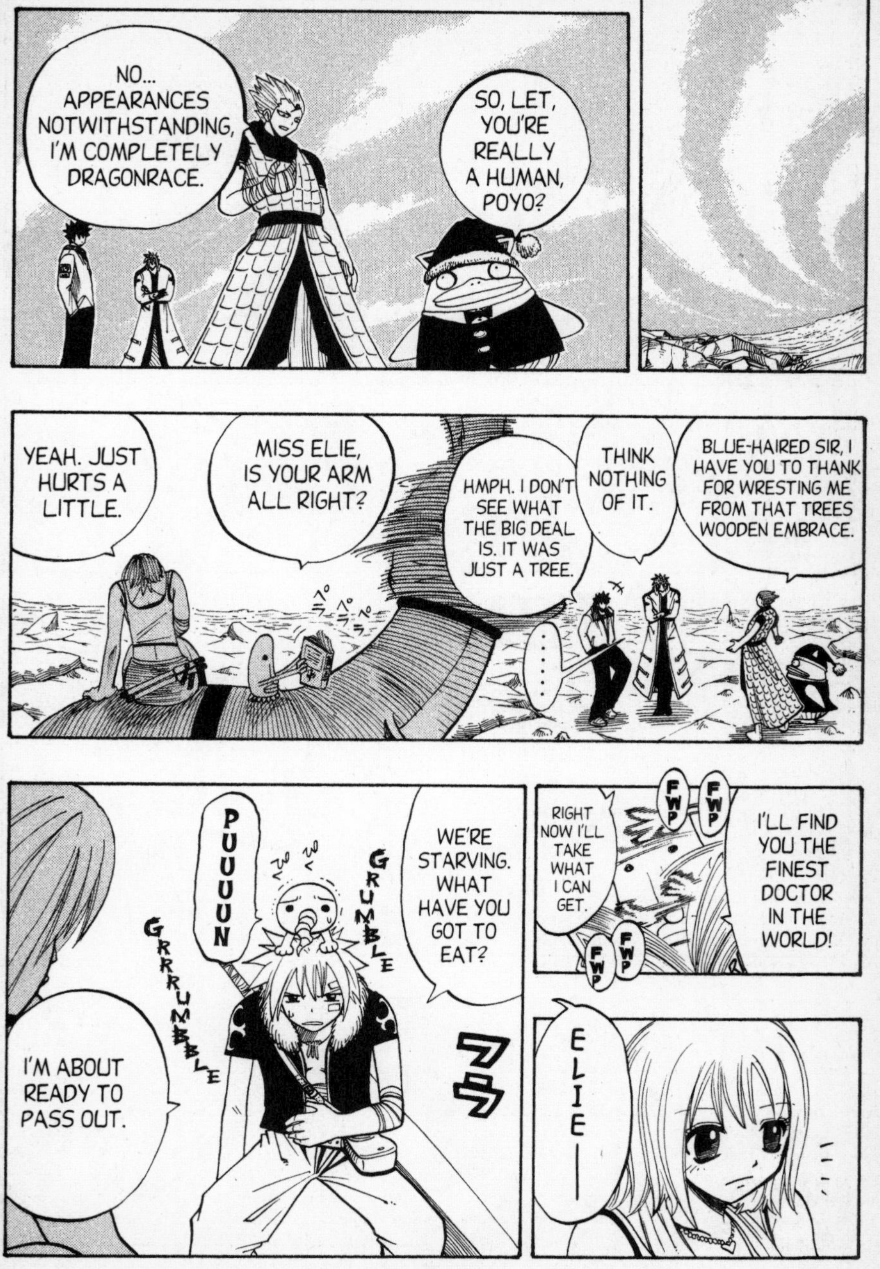
SO, LET, YOU'RE REALLY A HUMAN, POYO?
NO... APPEARANCES NOTWITHSTANDING, I'M COMPLETELY DRAGONRACE.
BLUE-HAIRED SIR, I HAVE YOU TO THANK FOR WRESTING ME FROM THAT TREES WOODEN EMBRACE.
THINK NOTHING OF IT.
HMPH. I DON'T SEE WHAT THE BIG DEAL IS. IT WAS JUST A TREE.
......
MISS ELIE, IS YOUR ARM ALL RIGHT?
YEAH. JUST HURTS A LITTLE.
I'LL FIND YOU THE FINEST DOCTOR IN THE WORLD!
FWP FWP
RIGHT NOW I'LL TAKE WHAT I CAN GET.
FWP FWP
ELIE—
WE'RE STARVING. WHAT HAVE YOU GOT TO EAT?
PUUUUN
GRUMBLE
GRRRUMBBLE
I'M ABOUT READY TO PASS OUT.

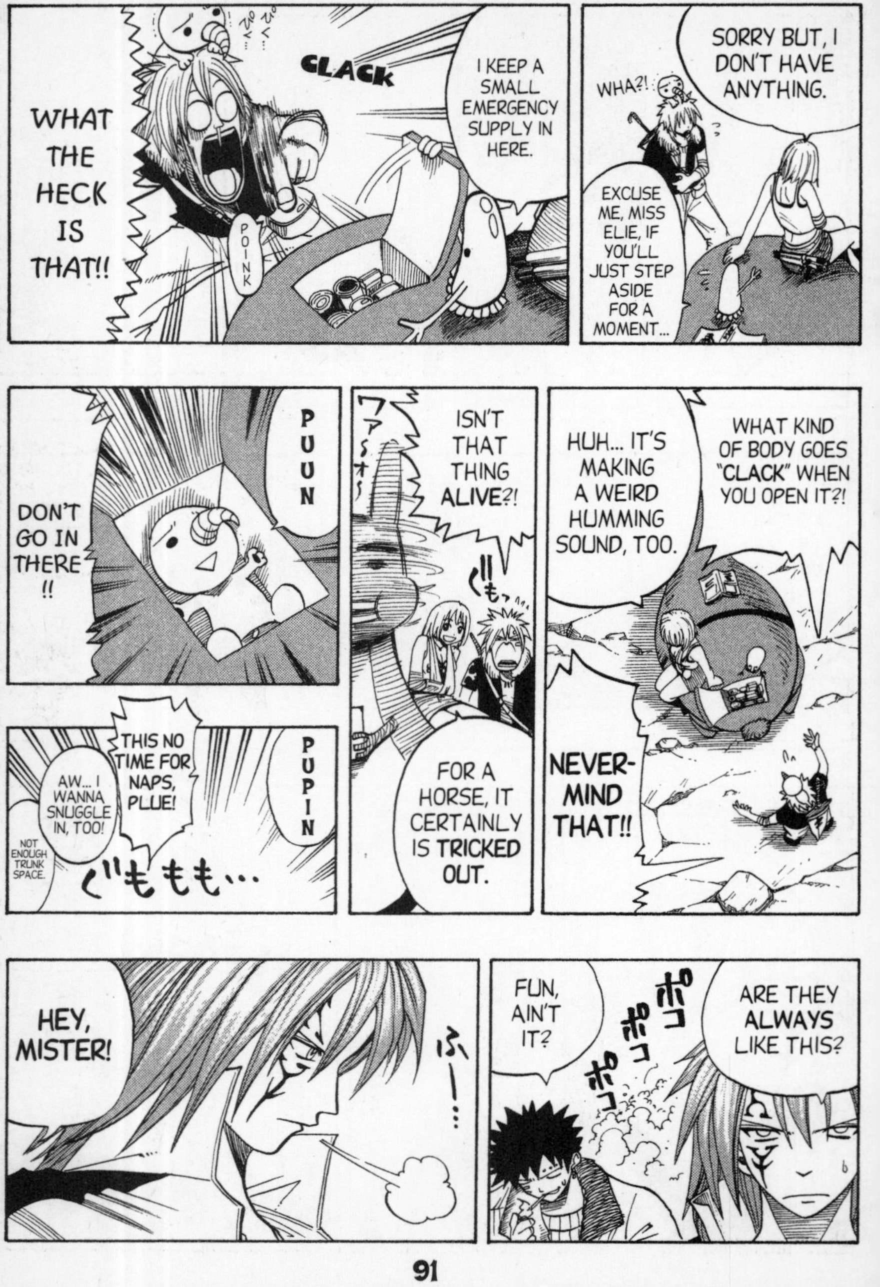
SORRY BUT, I DON'T HAVE ANYTHING.
WHA?!
EXCUSE ME, MISS ELIE, IF YOU'LL JUST STEP ASIDE FOR A MOMENT...
I KEEP A SMALL EMERGENCY SUPPLY IN HERE.
CLACK
WHAT THE HECK IS THAT!!
POINK
WHAT KIND OF BODY GOES "CLACK" WHEN YOU OPEN IT?!
HUH... IT'S MAKING A WEIRD HUMMING SOUND, TOO.
NEVER-MIND THAT!!
ISN'T THAT THING ALIVE?!
FOR A HORSE, IT CERTAINLY IS TRICKED OUT.
PUUN
DON'T GO IN THERE!!
PUPIN
THIS NO TIME FOR NAPS, PLUE!
AW... I WANNA SNUGGLE IN, TOO!
NOT ENOUGH TRUNK SPACE.
ぐもももも…
ARE THEY ALWAYS LIKE THIS?
ポコ
ポコ
ポコ
FUN, AIN'T IT?
HEY, MISTER!
ふー…

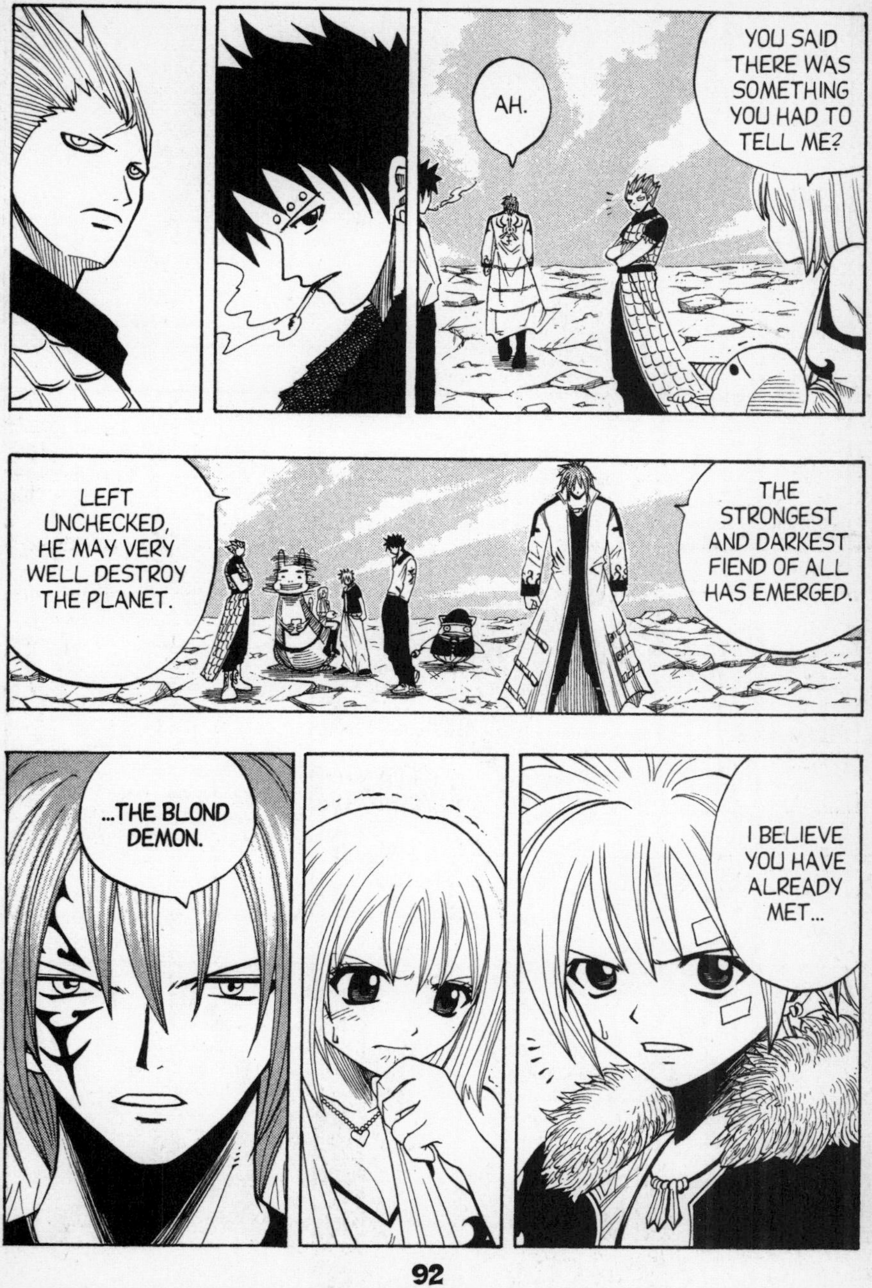
YOU SAID THERE WAS SOMETHING YOU HAD TO TELL ME?
AH.
THE STRONGEST AND DARKEST FIEND OF ALL HAS EMERGED.
LEFT UNCHECKED, HE MAY VERY WELL DESTROY THE PLANET.
I BELIEVE YOU HAVE ALREADY MET...
...THE BLOND DEMON.

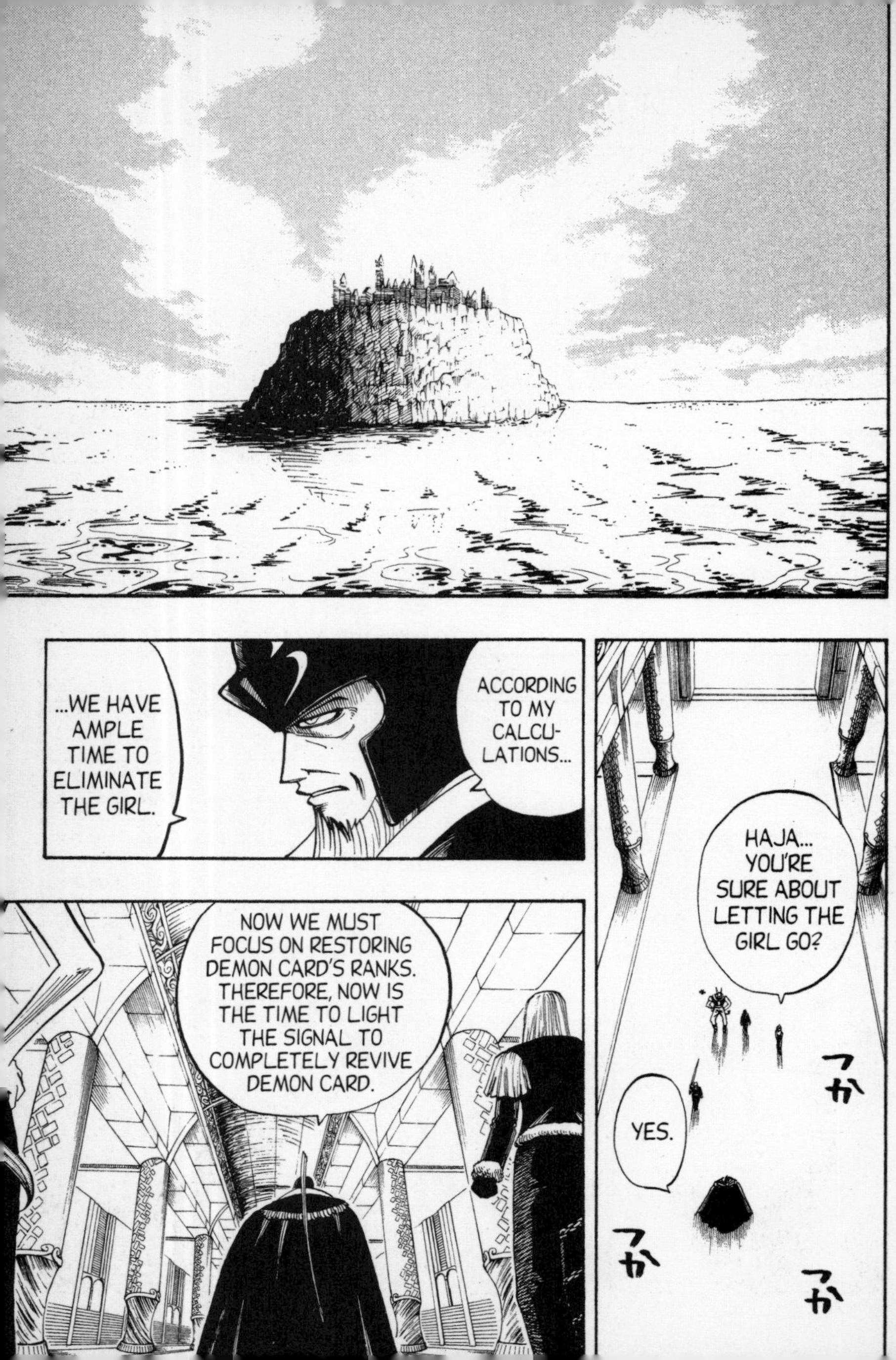
HAJA... YOU'RE SURE ABOUT LETTING THE GIRL GO?
YES.
つか
つか
つか
ACCORDING TO MY CALCU-LATIONS...
...WE HAVE AMPLE TIME TO ELIMINATE THE GIRL.
NOW WE MUST FOCUS ON RESTORING DEMON CARD'S RANKS. THEREFORE, NOW IS THE TIME TO LIGHT THE SIGNAL TO COMPLETELY REVIVE DEMON CARD.

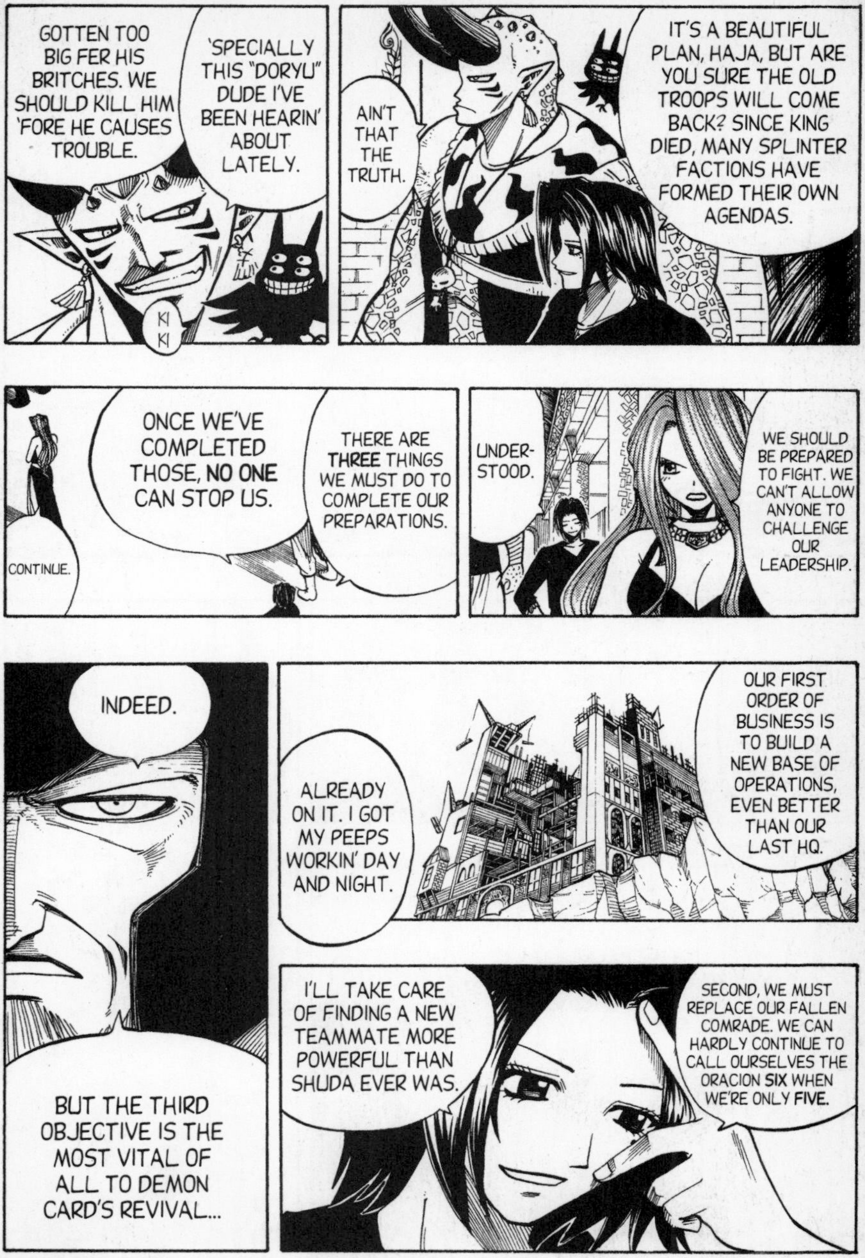
IT'S A BEAUTIFUL PLAN, HAJA, BUT ARE YOU SURE THE OLD TROOPS WILL COME BACK? SINCE KING DIED, MANY SPLINTER FACTIONS HAVE FORMED THEIR OWN AGENDAS.
AIN'T THAT THE TRUTH.
'SPECIALLY THIS "DORYU" DUDE I'VE BEEN HEARIN' ABOUT LATELY.
GOTTEN TOO BIG FER HIS BRITCHES. WE SHOULD KILL HIM 'FORE HE CAUSES TROUBLE.
KI KI
WE SHOULD BE PREPARED TO FIGHT. WE CAN'T ALLOW ANYONE TO CHALLENGE OUR LEADERSHIP.
UNDER-STOOD.
THERE ARE **THREE** THINGS WE MUST DO TO COMPLETE OUR PREPARATIONS.
ONCE WE'VE COMPLETED THOSE, **NO ONE** CAN STOP US.
CONTINUE.
OUR FIRST ORDER OF BUSINESS IS TO BUILD A NEW BASE OF OPERATIONS, EVEN BETTER THAN OUR LAST HQ.
ALREADY ON IT. I GOT MY PEEPS WORKIN' DAY AND NIGHT.
SECOND, WE MUST REPLACE OUR FALLEN COMRADE. WE CAN HARDLY CONTINUE TO CALL OURSELVES THE ORACION **SIX** WHEN WE'RE ONLY **FIVE**.
I'LL TAKE CARE OF FINDING A NEW TEAMMATE MORE POWERFUL THAN SHUDA EVER WAS.
INDEED.
BUT THE THIRD OBJECTIVE IS THE MOST VITAL OF ALL TO DEMON CARD'S REVIVAL...

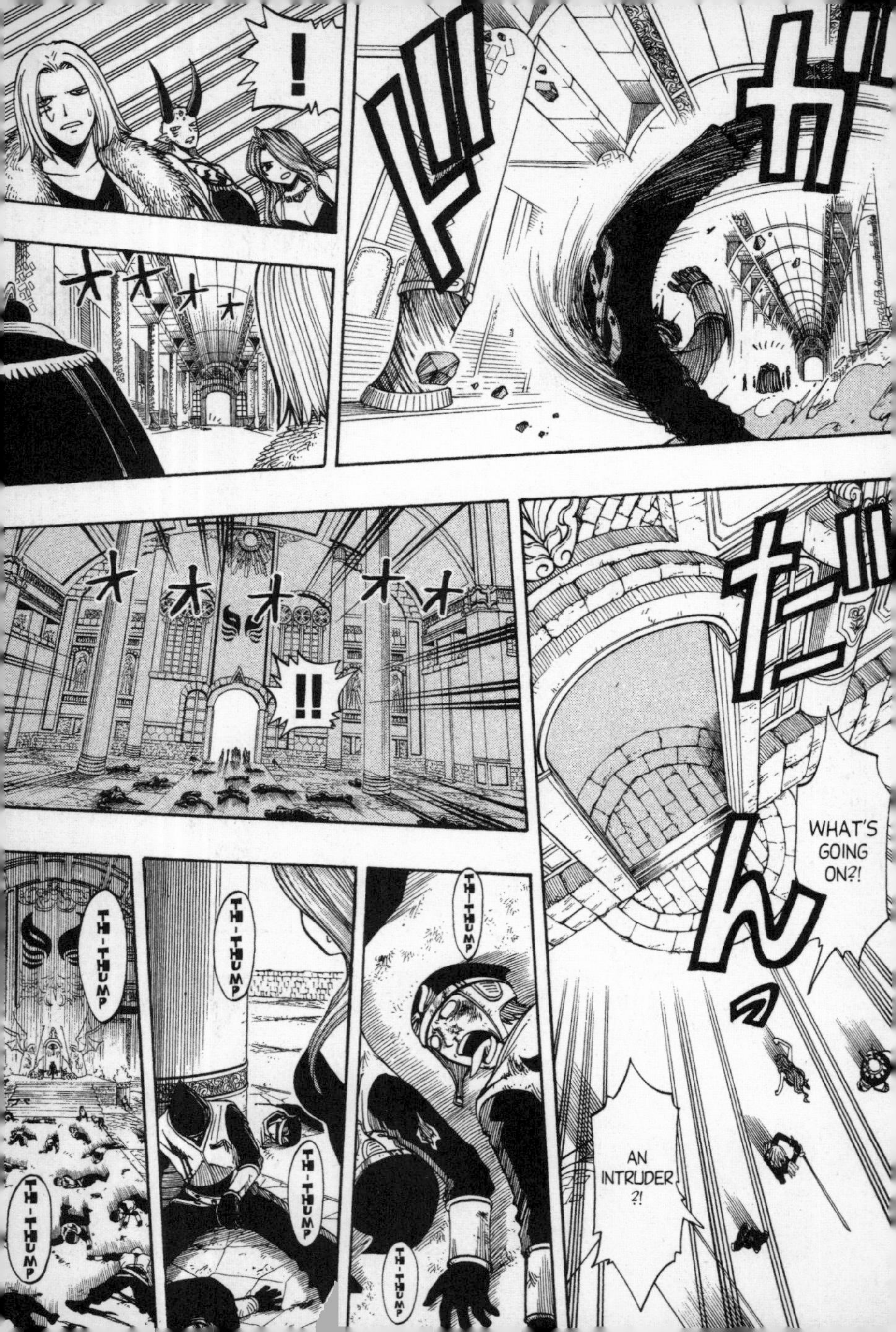
ドガ
!
オオオオ
たーん
WHAT'S GOING ON?!
AN INTRUDER ?!
オオオオオ
!!
THI-THUMP
THI-THUMP
THI-THUMP
THI-THUMP
THI-THUMP
THI-THUMP

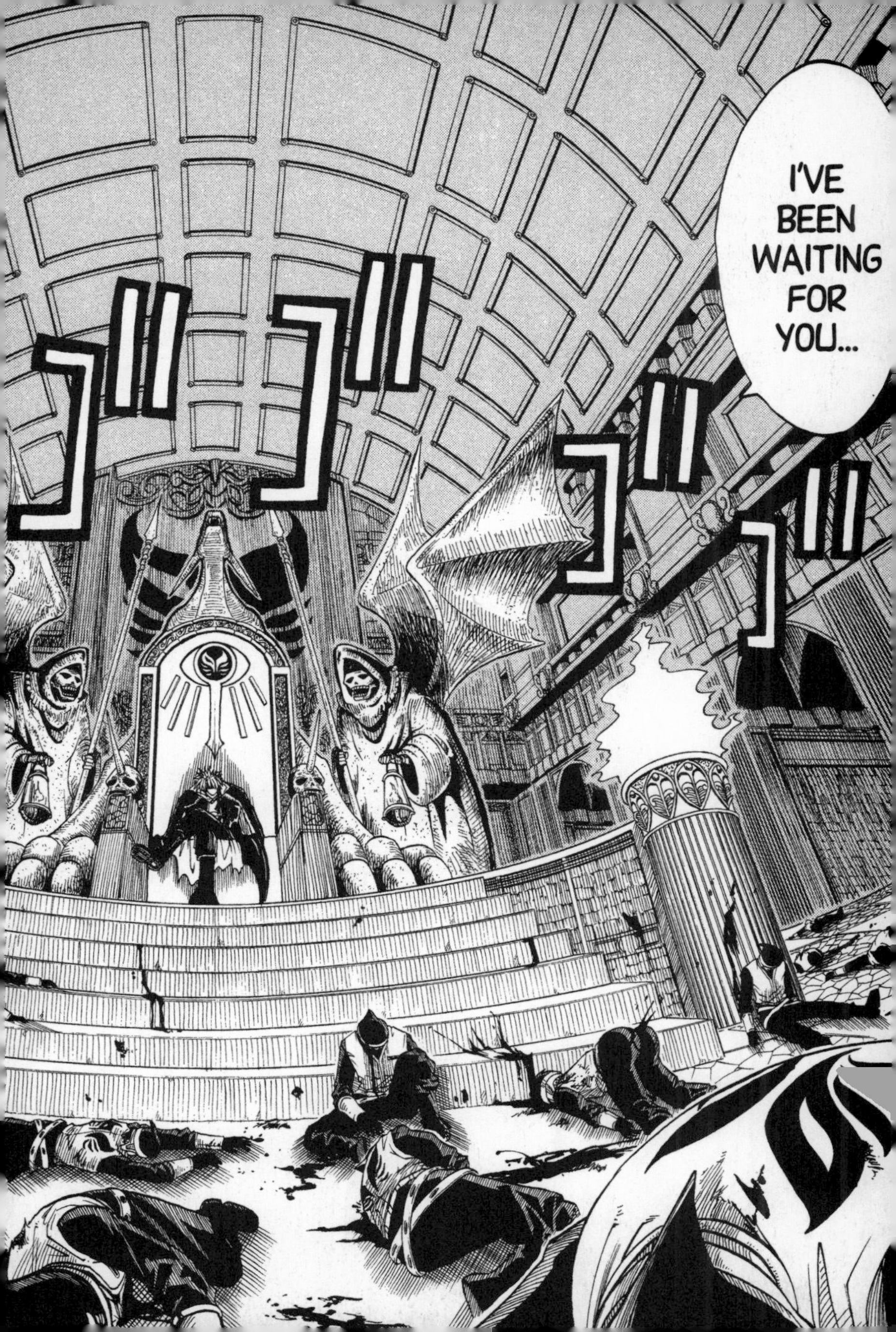
I'VE BEEN WAITING FOR YOU...

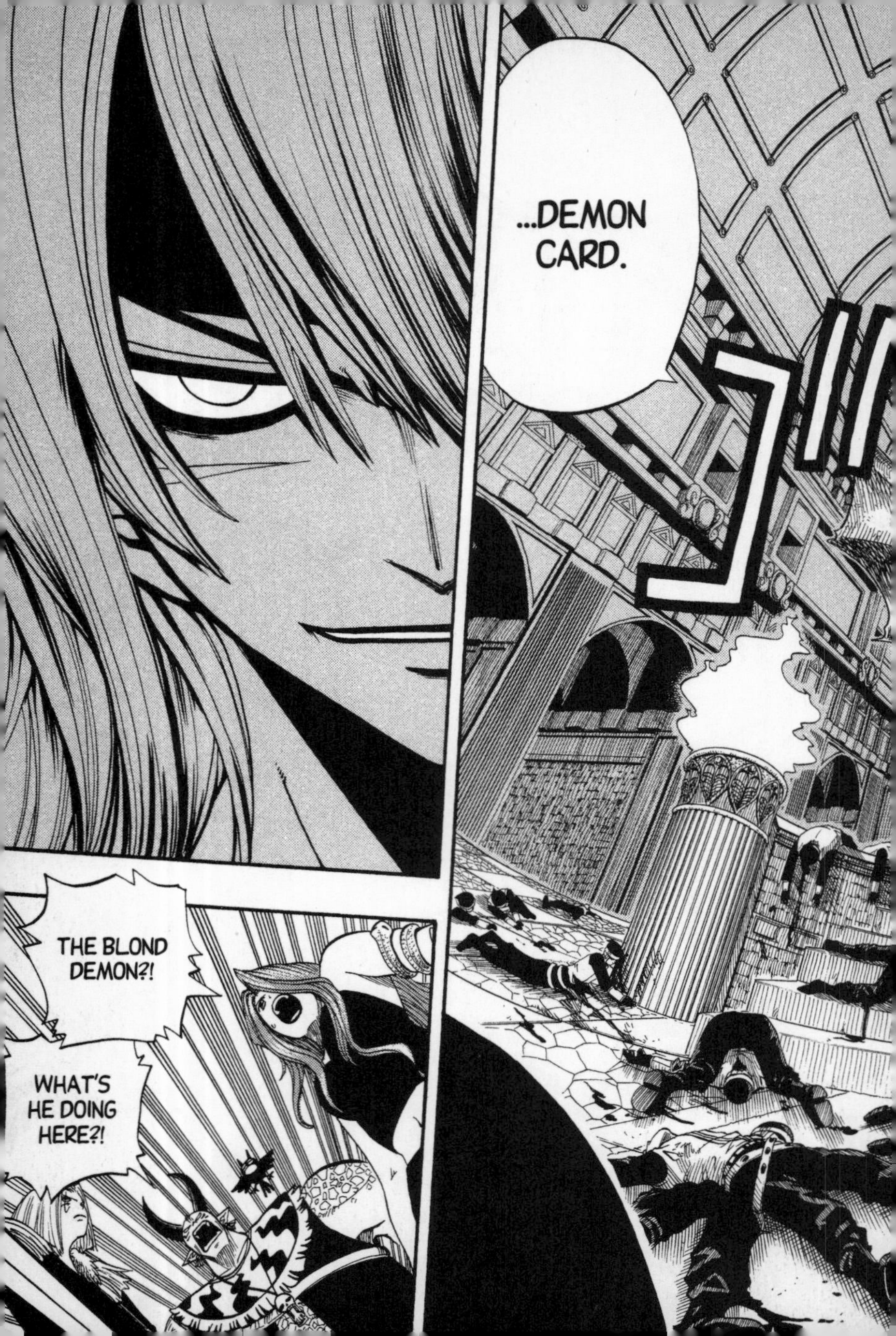
...DEMON CARD.
THE BLOND DEMON?!
WHAT'S HE DOING HERE?!

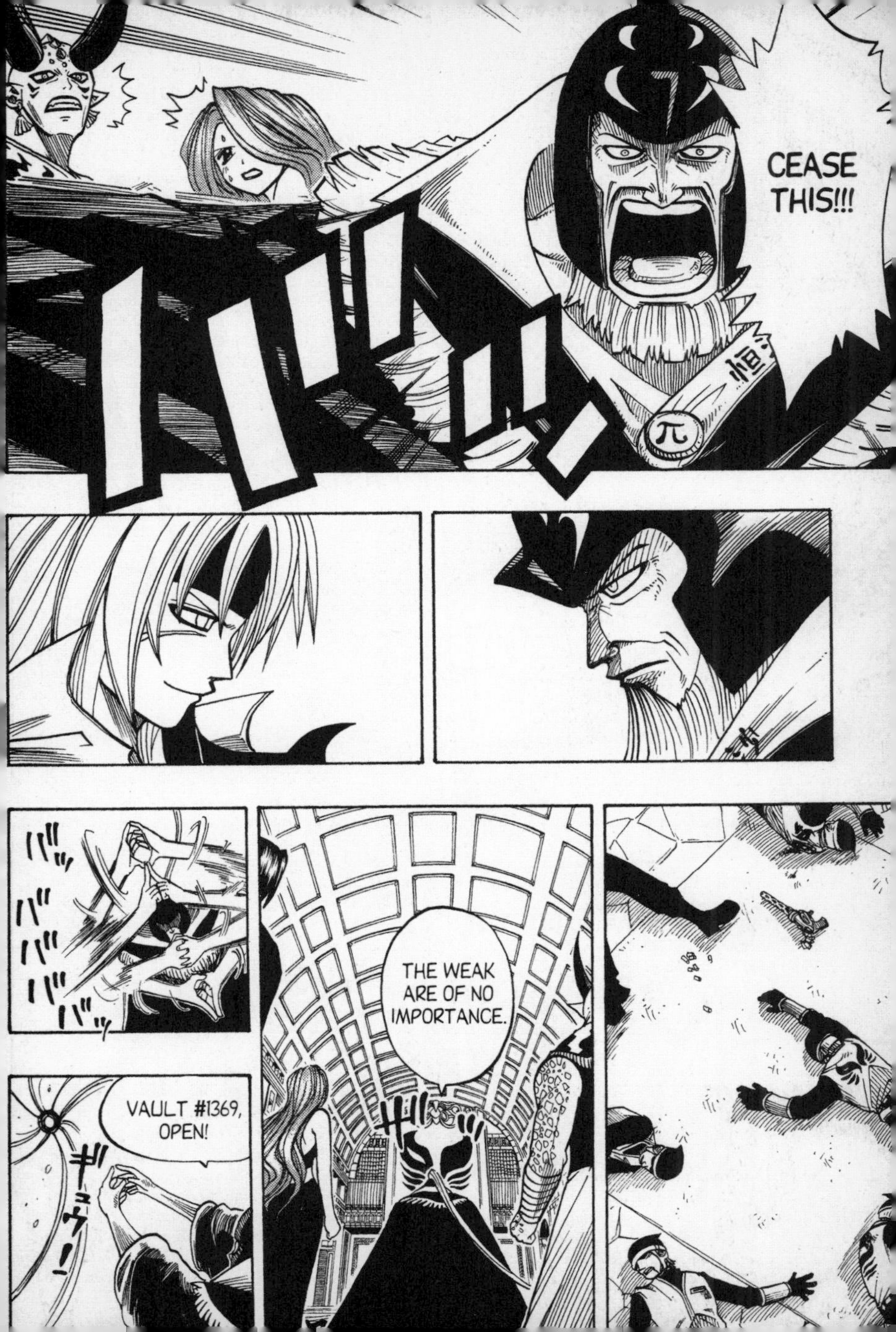
CEASE THIS!!!
THE WEAK ARE OF NO IMPORTANCE.
VAULT #1369, OPEN!

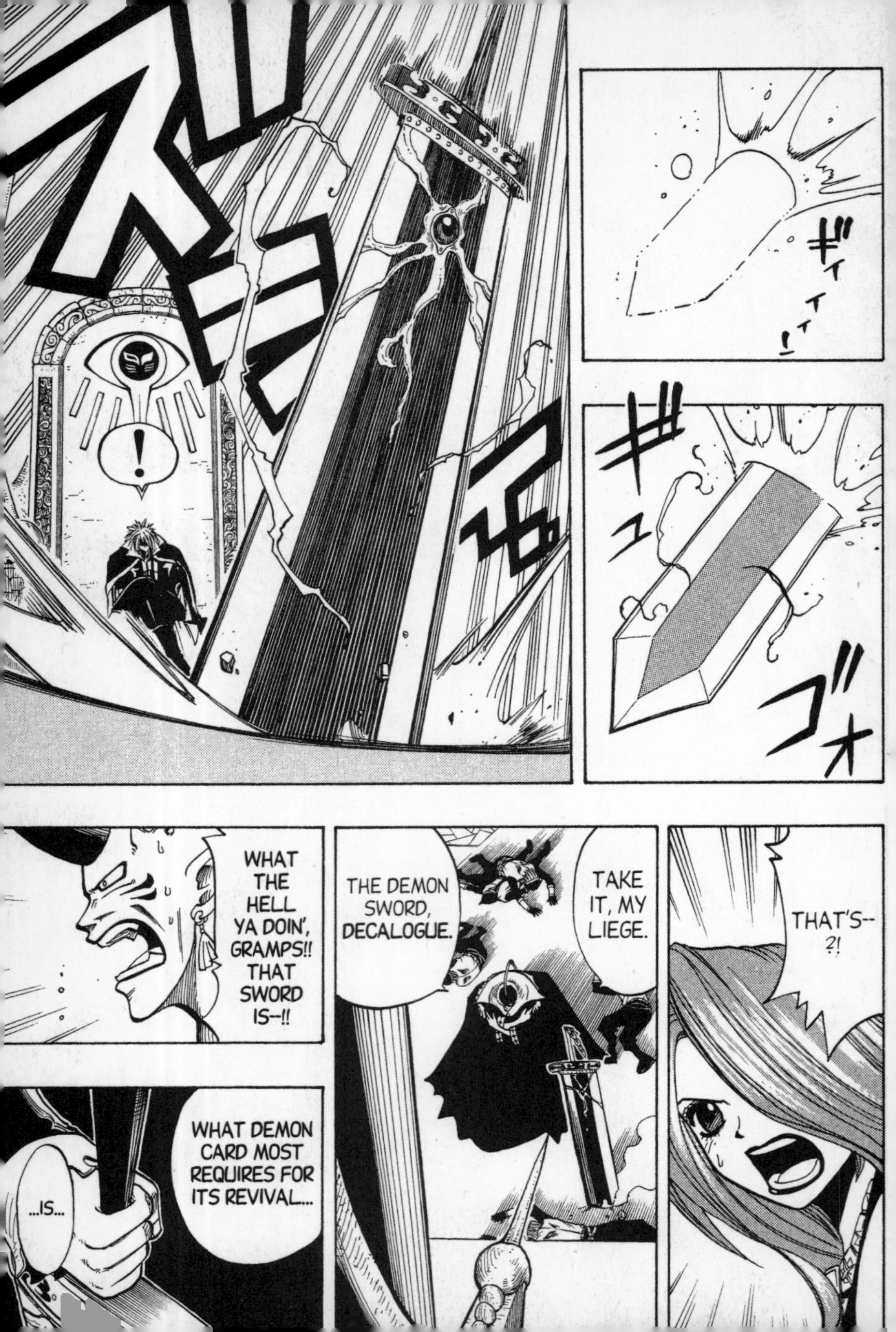
ギイイイ!
ギュ
ゴオ
THAT'S-- ?!
TAKE IT, MY LIEGE.
THE DEMON SWORD, DECALOGUE.
WHAT THE HELL YA DOIN', GRAMPS!! THAT SWORD IS--!!
WHAT DEMON CARD MOST REQUIRES FOR ITS REVIVAL...
...IS...

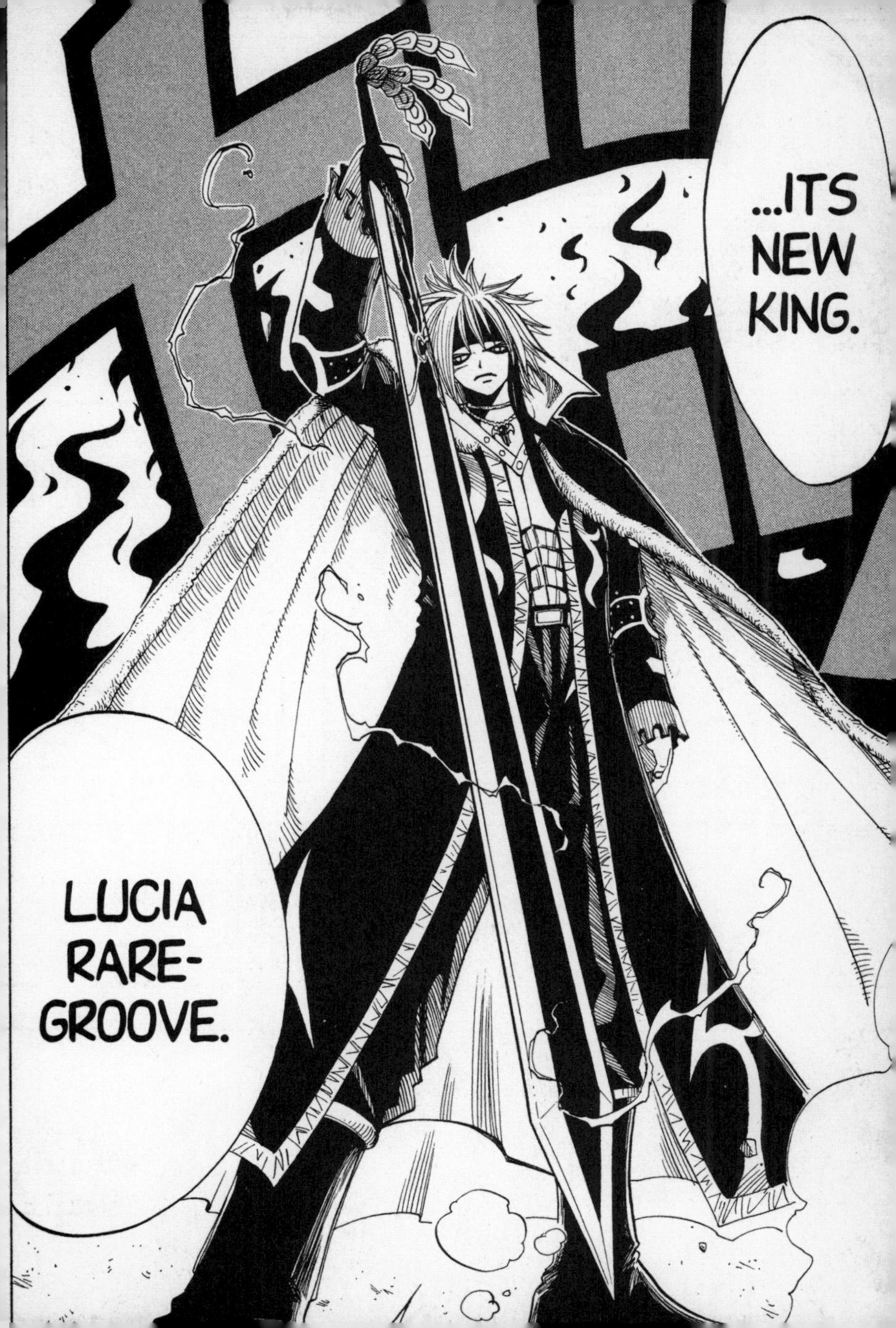
...ITS NEW KING.
LUCIA RARE-GROOVE.

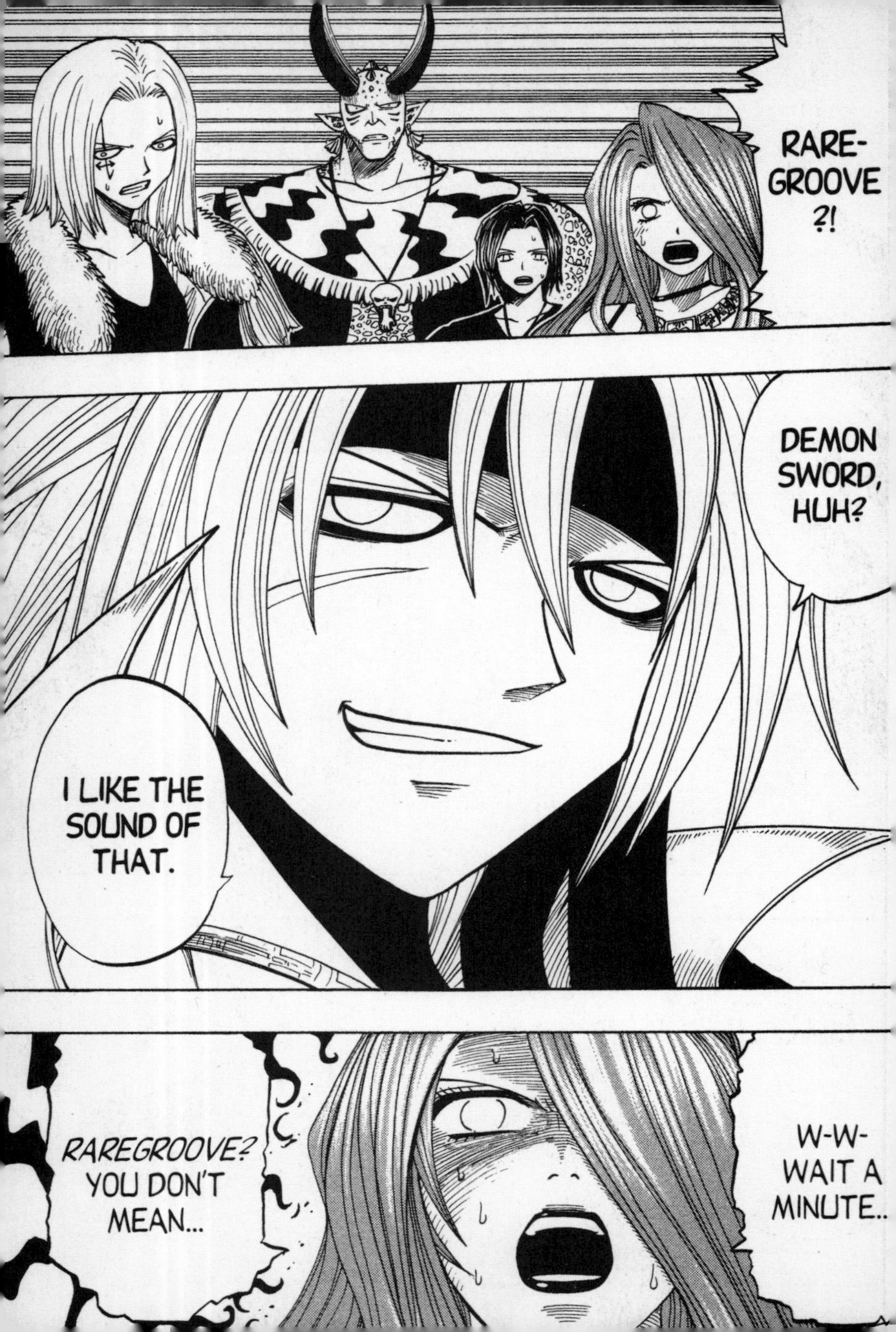
RARE-GROOVE ?!
DEMON SWORD, HUH?
I LIKE THE SOUND OF THAT.
W-W-WAIT A MINUTE...
RAREGROOVE? YOU DON'T MEAN...

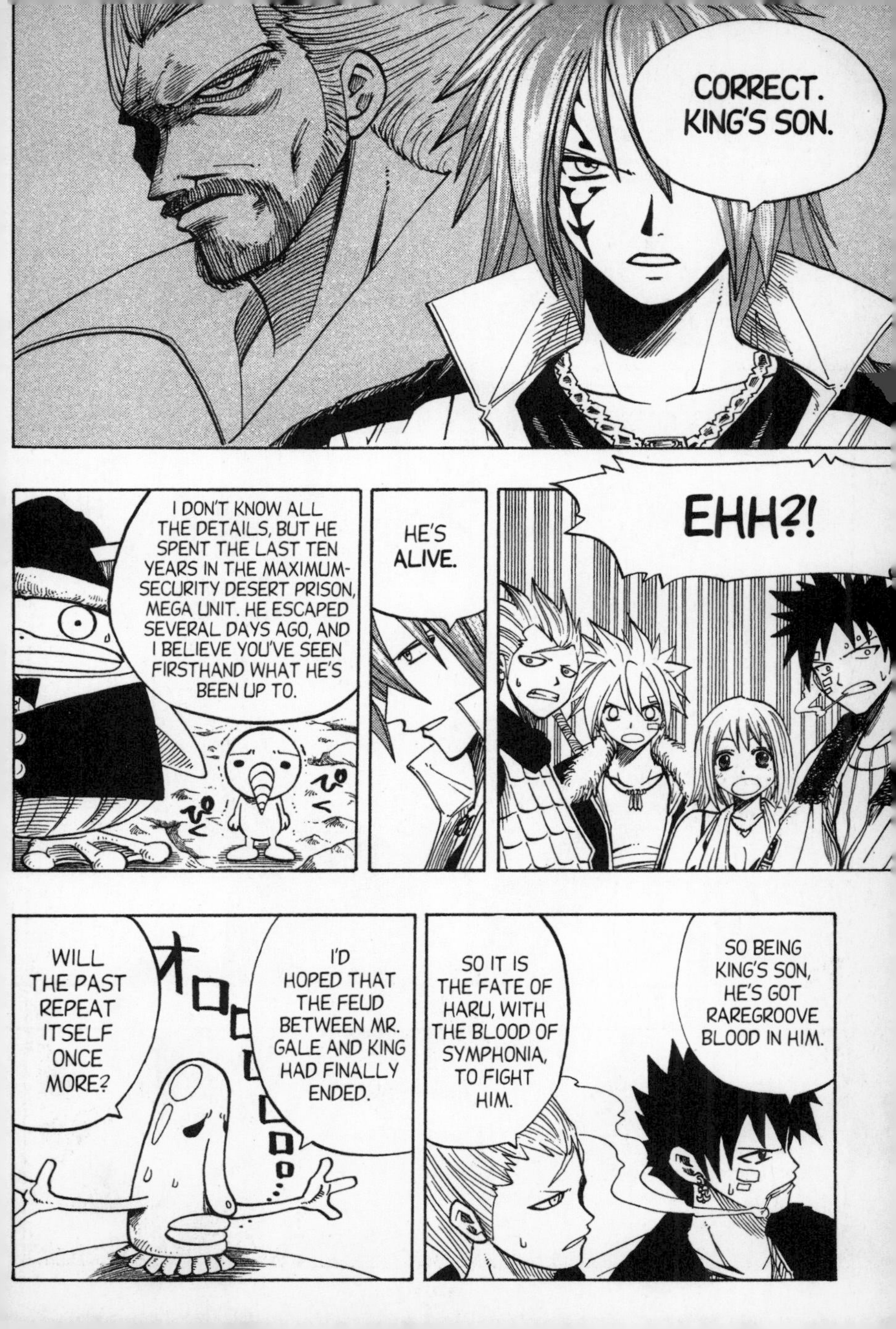
CORRECT. KING'S SON.
EHH?!
HE'S ALIVE.
I DON'T KNOW ALL THE DETAILS, BUT HE SPENT THE LAST TEN YEARS IN THE MAXIMUM-SECURITY DESERT PRISON, MEGA UNIT. HE ESCAPED SEVERAL DAYS AGO, AND I BELIEVE YOU'VE SEEN FIRSTHAND WHAT HE'S BEEN UP TO.
SO BEING KING'S SON, HE'S GOT RAREGROOVE BLOOD IN HIM.
SO IT IS THE FATE OF HARU, WITH THE BLOOD OF SYMPHONIA, TO FIGHT HIM.
I'D HOPED THAT THE FEUD BETWEEN MR. GALE AND KING HAD FINALLY ENDED.
WILL THE PAST REPEAT ITSELF ONCE MORE?

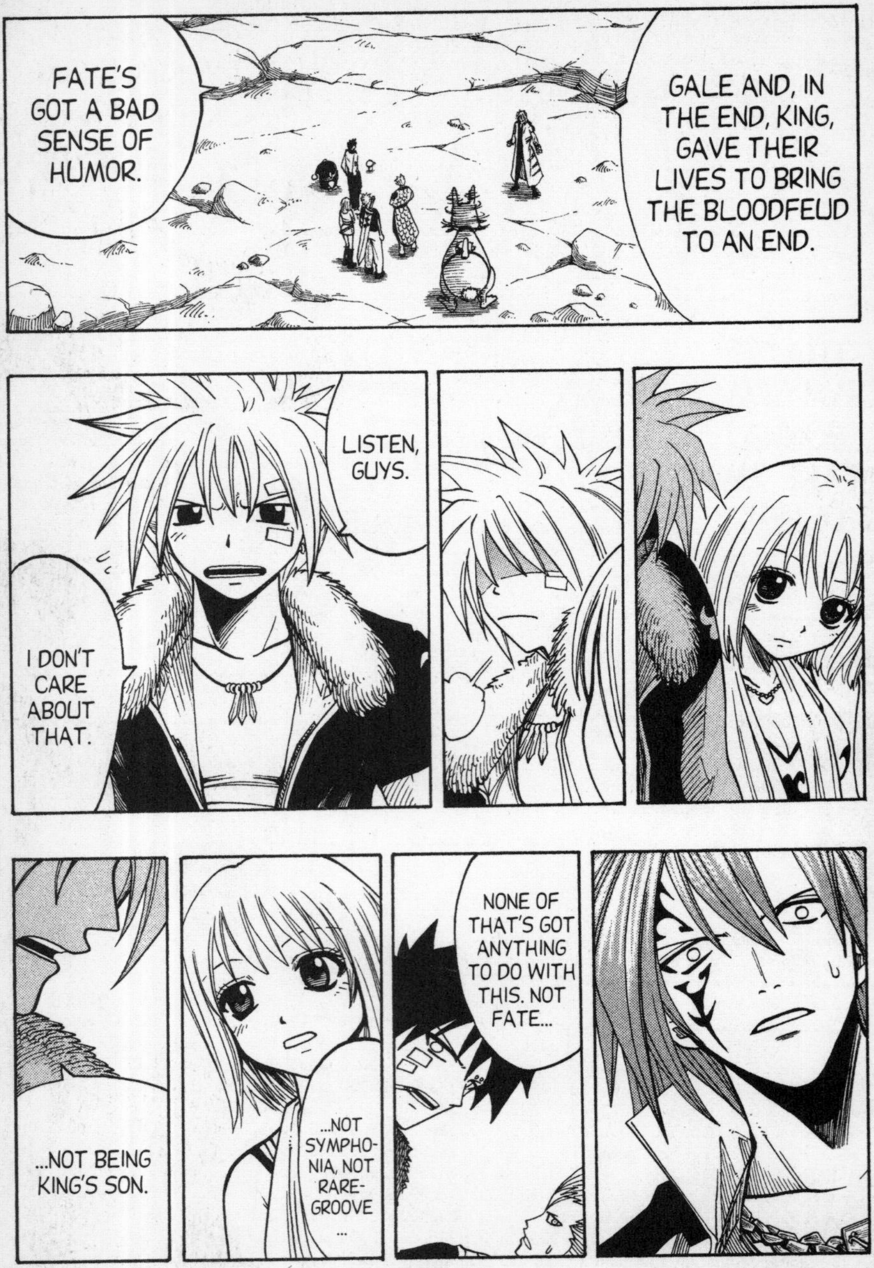
GALE AND, IN THE END, KING, GAVE THEIR LIVES TO BRING THE BLOODFEUD TO AN END.
FATE'S GOT A BAD SENSE OF HUMOR.
LISTEN, GUYS.
I DON'T CARE ABOUT THAT.
NONE OF THAT'S GOT ANYTHING TO DO WITH THIS. NOT FATE...
...NOT SYMPHO-NIA, NOT RARE-GROOVE ...
...NOT BEING KING'S SON.

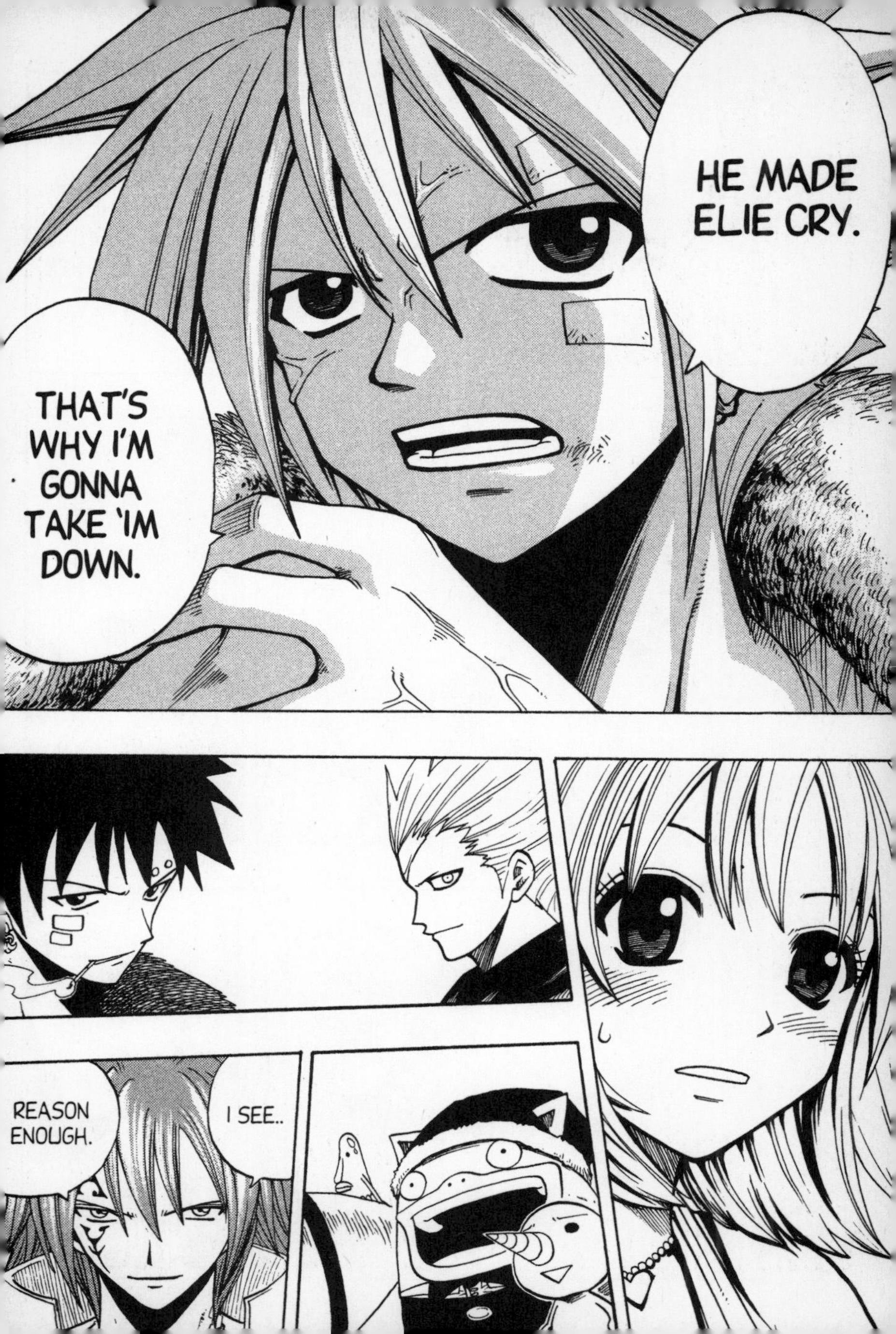
HE MADE ELIE CRY.
THAT'S WHY I'M GONNA TAKE 'IM DOWN.
I SEE..
REASON ENOUGH.

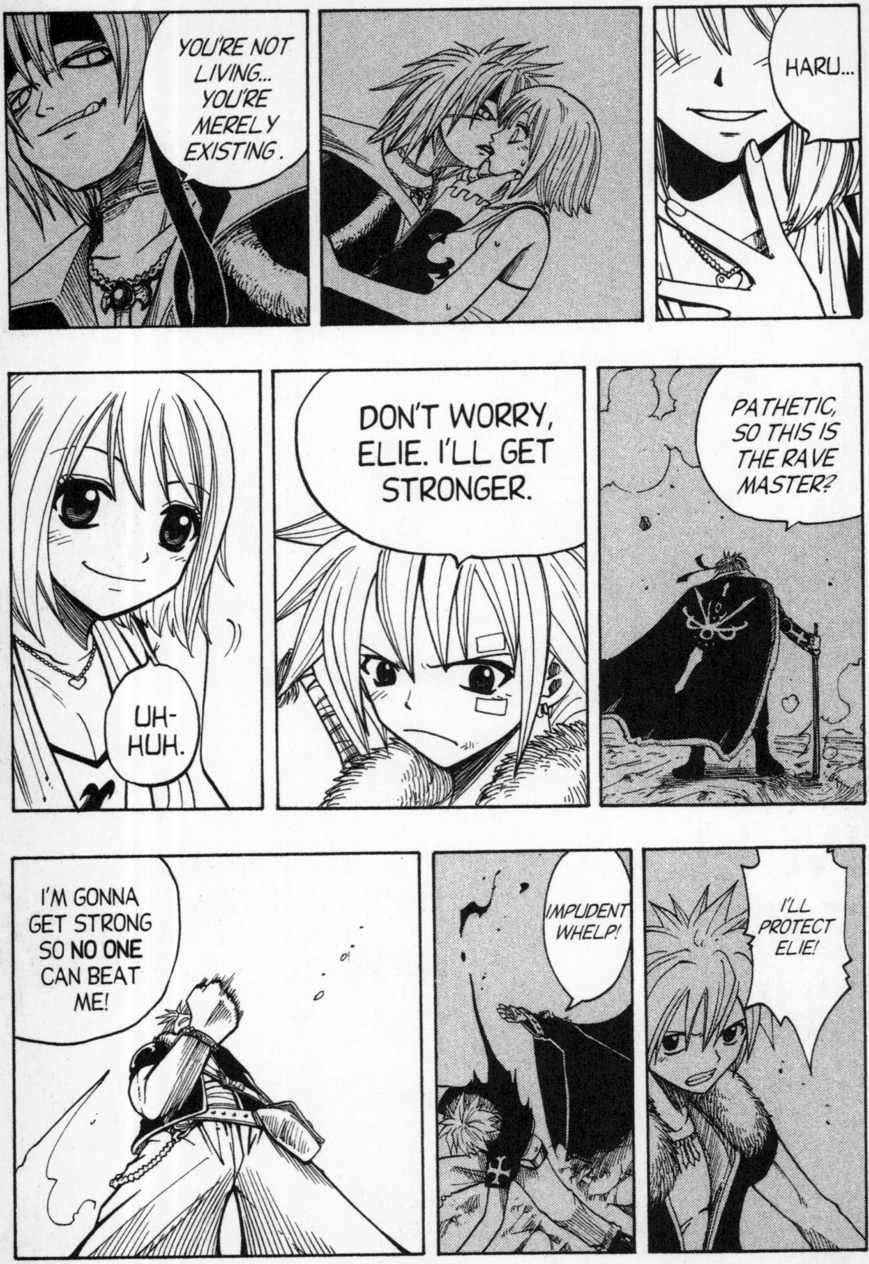
HARU...
YOU'RE NOT LIVING... YOU'RE MERELY EXISTING.
PATHETIC, SO THIS IS THE RAVE MASTER?
DON'T WORRY, ELIE. I'LL GET STRONGER.
UH-HUH.
I'LL PROTECT ELIE!
IMPUDENT WHELP!
I'M GONNA GET STRONG SO **NO ONE** CAN BEAT ME!

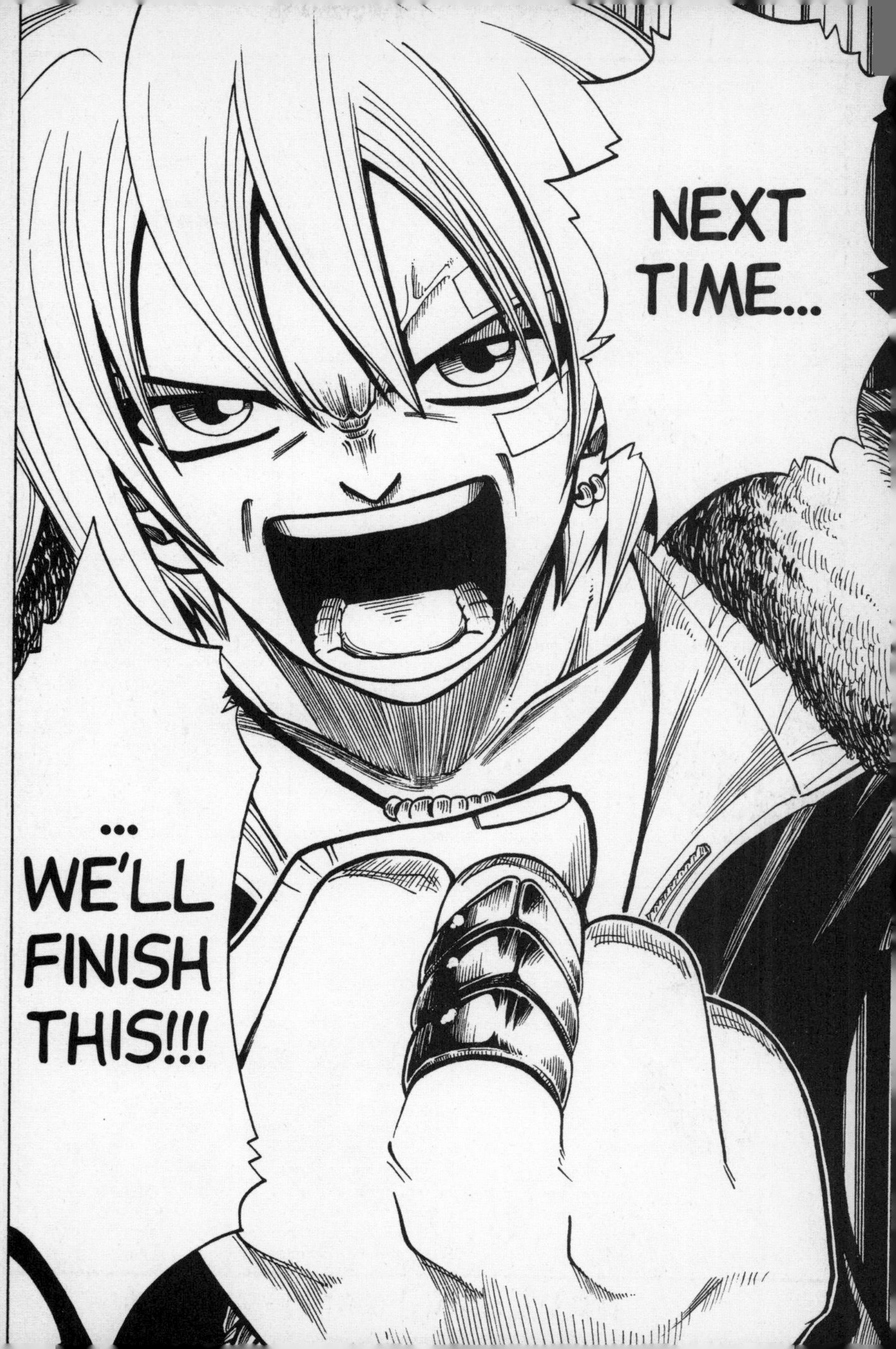
NEXT TIME...
...WE'LL FINISH THIS!!!

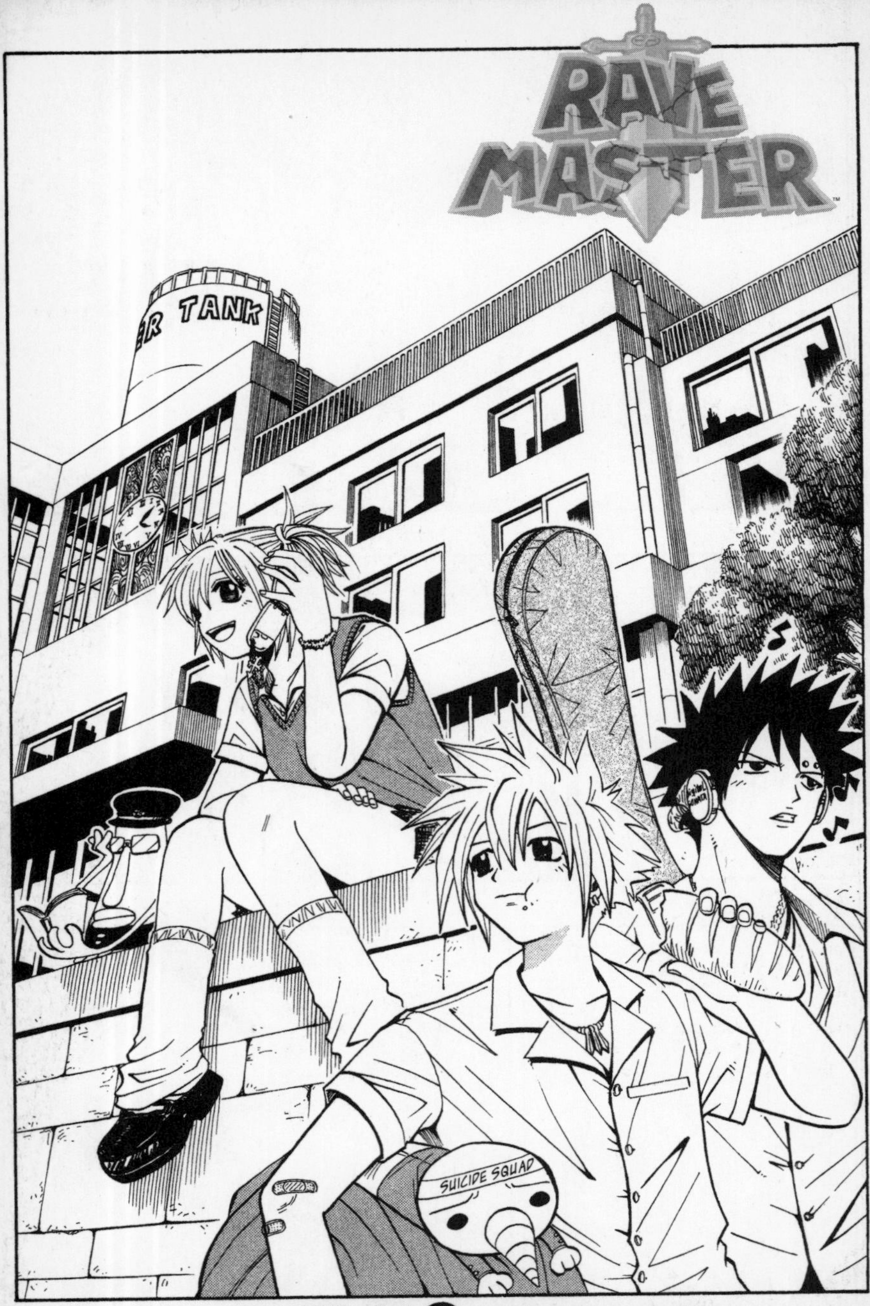
RAVE MASTER
ER TANK
SUICIDE SQUAD

RAVE:94 ✠ MEMORY DOOR

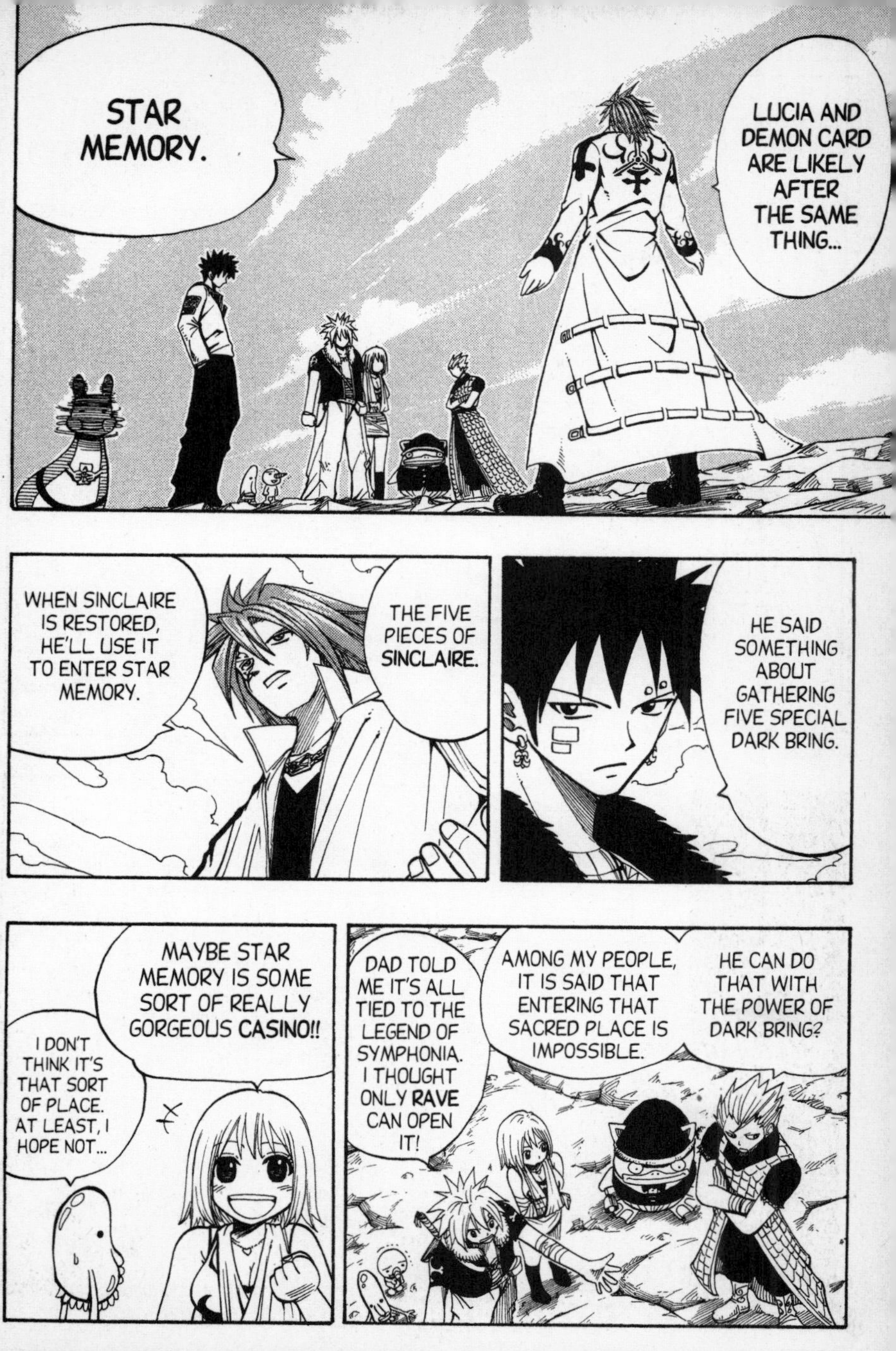
LUCIA AND DEMON CARD ARE LIKELY AFTER THE SAME THING...
STAR MEMORY.
HE SAID SOMETHING ABOUT GATHERING FIVE SPECIAL DARK BRING.
THE FIVE PIECES OF **SINCLAIRE.**
WHEN SINCLAIRE IS RESTORED, HE'LL USE IT TO ENTER STAR MEMORY.
HE CAN DO THAT WITH THE POWER OF DARK BRING?
AMONG MY PEOPLE, IT IS SAID THAT ENTERING THAT SACRED PLACE IS IMPOSSIBLE.
DAD TOLD ME IT'S ALL TIED TO THE LEGEND OF SYMPHONIA. I THOUGHT ONLY **RAVE** CAN OPEN IT!
MAYBE STAR MEMORY IS SOME SORT OF REALLY GORGEOUS **CASINO!!**
I DON'T THINK IT'S THAT SORT OF PLACE. AT LEAST, I HOPE NOT...

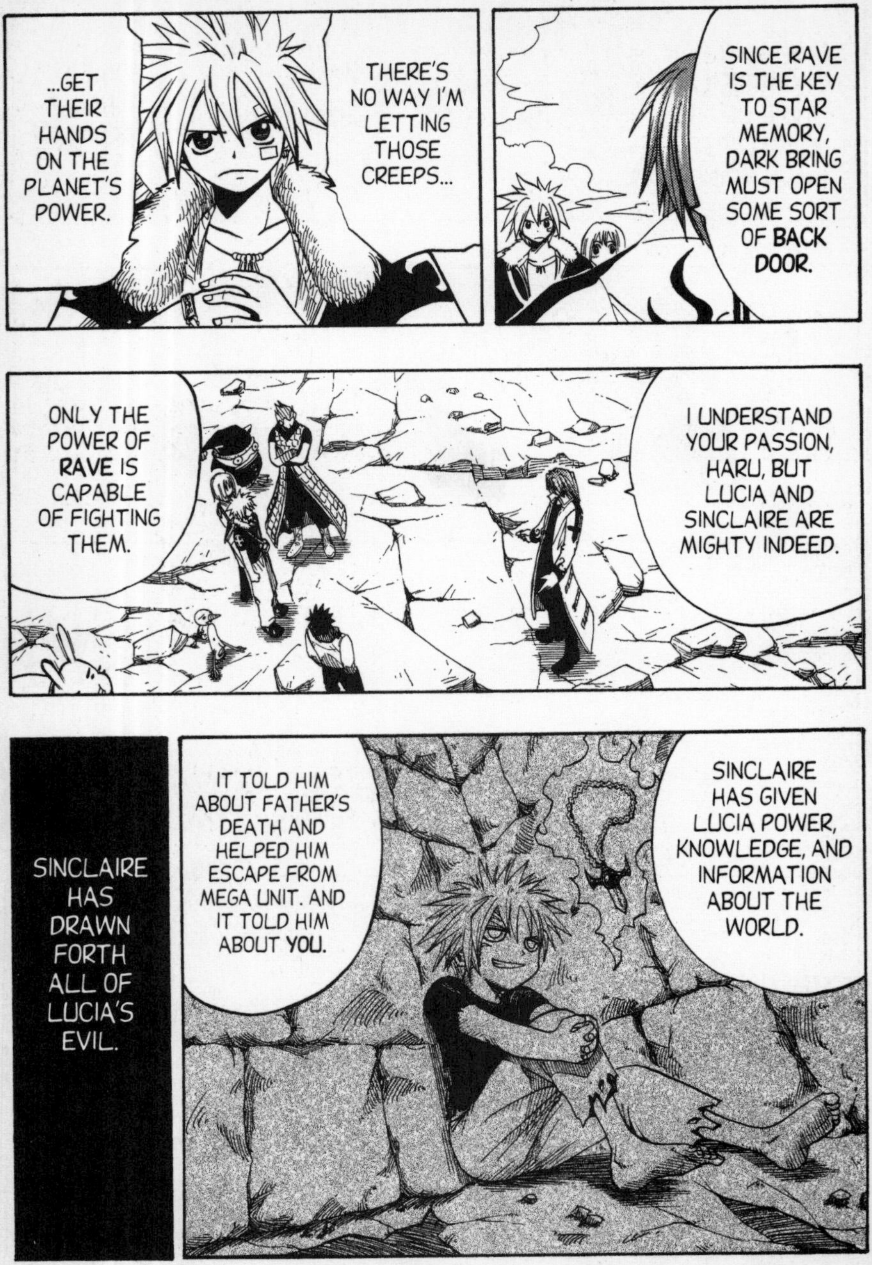
SINCE RAVE IS THE KEY TO STAR MEMORY, DARK BRING MUST OPEN SOME SORT OF BACK DOOR.
THERE'S NO WAY I'M LETTING THOSE CREEPS...
...GET THEIR HANDS ON THE PLANET'S POWER.
I UNDERSTAND YOUR PASSION, HARU, BUT LUCIA AND SINCLAIRE ARE MIGHTY INDEED.
ONLY THE POWER OF RAVE IS CAPABLE OF FIGHTING THEM.
SINCLAIRE HAS GIVEN LUCIA POWER, KNOWLEDGE, AND INFORMATION ABOUT THE WORLD.
IT TOLD HIM ABOUT FATHER'S DEATH AND HELPED HIM ESCAPE FROM MEGA UNIT. AND IT TOLD HIM ABOUT YOU.
SINCLAIRE HAS DRAWN FORTH ALL OF LUCIA'S EVIL.

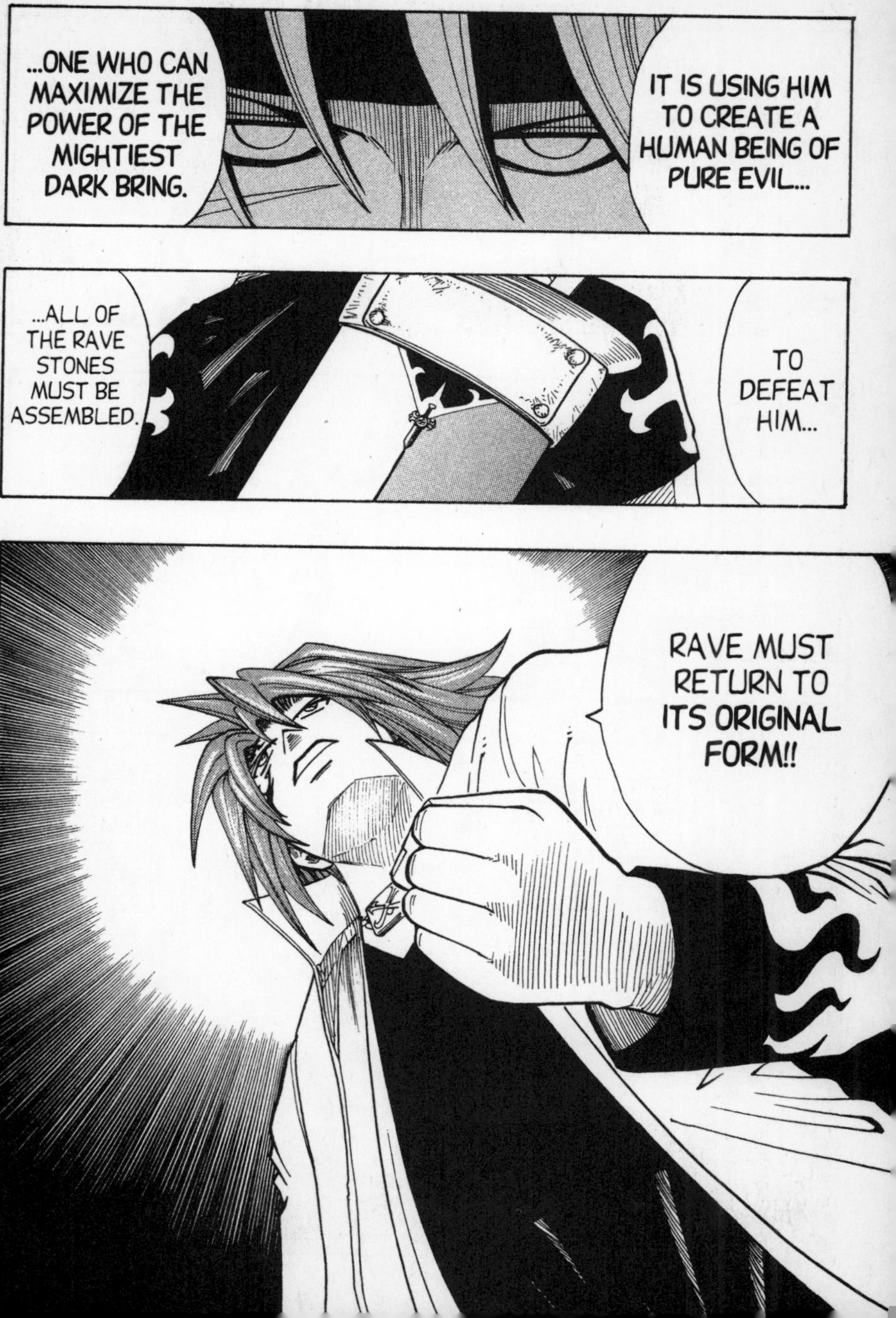
IT IS USING HIM TO CREATE A HUMAN BEING OF PURE EVIL...
...ONE WHO CAN MAXIMIZE THE POWER OF THE MIGHTIEST DARK BRING.
TO DEFEAT HIM...
...ALL OF THE RAVE STONES MUST BE ASSEMBLED.
RAVE MUST RETURN TO ITS ORIGINAL FORM!!

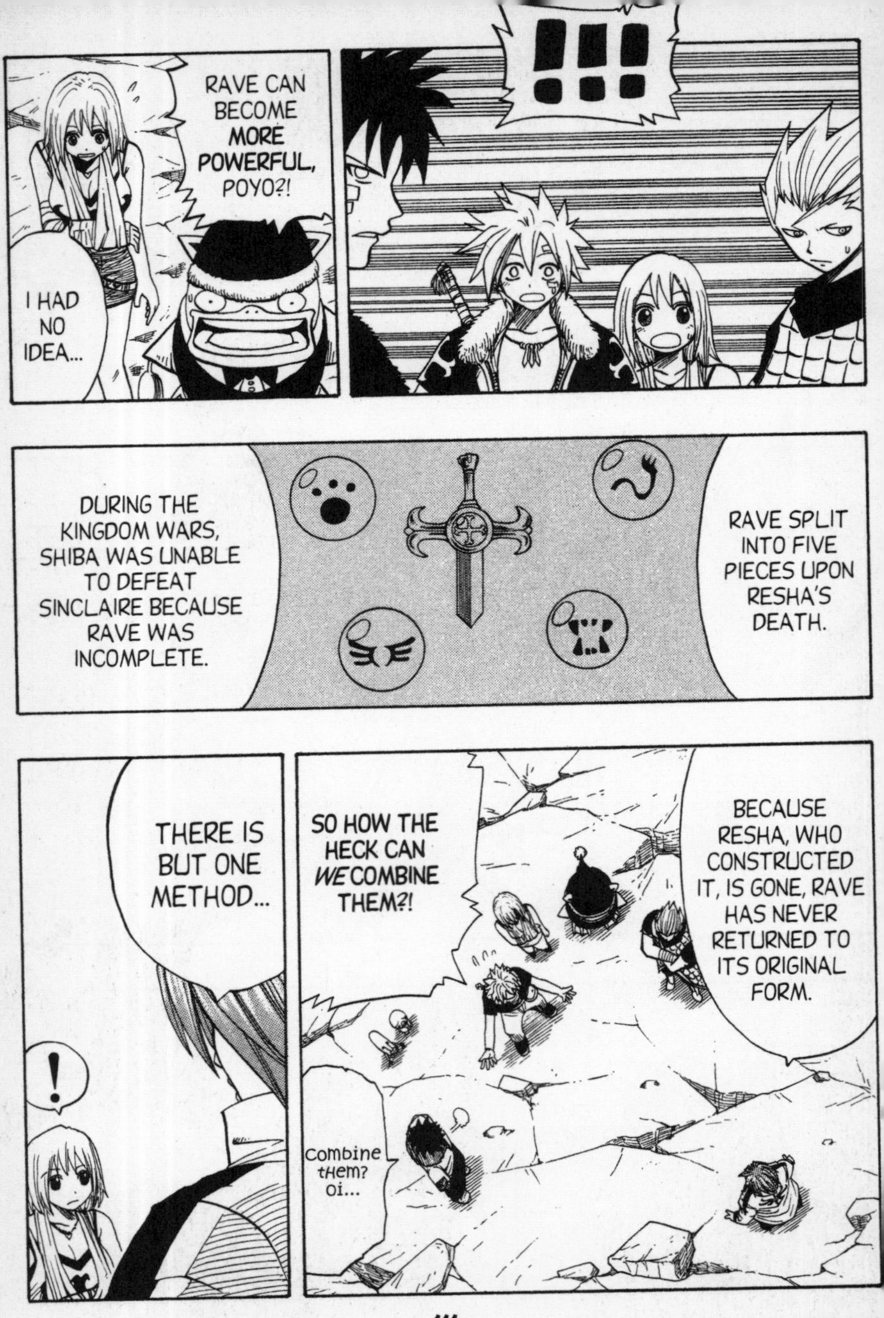
!!!
RAVE CAN BECOME **MORE POWERFUL**, POYO?!
I HAD NO IDEA...
RAVE SPLIT INTO FIVE PIECES UPON RESHA'S DEATH.
DURING THE KINGDOM WARS, SHIBA WAS UNABLE TO DEFEAT SINCLAIRE BECAUSE RAVE WAS INCOMPLETE.
BECAUSE RESHA, WHO CONSTRUCTED IT, IS GONE, RAVE HAS NEVER RETURNED TO ITS ORIGINAL FORM.
SO HOW THE HECK CAN *WE* COMBINE THEM?!
Combine them? Oi...
THERE IS BUT ONE METHOD...
!

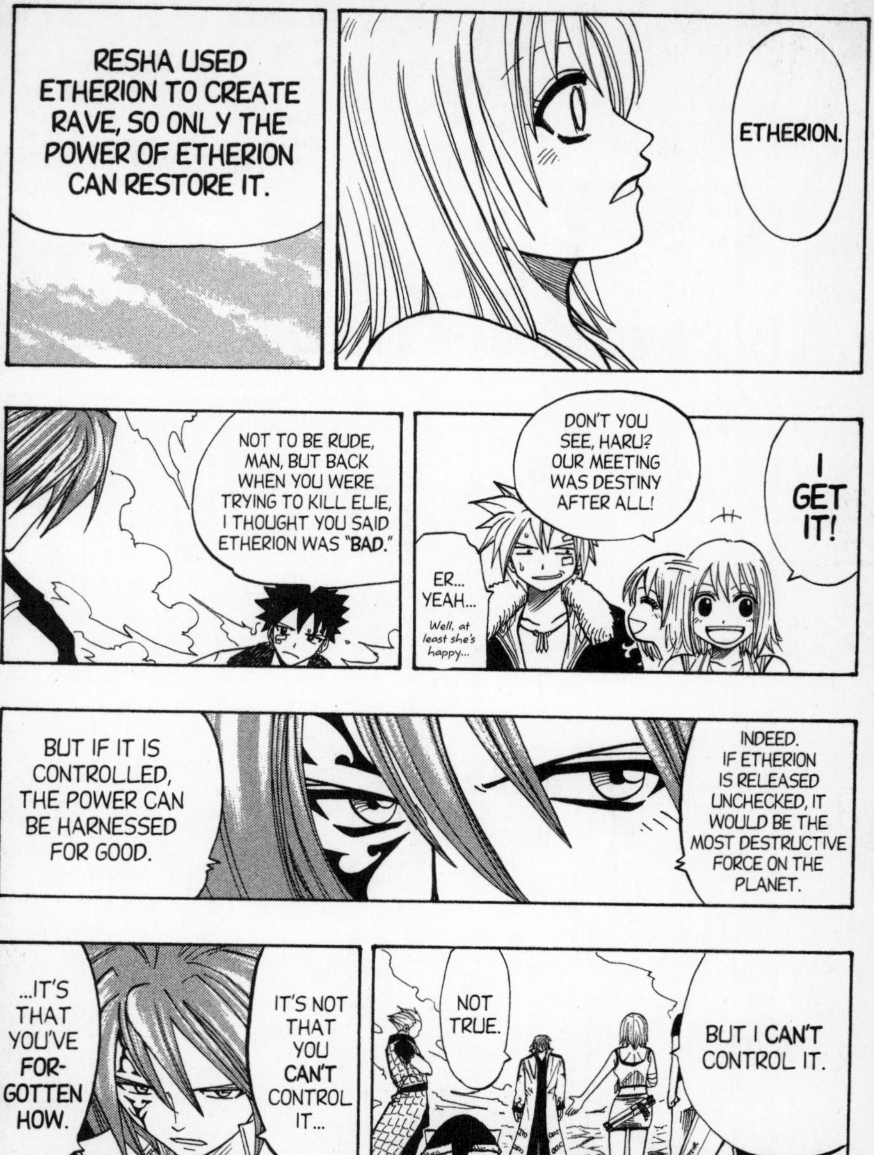
ETHERION.
RESHA USED ETHERION TO CREATE RAVE, SO ONLY THE POWER OF ETHERION CAN RESTORE IT.
I GET IT!
DON'T YOU SEE, HARU? OUR MEETING WAS DESTINY AFTER ALL!
ER... YEAH...
Well, at least she's happy...
NOT TO BE RUDE, MAN, BUT BACK WHEN YOU WERE TRYING TO KILL ELIE, I THOUGHT YOU SAID ETHERION WAS "BAD."
INDEED. IF ETHERION IS RELEASED UNCHECKED, IT WOULD BE THE MOST DESTRUCTIVE FORCE ON THE PLANET.
BUT IF IT IS CONTROLLED, THE POWER CAN BE HARNESSED FOR GOOD.
BUT I CAN'T CONTROL IT.
NOT TRUE.
IT'S NOT THAT YOU CAN'T CONTROL IT...
...IT'S THAT YOU'VE FOR-GOTTEN HOW.

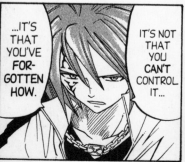

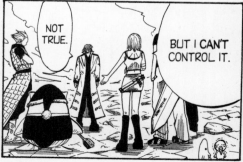

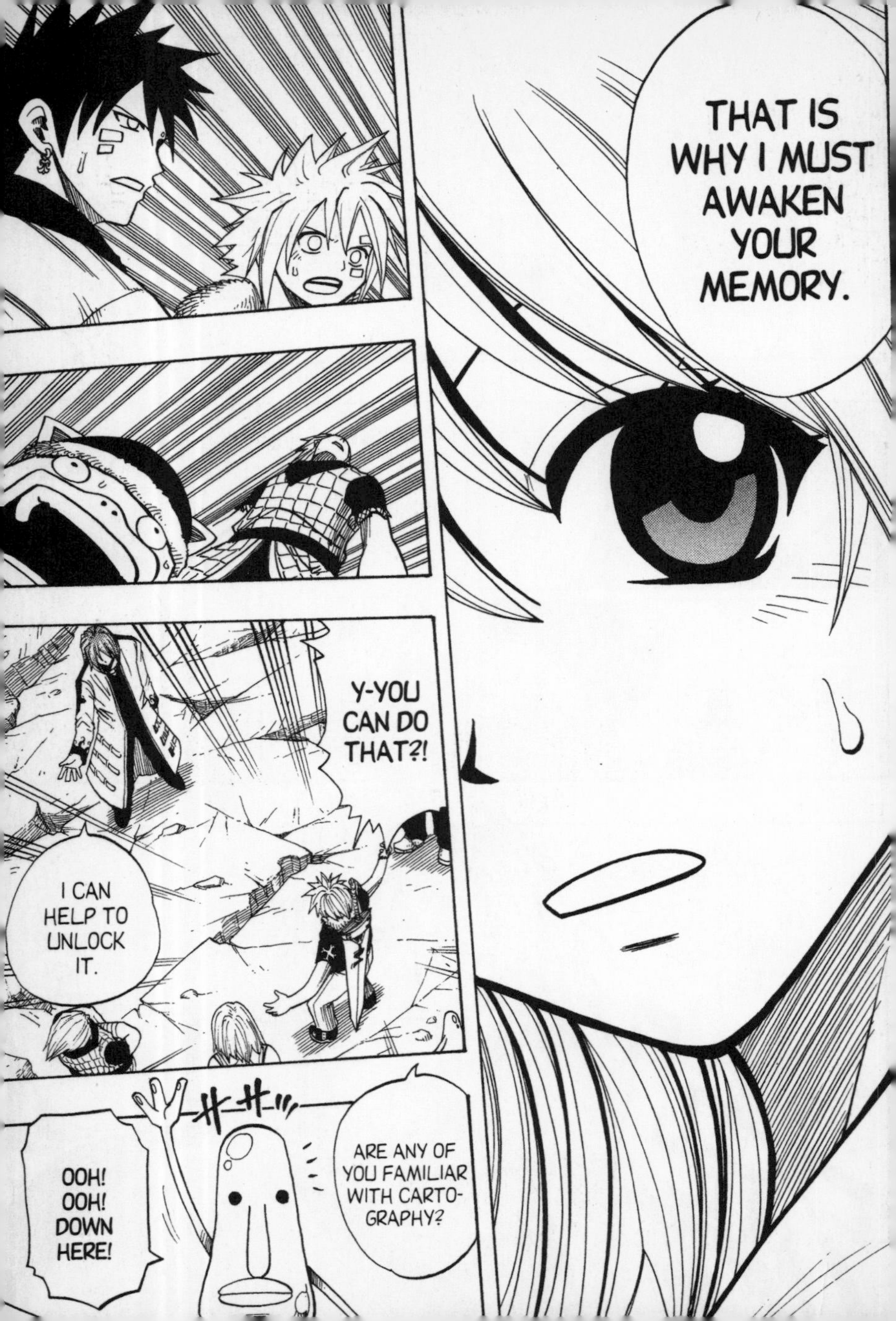
THAT IS WHY I MUST AWAKEN YOUR MEMORY.
Y-YOU CAN DO THAT?!
I CAN HELP TO UNLOCK IT.
ARE ANY OF YOU FAMILIAR WITH CARTO-GRAPHY?
OOH! OOH! DOWN HERE!

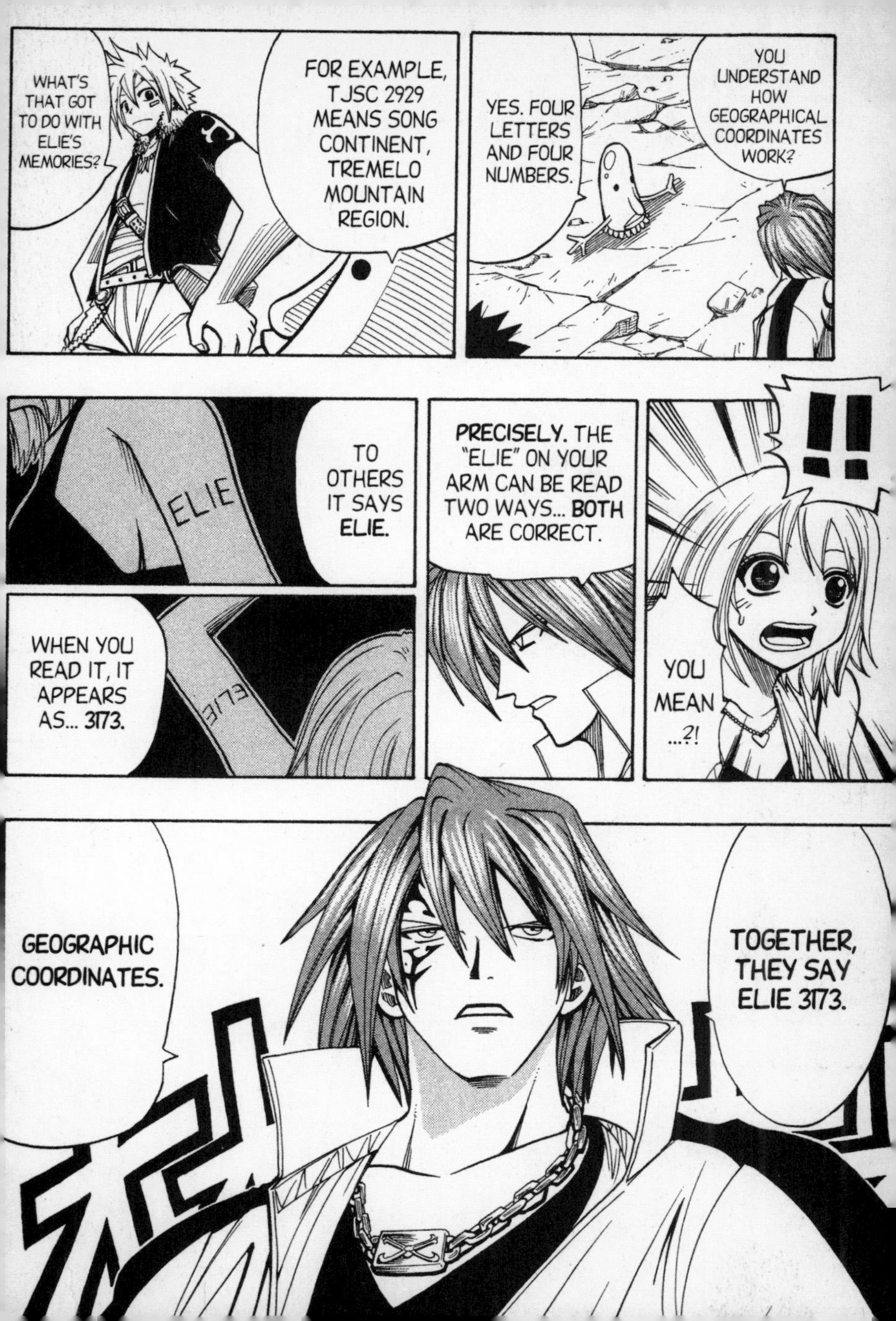
YOU UNDERSTAND HOW GEOGRAPHICAL COORDINATES WORK?
YES. FOUR LETTERS AND FOUR NUMBERS.
FOR EXAMPLE, TJSC 2929 MEANS SONG CONTINENT, TREMELO MOUNTAIN REGION.
WHAT'S THAT GOT TO DO WITH ELIE'S MEMORIES?
!!
YOU MEAN ...?!
PRECISELY. THE "ELIE" ON YOUR ARM CAN BE READ TWO WAYS... BOTH ARE CORRECT.
TO OTHERS IT SAYS ELIE.
ELIE
WHEN YOU READ IT, IT APPEARS AS... 3173.
TOGETHER, THEY SAY ELIE 3173.
GEOGRAPHIC COORDINATES.

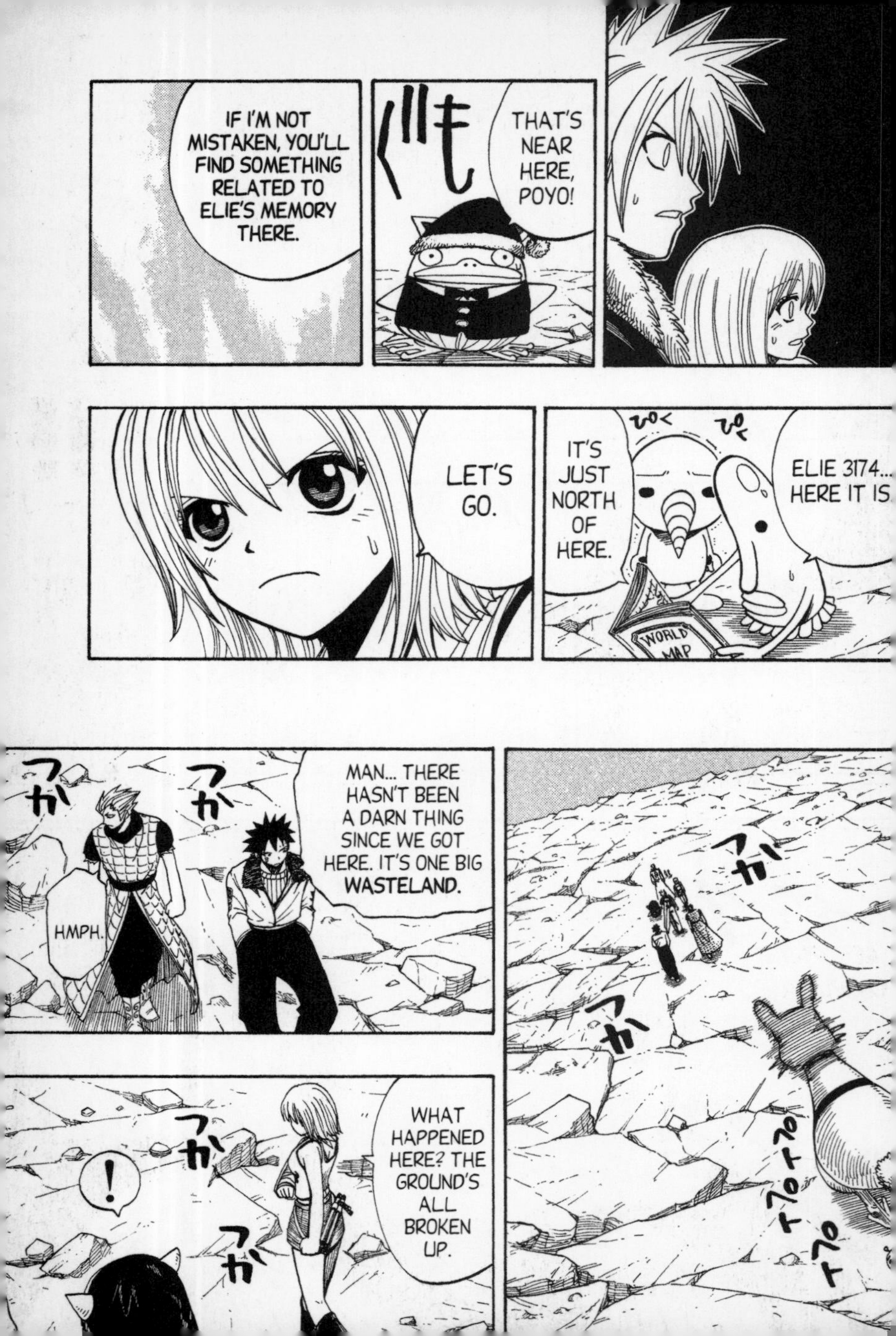
THAT'S NEAR HERE, POYO!
IF I'M NOT MISTAKEN, YOU'LL FIND SOMETHING RELATED TO ELIE'S MEMORY THERE.
ELIE 3174... HERE IT IS.
IT'S JUST NORTH OF HERE.
WORLD MAP
LET'S GO.
MAN... THERE HASN'T BEEN A DARN THING SINCE WE GOT HERE. IT'S ONE BIG **WASTELAND.**
HMPH.
WHAT HAPPENED HERE? THE GROUND'S ALL BROKEN UP.
!

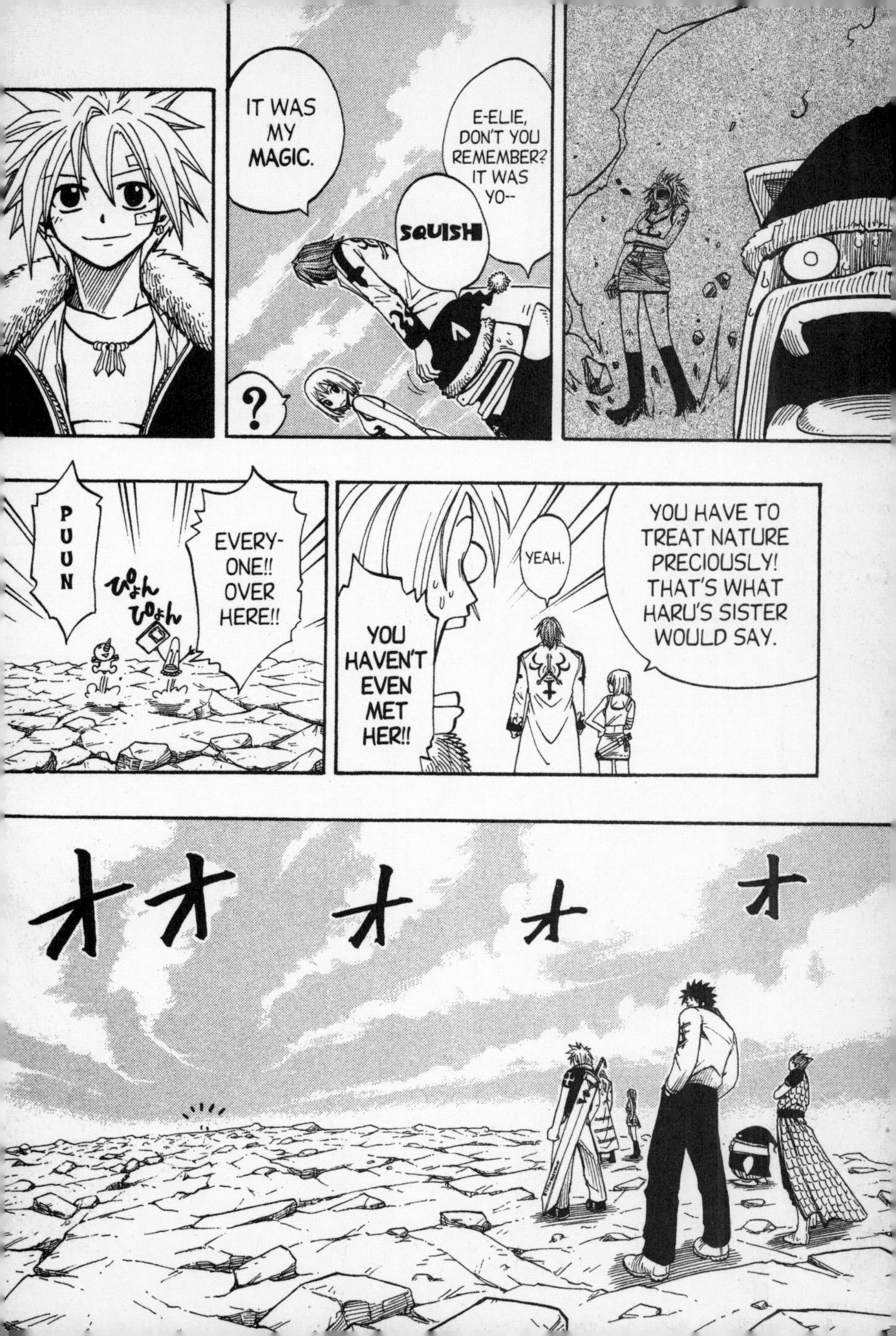
E-ELIE, DON'T YOU REMEMBER? IT WAS YO--
IT WAS MY MAGIC.
SQUISH
?
YOU HAVE TO TREAT NATURE PRECIOUSLY! THAT'S WHAT HARU'S SISTER WOULD SAY.
YEAH.
YOU HAVEN'T EVEN MET HER!!
EVERY-ONE!! OVER HERE!!
ぴょんぴょん
PUUN
オオオオオ

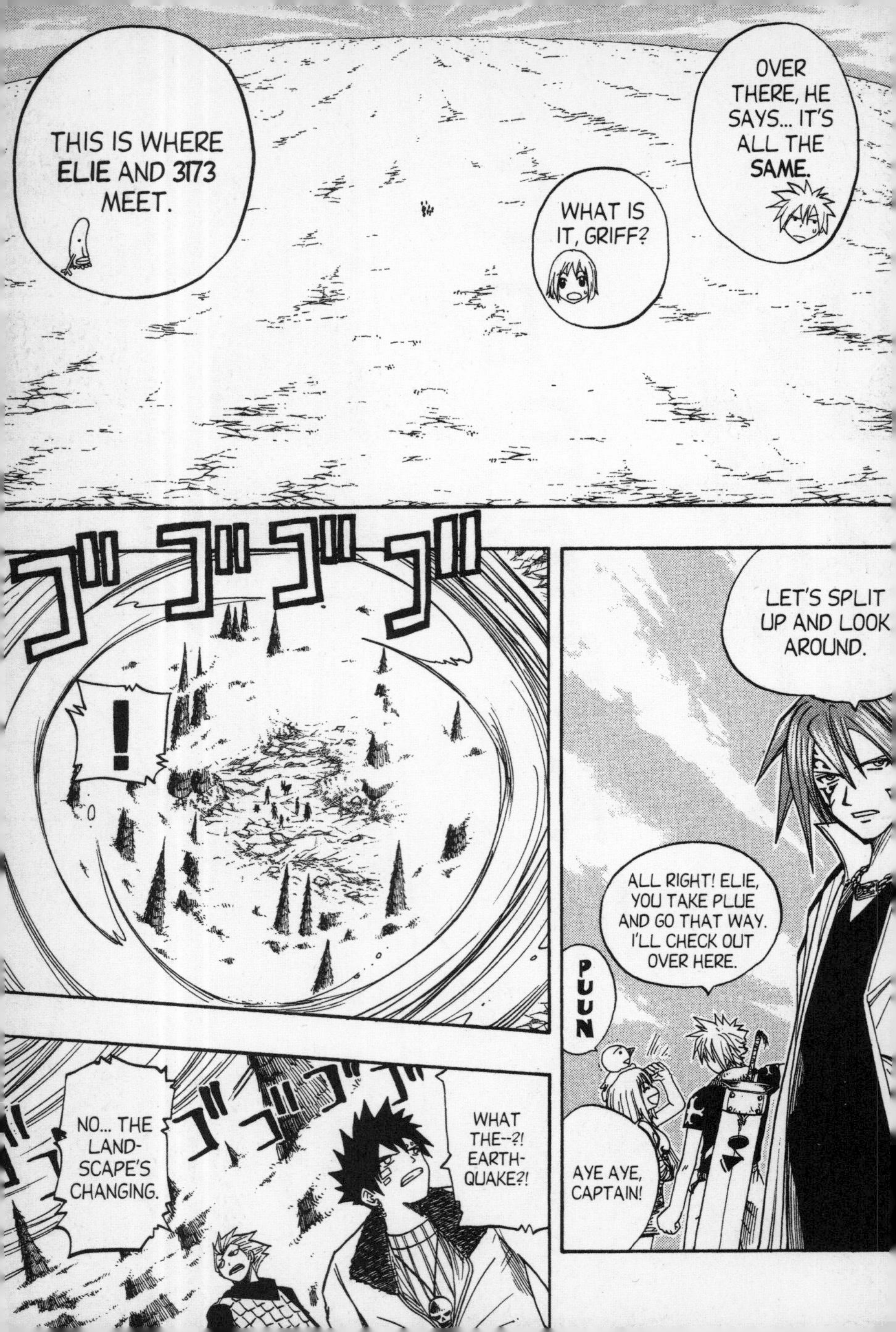
OVER THERE, HE SAYS... IT'S ALL THE SAME.
WHAT IS IT, GRIFF?
THIS IS WHERE ELIE AND 3173 MEET.
LET'S SPLIT UP AND LOOK AROUND.
ALL RIGHT! ELIE, YOU TAKE PLUE AND GO THAT WAY. I'LL CHECK OUT OVER HERE.
PUUN
AYE AYE, CAPTAIN!
ゴゴゴゴ
!
WHAT THE--?! EARTH-QUAKE?!
NO... THE LAND-SCAPE'S CHANGING.

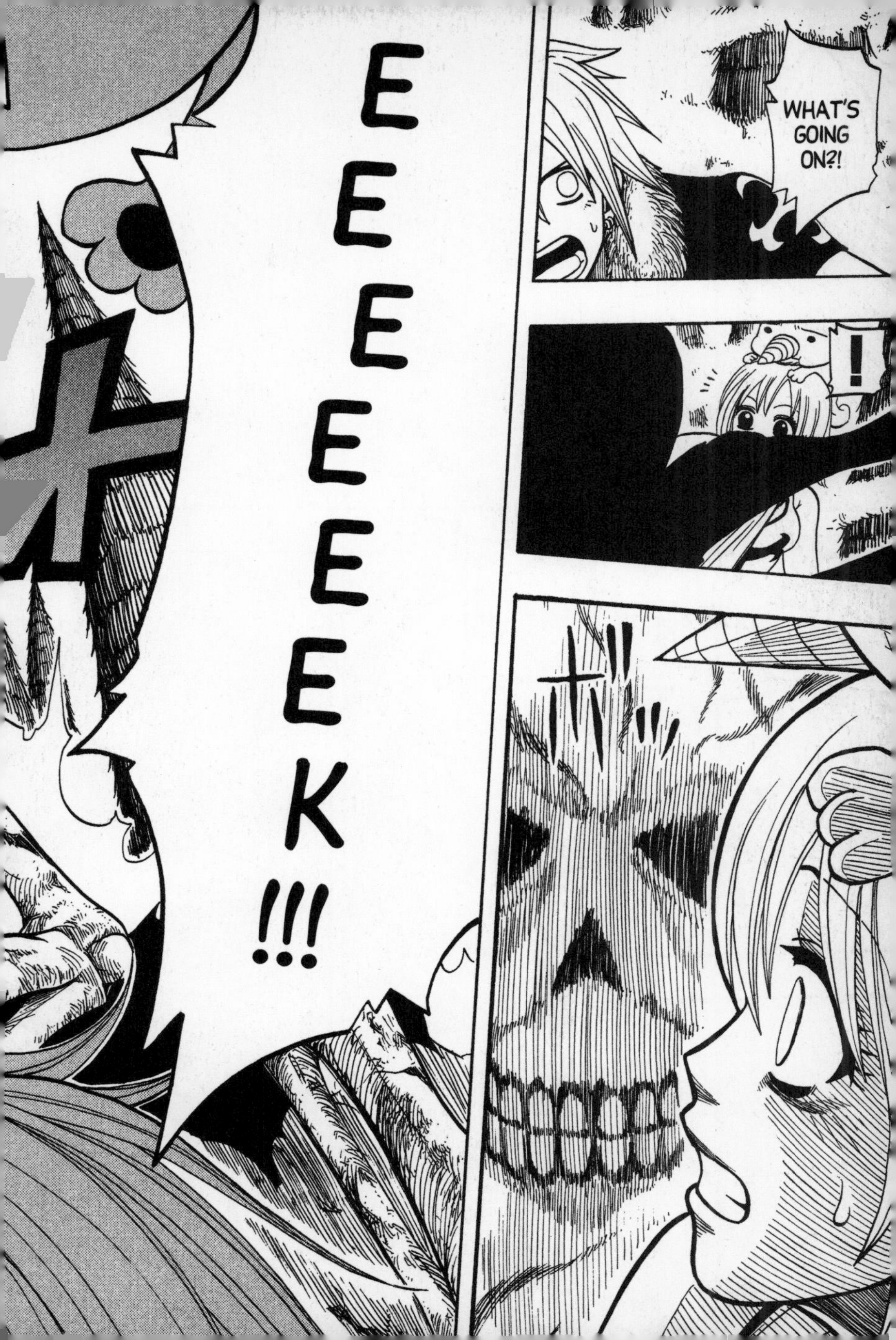
WHAT'S GOING ON?!
!
EEEEEEK!!!

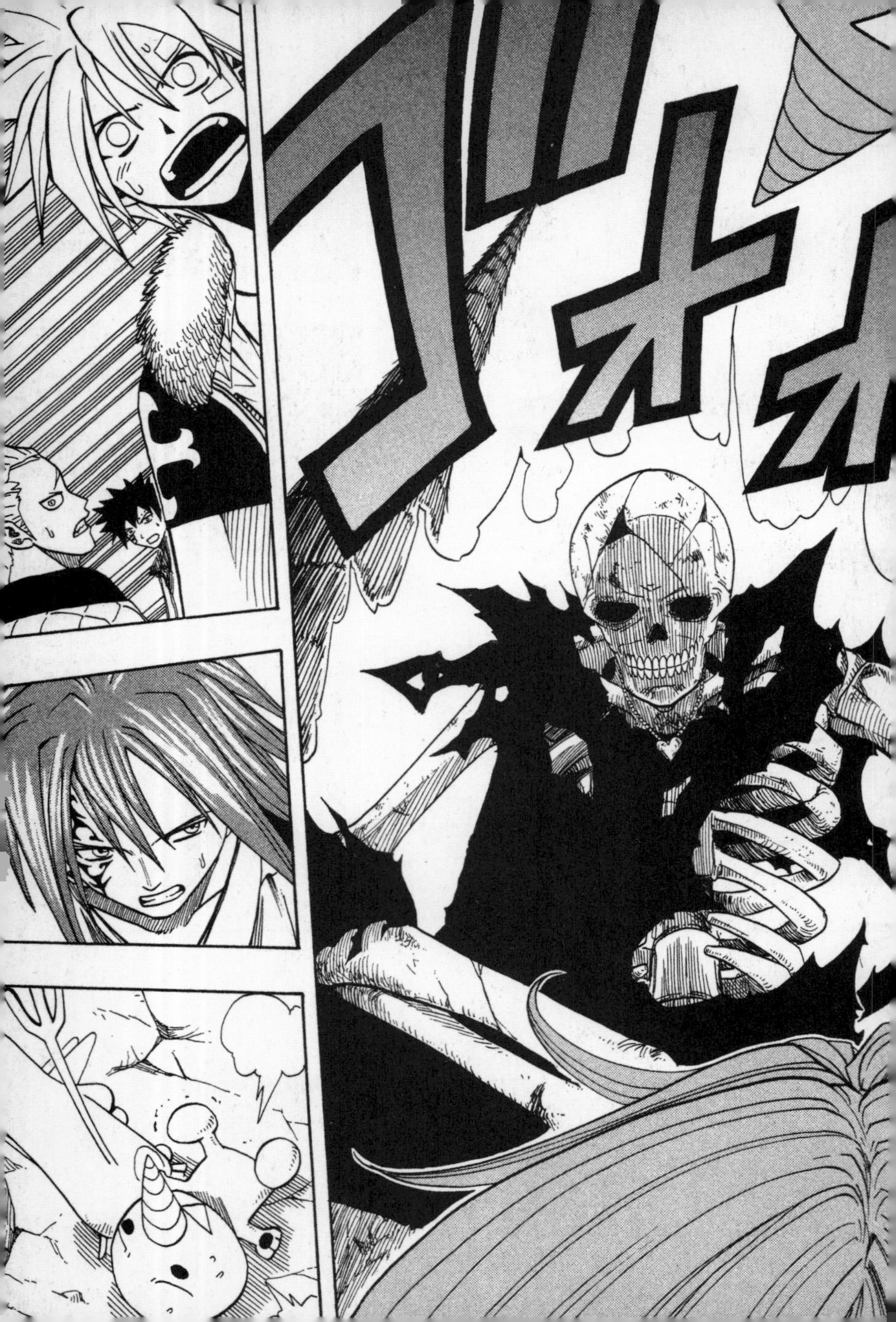
ゴオオ

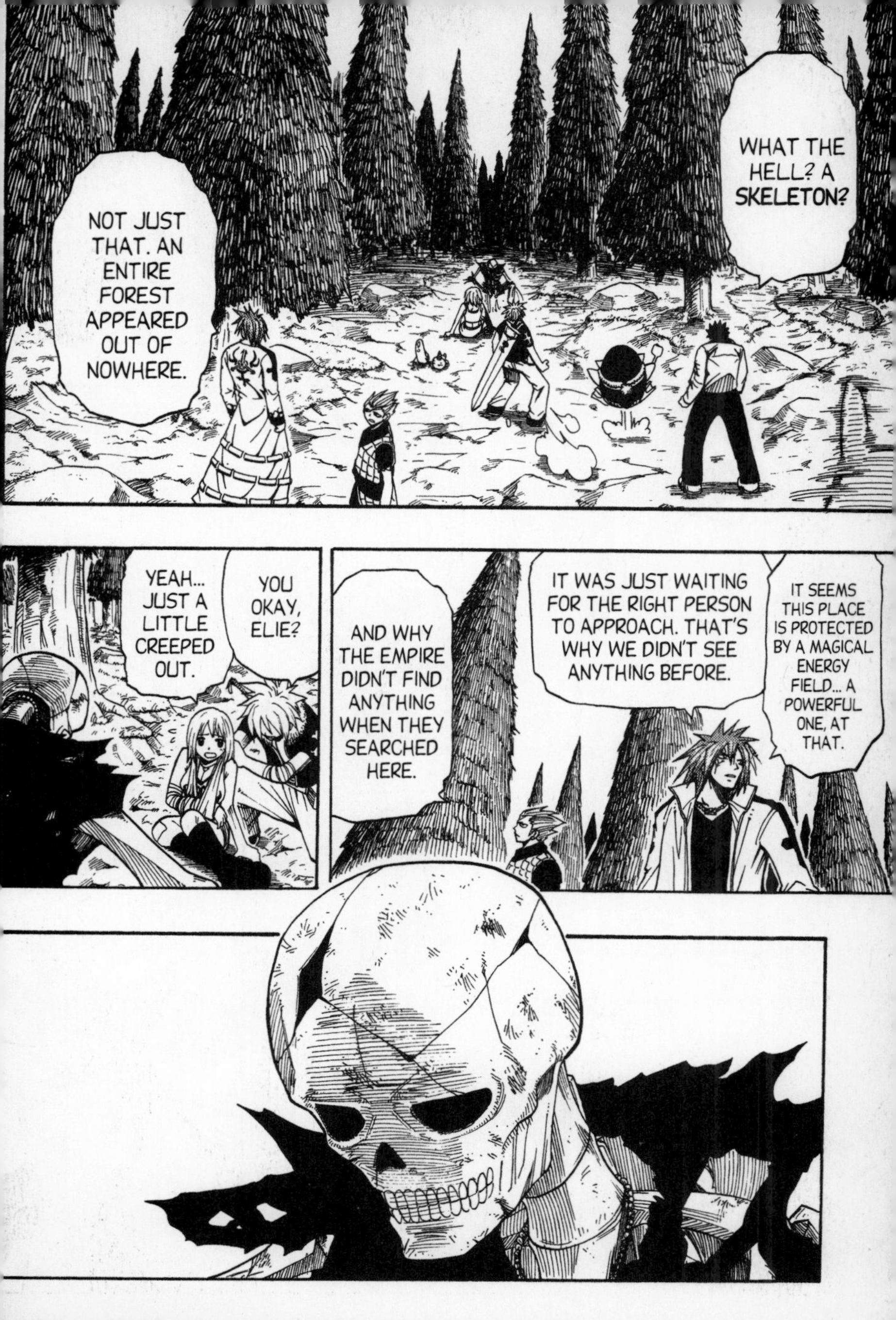

WHAT THE HELL? A SKELETON?
NOT JUST THAT. AN ENTIRE FOREST APPEARED OUT OF NOWHERE.
IT SEEMS THIS PLACE IS PROTECTED BY A MAGICAL ENERGY FIELD... A POWERFUL ONE, AT THAT.
IT WAS JUST WAITING FOR THE RIGHT PERSON TO APPROACH. THAT'S WHY WE DIDN'T SEE ANYTHING BEFORE.
AND WHY THE EMPIRE DIDN'T FIND ANYTHING WHEN THEY SEARCHED HERE.
YOU OKAY, ELIE?
YEAH... JUST A LITTLE CREEPED OUT.

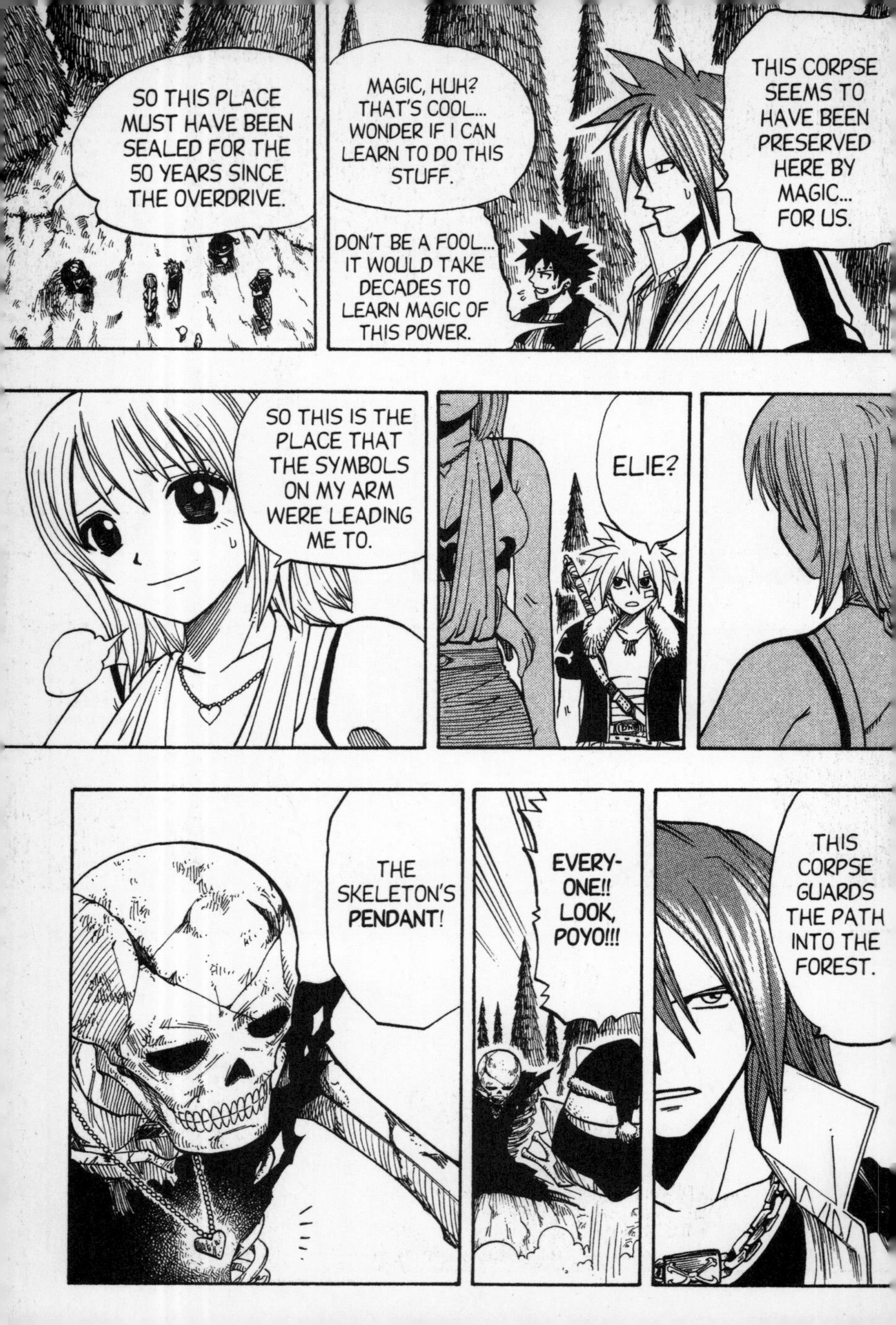
THIS CORPSE SEEMS TO HAVE BEEN PRESERVED HERE BY MAGIC... FOR US.
MAGIC, HUH? THAT'S COOL... WONDER IF I CAN LEARN TO DO THIS STUFF.
DON'T BE A FOOL... IT WOULD TAKE DECADES TO LEARN MAGIC OF THIS POWER.
SO THIS PLACE MUST HAVE BEEN SEALED FOR THE 50 YEARS SINCE THE OVERDRIVE.
ELIE?
SO THIS IS THE PLACE THAT THE SYMBOLS ON MY ARM WERE LEADING ME TO.
THIS CORPSE GUARDS THE PATH INTO THE FOREST.
EVERY-ONE!! LOOK, POYO!!!
THE SKELETON'S PENDANT!

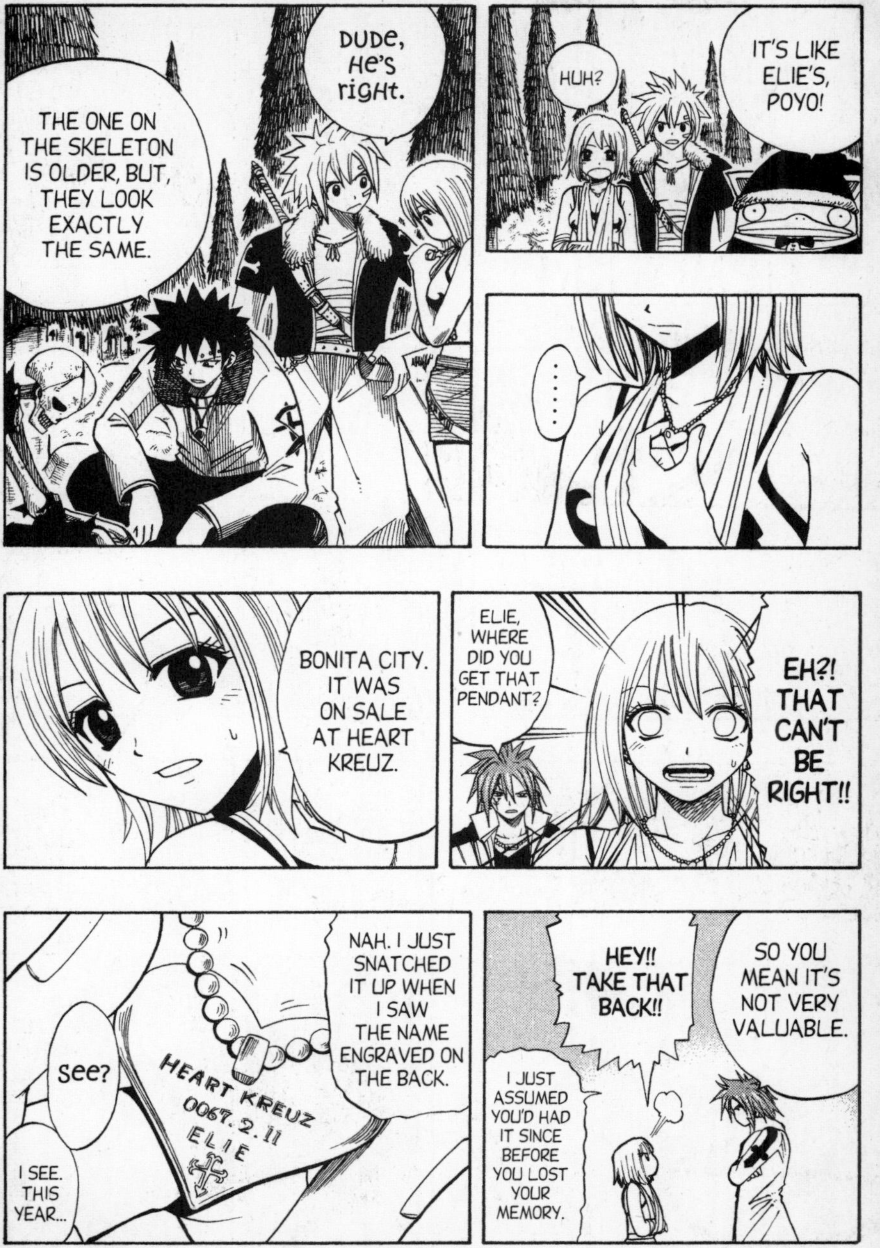
IT'S LIKE ELIE'S, POYO!
HUH?
......
DUDE, HE'S right.
THE ONE ON THE SKELETON IS OLDER, BUT, THEY LOOK EXACTLY THE SAME.
EH?! THAT CAN'T BE RIGHT!!
ELIE, WHERE DID YOU GET THAT PENDANT?
BONITA CITY. IT WAS ON SALE AT HEART KREUZ.
SO YOU MEAN IT'S NOT VERY VALUABLE.
HEY!! TAKE THAT BACK!!
I JUST ASSUMED YOU'D HAD IT SINCE BEFORE YOU LOST YOUR MEMORY.
NAH. I JUST SNATCHED IT UP WHEN I SAW THE NAME ENGRAVED ON THE BACK.
see?
HEART KREUZ 0067. 2. 11 ELIE
I SEE. THIS YEAR...

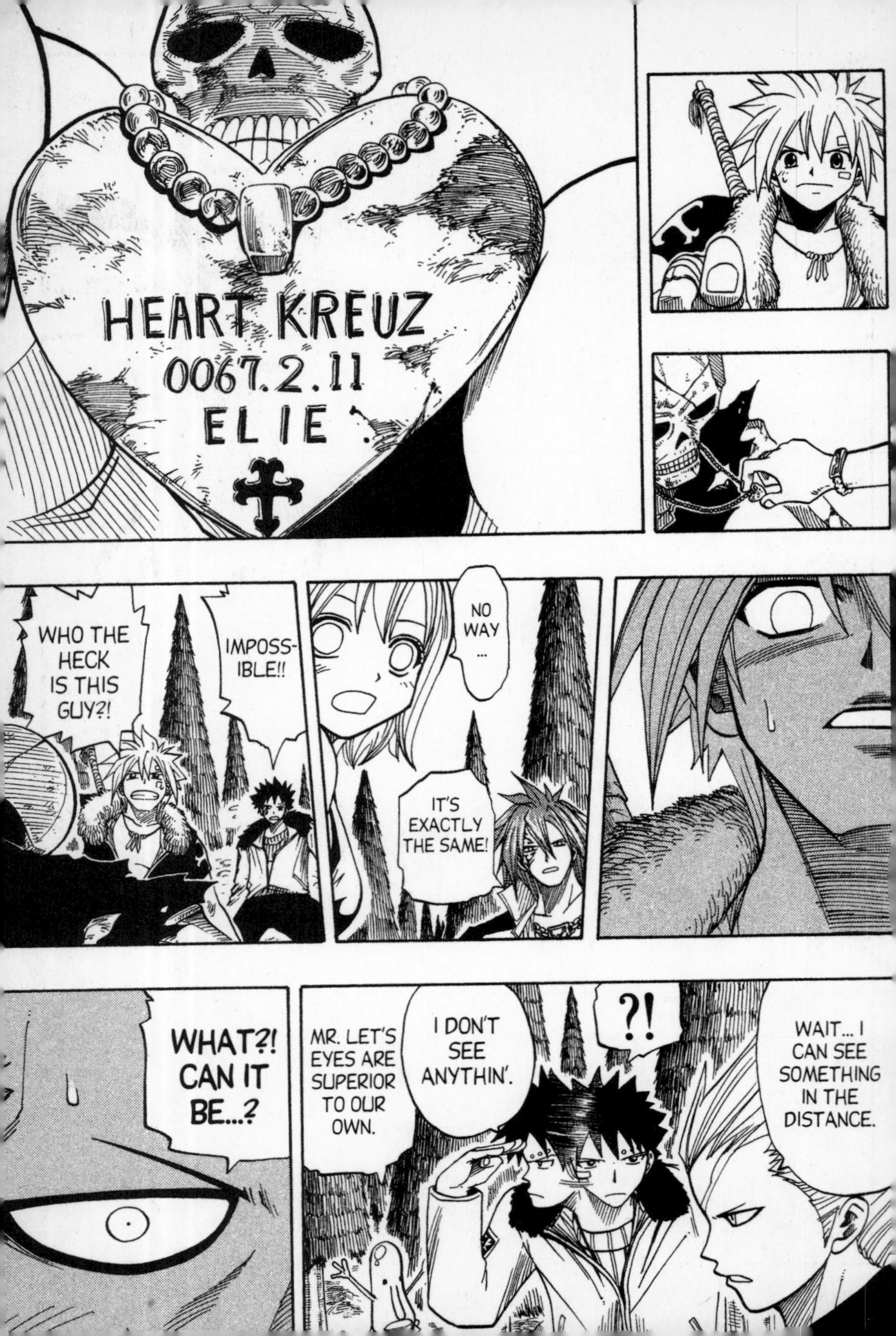
HEART KREUZ
0067.2.11
ELIE
NO WAY ...
IT'S EXACTLY THE SAME!
IMPOSS-IBLE!!
WHO THE HECK IS THIS GUY?!
WAIT... I CAN SEE SOMETHING IN THE DISTANCE.
?!
I DON'T SEE ANYTHIN'.
MR. LET'S EYES ARE SUPERIOR TO OUR OWN.
WHAT?! CAN IT BE...?

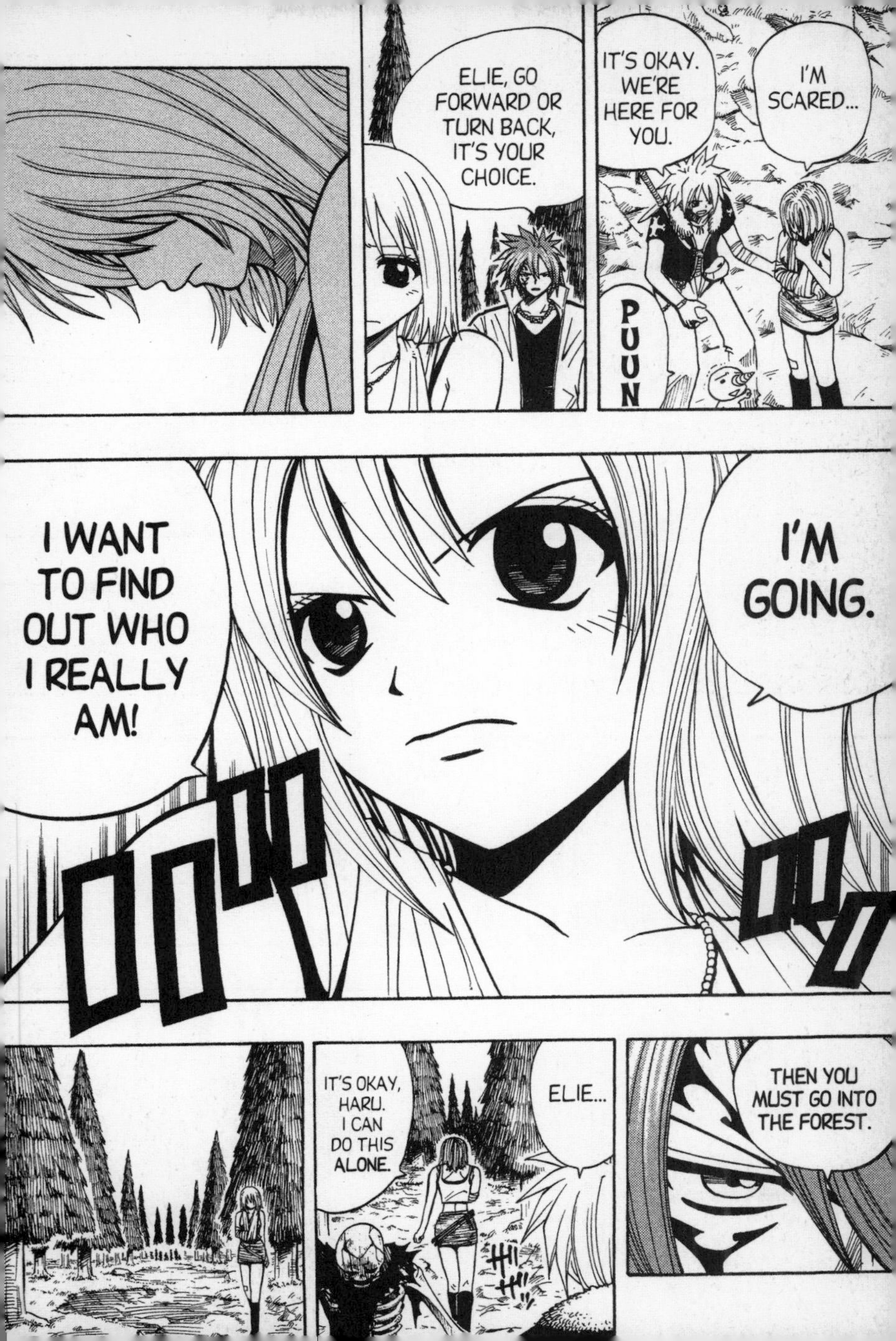
I'M SCARED...
IT'S OKAY. WE'RE HERE FOR YOU.
PUUN
ELIE, GO FORWARD OR TURN BACK, IT'S YOUR CHOICE.
I'M GOING.
I WANT TO FIND OUT WHO I REALLY AM!
THEN YOU MUST GO INTO THE FOREST.
ELIE...
IT'S OKAY, HARU. I CAN DO THIS ALONE.

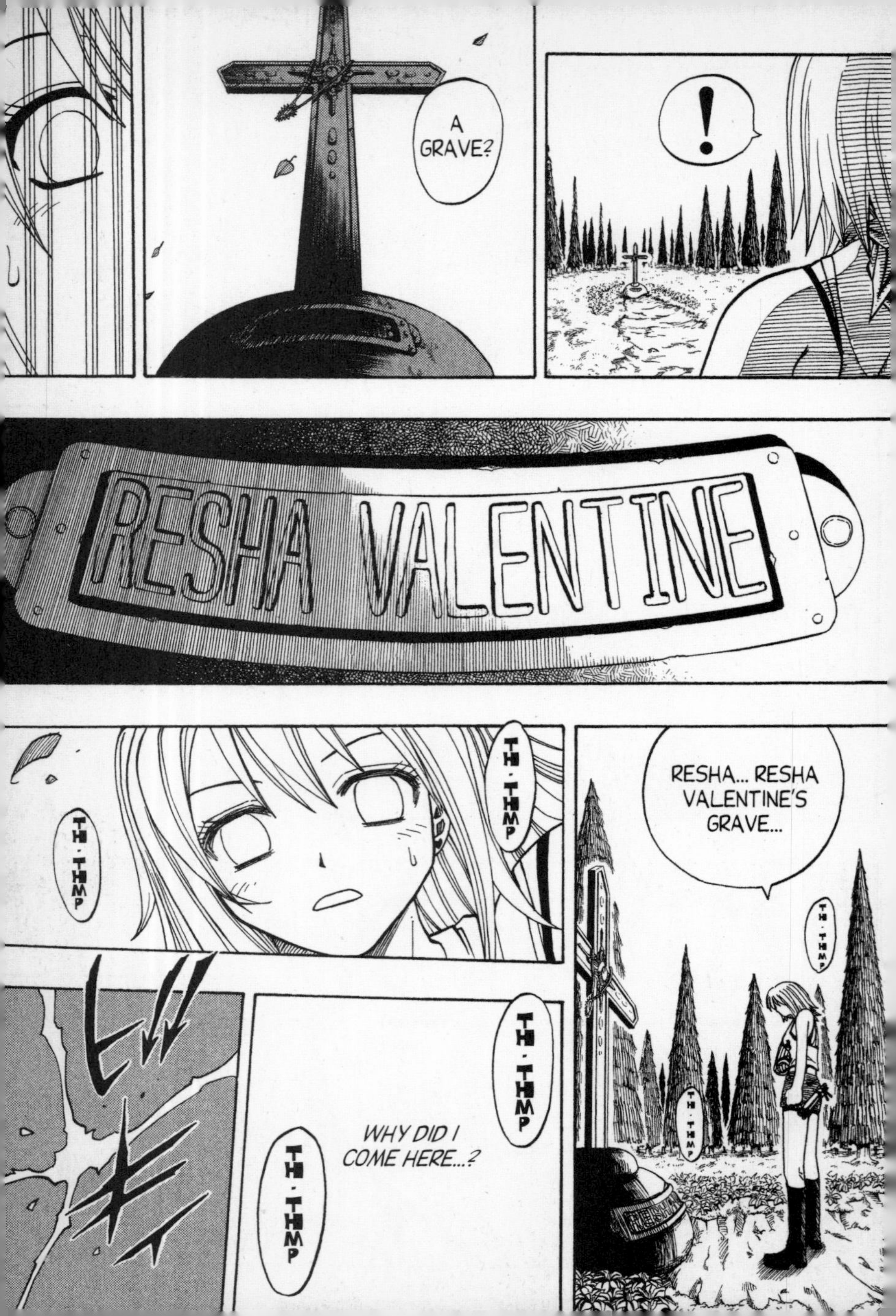
!
A GRAVE?
RESHA VALENTINE
RESHA... RESHA VALENTINE'S GRAVE...
TH-THMP
TH-THMP
TH-THMP
TH-THMP
TH-THMP
WHY DID I COME HERE...?
TH-THMP

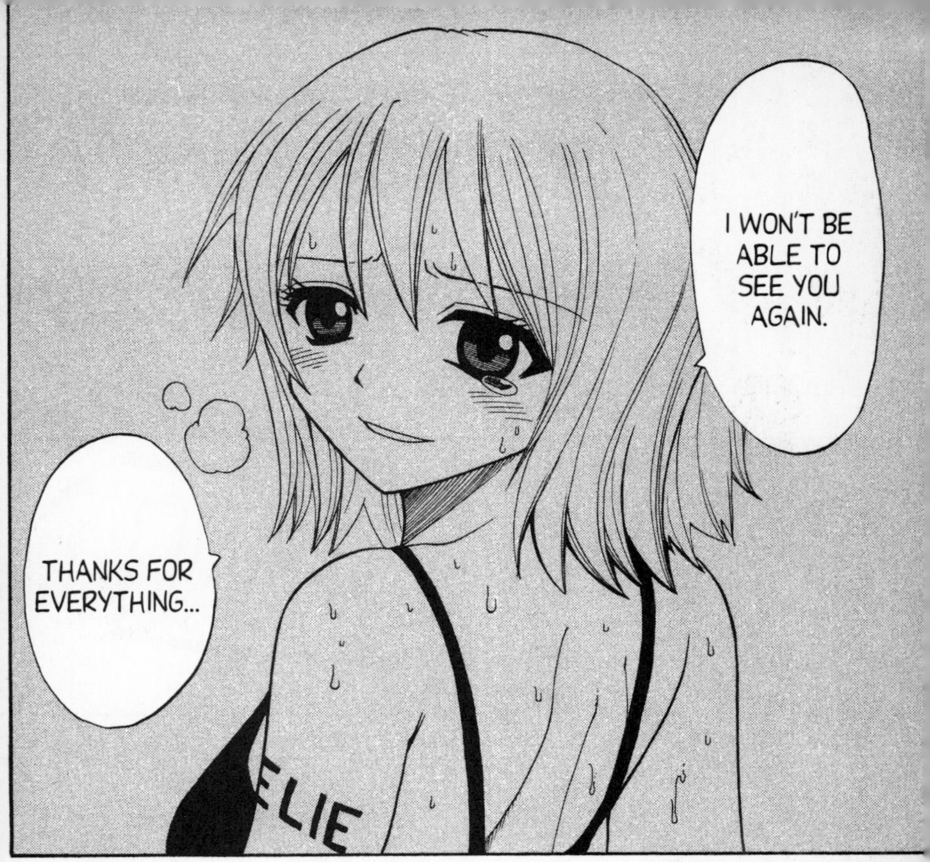
I WON'T BE ABLE TO SEE YOU AGAIN.
THANKS FOR EVERYTHING...
ELIE
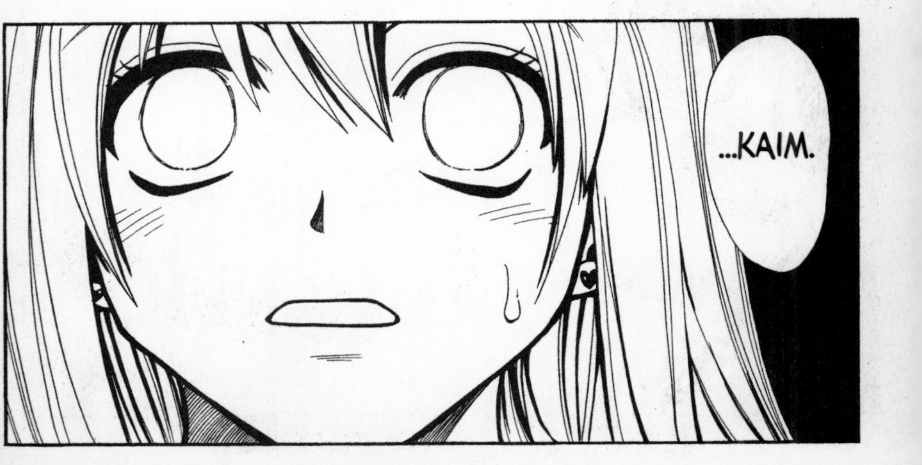
...KAIM.

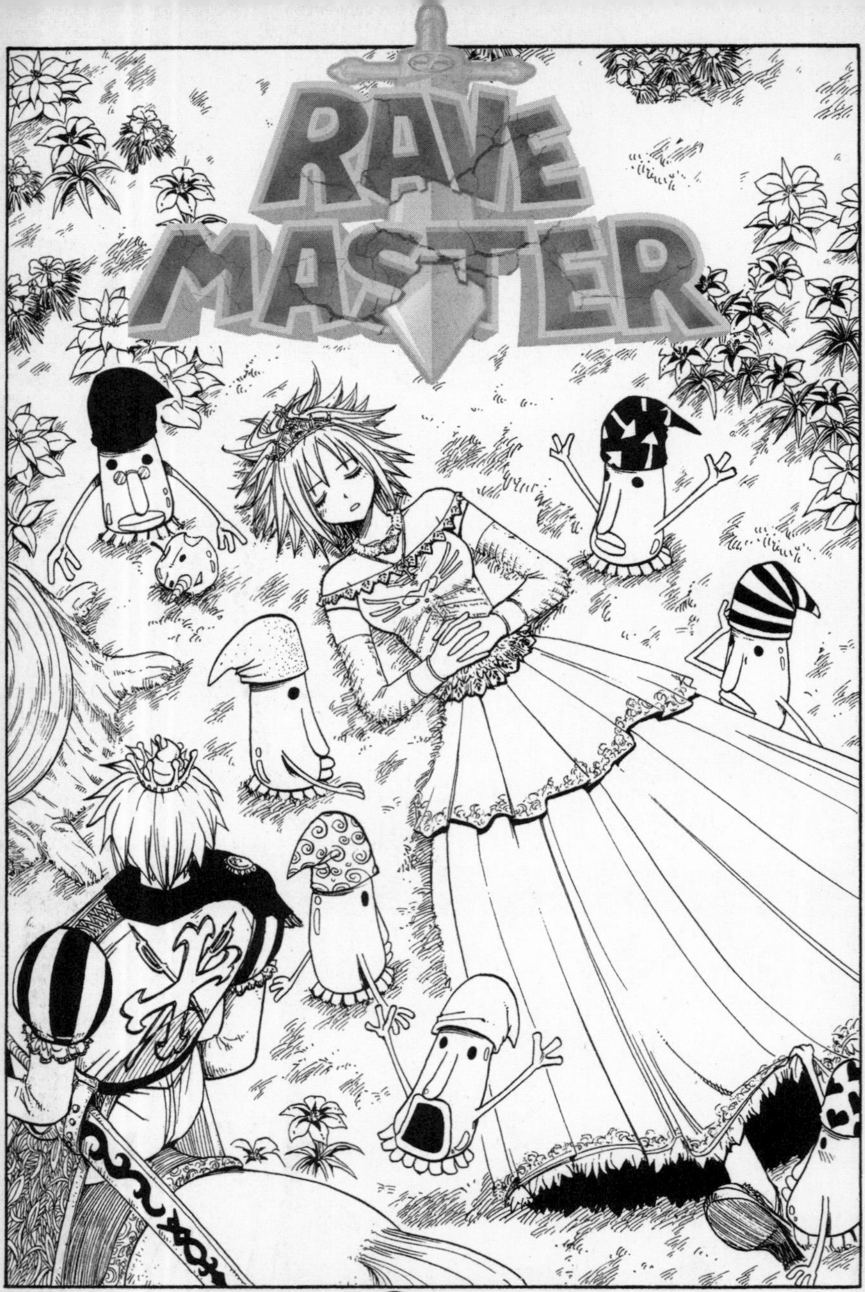
RAVE MASTER

RAVE:95 ✚ TWILIGHT VOW

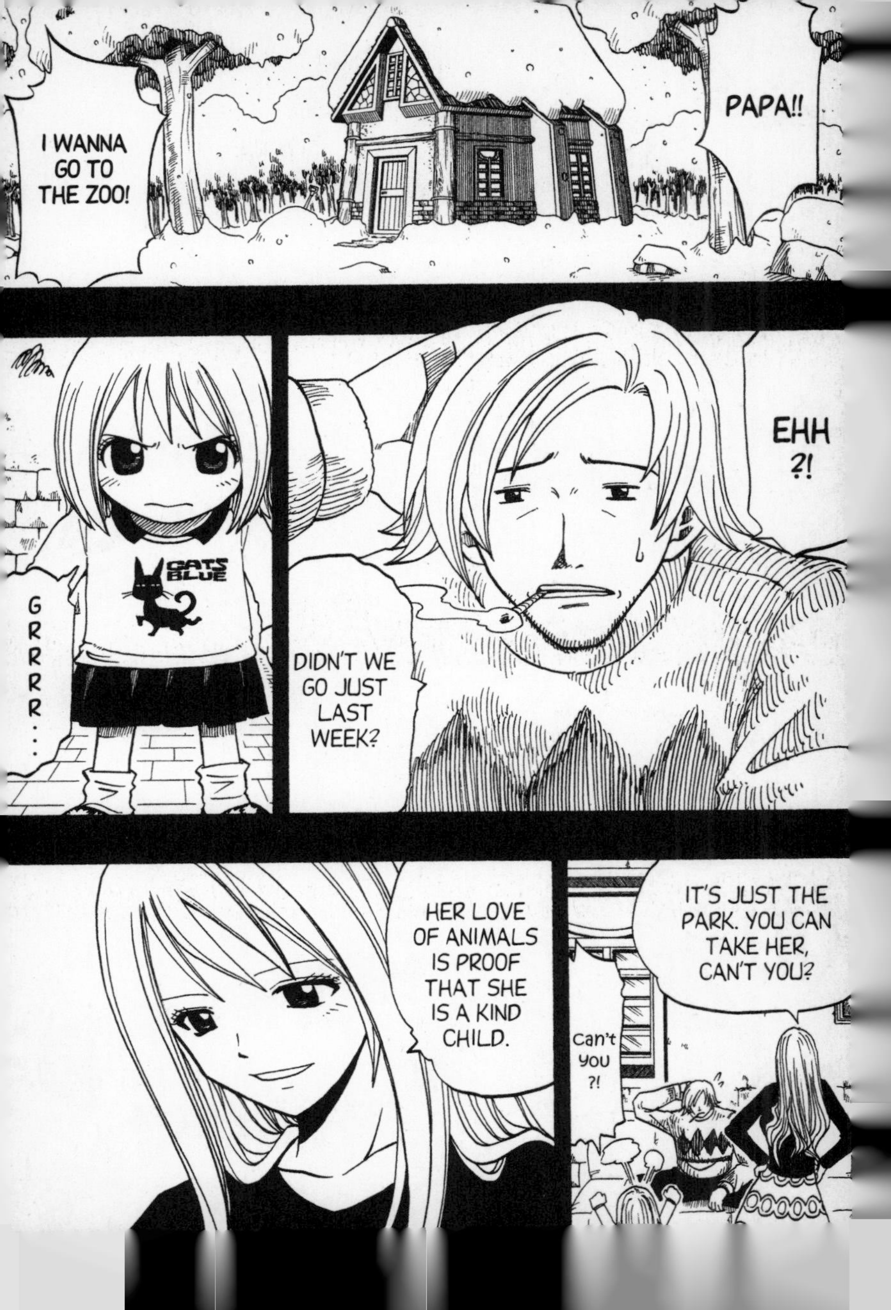
PAPA!!
I WANNA GO TO THE ZOO!
EHH ?!
DIDN'T WE GO JUST LAST WEEK?
GRRRR...
IT'S JUST THE PARK. YOU CAN TAKE HER, CAN'T YOU?
Can't you ?!
HER LOVE OF ANIMALS IS PROOF THAT SHE IS A KIND CHILD.

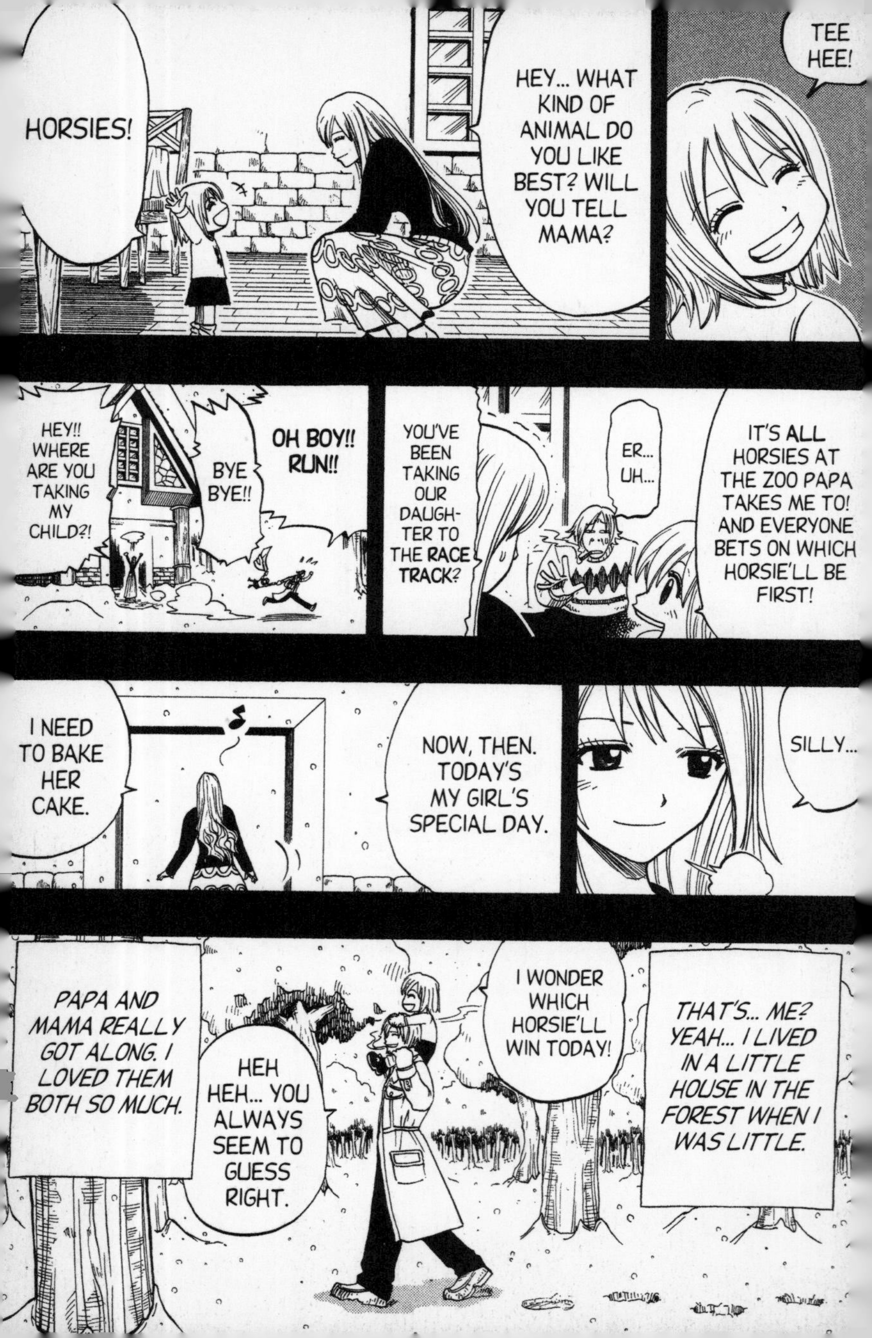
TEE HEE!
HEY... WHAT KIND OF ANIMAL DO YOU LIKE BEST? WILL YOU TELL MAMA?
HORSIES!
IT'S ALL HORSIES AT THE ZOO PAPA TAKES ME TO! AND EVERYONE BETS ON WHICH HORSIE'LL BE FIRST!
ER... UH...
YOU'VE BEEN TAKING OUR DAUGHTER TO THE RACE TRACK?
OH BOY!! RUN!!
BYE BYE!!
HEY!! WHERE ARE YOU TAKING MY CHILD?!
SILLY...
NOW, THEN. TODAY'S MY GIRL'S SPECIAL DAY.
I NEED TO BAKE HER CAKE.
THAT'S... ME? YEAH... I LIVED IN A LITTLE HOUSE IN THE FOREST WHEN I WAS LITTLE.
I WONDER WHICH HORSIE'LL WIN TODAY!
HEH HEH... YOU ALWAYS SEEM TO GUESS RIGHT.
PAPA AND MAMA REALLY GOT ALONG. I LOVED THEM BOTH SO MUCH.

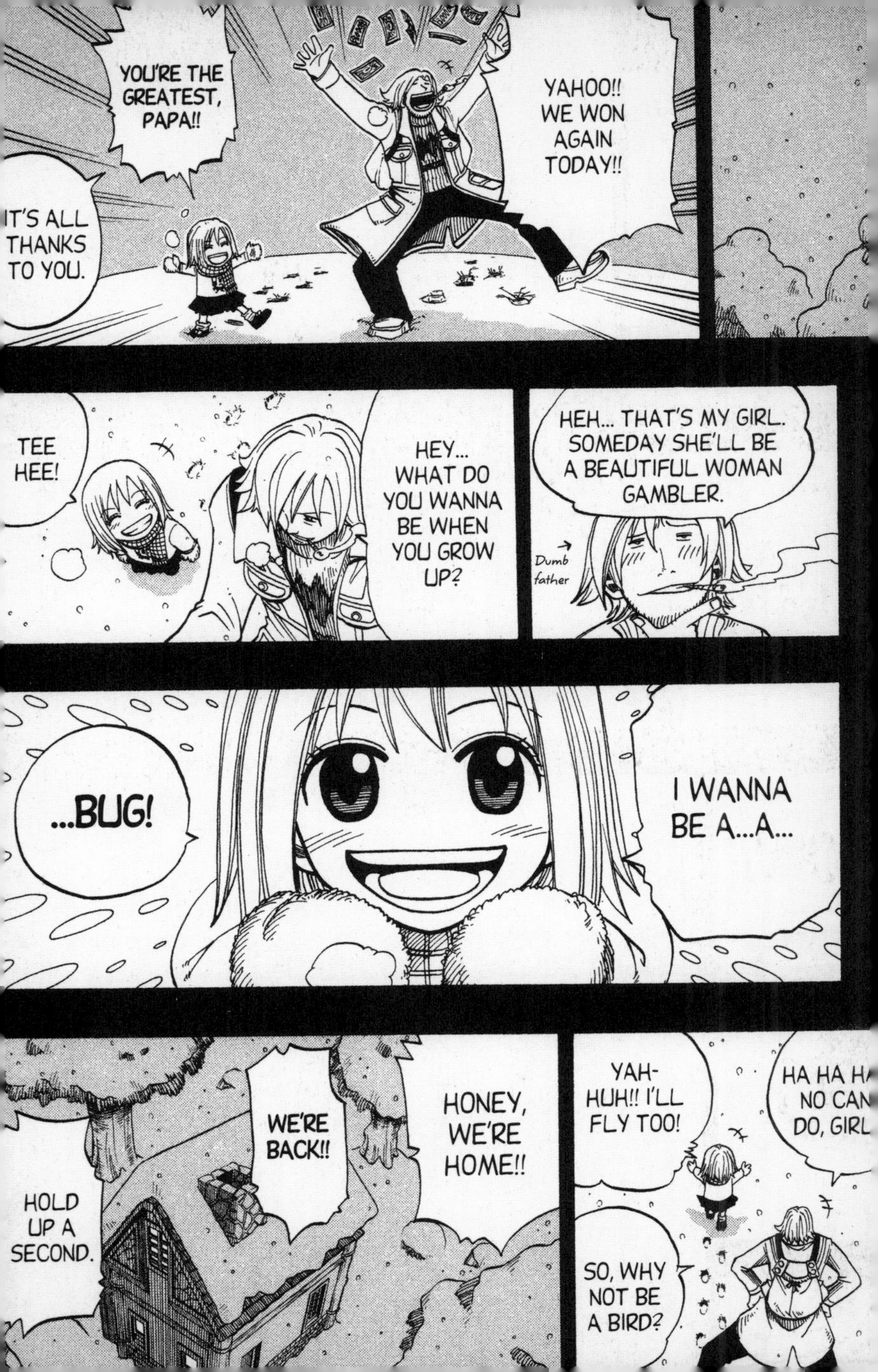
YAHOO!! WE WON AGAIN TODAY!!
YOU'RE THE GREATEST, PAPA!!
IT'S ALL THANKS TO YOU.
HEH... THAT'S MY GIRL. SOMEDAY SHE'LL BE A BEAUTIFUL WOMAN GAMBLER.
Dumb father
HEY... WHAT DO YOU WANNA BE WHEN YOU GROW UP?
TEE HEE!
I WANNA BE A...A...
...BUG!
HA HA H NO CAN DO, GIRL
YAH-HUH!! I'LL FLY TOO!
SO, WHY NOT BE A BIRD?
HONEY, WE'RE HOME!!
WE'RE BACK!!
HOLD UP A SECOND.

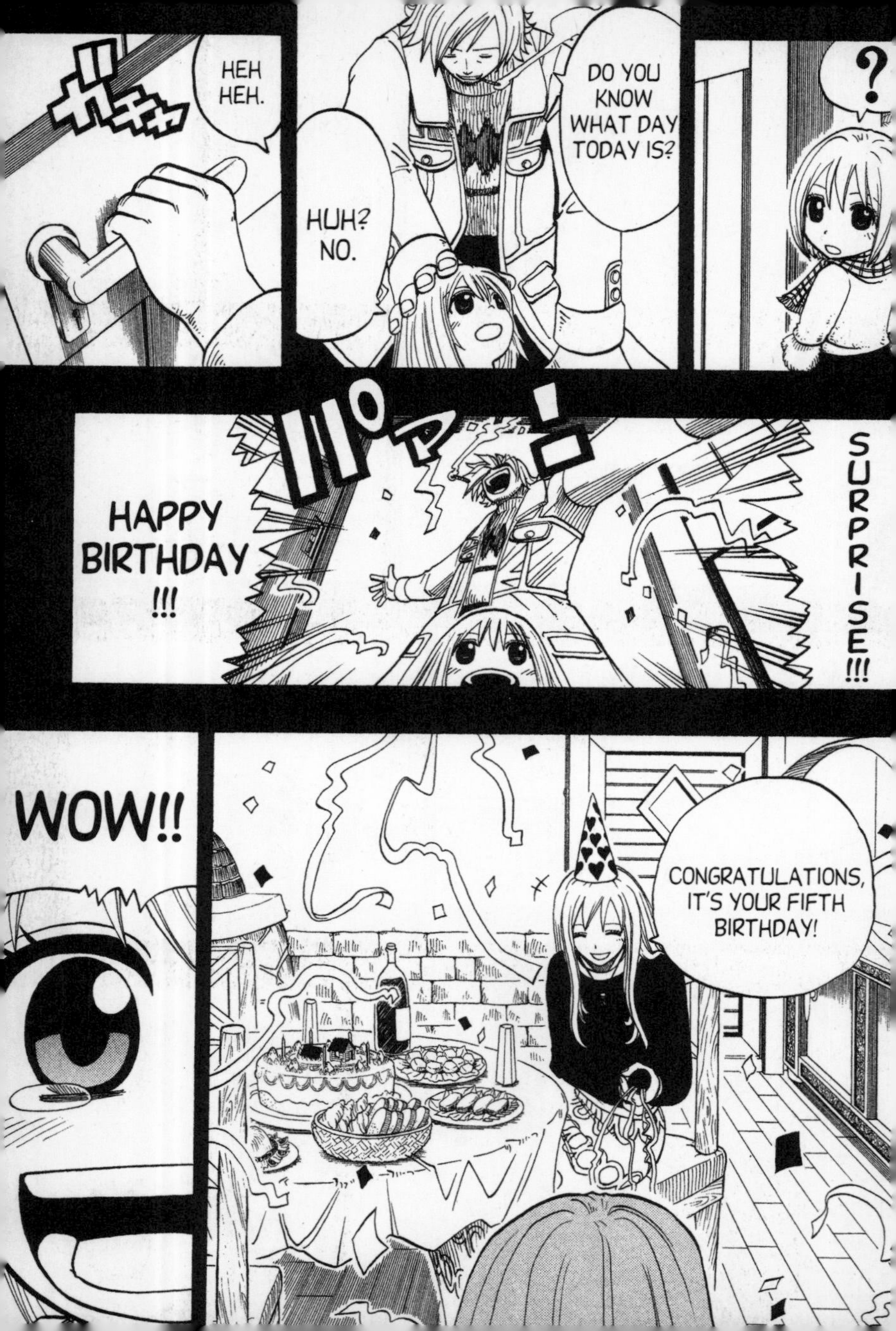
?
DO YOU KNOW WHAT DAY TODAY IS?
HUH? NO.
HEH HEH.
SURPRISE!!!
HAPPY BIRTHDAY!!!
CONGRATULATIONS, IT'S YOUR FIFTH BIRTHDAY!
WOW!!

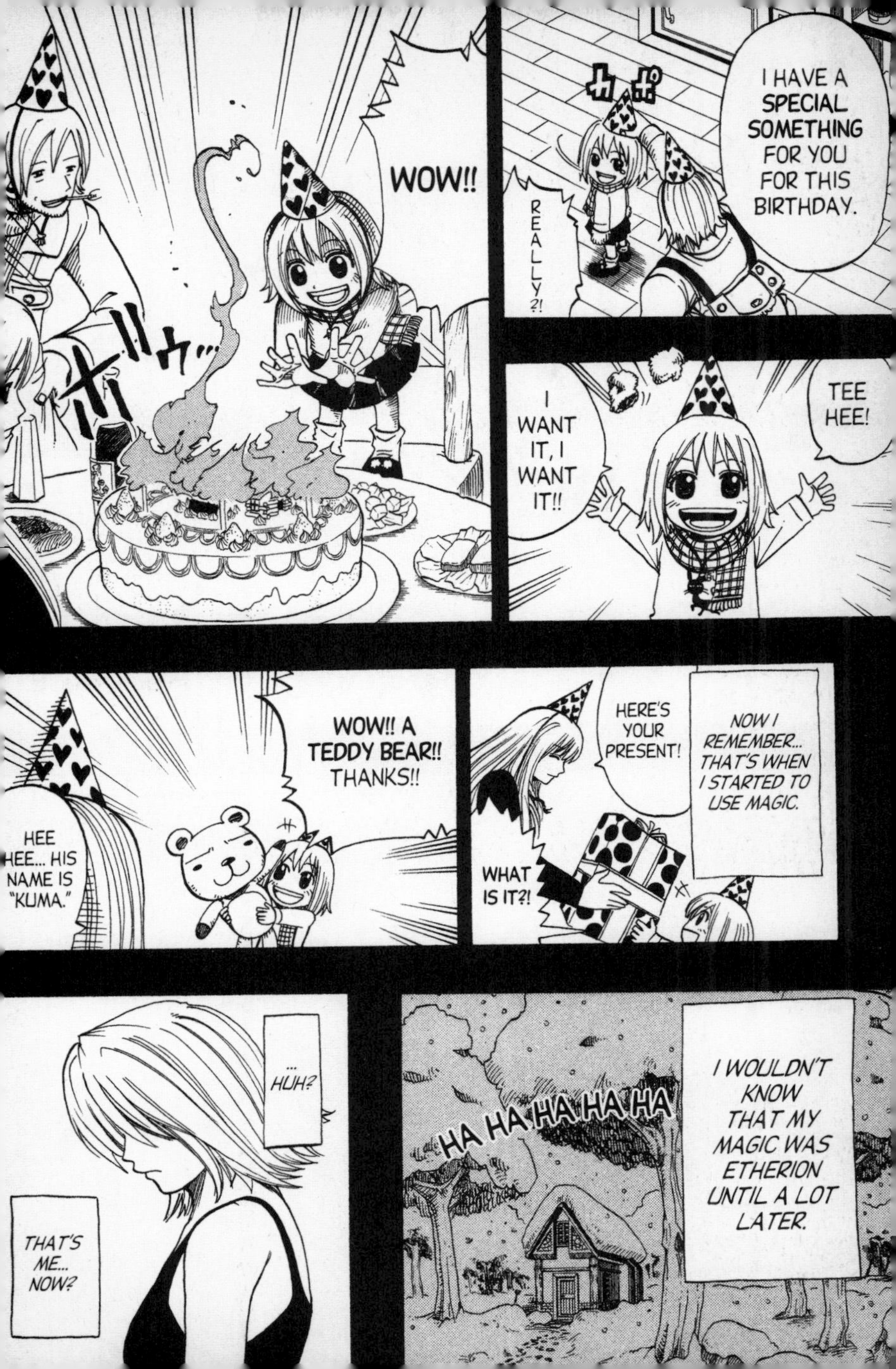
I HAVE A SPECIAL SOMETHING FOR YOU FOR THIS BIRTHDAY.
REALLY?!
TEE HEE!
I WANT IT, I WANT IT!!
WOW!!
NOW I REMEMBER... THAT'S WHEN I STARTED TO USE MAGIC.
HERE'S YOUR PRESENT!
WHAT IS IT?!
WOW!! A TEDDY BEAR!! THANKS!!
HEE HEE... HIS NAME IS "KUMA."
I WOULDN'T KNOW THAT MY MAGIC WAS ETHERION UNTIL A LOT LATER.
HA HA HA HA HA HA
... HUH?
THAT'S ME... NOW?

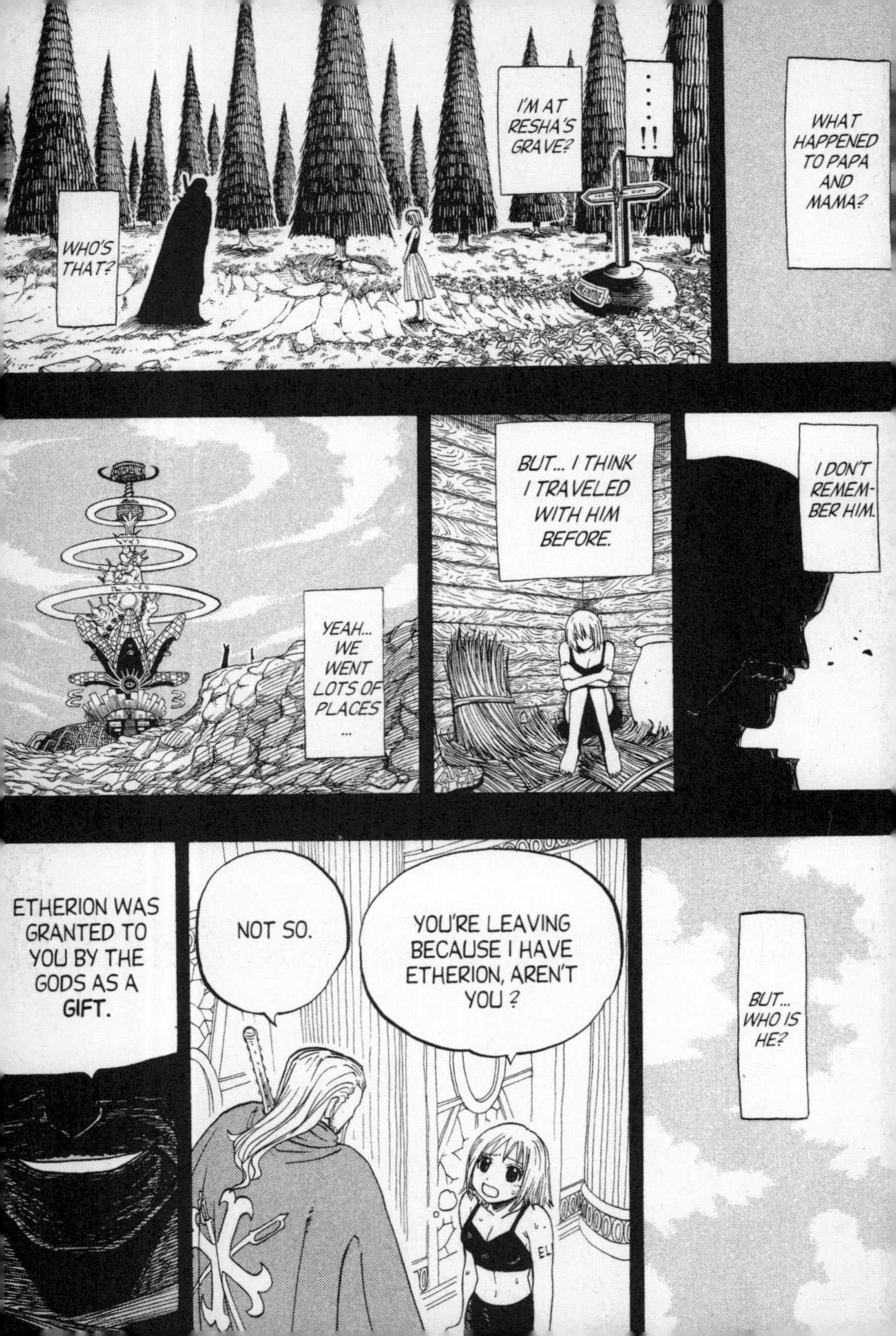
WHAT HAPPENED TO PAPA AND MAMA?
. . . . !!
I'M AT RESHA'S GRAVE?
VALENTINE
WHO'S THAT?
I DON'T REMEMBER HIM.
BUT... I THINK I TRAVELED WITH HIM BEFORE.
YEAH... WE WENT LOTS OF PLACES ...
BUT... WHO IS HE?
YOU'RE LEAVING BECAUSE I HAVE ETHERION, AREN'T YOU?
NOT SO.
ETHERION WAS GRANTED TO YOU BY THE GODS AS A GIFT.

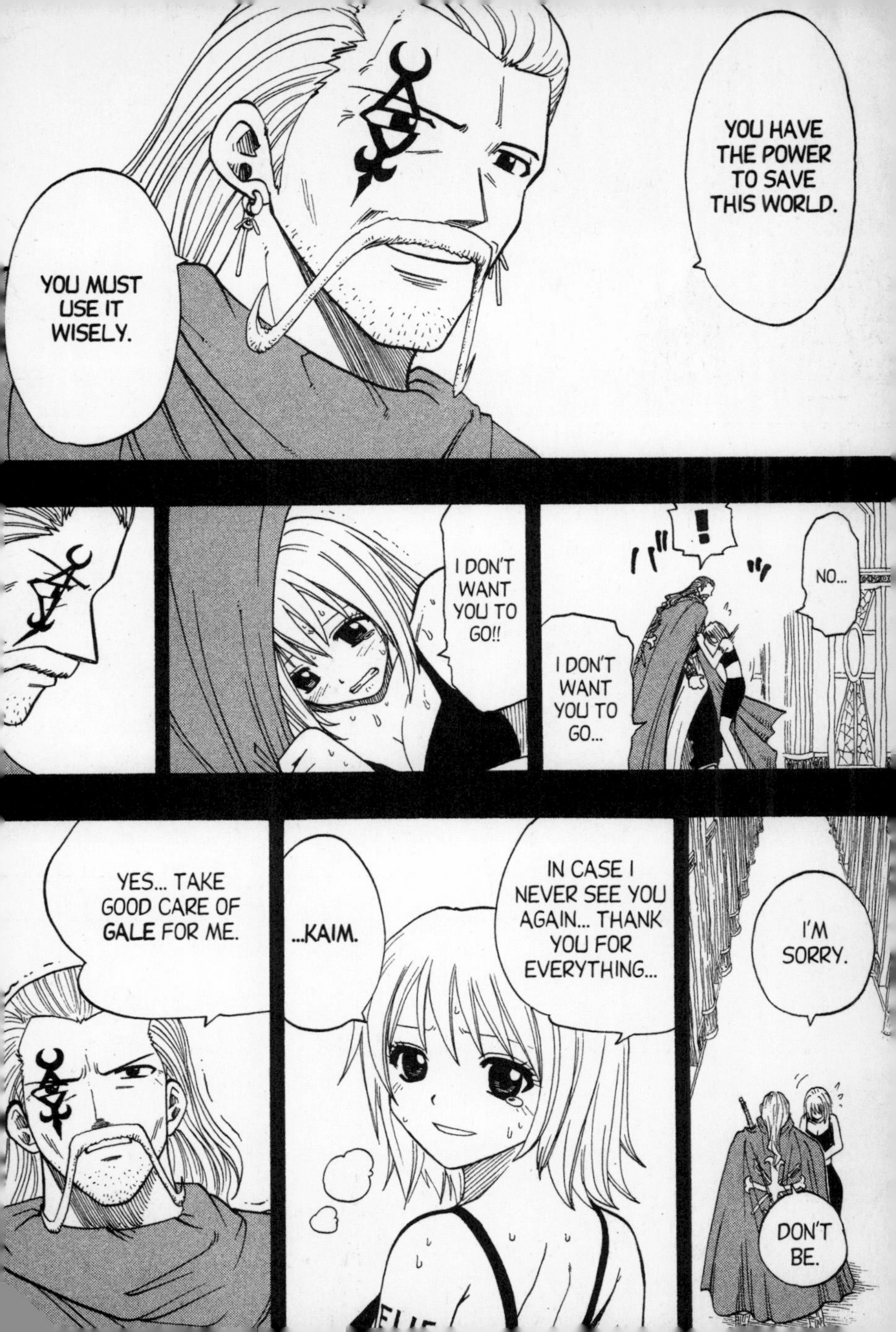
YOU HAVE THE POWER TO SAVE THIS WORLD.
YOU MUST USE IT WISELY.
!
NO...
I DON'T WANT YOU TO GO...
I DON'T WANT YOU TO GO!!
I'M SORRY.
DON'T BE.
IN CASE I NEVER SEE YOU AGAIN... THANK YOU FOR EVERYTHING...
...KAIM.
YES... TAKE GOOD CARE OF GALE FOR ME.

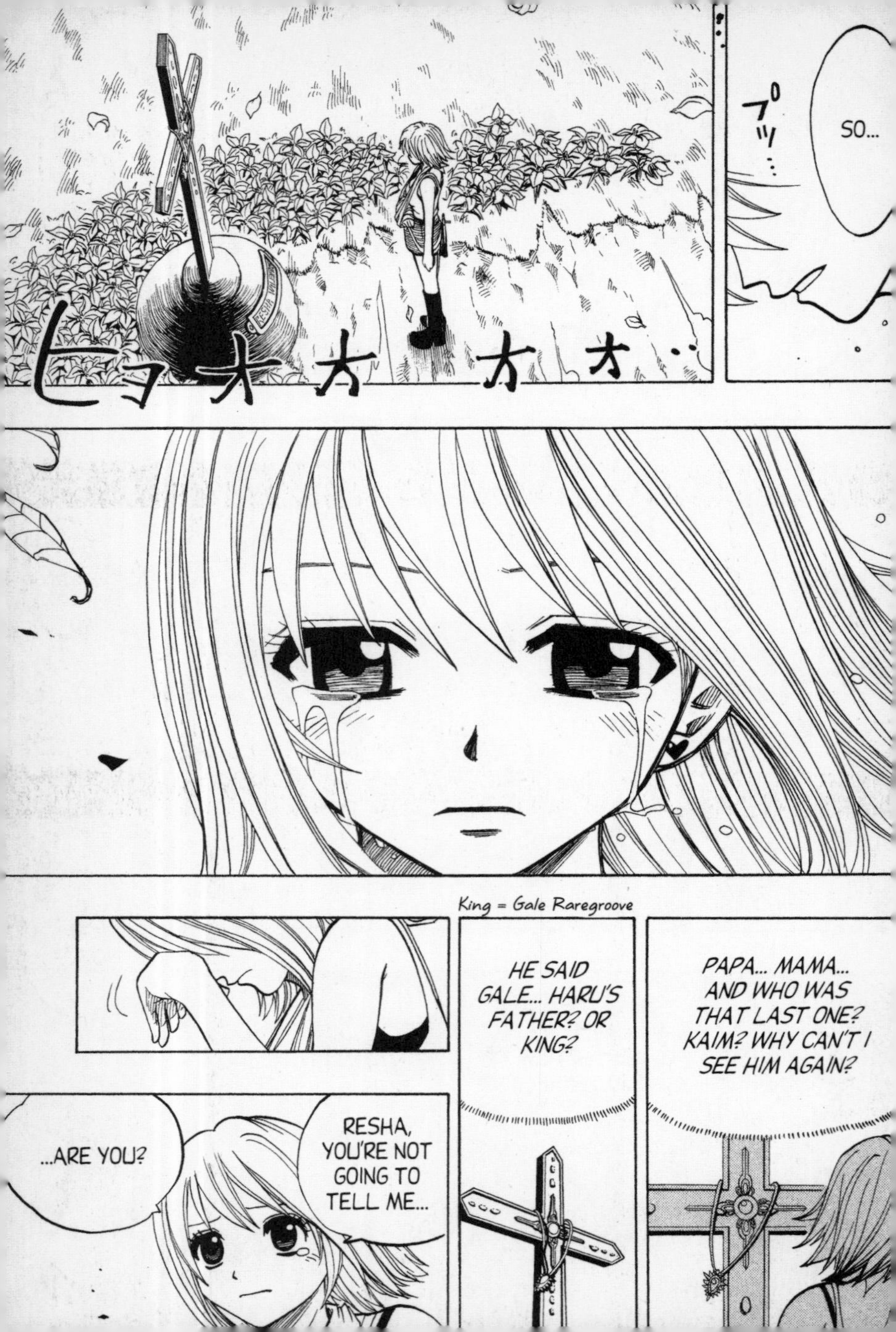

プッ…
SO...
ヒョオオオオ‥
PAPA... MAMA... AND WHO WAS THAT LAST ONE? KAIM? WHY CAN'T I SEE HIM AGAIN?
King = Gale Raregroove
HE SAID GALE... HARU'S FATHER? OR KING?
RESHA, YOU'RE NOT GOING TO TELL ME...
...ARE YOU?

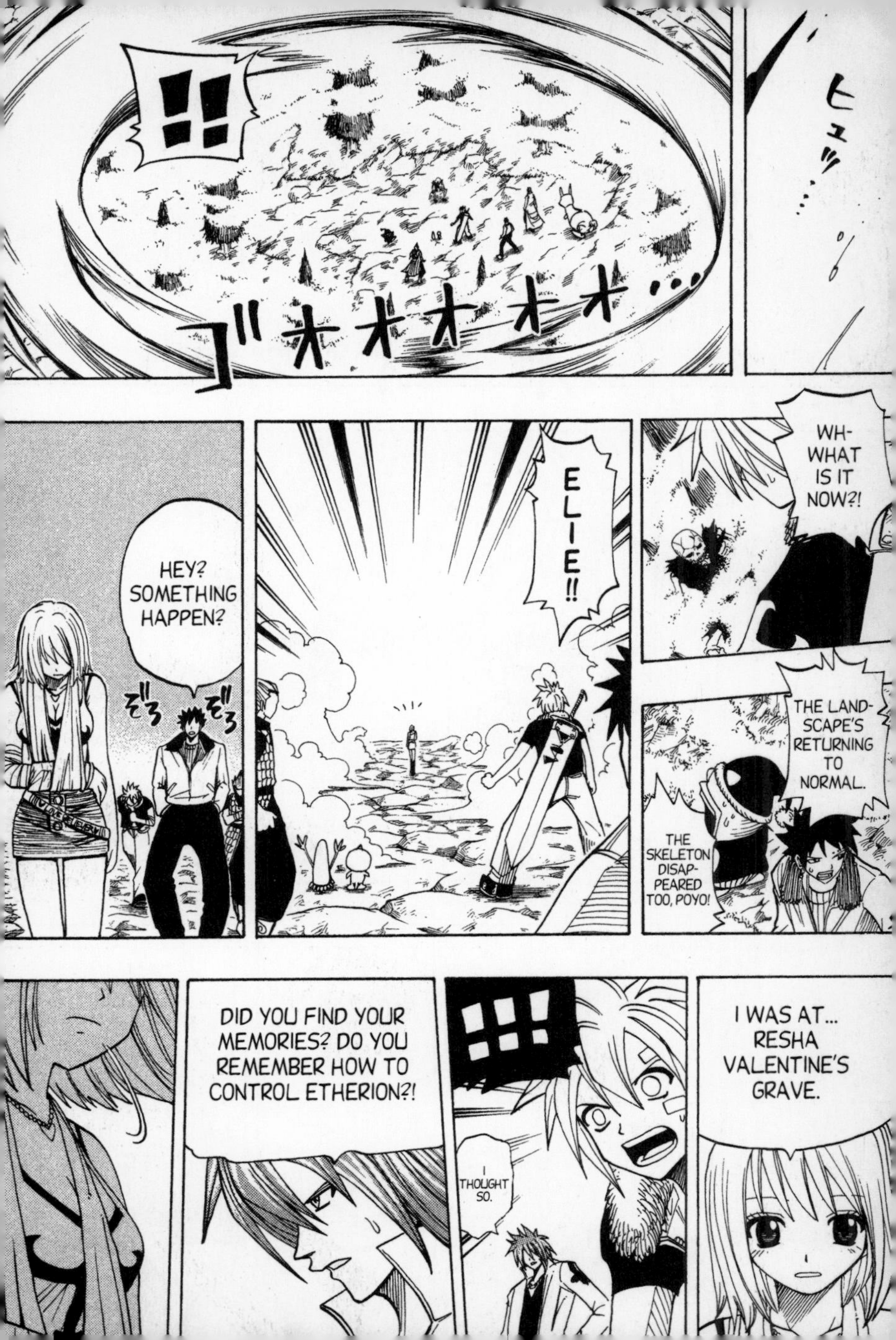
ヒュッ…
!!
ゴォオオオオ…
WH- WHAT IS IT NOW?!
THE LAND-SCAPE'S RETURNING TO NORMAL.
THE SKELETON DISAP-PEARED TOO, POYO!
ELIE!!
HEY? SOMETHING HAPPEN?
ぞろ ぞろ
I WAS AT... RESHA VALENTINE'S GRAVE.
I THOUGHT SO.
DID YOU FIND YOUR MEMORIES? DO YOU REMEMBER HOW TO CONTROL ETHERION?!

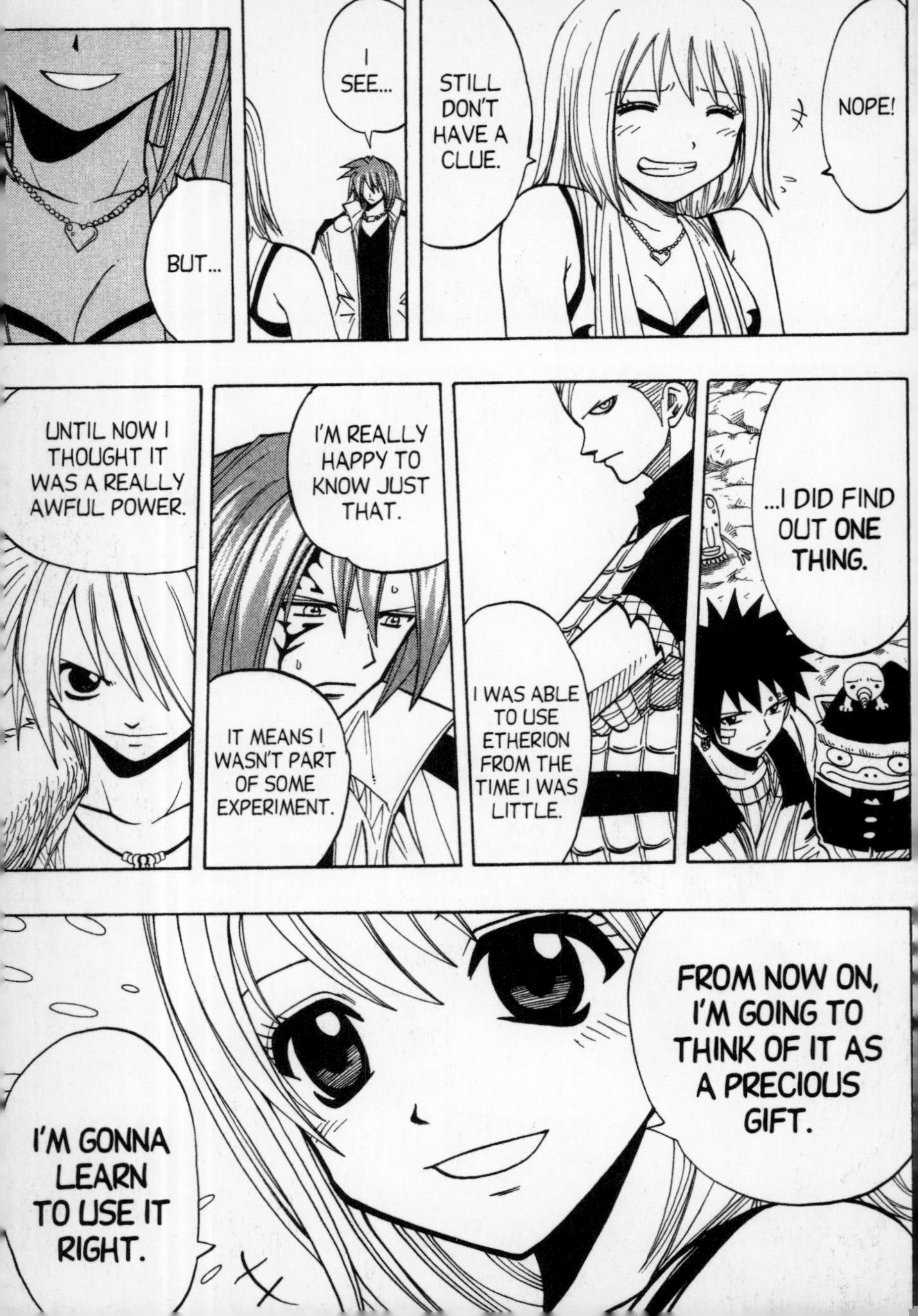
NOPE!
STILL DON'T HAVE A CLUE.
I SEE...
BUT...
...I DID FIND OUT ONE THING.
I WAS ABLE TO USE ETHERION FROM THE TIME I WAS LITTLE.
I'M REALLY HAPPY TO KNOW JUST THAT.
IT MEANS I WASN'T PART OF SOME EXPERIMENT.
UNTIL NOW I THOUGHT IT WAS A REALLY AWFUL POWER.
FROM NOW ON, I'M GOING TO THINK OF IT AS A PRECIOUS GIFT.
I'M GONNA LEARN TO USE IT RIGHT.

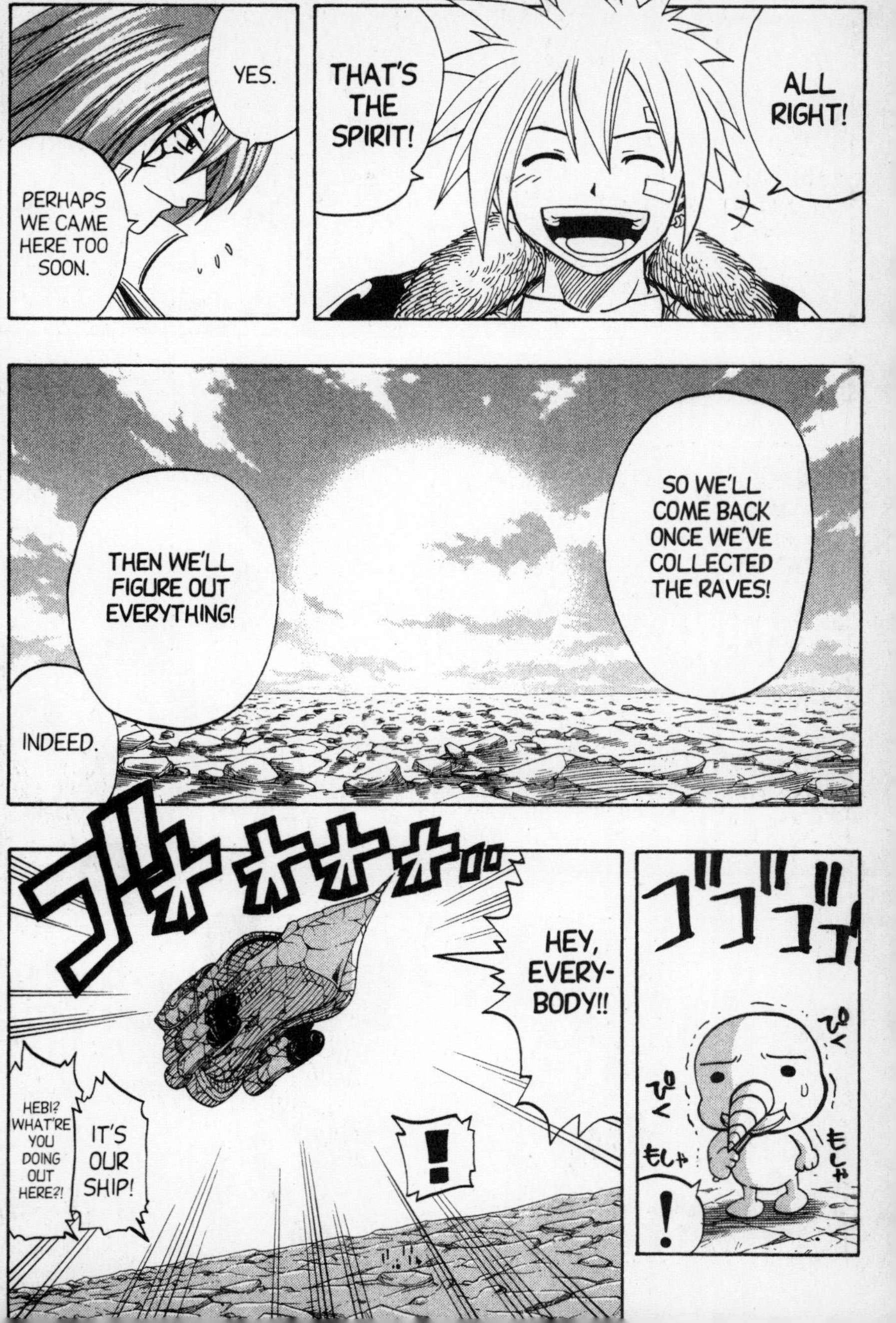
ALL RIGHT!
THAT'S THE SPIRIT!
YES.
PERHAPS WE CAME HERE TOO SOON.
SO WE'LL COME BACK ONCE WE'VE COLLECTED THE RAVES!
THEN WE'LL FIGURE OUT EVERYTHING!
INDEED.
ゴゴゴ
ぴく
ぴく
もしゃ
もしゃ
!
ブォオオオ
HEY, EVERY-BODY!!
!
IT'S OUR SHIP!
HEBI? WHAT'RE YOU DOING OUT HERE?!

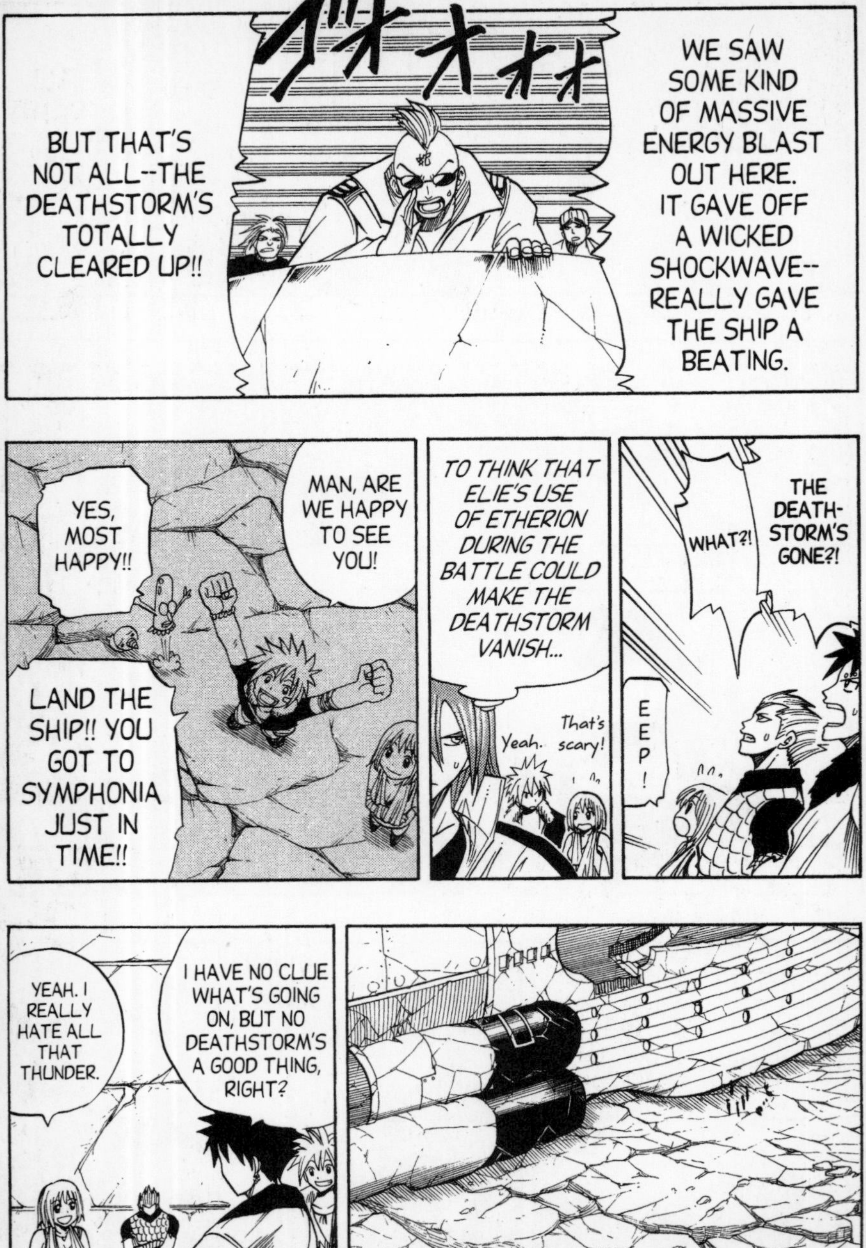
グオオオオ
WE SAW SOME KIND OF MASSIVE ENERGY BLAST OUT HERE. IT GAVE OFF A WICKED SHOCKWAVE--REALLY GAVE THE SHIP A BEATING.
BUT THAT'S NOT ALL--THE DEATHSTORM'S TOTALLY CLEARED UP!!
THE DEATH-STORM'S GONE?!
WHAT?!
EEP!
TO THINK THAT ELIE'S USE OF ETHERION DURING THE BATTLE COULD MAKE THE DEATHSTORM VANISH...
That's scary!
Yeah.
MAN, ARE WE HAPPY TO SEE YOU!
YES, MOST HAPPY!!
LAND THE SHIP!! YOU GOT TO SYMPHONIA JUST IN TIME!!
I HAVE NO CLUE WHAT'S GOING ON, BUT NO DEATHSTORM'S A GOOD THING, RIGHT?
YEAH. I REALLY HATE ALL THAT THUNDER.

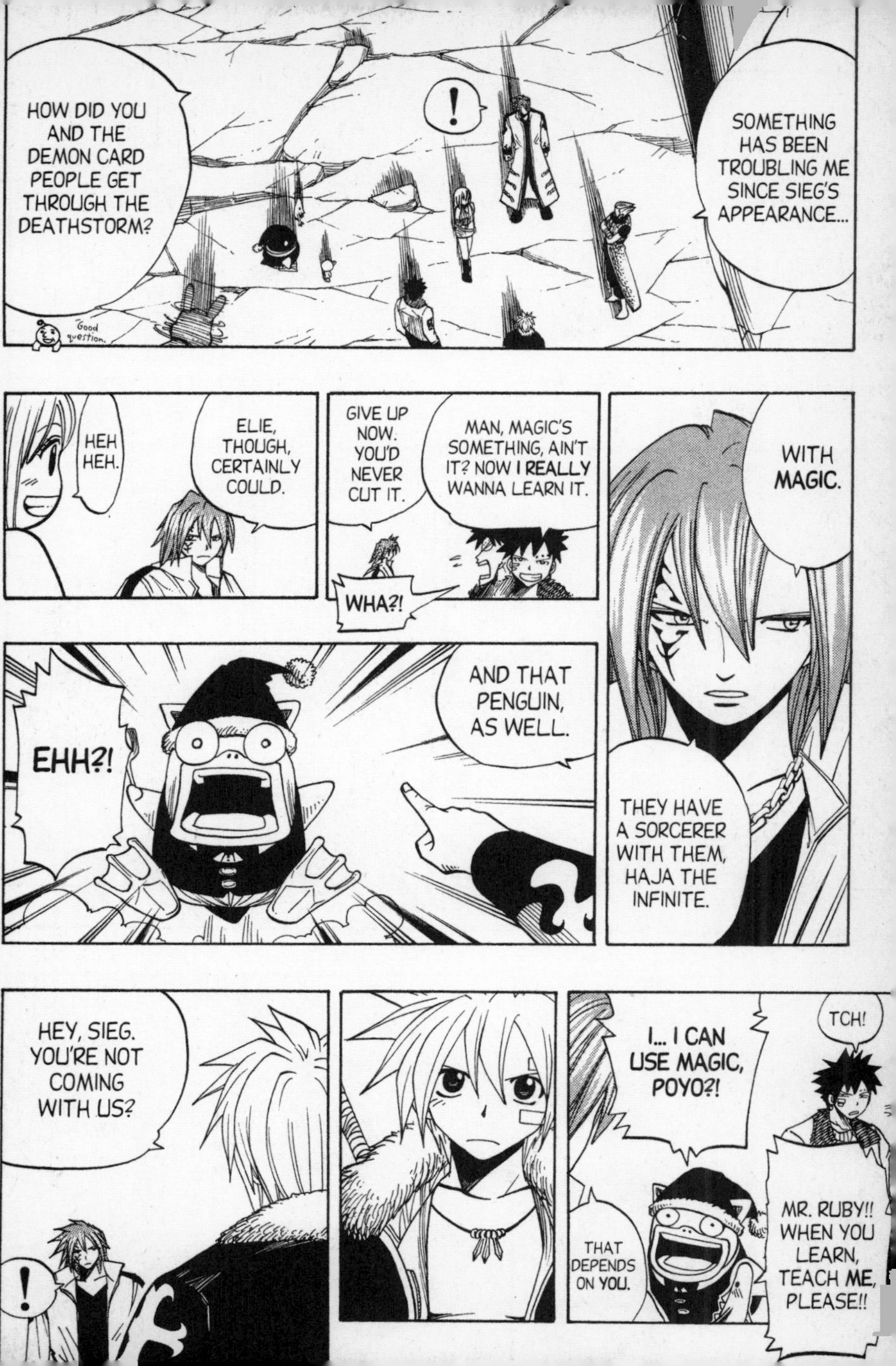
SOMETHING HAS BEEN TROUBLING ME SINCE SIEG'S APPEARANCE...
!
HOW DID YOU AND THE DEMON CARD PEOPLE GET THROUGH THE DEATHSTORM?
"Good question.
WITH MAGIC.
THEY HAVE A SORCERER WITH THEM, HAJA THE INFINITE.
MAN, MAGIC'S SOMETHING, AIN'T IT? NOW I REALLY WANNA LEARN IT.
GIVE UP NOW. YOU'D NEVER CUT IT.
WHA?!
ELIE, THOUGH, CERTAINLY COULD.
HEH HEH.
AND THAT PENGUIN, AS WELL.
EHH?!
TCH!
I... I CAN USE MAGIC, POYO?!
MR. RUBY!! WHEN YOU LEARN, TEACH ME, PLEASE!!
THAT DEPENDS ON YOU.
HEY, SIEG. YOU'RE NOT COMING WITH US?
!

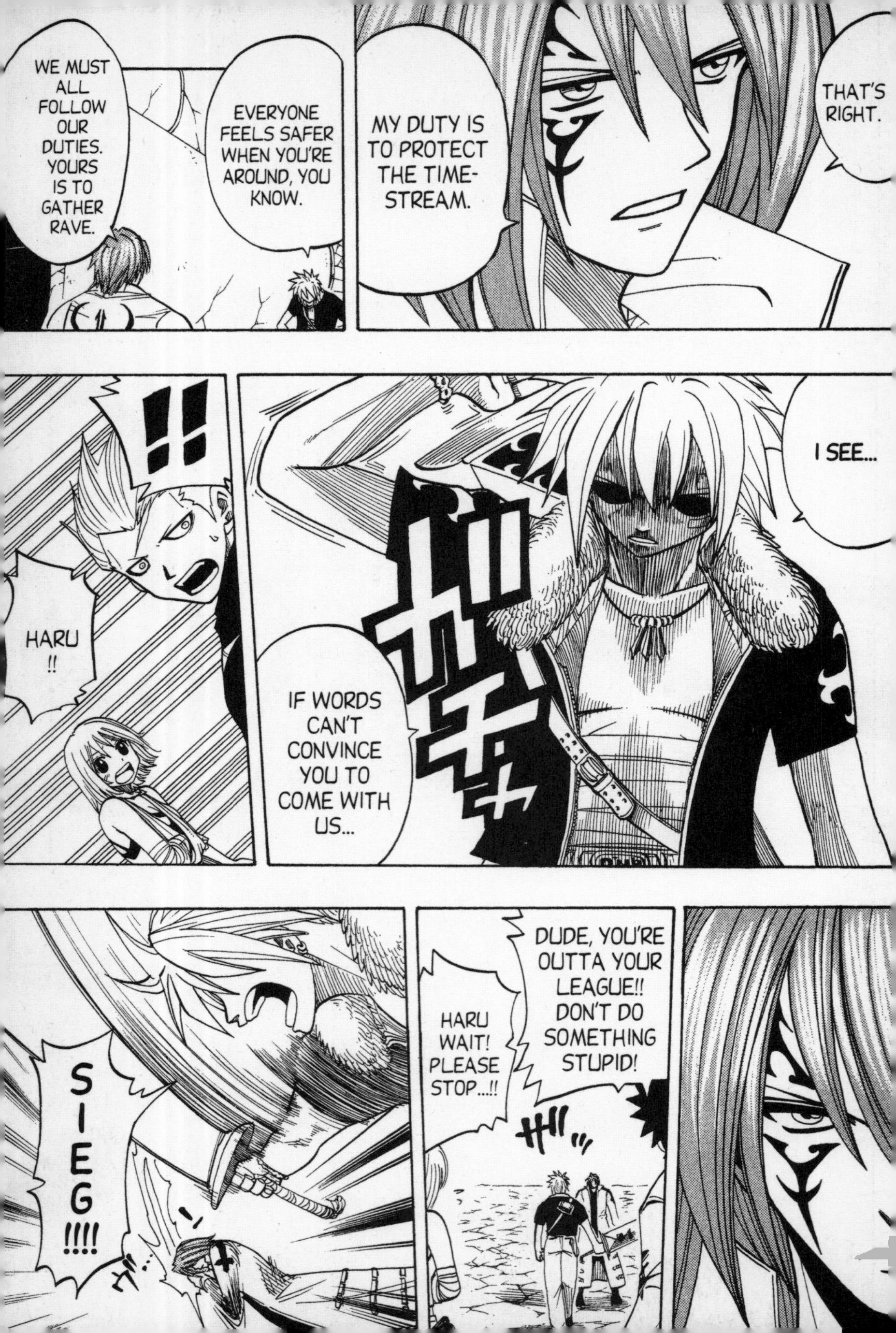
THAT'S RIGHT.
MY DUTY IS TO PROTECT THE TIME-STREAM.
EVERYONE FEELS SAFER WHEN YOU'RE AROUND, YOU KNOW.
WE MUST ALL FOLLOW OUR DUTIES. YOURS IS TO GATHER RAVE.
I SEE...
IF WORDS CAN'T CONVINCE YOU TO COME WITH US...
!!
HARU !!
DUDE, YOU'RE OUTTA YOUR LEAGUE!! DON'T DO SOMETHING STUPID!
HARU WAIT! PLEASE STOP...!!
SIEG!!!!

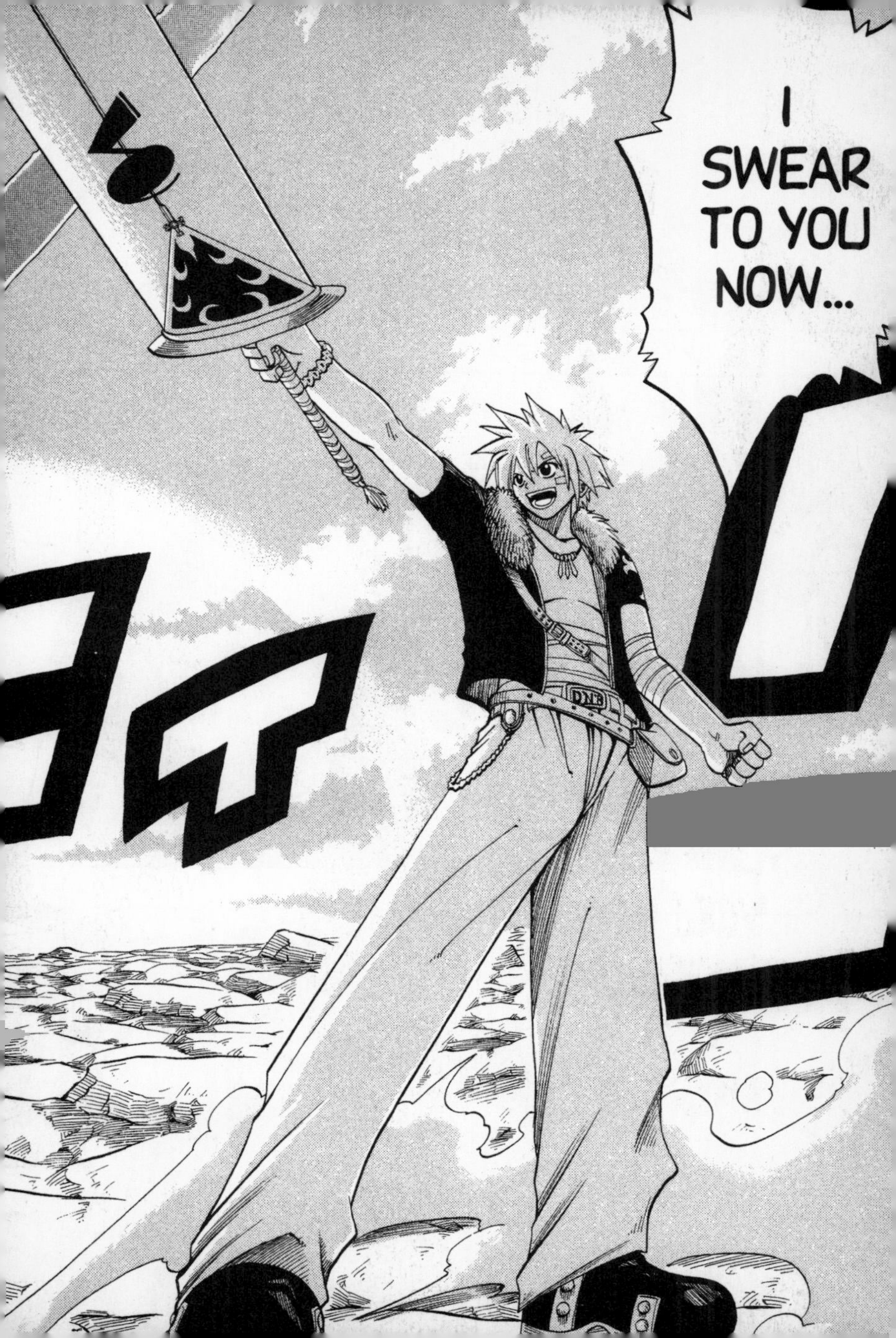
I SWEAR TO YOU NOW...

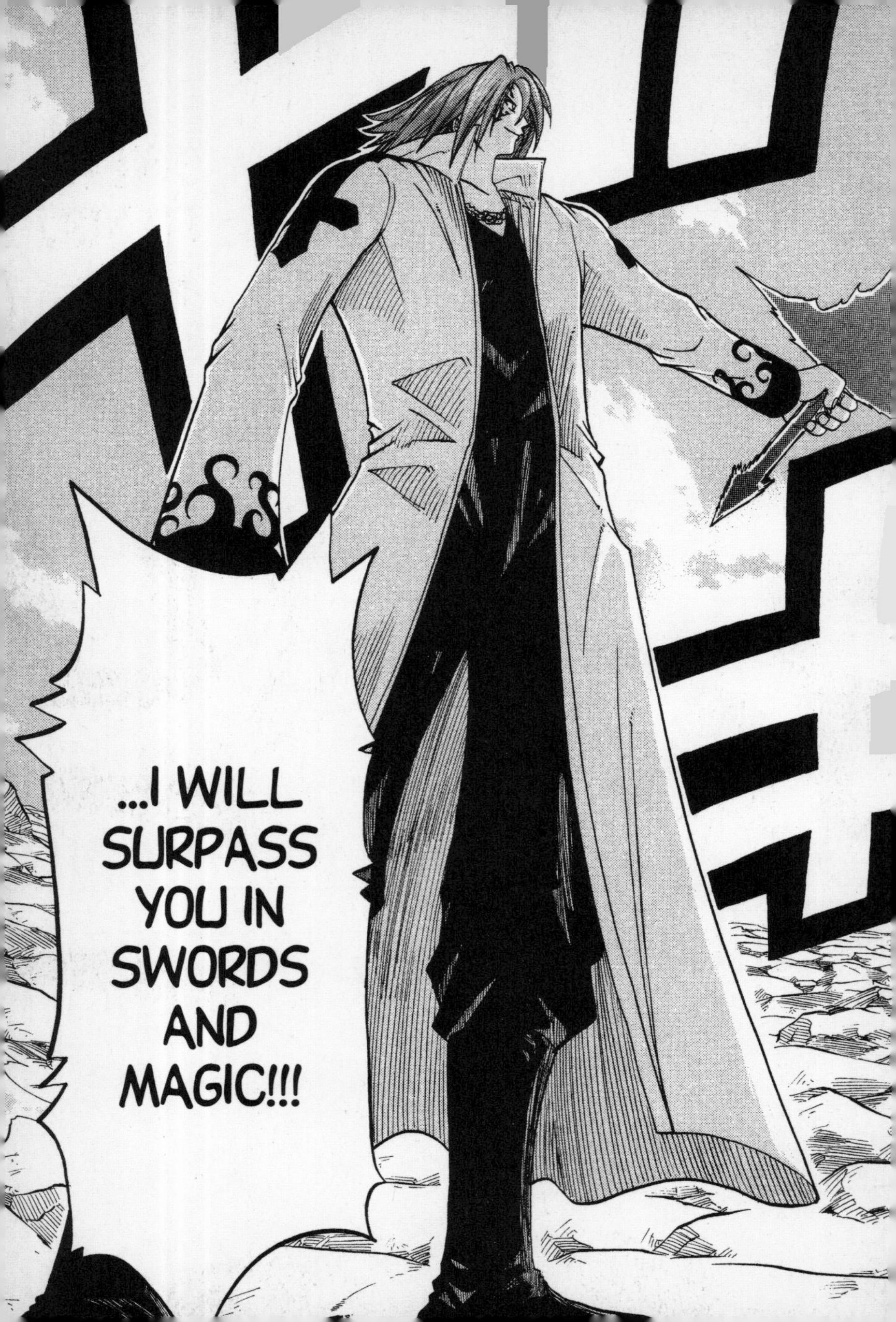
...I WILL SURPASS YOU IN SWORDS AND MAGIC!!!

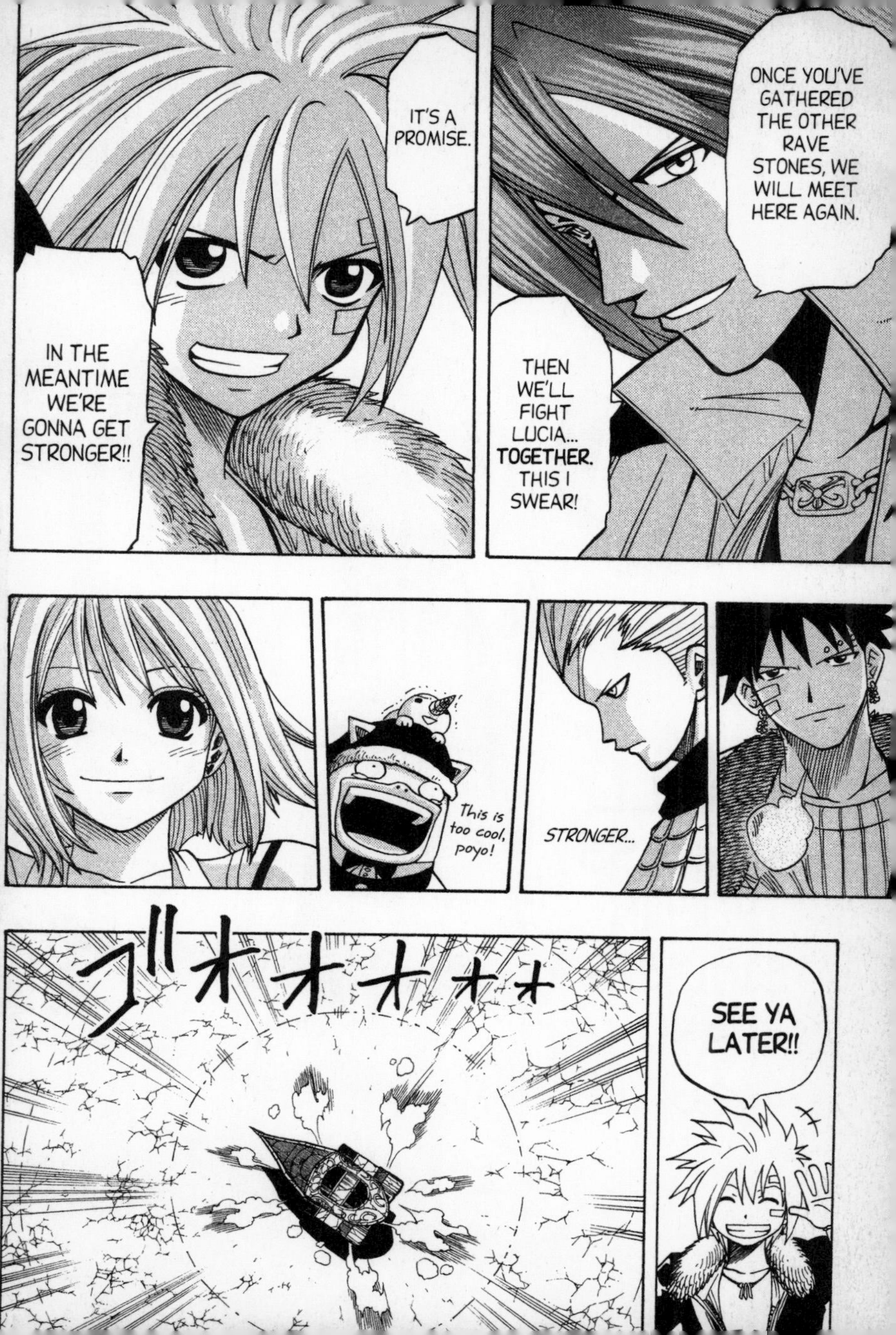
ONCE YOU'VE GATHERED THE OTHER RAVE STONES, WE WILL MEET HERE AGAIN.
THEN WE'LL FIGHT LUCIA... TOGETHER. THIS I SWEAR!
IT'S A PROMISE.
IN THE MEANTIME WE'RE GONNA GET STRONGER!!
STRONGER...
This is too cool, poyo!
SEE YA LATER!!
ゴオオオオオ

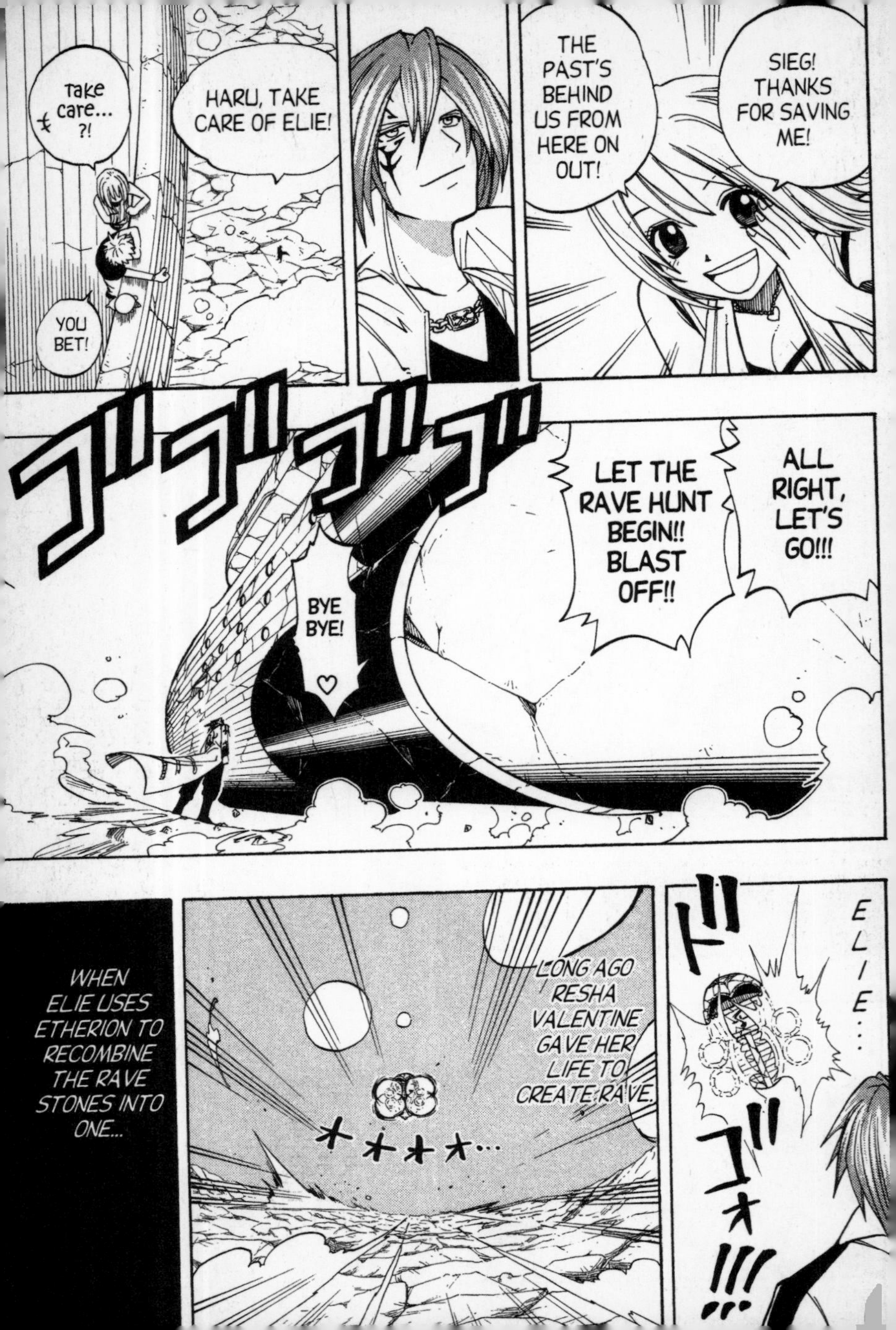
SIEG! THANKS FOR SAVING ME!
THE PAST'S BEHIND US FROM HERE ON OUT!
HARU, TAKE CARE OF ELIE!
Take care... ?!
YOU BET!
ブブブブ
ALL RIGHT, LET'S GO!!!
LET THE RAVE HUNT BEGIN!! BLAST OFF!!
BYE BYE! ♡
ド
ELIE...
ゴォ!!!
LONG AGO RESHA VALENTINE GAVE HER LIFE TO CREATE RAVE.
ォォォォ...
WHEN ELIE USES ETHERION TO RECOMBINE THE RAVE STONES INTO ONE...

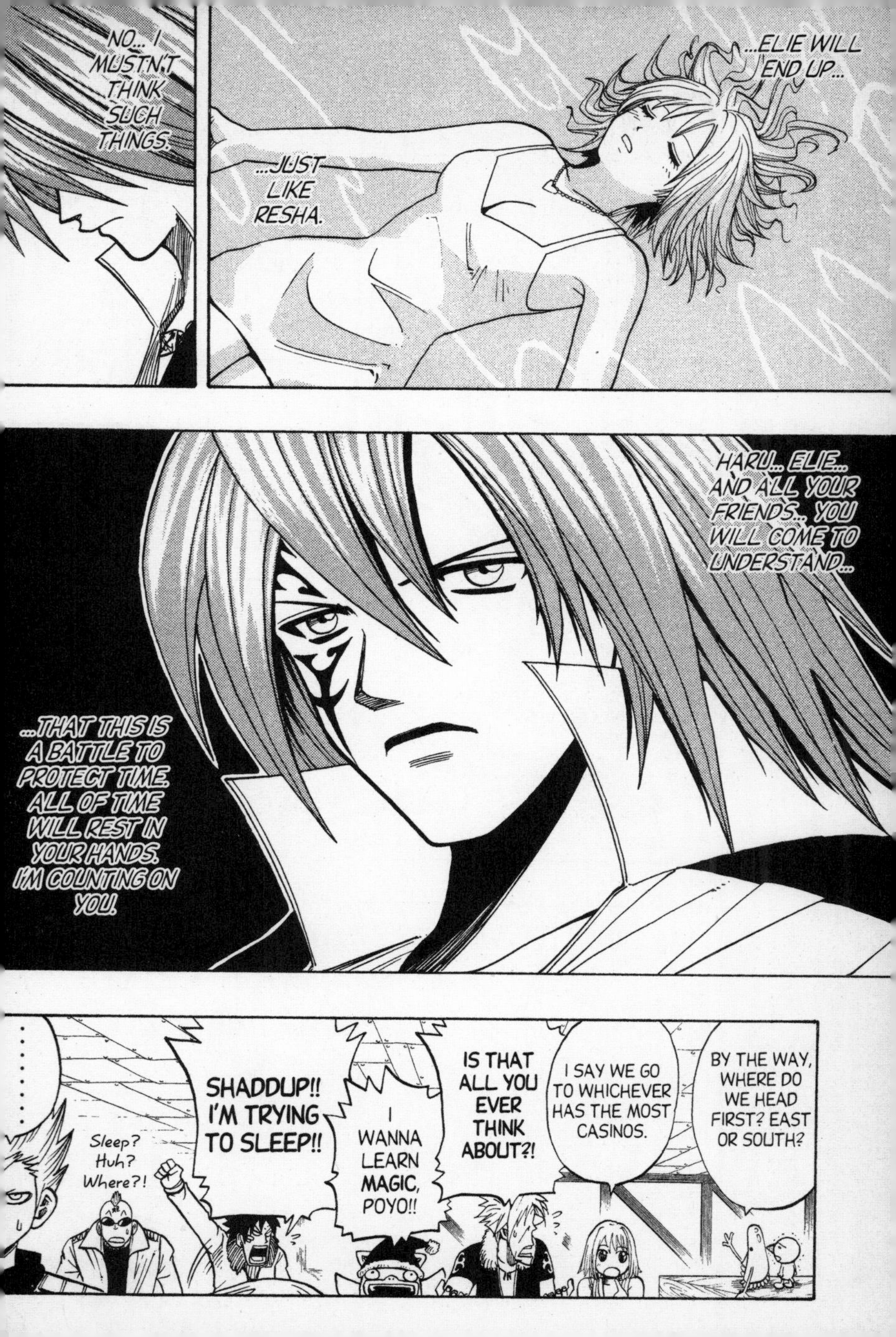
...ELIE WILL END UP...
...JUST LIKE RESHA.
NO... I MUSTN'T THINK SUCH THINGS.
HARU... ELIE... AND ALL YOUR FRIENDS... YOU WILL COME TO UNDERSTAND...
...THAT THIS IS A BATTLE TO PROTECT TIME. ALL OF TIME WILL REST IN YOUR HANDS. I'M COUNTING ON YOU.
BY THE WAY, WHERE DO WE HEAD FIRST? EAST OR SOUTH?
I SAY WE GO TO WHICHEVER HAS THE MOST CASINOS.
IS THAT ALL YOU EVER THINK ABOUT?!
I WANNA LEARN MAGIC, POYO!!
SHADDUP!! I'M TRYING TO SLEEP!!
Sleep? Huh? Where?!
....

Q&A CORNER!!

Q. TELL US HOW YOU CAME UP WITH NAMES FOR THE ORACION SIX.

A. SURE... HERE WE GO!

SHUDA: THIS ONE'S BASED ON TWO NAMES I PICKED UP FROM A FIGHTING GAME, "JUDO" AND "JEDA". I PLAYED AROUND WITH THEM AND THOUGHT THE RESULT WAS PRETTY COOL.

REINA: MEANS "QUEEN" IN SPANISH. SHE WAS ALWAYS AROUND KING, LIKE A QUEEN, HENCE REINA. IN SPANISH, KING'S REAL NAME IS "REY," AND JEGAN'S JACK IS "RITTA".

JEGAN: A "J" NAME BASED ON THE "JACK" I MENTIONED ABOVE. AT FIRST, I WANTED EVERYONE'S NAMES TO FIT WITH THE IDEA OF "DEMON CARD," BUT I COULDN'T THINK OF ENOUGH NAMES TO STICK WITH IT.

BERIAL: THIS IS AN ACTUAL DEMON'S NAME. I WAS READING A BOOK ABOUT DEMONS AND THIS NAME STUCK IN MY MIND. I THOUGHT IT FIT.

IULIUS: I DON'T REMEMBER EXACTLY BUT, I THINK IT MEANS AUGUST IN SOME LANGUAGE OR OTHER. THERE'S NO SPECIAL RELATIONSHIP TO THE CHARACTER. IT SOUNDED GOOD, SO I USED IT. (ACTUALLY, MASHIMA-SENSEI, THAT'S "JULY," AND IT'S LATIN. -ED.)

LUCIA: AGAIN, THIS IS JUST A NAME THAT SOUNDED GOOD. WHAT IT MEANS... WELL, THAT'S IN THE DETAILED CHARACTER INFO ON P. 190.

BY THE WAY, THE WORD ORACION IS THE SPANISH WORD FOR "PRAYER," SO THEIR NAME TRANSLATES TO "THE SIX PRAYERS."

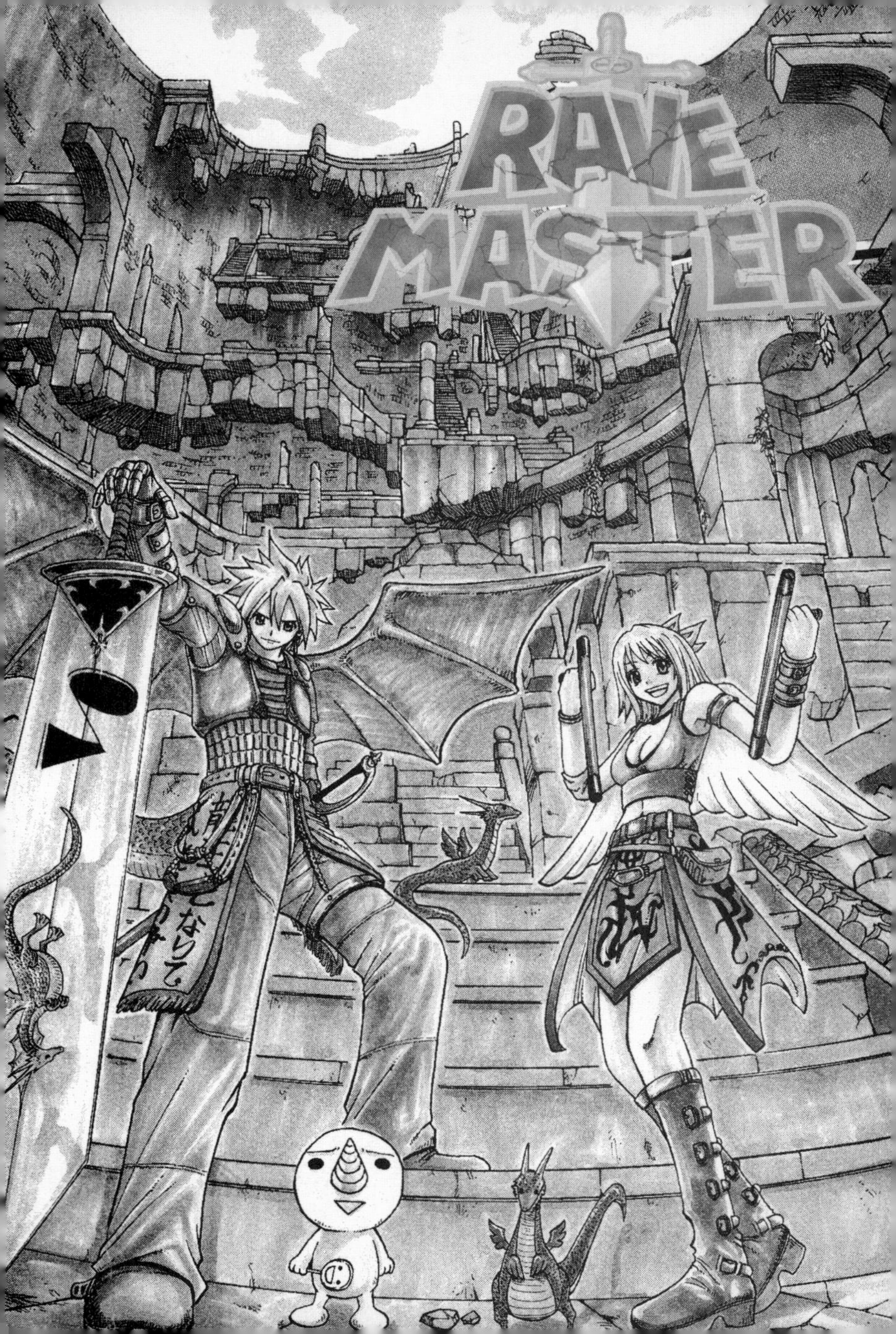
RAVE
MASTER

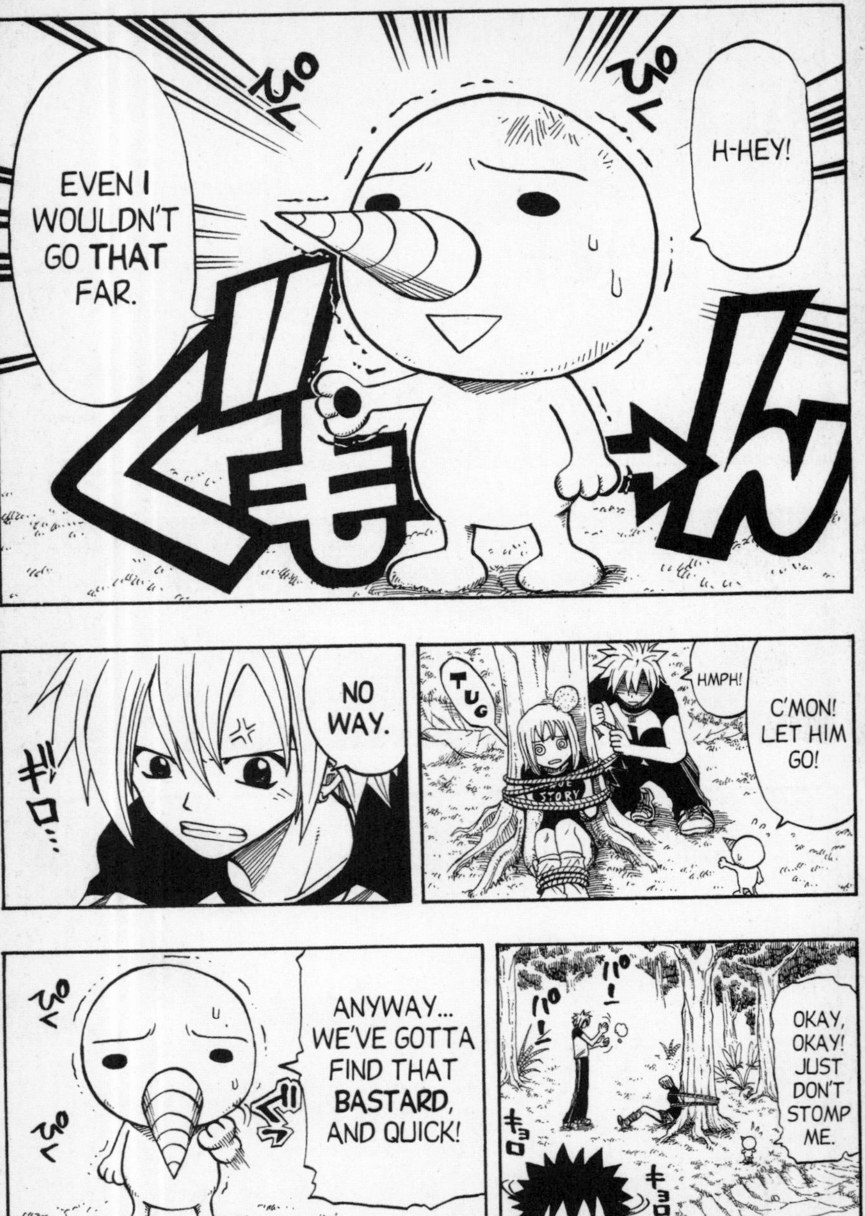
H-HEY!
EVEN I WOULDN'T GO THAT FAR.
C'MON! LET HIM GO!
HMPH!
TUG
NO WAY.
OKAY, OKAY! JUST DON'T STOMP ME.
ANYWAY... WE'VE GOTTA FIND THAT BASTARD, AND QUICK!

RAVE:96 ✚ THE SEARCH FOR ALICE!

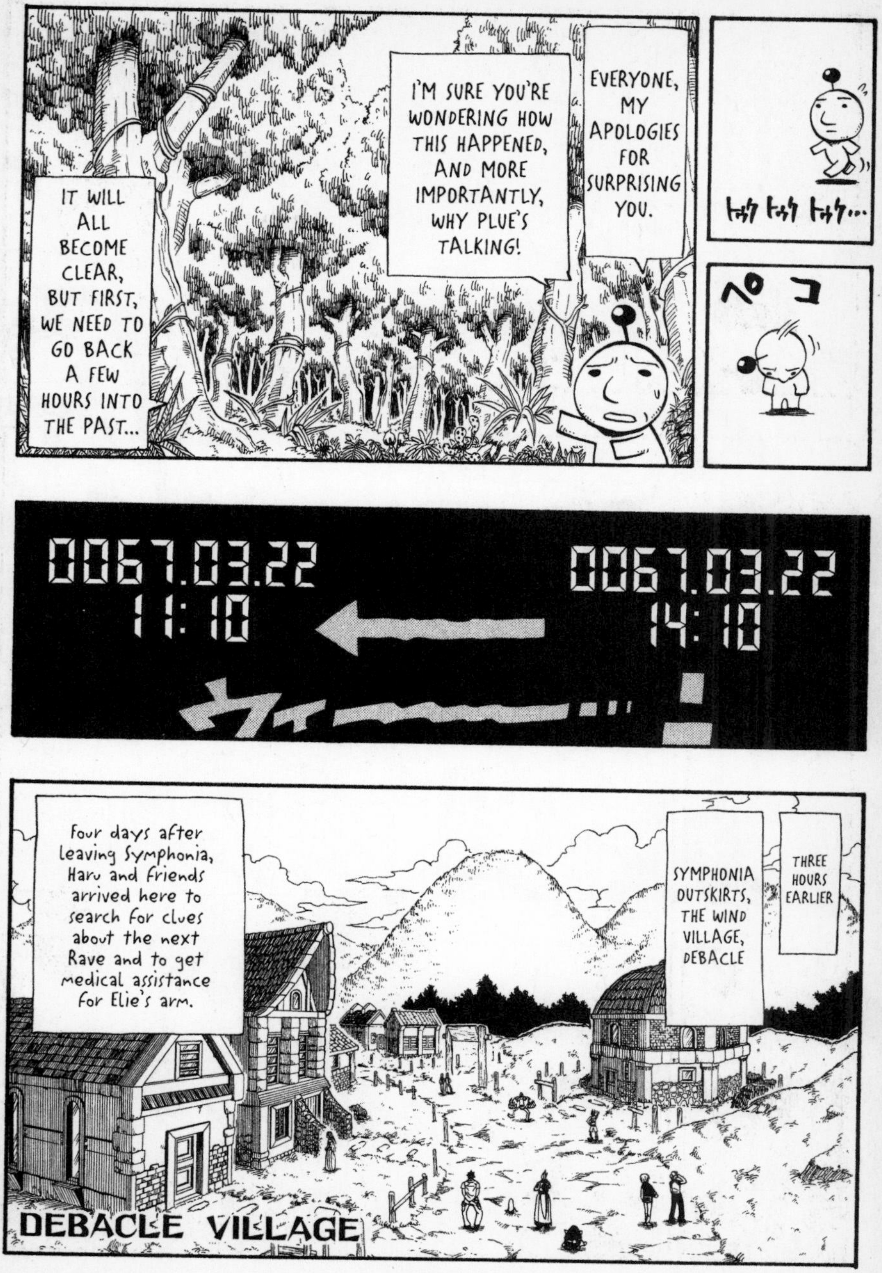
トゥク トゥク トゥク…
ペコ
EVERYONE, MY APOLOGIES FOR SURPRISING YOU.
I'M SURE YOU'RE WONDERING HOW THIS HAPPENED, AND MORE IMPORTANTLY, WHY PLUE'S TALKING!
IT WILL ALL BECOME CLEAR, BUT FIRST, WE NEED TO GO BACK A FEW HOURS INTO THE PAST...
0067.03.22 14:10
0067.03.22 11:10
ウィーーー…!
THREE HOURS EARLIER
SYMPHONIA OUTSKIRTS, THE WIND VILLAGE, DEBACLE
Four days after leaving Symphonia, Haru and friends arrived here to search for clues about the next Rave and to get medical assistance for Elie's arm.
DEBACLE VILLAGE

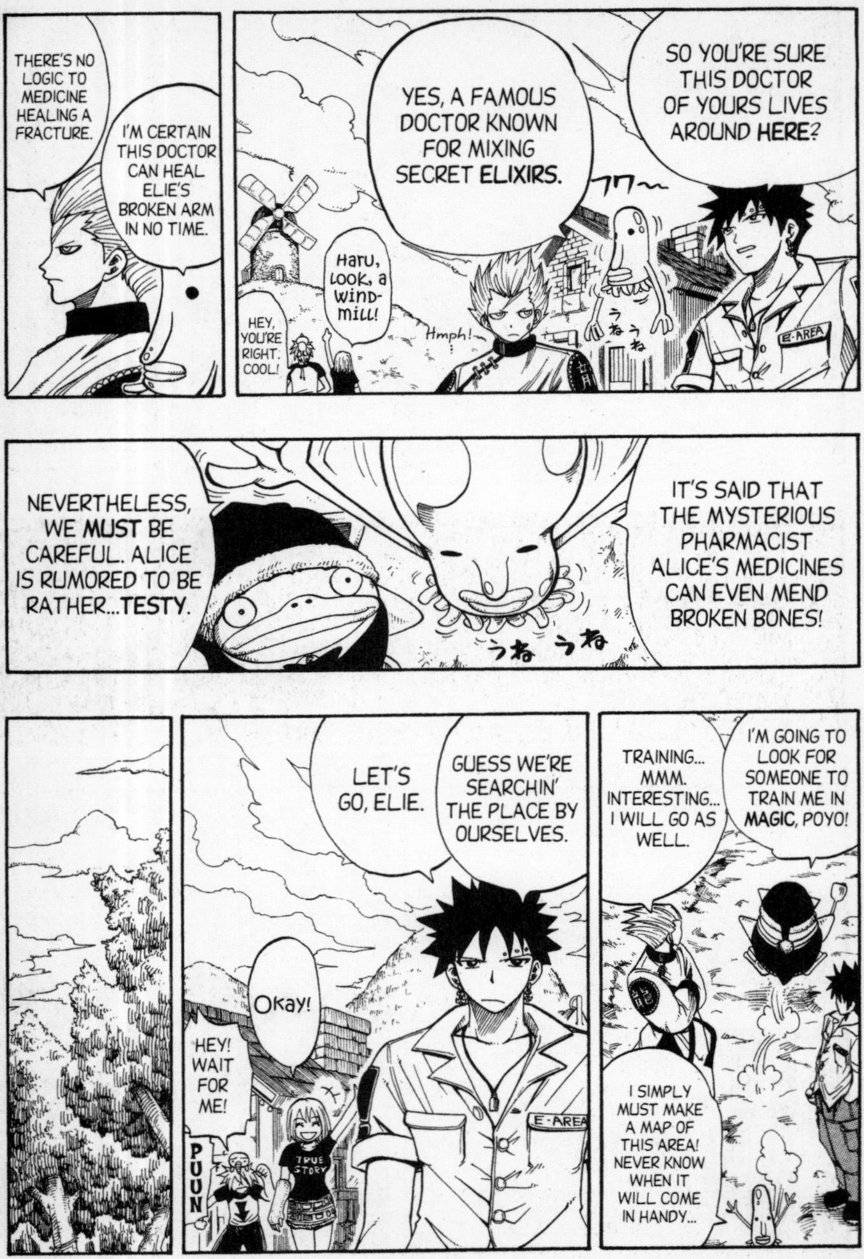
SO YOU'RE SURE THIS DOCTOR OF YOURS LIVES AROUND **HERE**?
YES, A FAMOUS DOCTOR KNOWN FOR MIXING SECRET **ELIXIRS**.
フワ〜
E-AREA
うねうね
Hmph!
Haru, look, a wind-mill!
HEY, YOU'RE RIGHT. COOL!
THERE'S NO LOGIC TO MEDICINE HEALING A FRACTURE.
I'M CERTAIN THIS DOCTOR CAN HEAL ELIE'S BROKEN ARM IN NO TIME.
IT'S SAID THAT THE MYSTERIOUS PHARMACIST ALICE'S MEDICINES CAN EVEN MEND BROKEN BONES!
うね うね
NEVERTHELESS, WE **MUST** BE CAREFUL. ALICE IS RUMORED TO BE RATHER...**TESTY**.
I'M GOING TO LOOK FOR SOMEONE TO TRAIN ME IN **MAGIC**, POYO!
TRAINING... MMM. INTERESTING... I WILL GO AS WELL.
I SIMPLY MUST MAKE A MAP OF THIS AREA! NEVER KNOW WHEN IT WILL COME IN HANDY...
GUESS WE'RE SEARCHIN' THE PLACE BY OURSELVES.
LET'S GO, ELIE.
E-AREA
Okay!
TRUE STORY
HEY! WAIT FOR ME!
PUUN

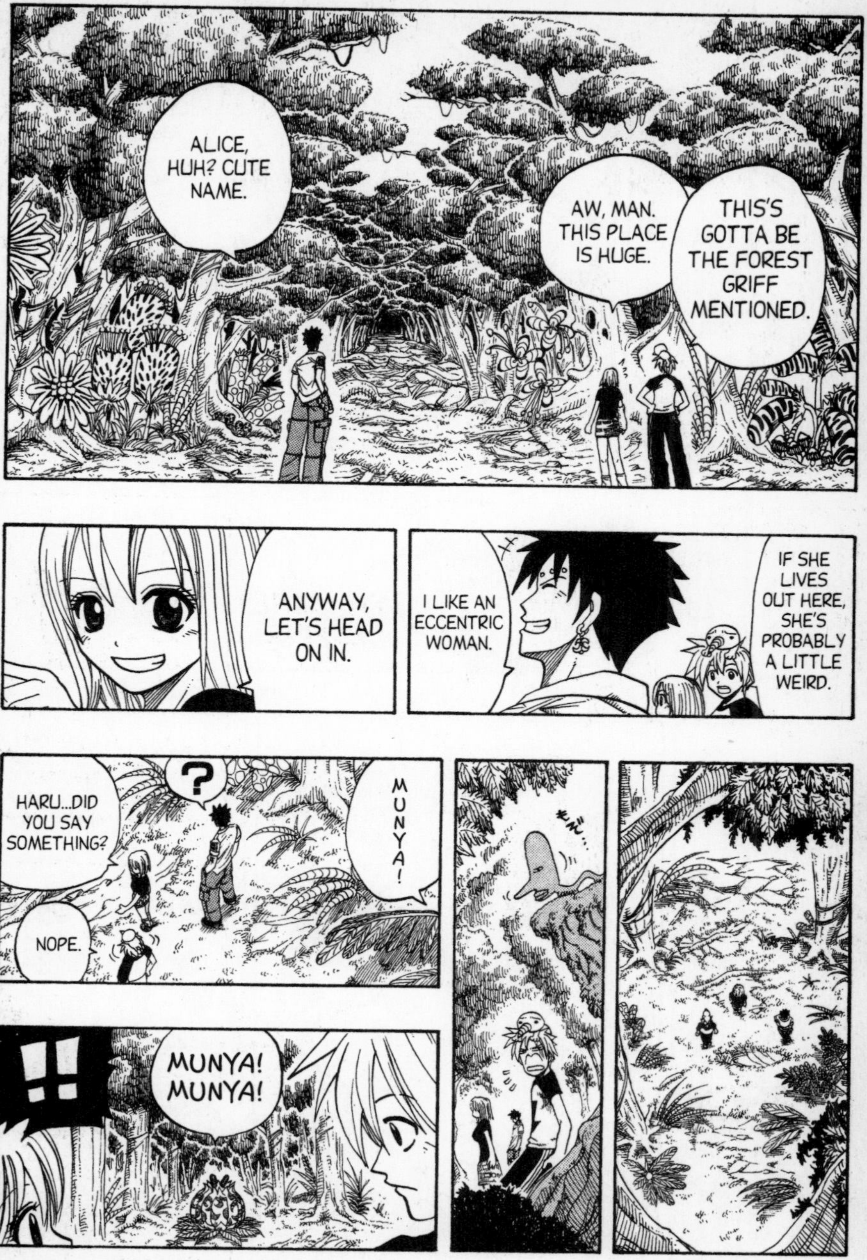
THIS'S GOTTA BE THE FOREST GRIFF MENTIONED.
AW, MAN. THIS PLACE IS HUGE.
ALICE, HUH? CUTE NAME.
IF SHE LIVES OUT HERE, SHE'S PROBABLY A LITTLE WEIRD.
I LIKE AN ECCENTRIC WOMAN.
ANYWAY, LET'S HEAD ON IN.
MUNYA!
?
HARU...DID YOU SAY SOMETHING?
NOPE.
MUNYA! MUNYA!
!!

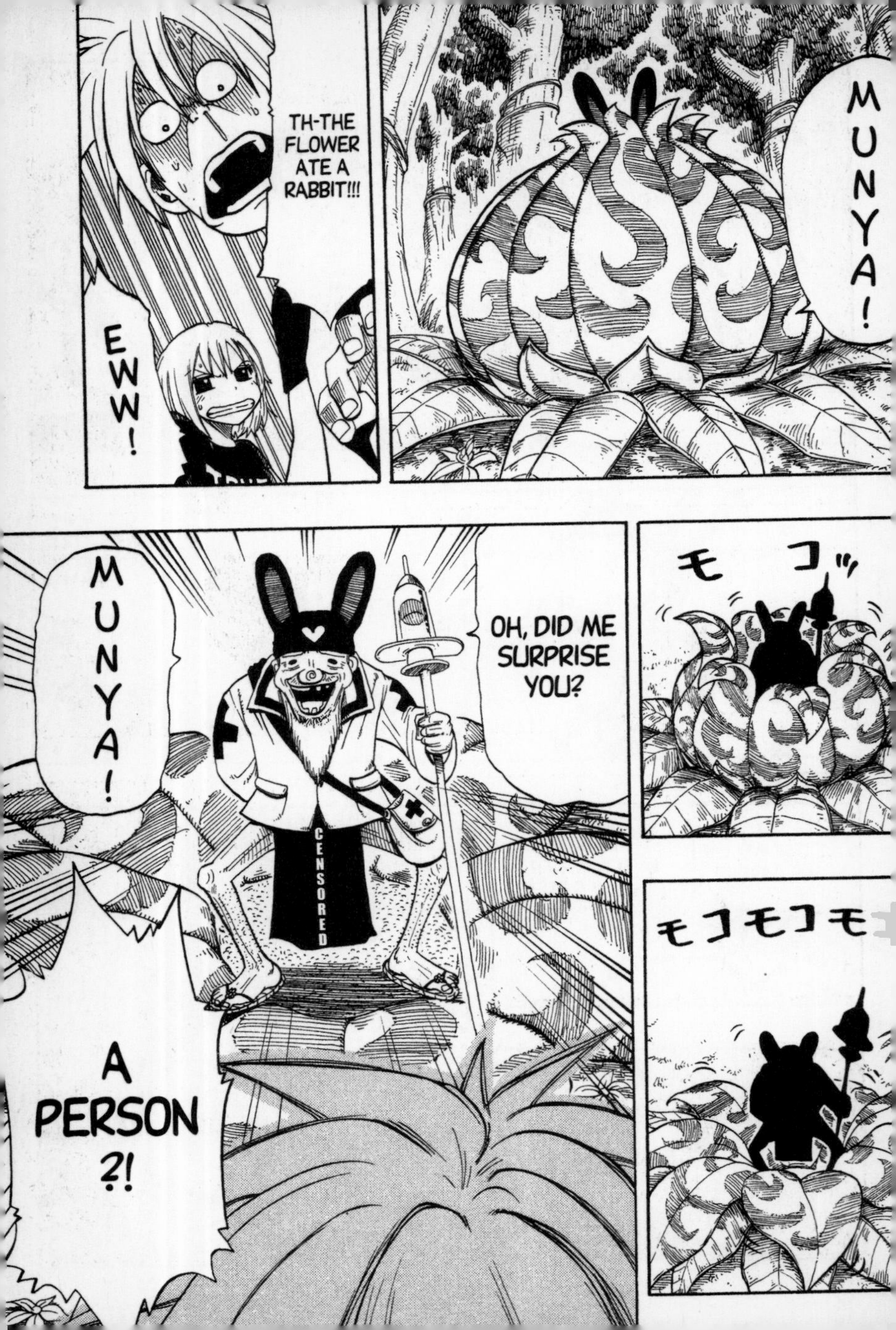
MUNYA!
TH-THE FLOWER ATE A RABBIT!!!
EWW!
モコッ
モコモコモ
OH, DID ME SURPRISE YOU?
MUNYA!
CENSORED
A PERSON ?!

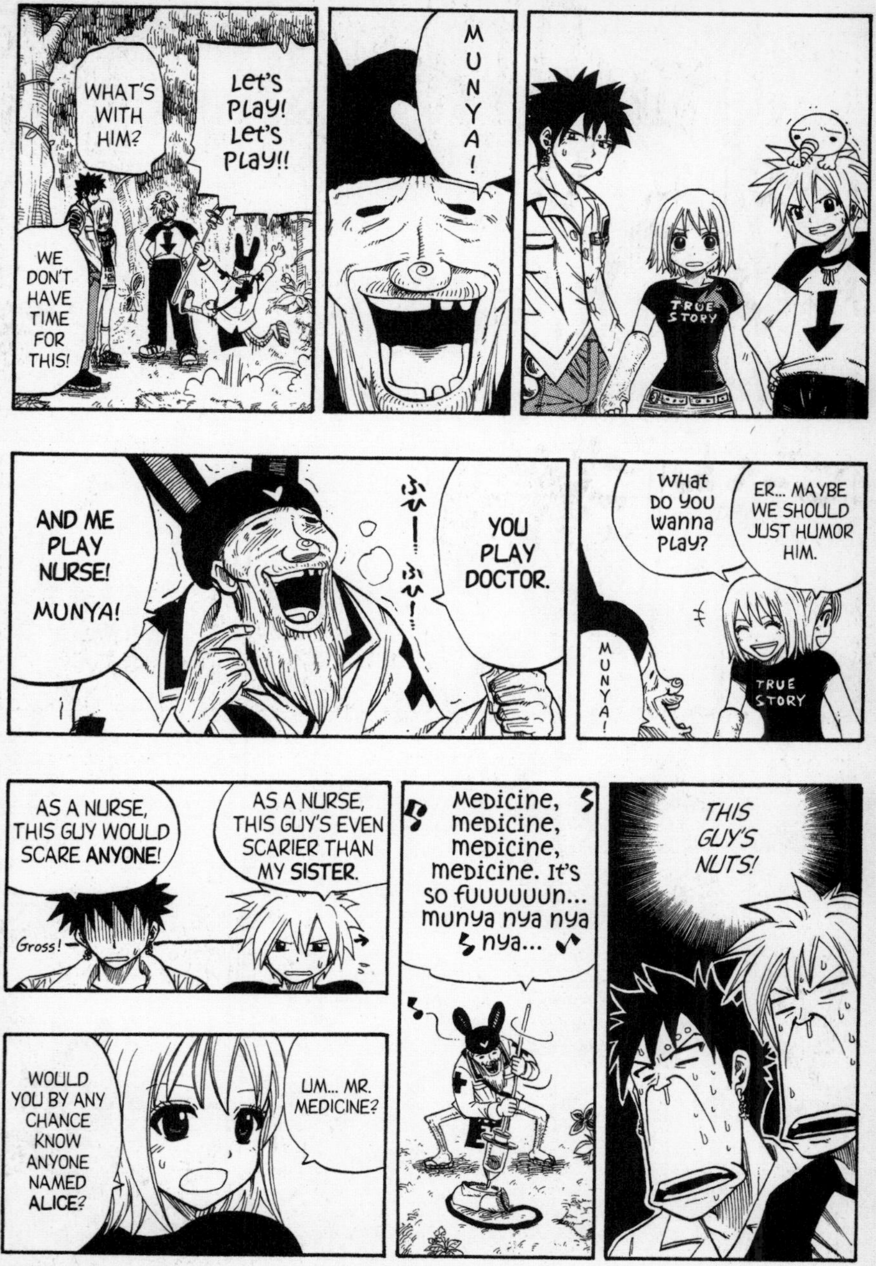
MUNYA!
Let's play! Let's play!!
WHAT'S WITH HIM?
WE DON'T HAVE TIME FOR THIS!
ER... MAYBE WE SHOULD JUST HUMOR HIM.
WHAT DO YOU wanna play?
MUNYA!
YOU PLAY DOCTOR.
ふひ！ふひ！
AND ME PLAY NURSE!
MUNYA!
THIS GUY'S NUTS!
Medicine, medicine, medicine, medicine. It's so fuuuuuun... munya nya nya nya...
AS A NURSE, THIS GUY'S EVEN SCARIER THAN MY SISTER.
AS A NURSE, THIS GUY WOULD SCARE ANYONE!
Gross!
UM... MR. MEDICINE?
WOULD YOU BY ANY CHANCE KNOW ANYONE NAMED ALICE?

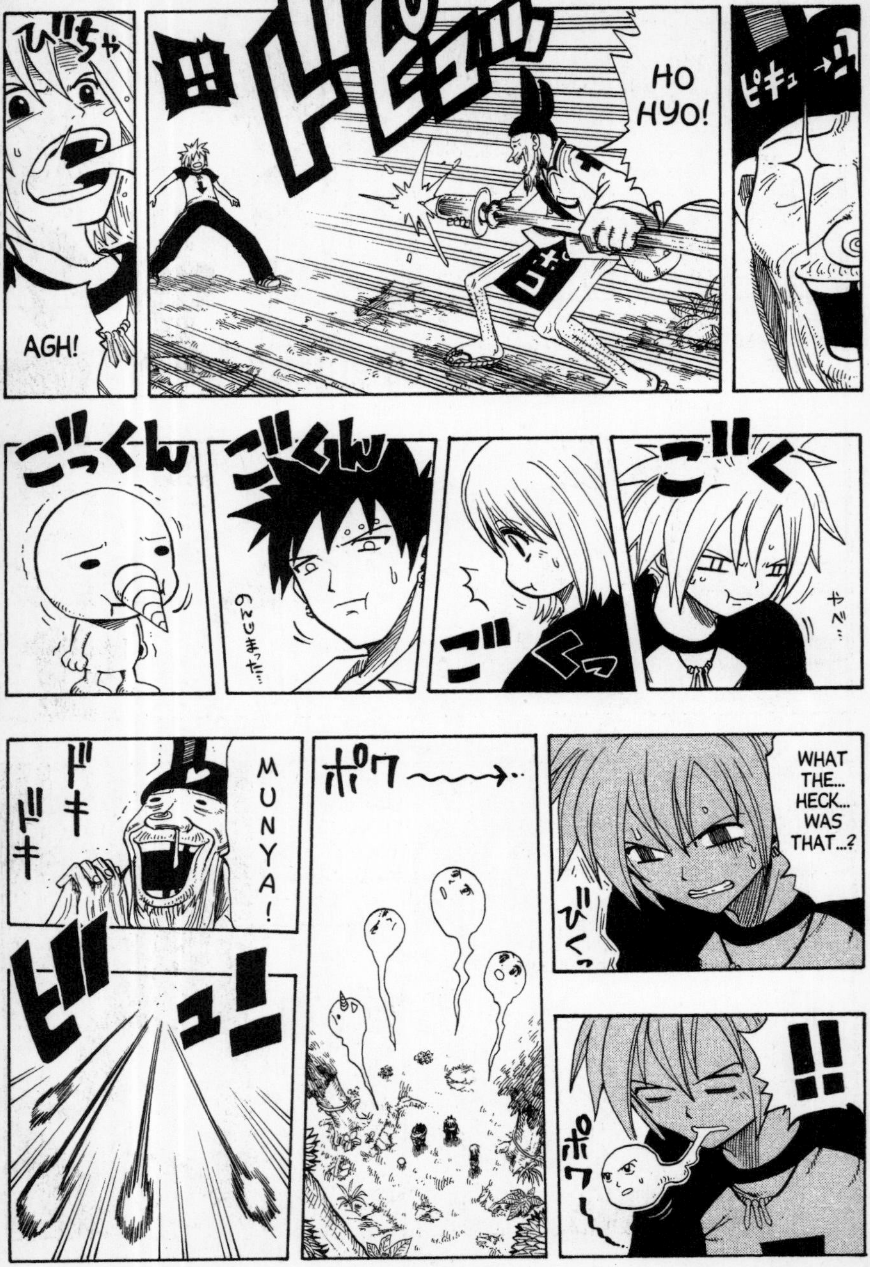

HO HYO!
AGH!
やべ…
ごくっ
ごくん
のんじまった…
ごっくん
WHAT THE... HECK... WAS THAT...?
びくっ
!!
ポワ〜
ポワ〜
ドキドキ
MUNYA!

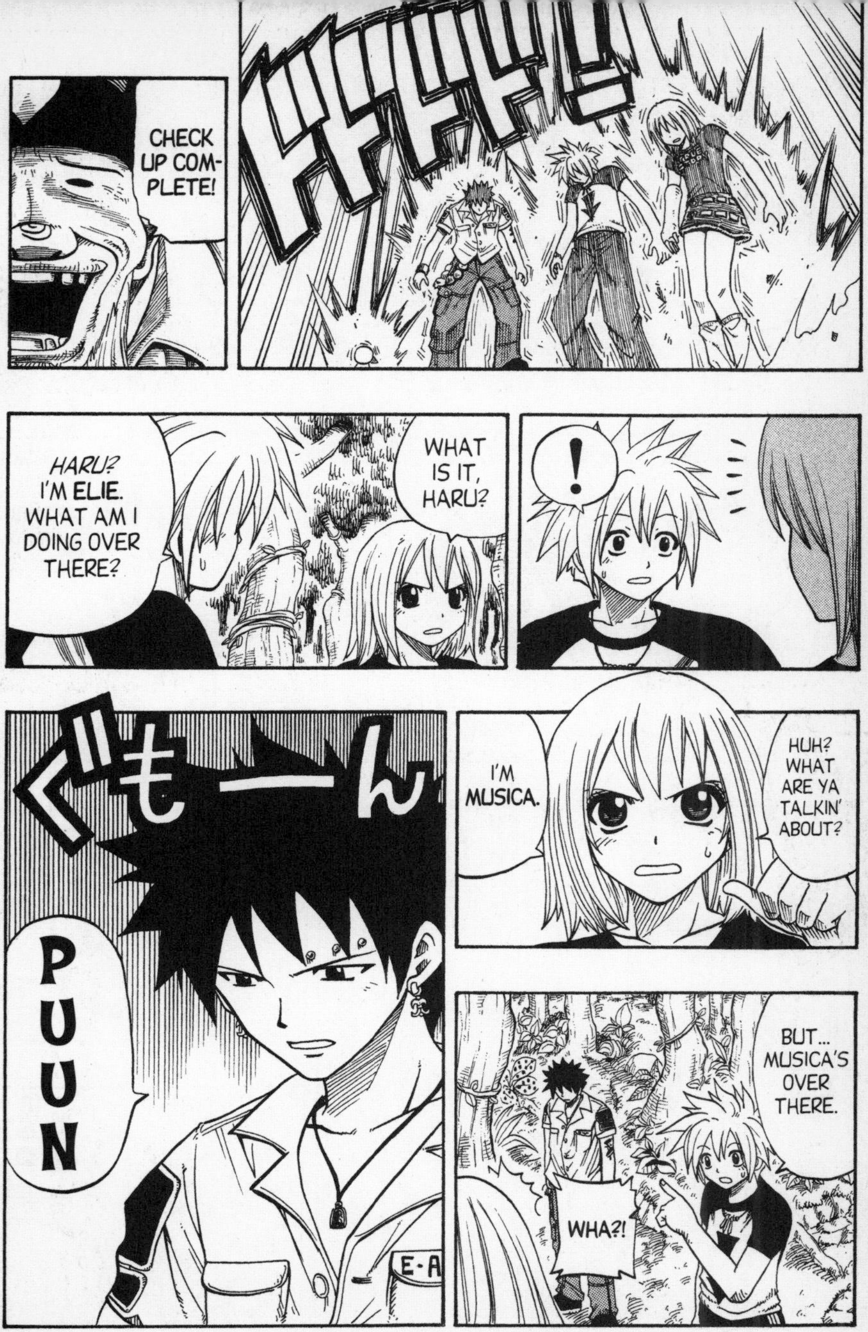
CHECK UP COM-PLETE!
!
WHAT IS IT, HARU?
HARU? I'M ELIE. WHAT AM I DOING OVER THERE?
HUH? WHAT ARE YA TALKIN' ABOUT?
I'M MUSICA.
BUT... MUSICA'S OVER THERE.
WHA?!
ぐもーん
PUUN

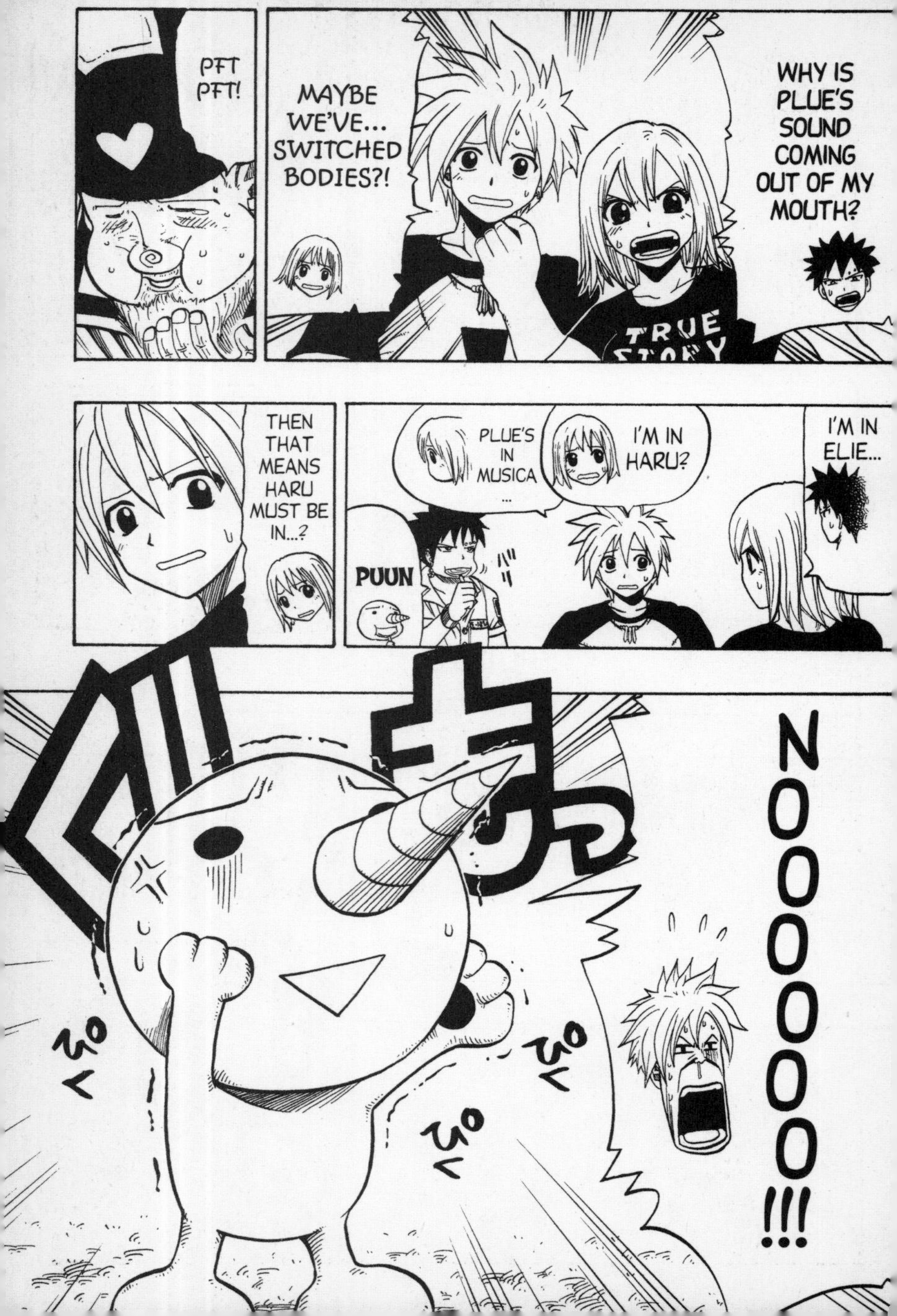

WHY IS PLUE'S SOUND COMING OUT OF MY MOUTH?
MAYBE WE'VE... SWITCHED BODIES?!
PFT PFT!
I'M IN ELIE...
I'M IN HARU?
PLUE'S IN MUSICA ...
PUUN
THEN THAT MEANS HARU MUST BE IN...?
NOOOOOO!!!

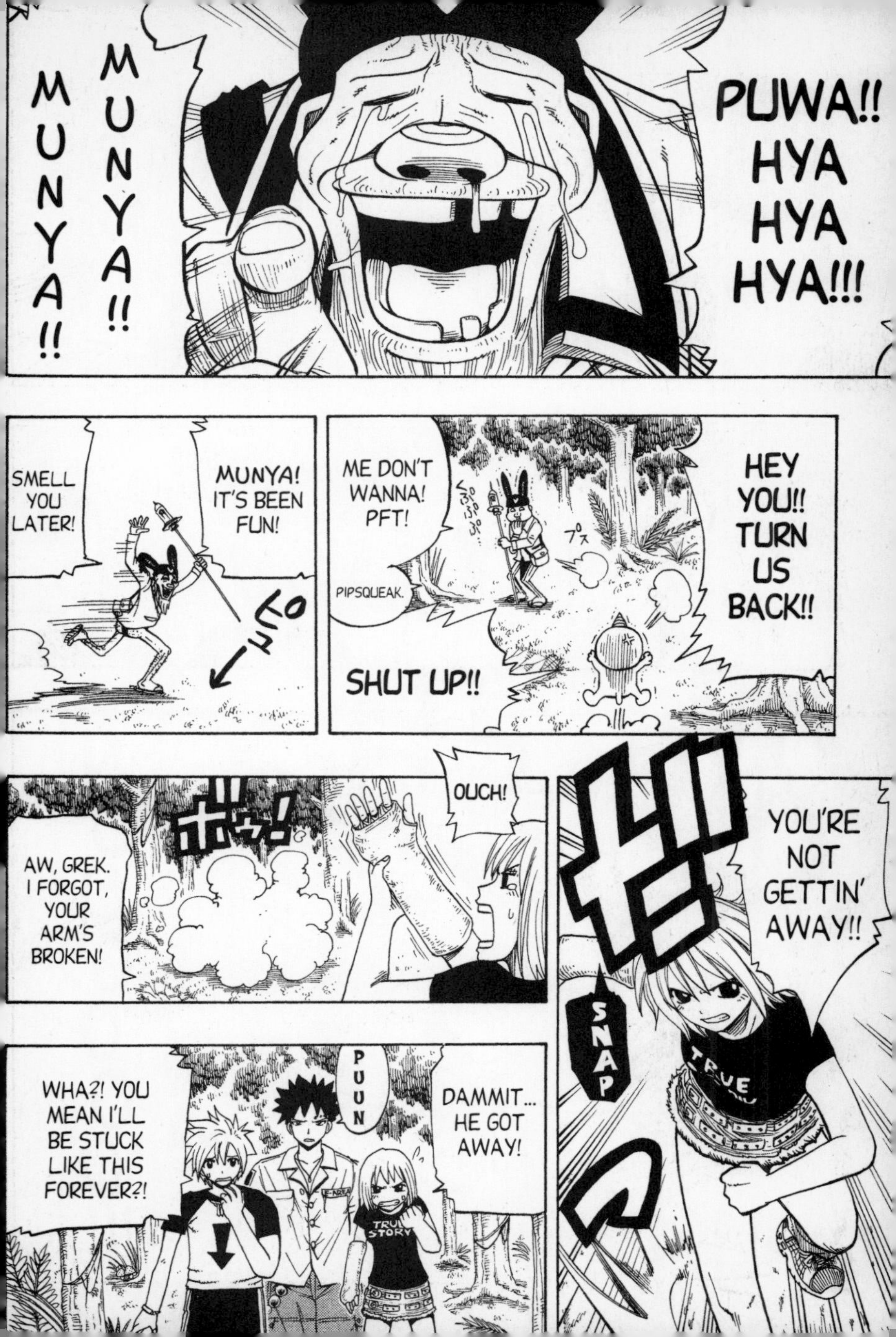
PUWA!! HYA HYA HYA!!!
MUNYA!!
MUNYA!!
HEY YOU!! TURN US BACK!!
ME DON'T WANNA! PFT!
PIPSQUEAK.
SHUT UP!!
MUNYA! IT'S BEEN FUN!
SMELL YOU LATER!
YOU'RE NOT GETTIN' AWAY!!
SNAP
OUCH!
AW, GREK. I FORGOT, YOUR ARM'S BROKEN!
PUUN
DAMMIT... HE GOT AWAY!
WHA?! YOU MEAN I'LL BE STUCK LIKE THIS FOREVER?!

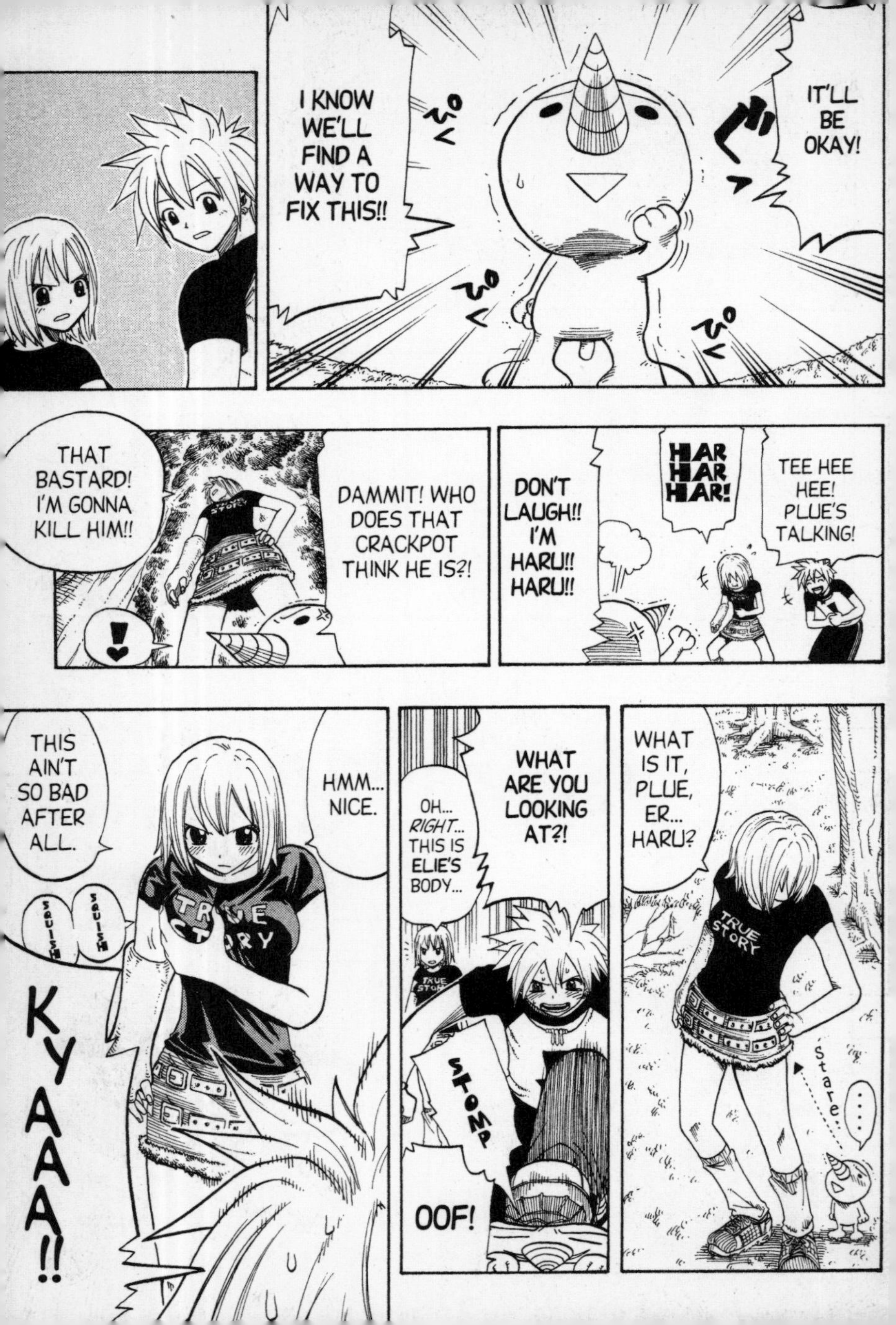
IT'LL BE OKAY!
I KNOW WE'LL FIND A WAY TO FIX THIS!!
TEE HEE HEE! PLUE'S TALKING!
HAR HAR HAR!
DON'T LAUGH!! I'M HARU!! HARU!!
DAMMIT! WHO DOES THAT CRACKPOT THINK HE IS?!
THAT BASTARD! I'M GONNA KILL HIM!!
!
WHAT IS IT, PLUE, ER... HARU?
Stare...
...
WHAT ARE YOU LOOKING AT?!
OH... *RIGHT*... THIS IS ELIE'S BODY...
STOMP
OOF!
HMM... NICE.
THIS AIN'T SO BAD AFTER ALL.
SQUISH
SQUISH
KYAAA!!

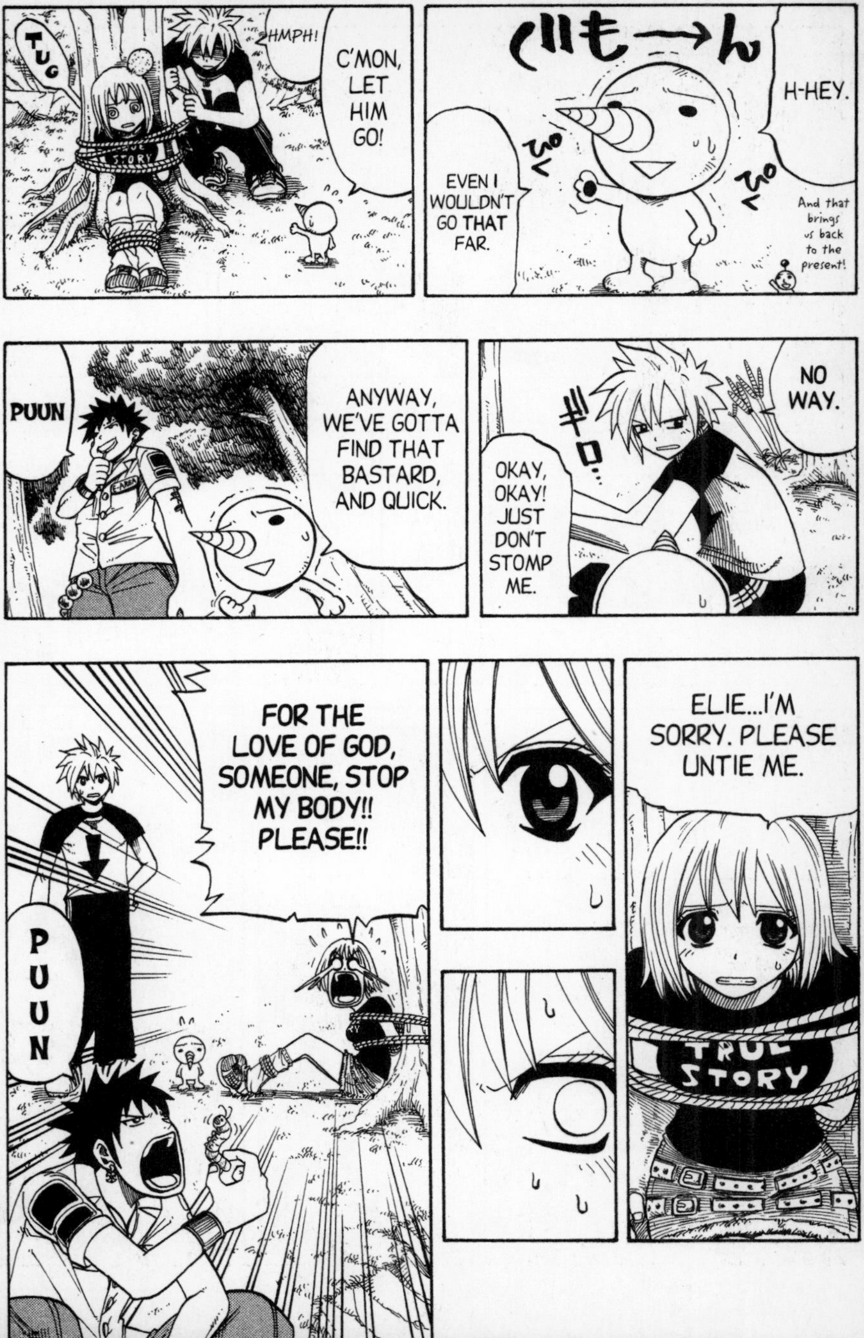
H-HEY.
EVEN I WOULDN'T GO THAT FAR.
ぴくぴく
And that brings us back to the present!
C'MON, LET HIM GO!
HMPH!
TUG
NO WAY.
ギロ
OKAY, OKAY! JUST DON'T STOMP ME.
ANYWAY, WE'VE GOTTA FIND THAT BASTARD, AND QUICK.
PUUN
ELIE...I'M SORRY. PLEASE UNTIE ME.
TRUE STORY
FOR THE LOVE OF GOD, SOMEONE, STOP MY BODY!! PLEASE!!
PUUN

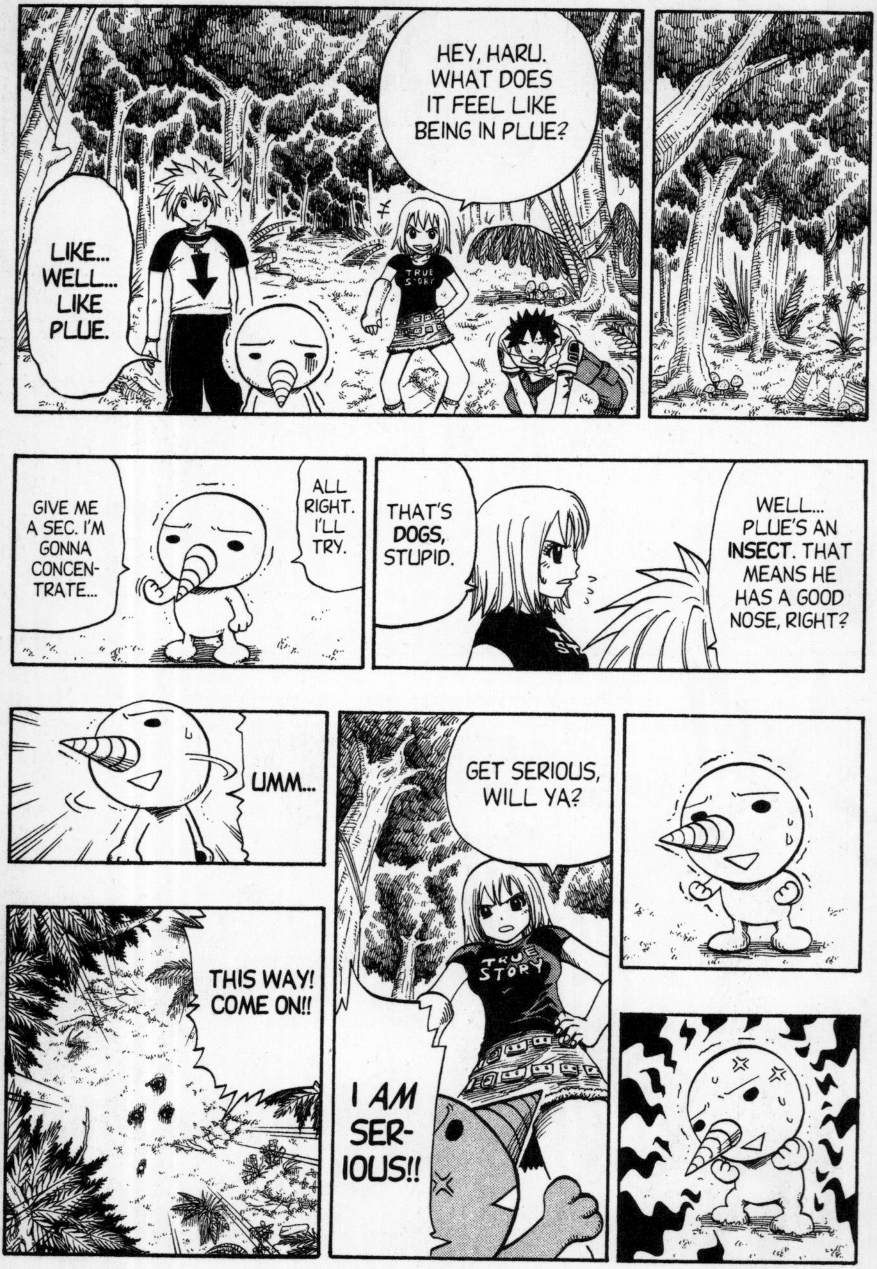
HEY, HARU. WHAT DOES IT FEEL LIKE BEING IN PLUE?
LIKE... WELL... LIKE PLUE.
WELL... PLUE'S AN **INSECT**. THAT MEANS HE HAS A GOOD NOSE, RIGHT?
THAT'S **DOGS**, STUPID.
ALL RIGHT. I'LL TRY.
GIVE ME A SEC. I'M GONNA CONCEN-TRATE...
GET SERIOUS, WILL YA?
I *AM* SER-IOUS!!
UMM...
THIS WAY! COME ON!!

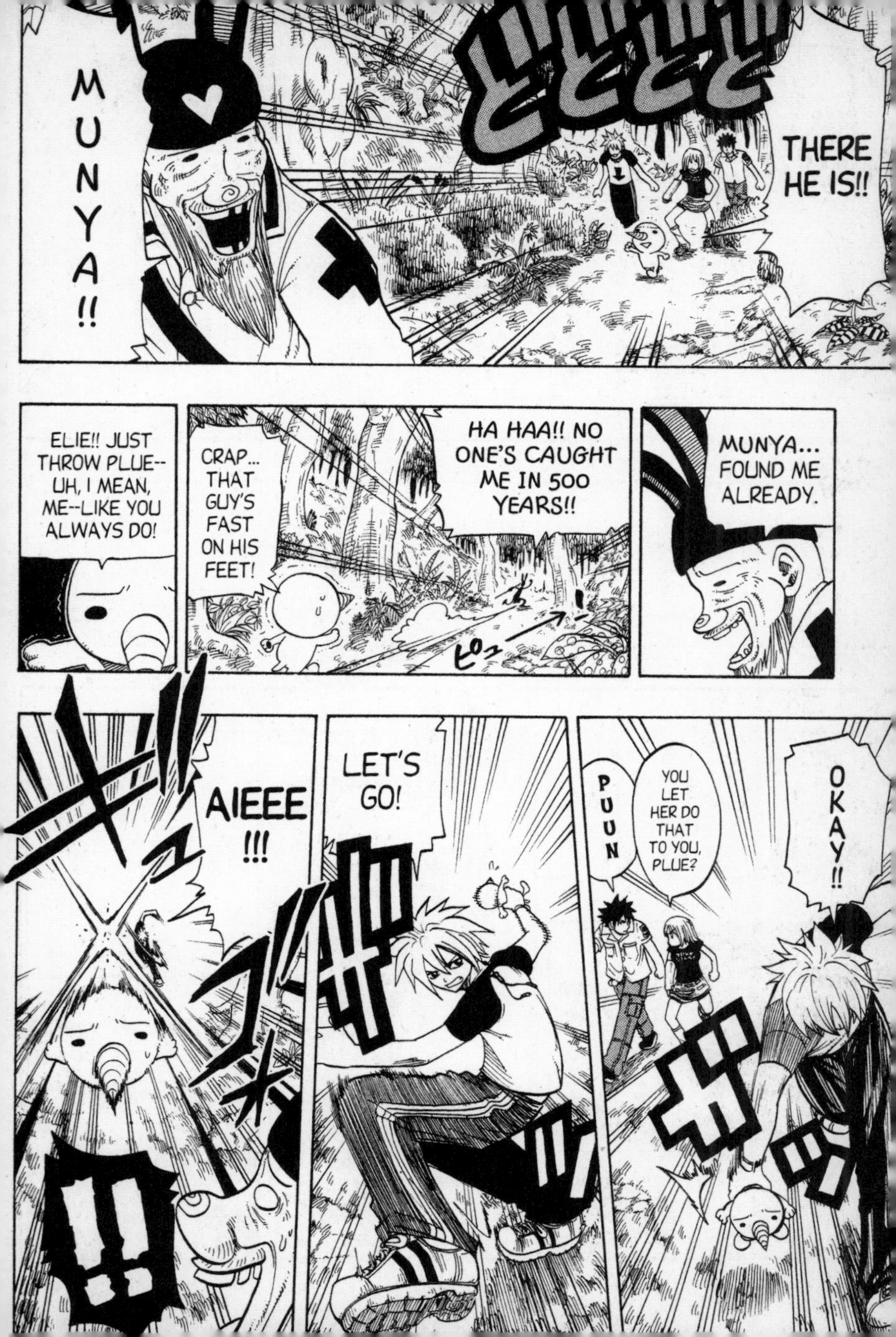
THERE HE IS!!
MUNYA!!
MUNYA... FOUND ME ALREADY.
HA HAA!! NO ONE'S CAUGHT ME IN 500 YEARS!!
CRAP... THAT GUY'S FAST ON HIS FEET!
ピュ
ELIE!! JUST THROW PLUE-- UH, I MEAN, ME--LIKE YOU ALWAYS DO!
OKAY!!
YOU LET HER DO THAT TO YOU, PLUE?
PUUN
LET'S GO!
AIEEE!!!

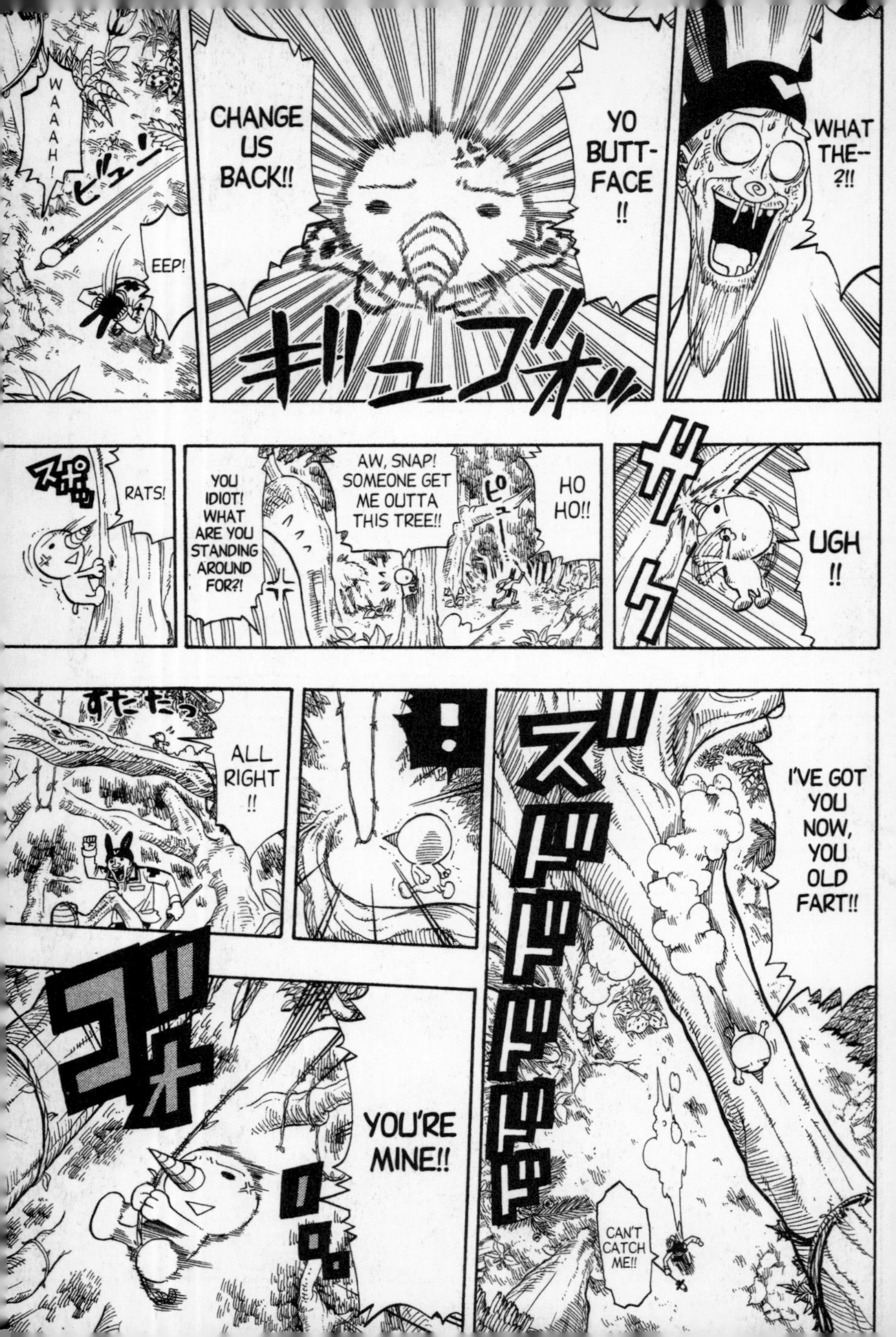
WHAT THE--?!!
YO BUTT-FACE!!
CHANGE US BACK!!
WAAAAH!
ビューッ
EEP!
UGH!!
HO HO!!
AW, SNAP! SOMEONE GET ME OUTTA THIS TREE!!
YOU IDIOT! WHAT ARE YOU STANDING AROUND FOR?!
RATS!
I'VE GOT YOU NOW, YOU OLD FART!!
CAN'T CATCH ME!!
ALL RIGHT!!
YOU'RE MINE!!

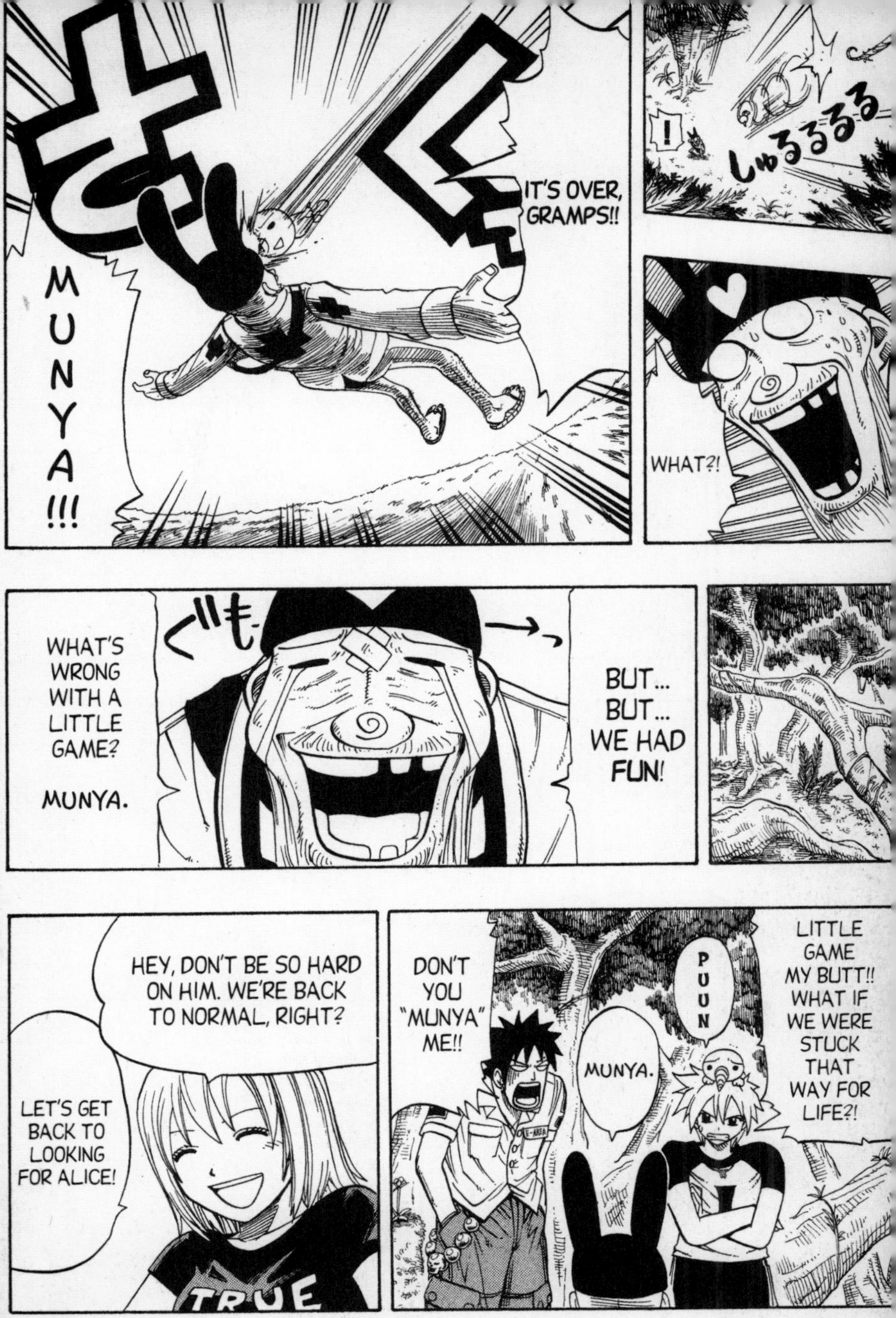
しゅるるるる
!
WHAT?!
IT'S OVER, GRAMPS!!
MUNYA!!!
BUT... BUT... WE HAD FUN!
WHAT'S WRONG WITH A LITTLE GAME?
MUNYA.
LITTLE GAME MY BUTT!! WHAT IF WE WERE STUCK THAT WAY FOR LIFE?!
PUUN
DON'T YOU "MUNYA" ME!!
MUNYA.
HEY, DON'T BE SO HARD ON HIM. WE'RE BACK TO NORMAL, RIGHT?
LET'S GET BACK TO LOOKING FOR ALICE!
TRUE

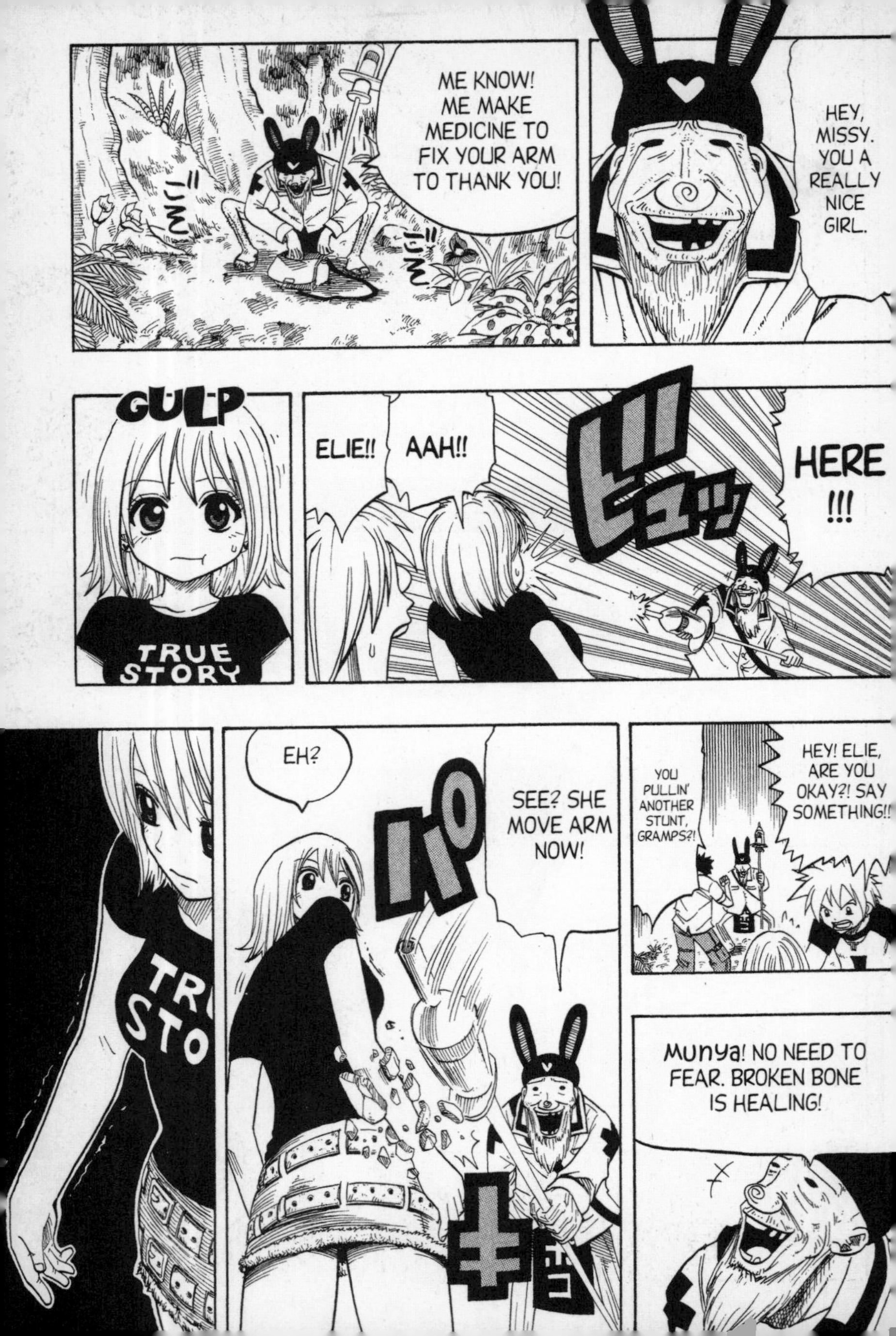
HEY, MISSY. YOU A REALLY NICE GIRL.
ME KNOW! ME MAKE MEDICINE TO FIX YOUR ARM TO THANK YOU!
HERE !!!
AAH!!
ELIE!!
GULP
TRUE STORY
HEY! ELIE, ARE YOU OKAY?! SAY SOMETHING!!
YOU PULLIN' ANOTHER STUNT, GRAMPS?!
Munya! NO NEED TO FEAR. BROKEN BONE IS HEALING!
SEE? SHE MOVE ARM NOW!
EH?
TRUE STORY

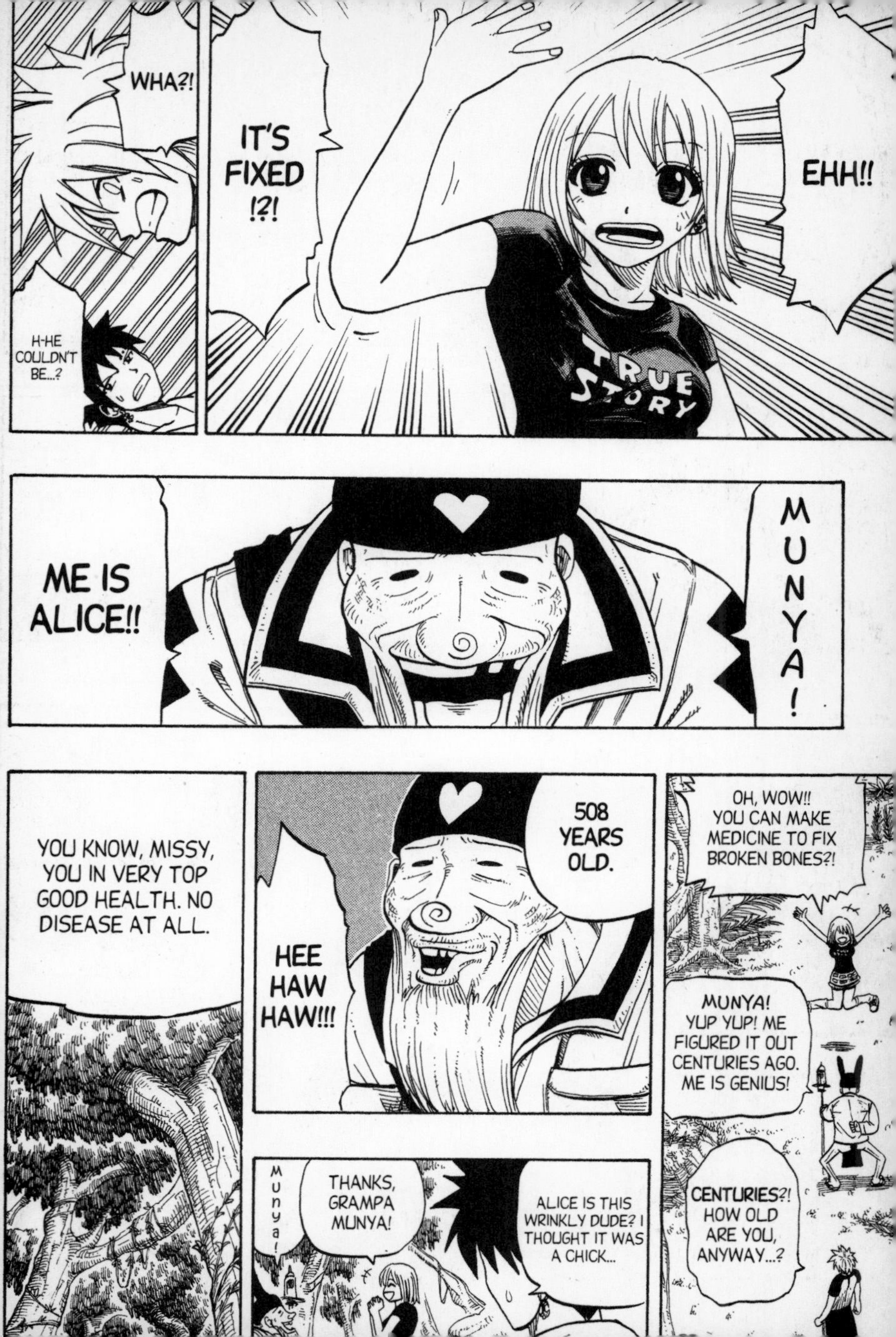
EHH!!
IT'S FIXED !?!
WHA?!
H-HE COULDN'T BE...?
MUNYA!
ME IS ALICE!!
OH, WOW!! YOU CAN MAKE MEDICINE TO FIX BROKEN BONES?!
MUNYA! YUP YUP! ME FIGURED IT OUT CENTURIES AGO. ME IS GENIUS!
CENTURIES?! HOW OLD ARE YOU, ANYWAY...?
508 YEARS OLD.
HEE HAW HAW!!!
ALICE IS THIS WRINKLY DUDE? I THOUGHT IT WAS A CHICK...
THANKS, GRAMPA MUNYA!
Munya!
YOU KNOW, MISSY, YOU IN VERY TOP GOOD HEALTH. NO DISEASE AT ALL.

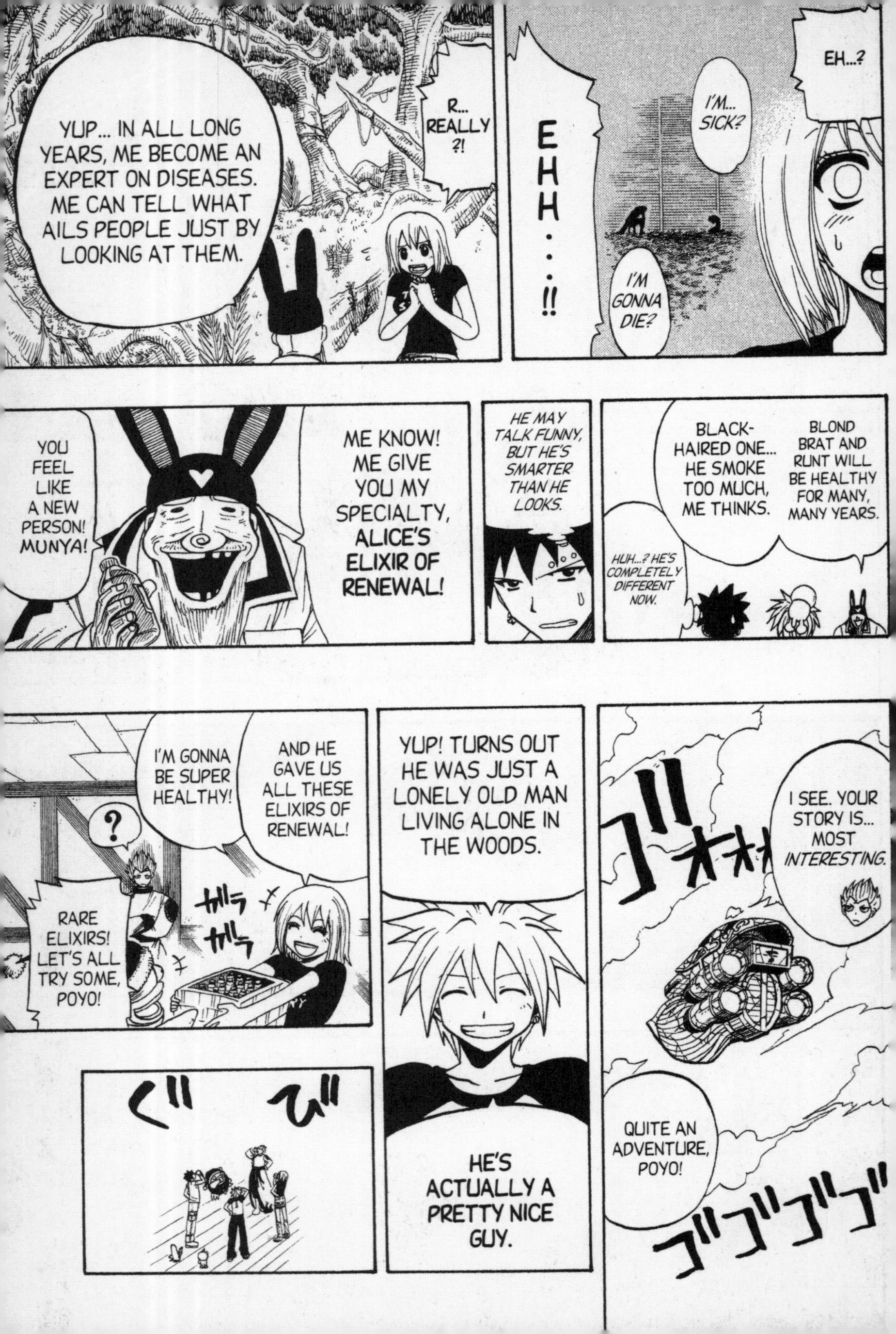
EH...?
I'M... SICK?
I'M GONNA DIE?
EHH...!!
R... REALLY?!
YUP... IN ALL LONG YEARS, ME BECOME AN EXPERT ON DISEASES. ME CAN TELL WHAT AILS PEOPLE JUST BY LOOKING AT THEM.
BLOND BRAT AND RUNT WILL BE HEALTHY FOR MANY, MANY YEARS.
BLACK-HAIRED ONE... HE SMOKE TOO MUCH, ME THINKS.
HUH...? HE'S COMPLETELY DIFFERENT NOW.
HE MAY TALK FUNNY, BUT HE'S SMARTER THAN HE LOOKS.
ME KNOW! ME GIVE YOU MY SPECIALTY, ALICE'S ELIXIR OF RENEWAL!
YOU FEEL LIKE A NEW PERSON! MUNYA!
I SEE. YOUR STORY IS... MOST INTERESTING.
ゴオオオ
QUITE AN ADVENTURE, POYO!
ゴゴゴゴ
YUP! TURNS OUT HE WAS JUST A LONELY OLD MAN LIVING ALONE IN THE WOODS.
HE'S ACTUALLY A PRETTY NICE GUY.
AND HE GAVE US ALL THESE ELIXIRS OF RENEWAL!
I'M GONNA BE SUPER HEALTHY!
?
ガラ ガラ
RARE ELIXIRS! LET'S ALL TRY SOME, POYO!
ぐび ぐび

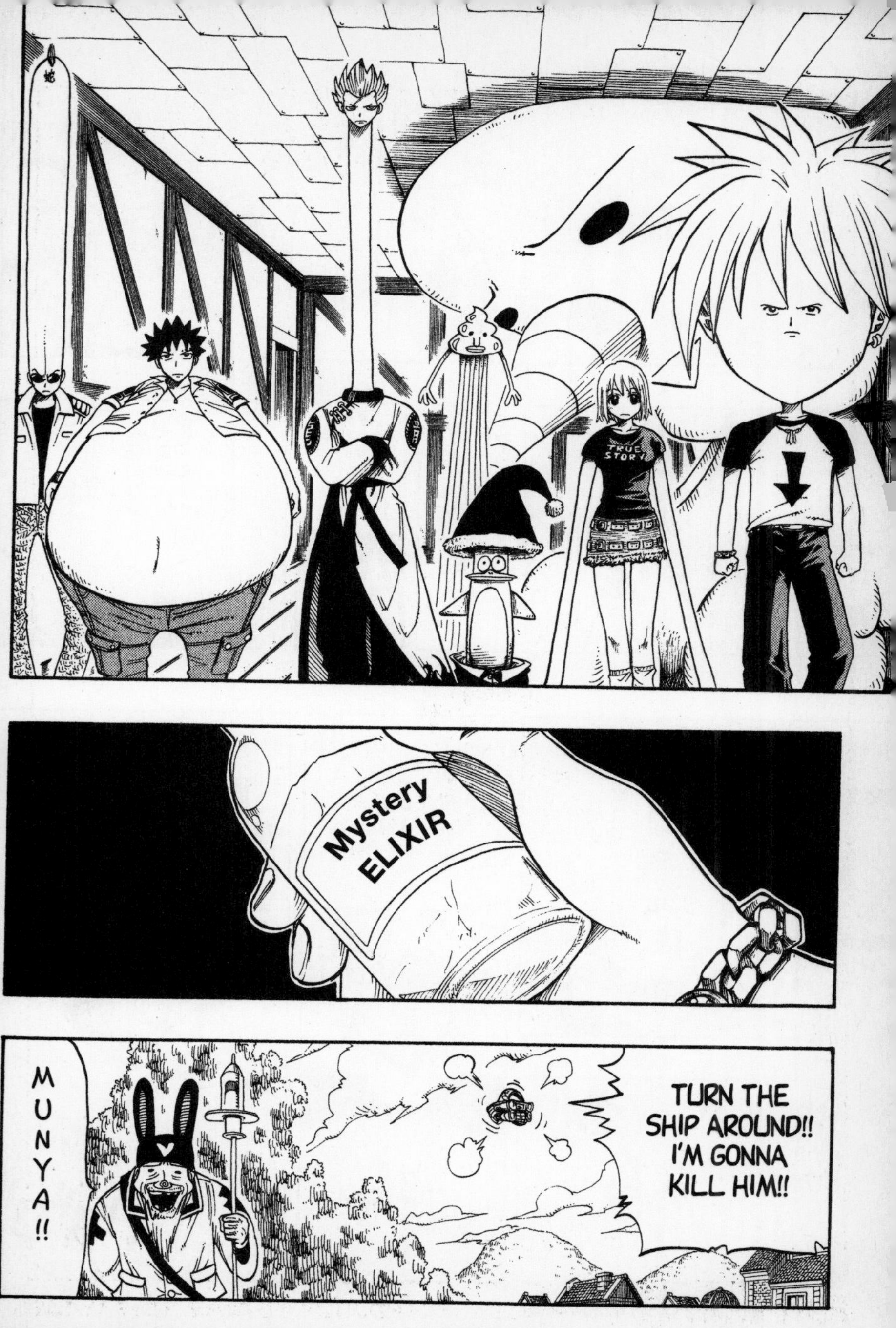
TRUE STORY
Mystery ELIXIR
TURN THE SHIP AROUND!! I'M GONNA KILL HIM!!
MUNYA!!

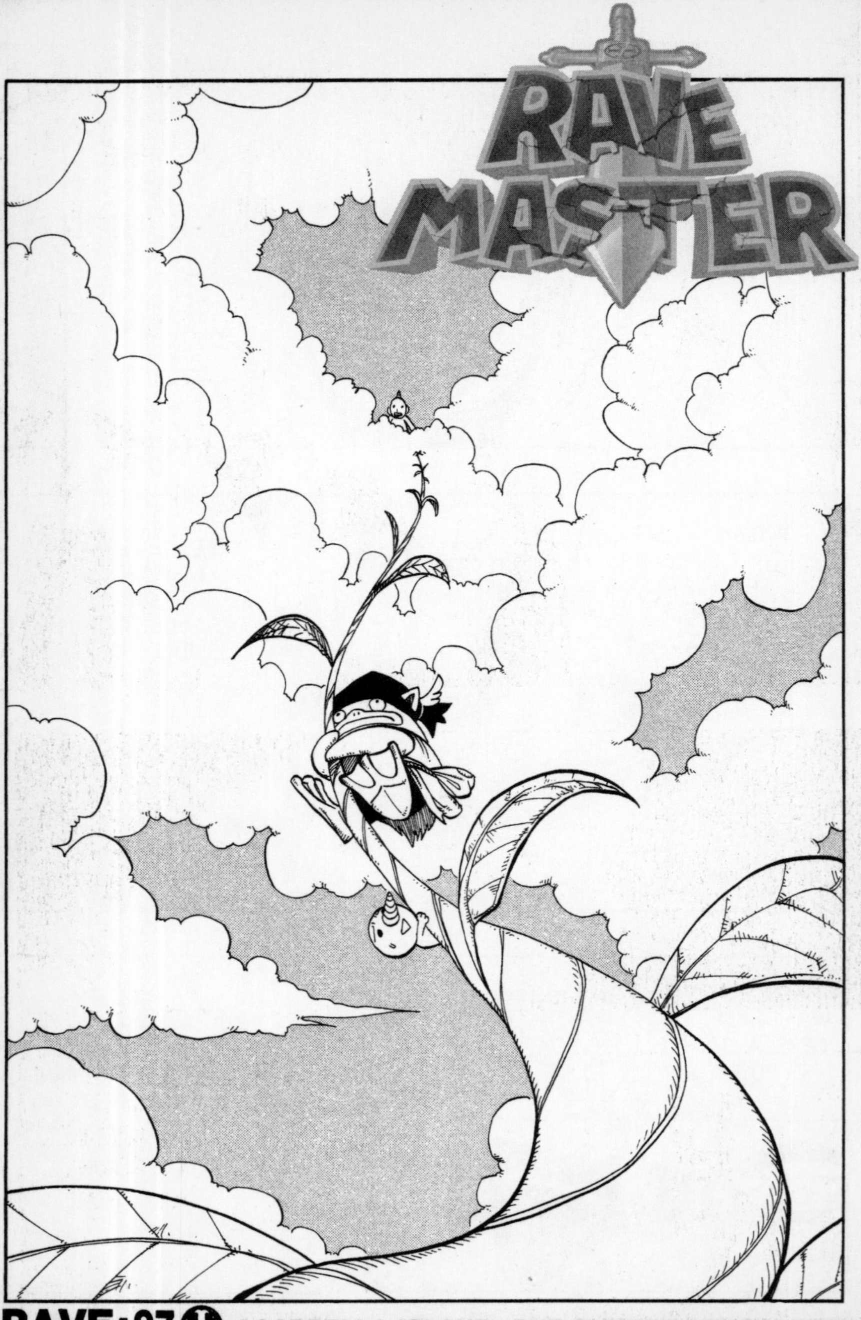
RAVE MASTER

RAVE:97 ACAPPELLA ISLAND: OUR FUTURE REVEALED?!

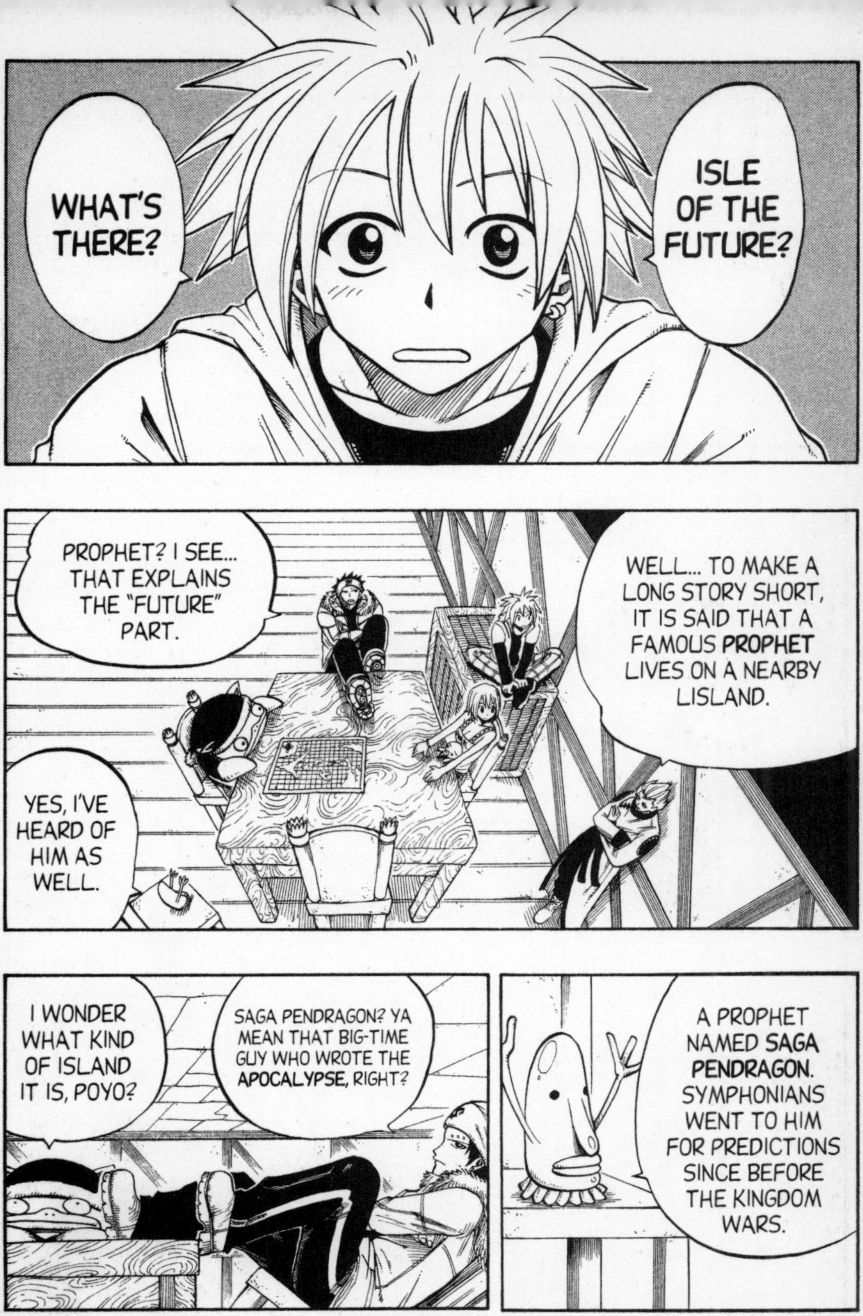
ISLE OF THE FUTURE?
WHAT'S THERE?
WELL... TO MAKE A LONG STORY SHORT, IT IS SAID THAT A FAMOUS PROPHET LIVES ON A NEARBY LISLAND.
PROPHET? I SEE... THAT EXPLAINS THE "FUTURE" PART.
YES, I'VE HEARD OF HIM AS WELL.
A PROPHET NAMED SAGA PENDRAGON. SYMPHONIANS WENT TO HIM FOR PREDICTIONS SINCE BEFORE THE KINGDOM WARS.
SAGA PENDRAGON? YA MEAN THAT BIG-TIME GUY WHO WROTE THE APOCALYPSE, RIGHT?
I WONDER WHAT KIND OF ISLAND IT IS, POYO?

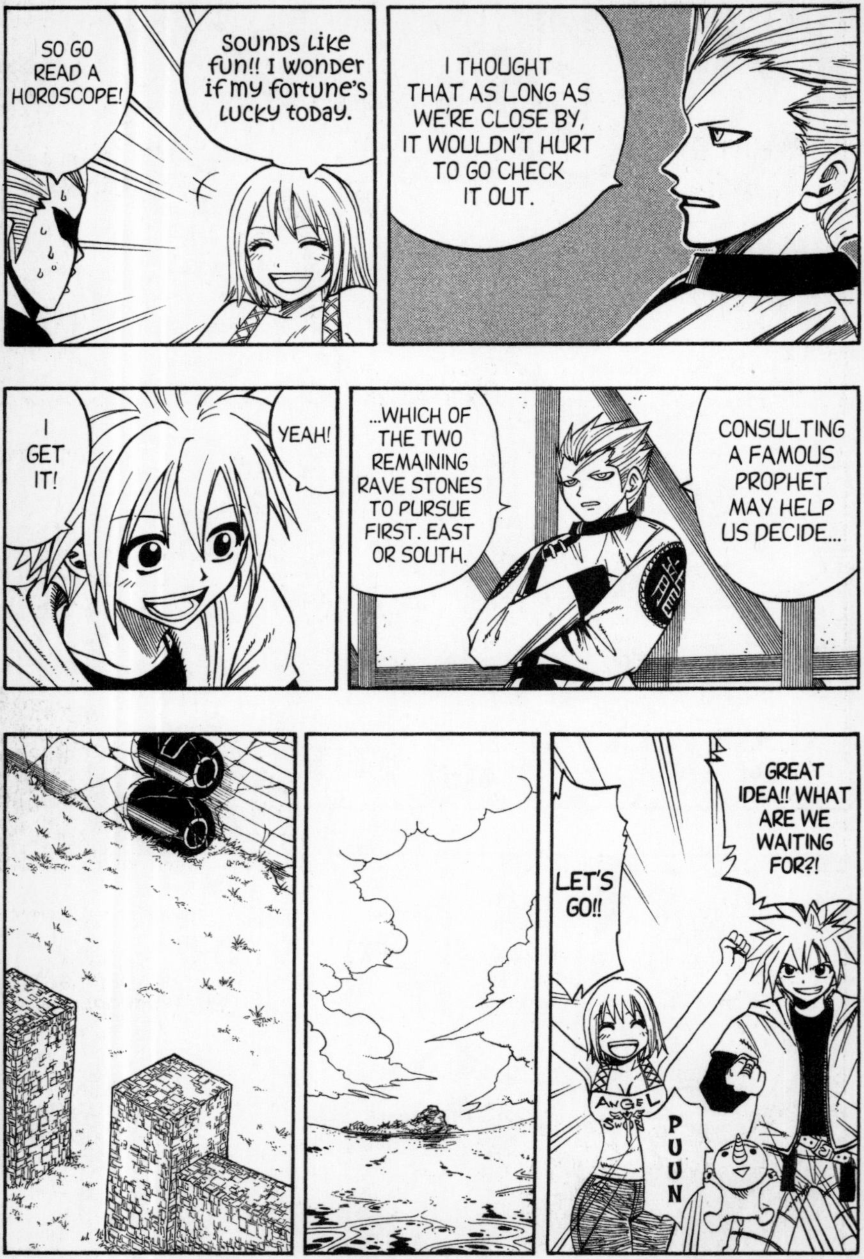
I THOUGHT THAT AS LONG AS WE'RE CLOSE BY, IT WOULDN'T HURT TO GO CHECK IT OUT.
SOUNDS LIKE fun!! I wonder if my fortune's LUCKY today.
SO GO READ A HOROSCOPE!
CONSULTING A FAMOUS PROPHET MAY HELP US DECIDE...
...WHICH OF THE TWO REMAINING RAVE STONES TO PURSUE FIRST. EAST OR SOUTH.
YEAH!
I GET IT!
GREAT IDEA!! WHAT ARE WE WAITING FOR?!
LET'S GO!!
ANGEL
PUUN

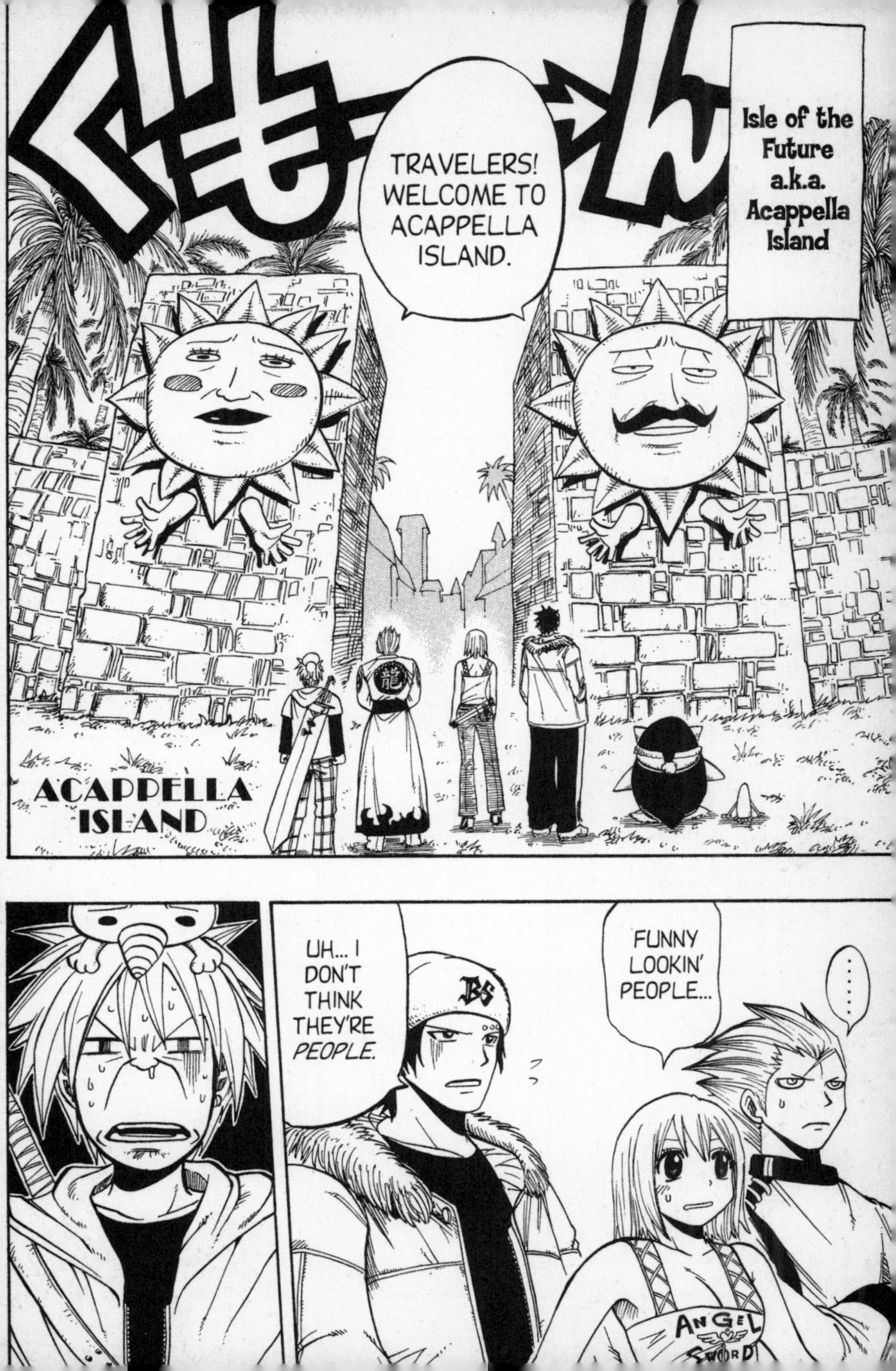
Isle of the Future a.k.a. Acappella Island
TRAVELERS! WELCOME TO ACAPPELLA ISLAND.
ACAPPELLA ISLAND
......
FUNNY LOOKIN' PEOPLE...
UH... I DON'T THINK THEY'RE *PEOPLE.*

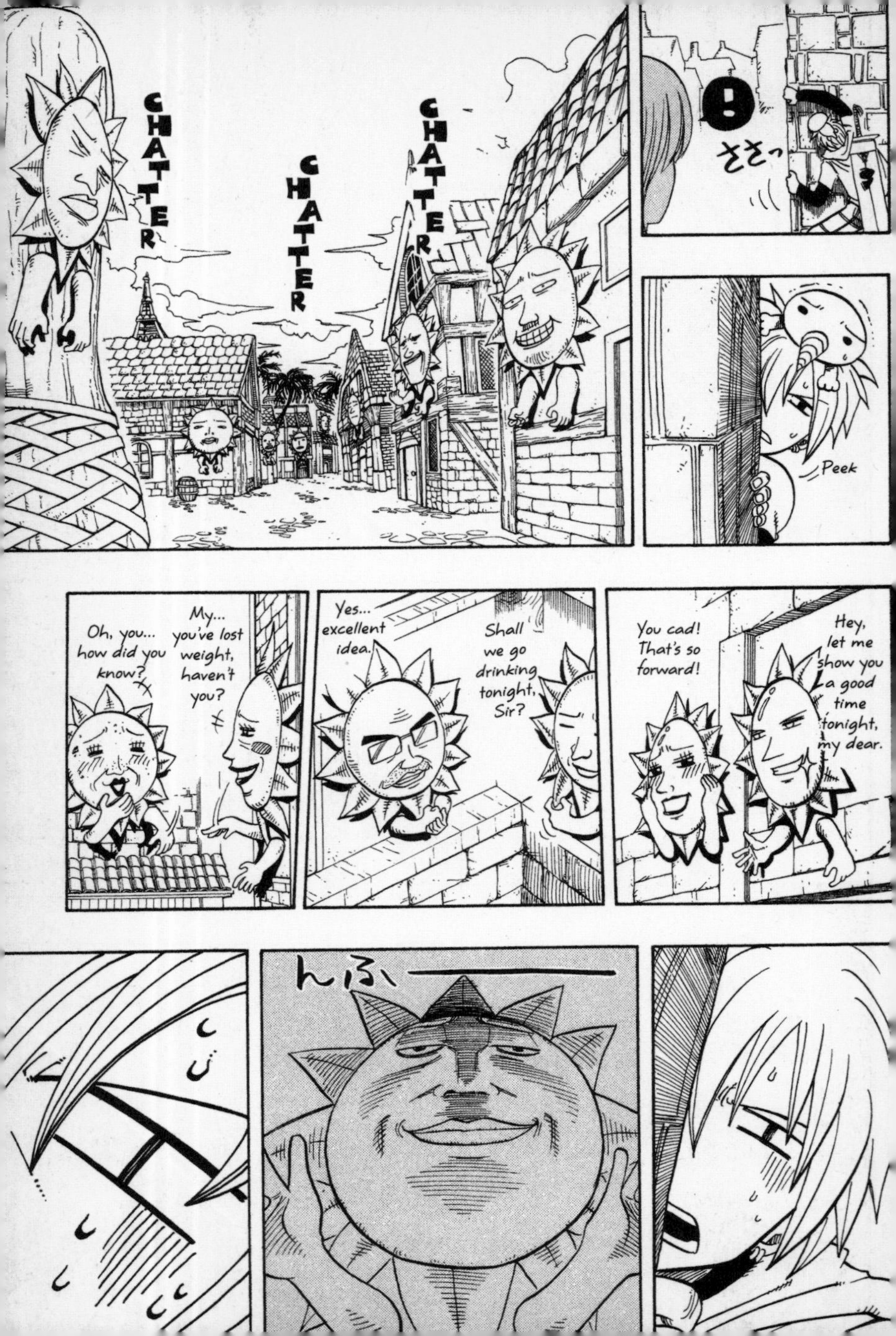
!
ささっ
Peek
CHATTER
CHATTER
CHATTER
Hey, let me show you a good time tonight, my dear.
You cad! That's so forward!
Shall we go drinking tonight, Sir?
Yes... excellent idea.
My... you've lost weight, haven't you?
Oh, you... how did you know?
んふ――

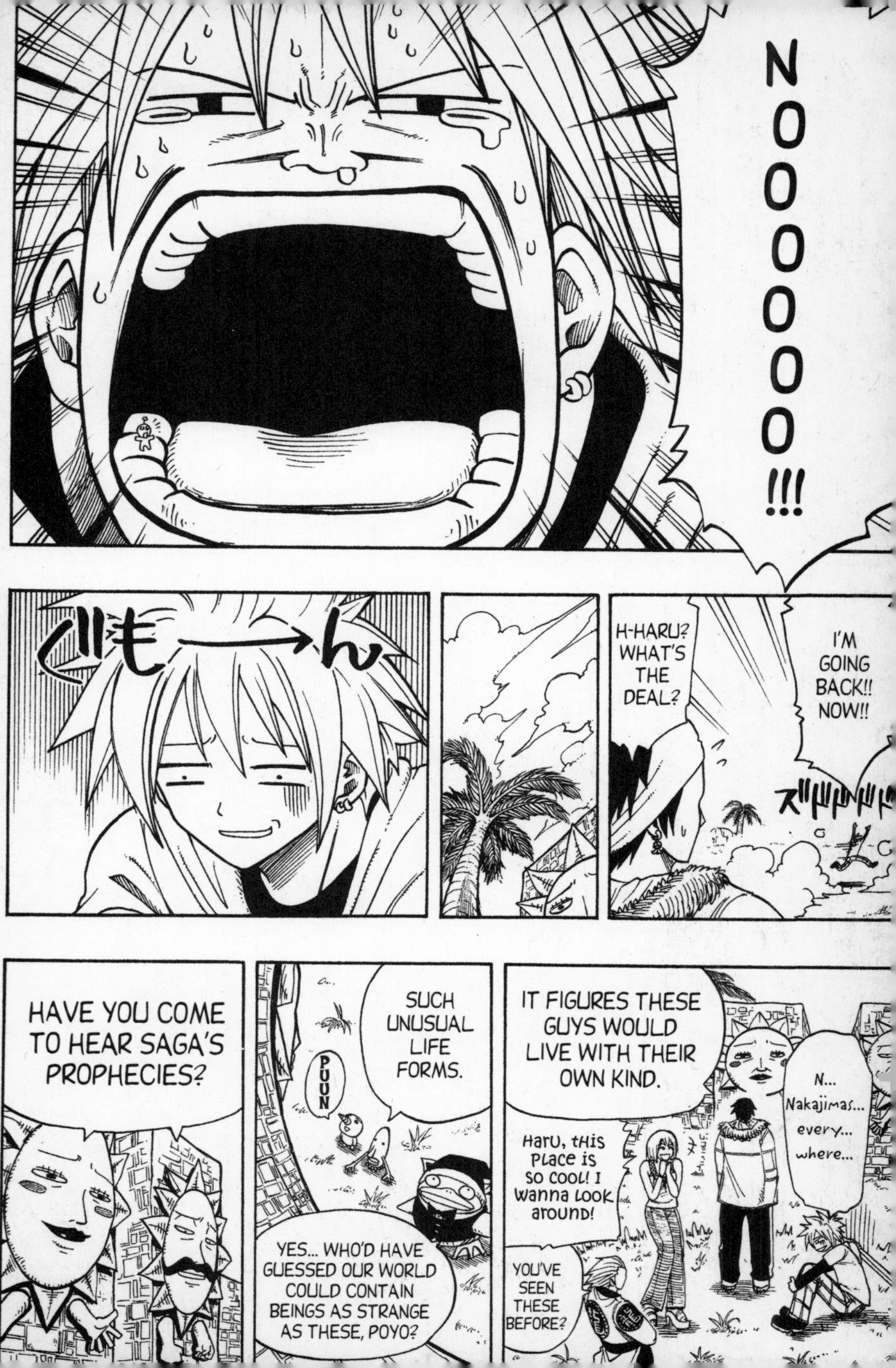
NOOOOOO!!!
I'M GOING BACK!! NOW!!
H-HARU? WHAT'S THE DEAL?
ぐもーん
N... Nakajimas... every... where...
IT FIGURES THESE GUYS WOULD LIVE WITH THEIR OWN KIND.
Haru, this place is so cool! I wanna look around!
YOU'VE SEEN THESE BEFORE?
SUCH UNUSUAL LIFE FORMS.
PUUN
YES... WHO'D HAVE GUESSED OUR WORLD COULD CONTAIN BEINGS AS STRANGE AS THESE, POYO?
HAVE YOU COME TO HEAR SAGA'S PROPHECIES?

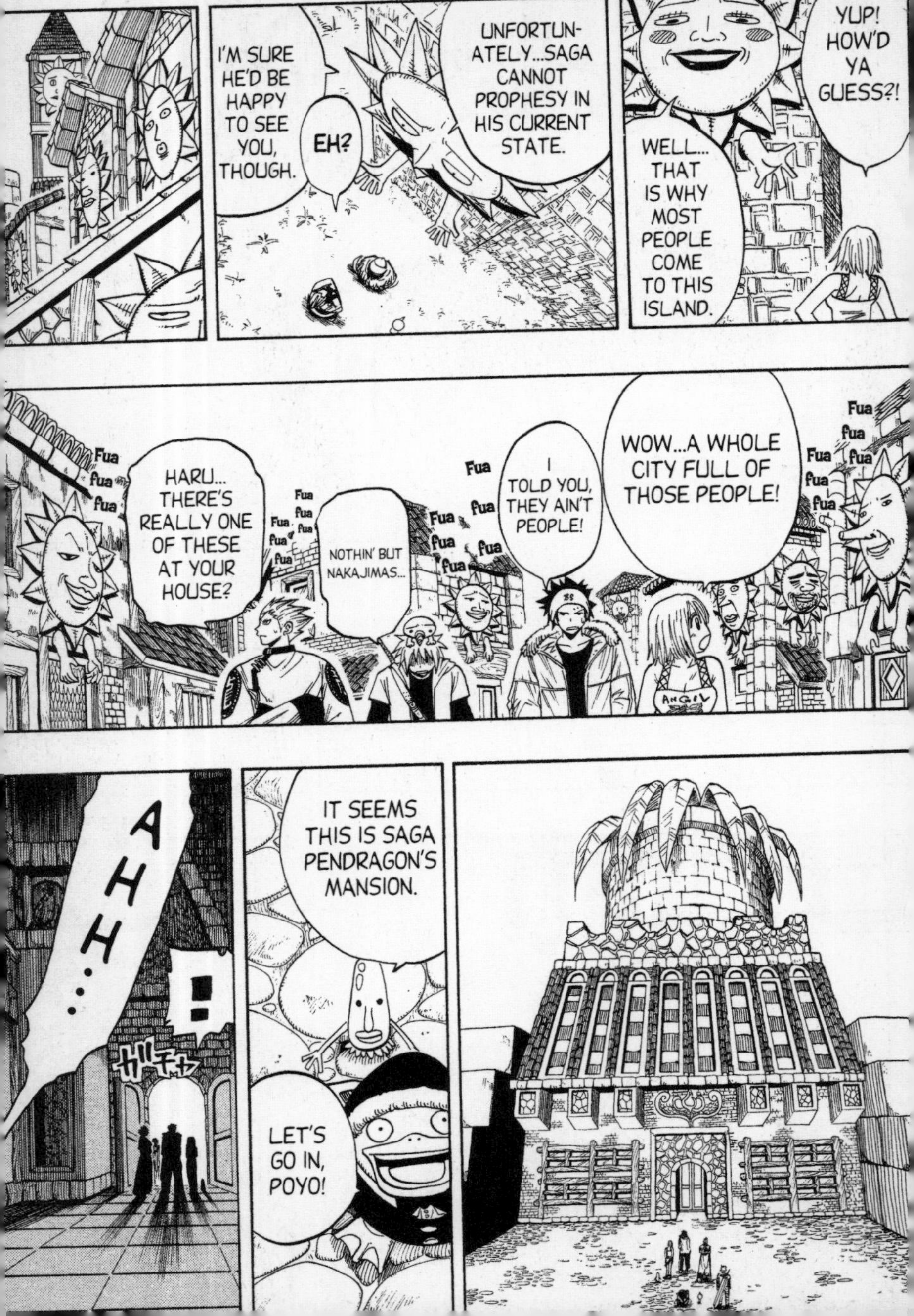
YUP! HOW'D YA GUESS?!
WELL... THAT IS WHY MOST PEOPLE COME TO THIS ISLAND.
UNFORTUN-ATELY...SAGA CANNOT PROPHESY IN HIS CURRENT STATE.
EH?
I'M SURE HE'D BE HAPPY TO SEE YOU, THOUGH.
Fua fua Fua fua fua fua
WOW...A WHOLE CITY FULL OF THOSE PEOPLE!
I TOLD YOU, THEY AIN'T PEOPLE!
Fua fua Fua fua fua fua
NOTHIN' BUT NAKAJIMAS...
Fua fua fua Fua fua fua
HARU... THERE'S REALLY ONE OF THESE AT YOUR HOUSE?
Fua fua fua
IT SEEMS THIS IS SAGA PENDRAGON'S MANSION.
LET'S GO IN, POYO!
AHH...!
ガチャ

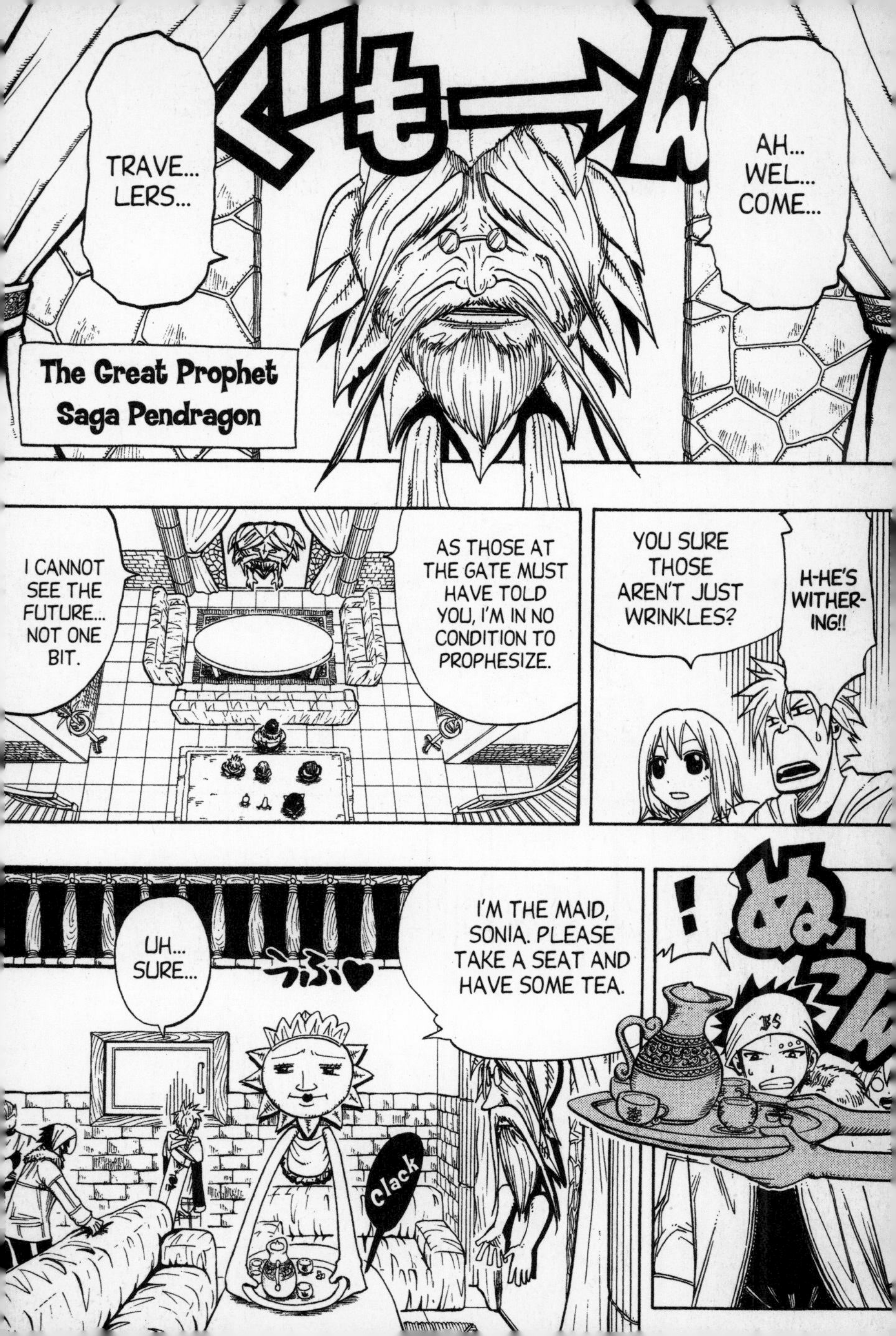
AH... WEL... COME...
TRAVE... LERS...
The Great Prophet Saga Pendragon
H-HE'S WITHER-ING!!
YOU SURE THOSE AREN'T JUST WRINKLES?
AS THOSE AT THE GATE MUST HAVE TOLD YOU, I'M IN NO CONDITION TO PROPHESIZE.
I CANNOT SEE THE FUTURE... NOT ONE BIT.
!
I'M THE MAID, SONIA. PLEASE TAKE A SEAT AND HAVE SOME TEA.
うふ♥
UH... SURE...
clack

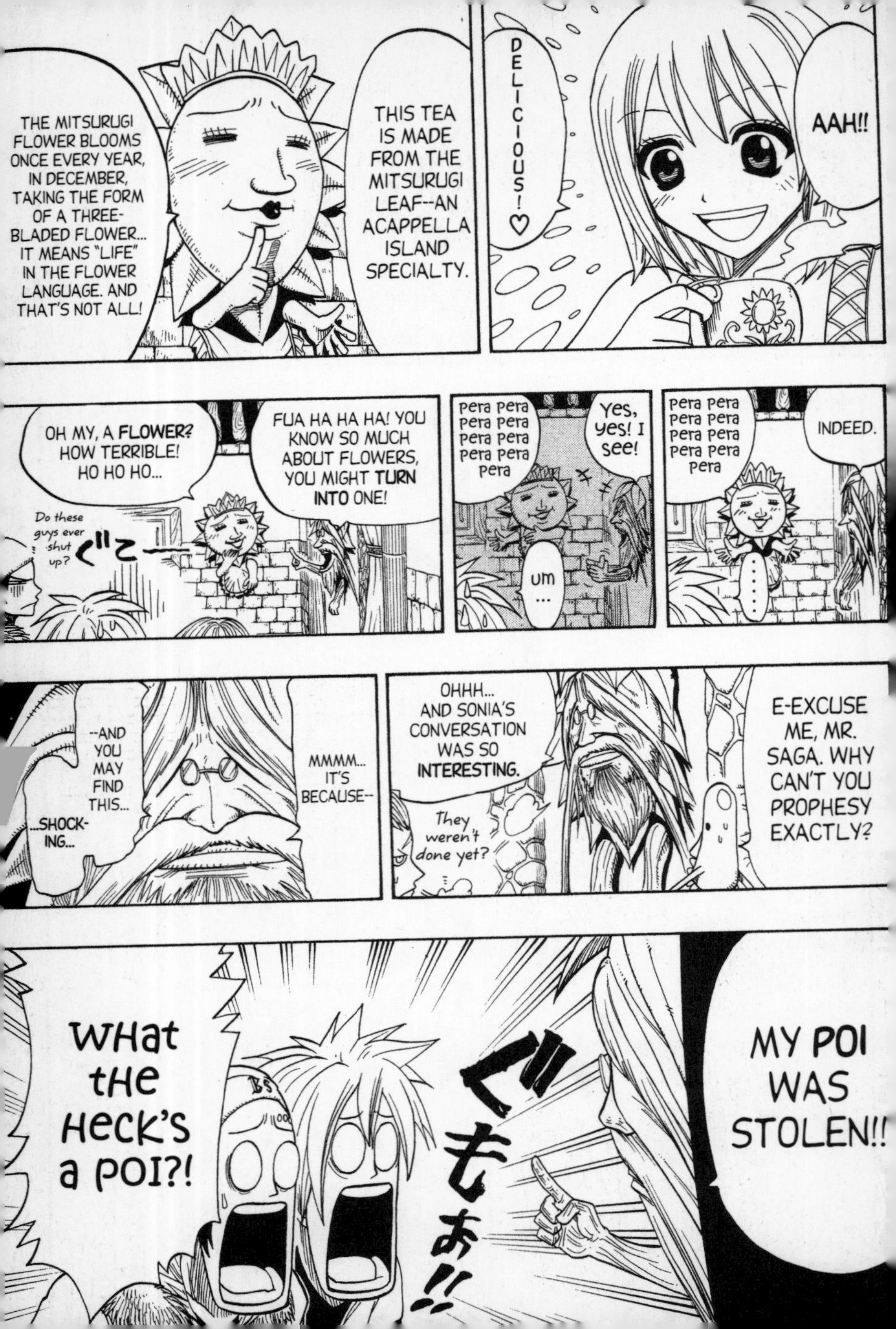
AAH!!
DELICIOUS! ♡
THIS TEA IS MADE FROM THE MITSURUGI LEAF--AN ACAPPELLA ISLAND SPECIALTY.
THE MITSURUGI FLOWER BLOOMS ONCE EVERY YEAR, IN DECEMBER, TAKING THE FORM OF A THREE-BLADED FLOWER... IT MEANS "LIFE" IN THE FLOWER LANGUAGE. AND THAT'S NOT ALL!
INDEED.
pera pera pera pera pera pera pera pera pera
......
Yes, yes! I see!
pera pera pera pera pera pera pera pera pera
um ...
FUA HA HA HA! YOU KNOW SO MUCH ABOUT FLOWERS, YOU MIGHT TURN INTO ONE!
OH MY, A FLOWER? HOW TERRIBLE! HO HO HO...
Do these guys ever shut up?
E-EXCUSE ME, MR. SAGA. WHY CAN'T YOU PROPHESY EXACTLY?
OHHH... AND SONIA'S CONVERSATION WAS SO INTERESTING.
They weren't done yet?
MMMM... IT'S BECAUSE--
--AND YOU MAY FIND THIS...
...SHOCKING...
MY POI WAS STOLEN!!
ぐもぉ!!
What the heck's a POI?!

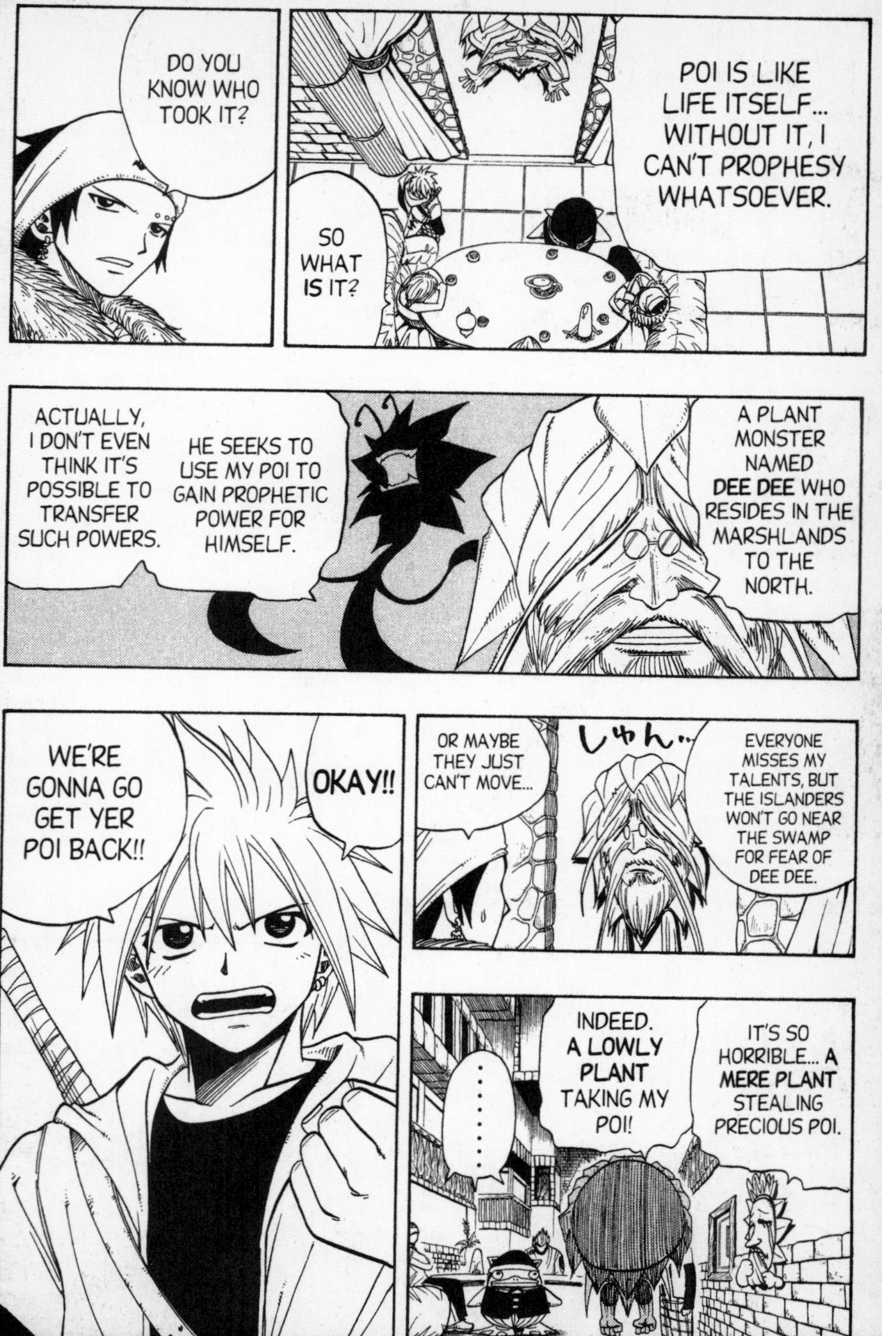
POI IS LIKE LIFE ITSELF... WITHOUT IT, I CAN'T PROPHESY WHATSOEVER.
SO WHAT IS IT?
DO YOU KNOW WHO TOOK IT?
A PLANT MONSTER NAMED DEE DEE WHO RESIDES IN THE MARSHLANDS TO THE NORTH.
HE SEEKS TO USE MY POI TO GAIN PROPHETIC POWER FOR HIMSELF.
ACTUALLY, I DON'T EVEN THINK IT'S POSSIBLE TO TRANSFER SUCH POWERS.
EVERYONE MISSES MY TALENTS, BUT THE ISLANDERS WON'T GO NEAR THE SWAMP FOR FEAR OF DEE DEE.
しゃん…
OR MAYBE THEY JUST CAN'T MOVE...
IT'S SO HORRIBLE... A MERE PLANT STEALING PRECIOUS POI.
INDEED. A LOWLY PLANT TAKING MY POI!
......
OKAY!!
WE'RE GONNA GO GET YER POI BACK!!

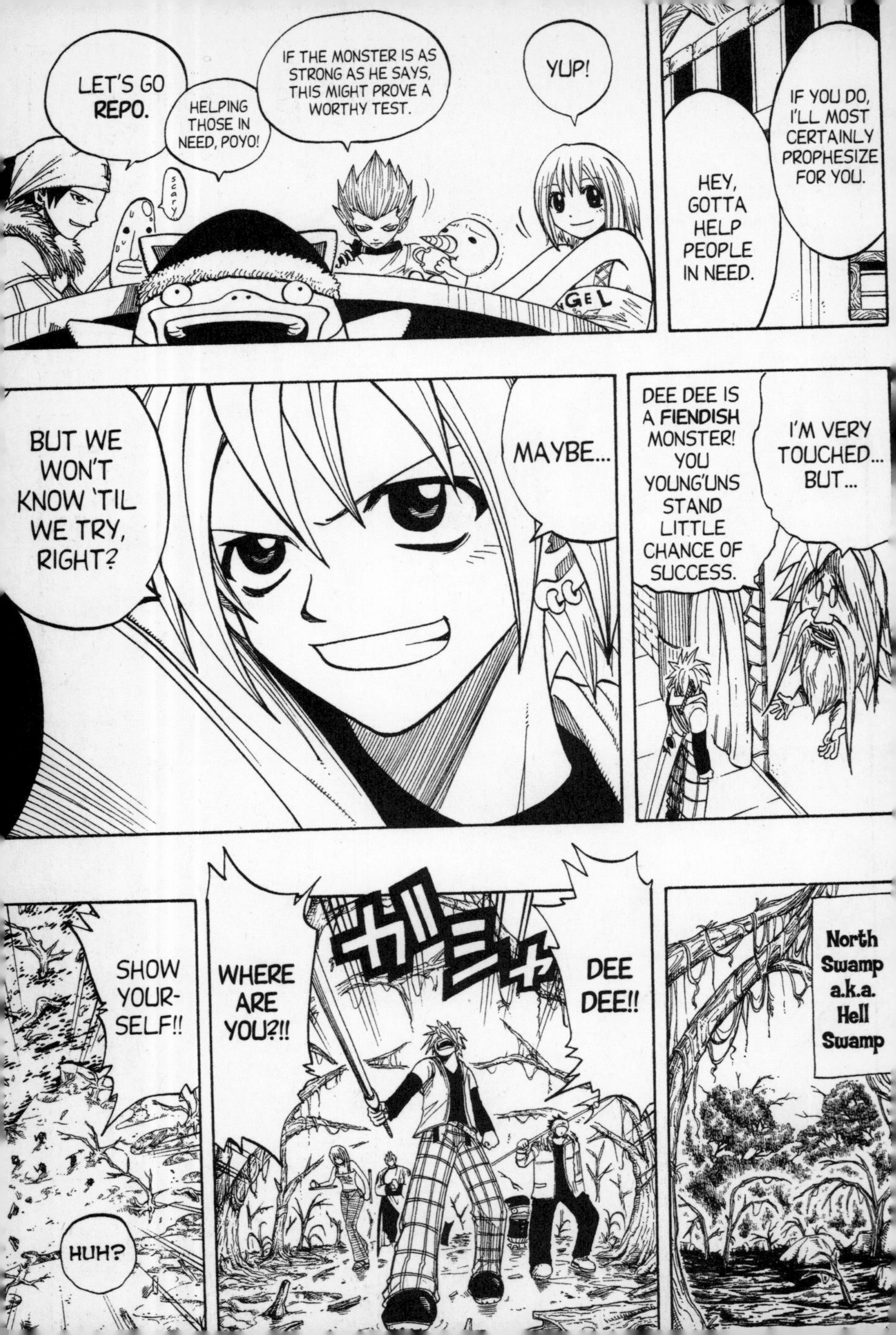
IF YOU DO, I'LL MOST CERTAINLY PROPHESIZE FOR YOU.
HEY, GOTTA HELP PEOPLE IN NEED.
YUP!
IF THE MONSTER IS AS STRONG AS HE SAYS, THIS MIGHT PROVE A WORTHY TEST.
HELPING THOSE IN NEED, POYO!
LET'S GO **REPO.**
scary
I'M VERY TOUCHED... BUT...
DEE DEE IS A **FIENDISH** MONSTER! YOU YOUNG'UNS STAND LITTLE CHANCE OF SUCCESS.
MAYBE...
BUT WE WON'T KNOW 'TIL WE TRY, RIGHT?
North Swamp a.k.a. Hell Swamp
DEE DEE!!
ガシャ
WHERE ARE YOU?!!
SHOW YOURSELF!!
HUH?

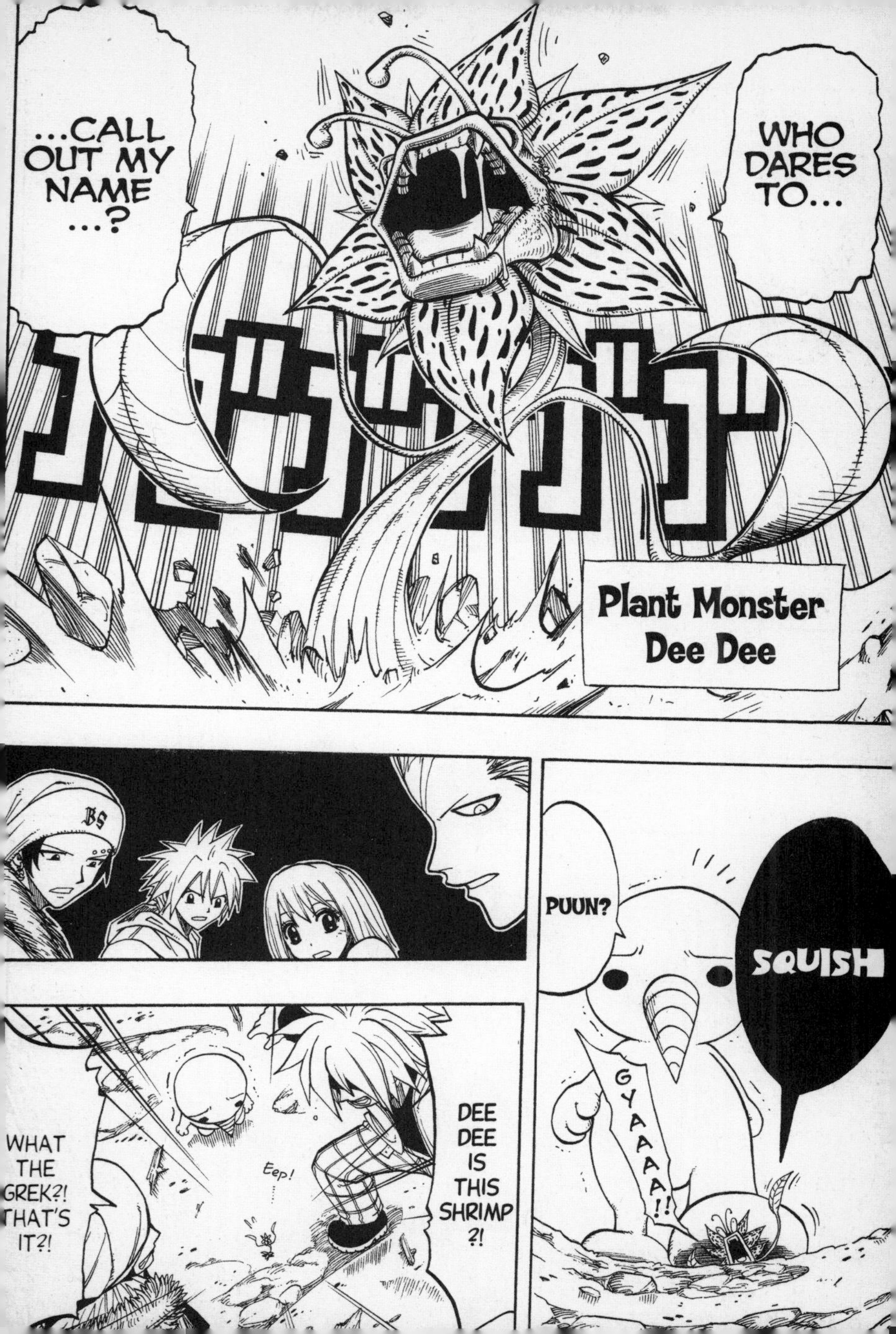
WHO DARES TO...
...CALL OUT MY NAME ...?
Plant Monster Dee Dee
PUUN?
SQUISH
GYAAAA!!
DEE DEE IS THIS SHRIMP?!
Eep!
WHAT THE GREK?! THAT'S IT?!

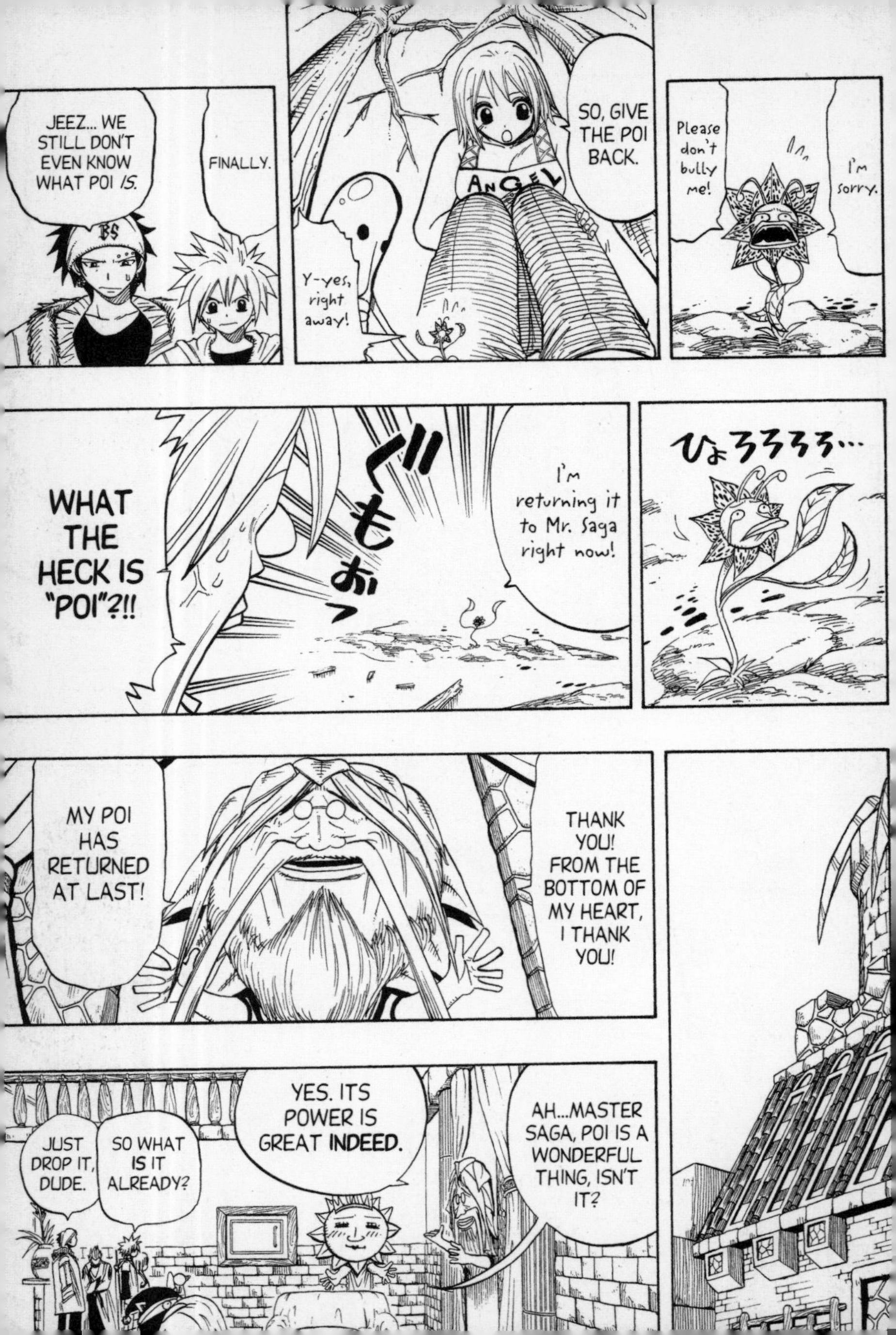
I'm sorry.
Please don't bully me!
SO, GIVE THE POI BACK.
Y-yes, right away!
FINALLY.
JEEZ... WE STILL DON'T EVEN KNOW WHAT POI IS.
ひょろろろろ…
I'm returning it to Mr. Saga right now!
ぐもぉっ
WHAT THE HECK IS "POI"?!!
THANK YOU! FROM THE BOTTOM OF MY HEART, I THANK YOU!
MY POI HAS RETURNED AT LAST!
AH...MASTER SAGA, POI IS A WONDERFUL THING, ISN'T IT?
YES. ITS POWER IS GREAT INDEED.
SO WHAT IS IT ALREADY?
JUST DROP IT, DUDE.

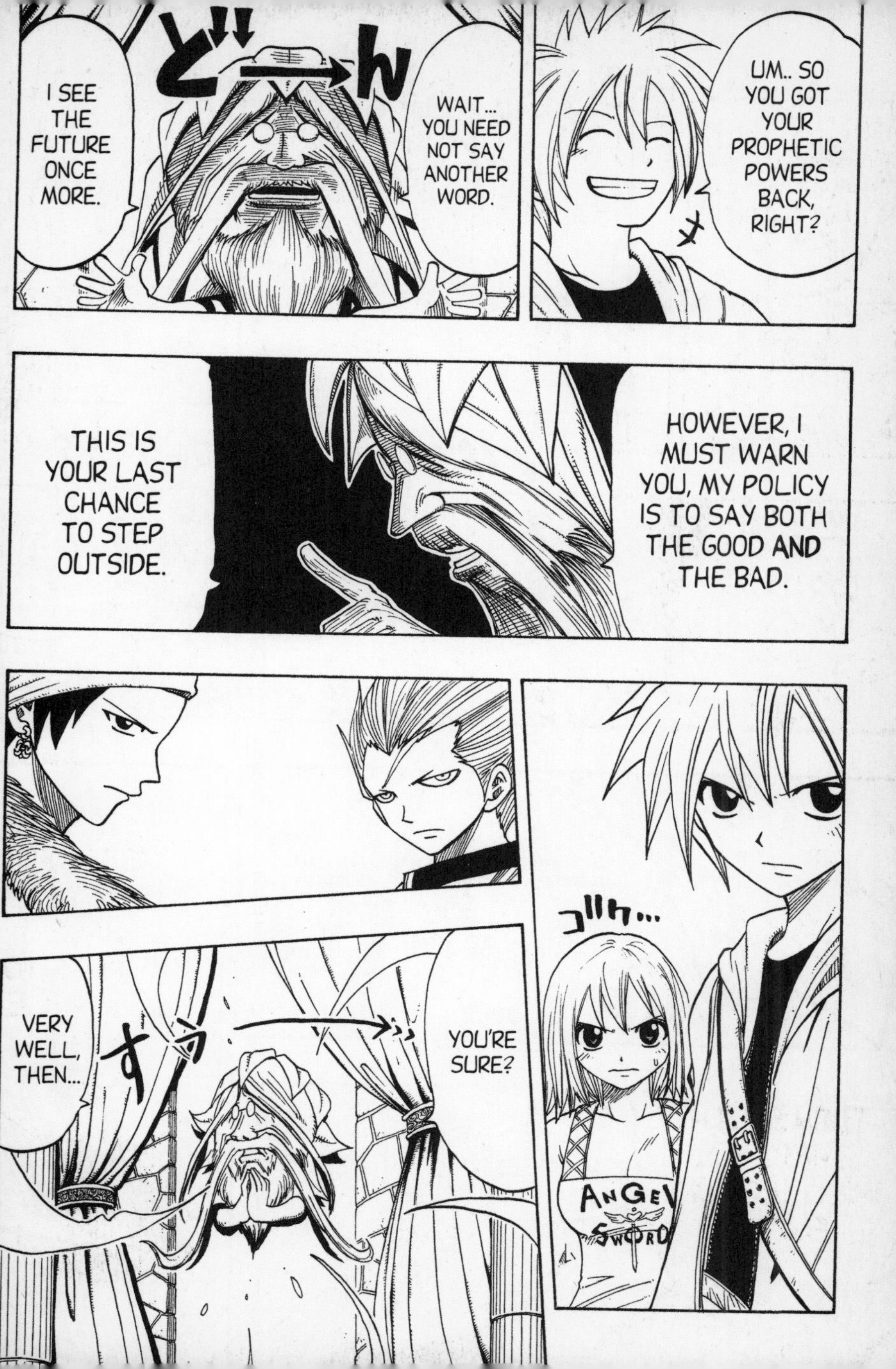
UM.. SO YOU GOT YOUR PROPHETIC POWERS BACK, RIGHT?
どーん
WAIT... YOU NEED NOT SAY ANOTHER WORD.
I SEE THE FUTURE ONCE MORE.
HOWEVER, I MUST WARN YOU, MY POLICY IS TO SAY BOTH THE GOOD AND THE BAD.
THIS IS YOUR LAST CHANCE TO STEP OUTSIDE.
YOU'RE SURE?
VERY WELL, THEN...

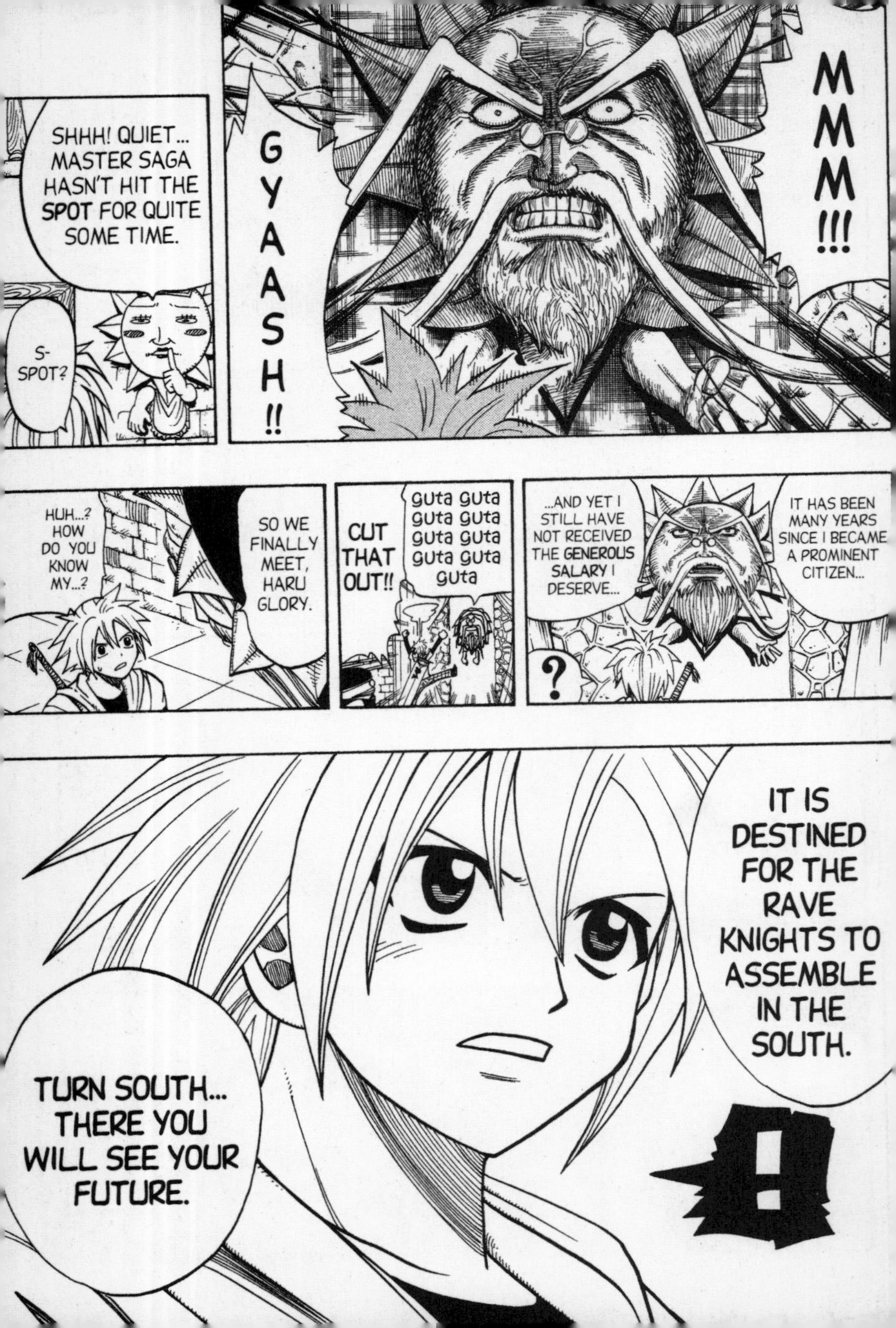
MMM!!!
GYAASH!!
SHHH! QUIET... MASTER SAGA HASN'T HIT THE SPOT FOR QUITE SOME TIME.
S-SPOT?
IT HAS BEEN MANY YEARS SINCE I BECAME A PROMINENT CITIZEN...
...AND YET I STILL HAVE NOT RECEIVED THE GENEROUS SALARY I DESERVE...
?
guta guta guta guta guta guta guta guta guta
CUT THAT OUT!!
SO WE FINALLY MEET, HARU GLORY.
HUH...? HOW DO YOU KNOW MY...?
IT IS DESTINED FOR THE RAVE KNIGHTS TO ASSEMBLE IN THE SOUTH.
!
TURN SOUTH... THERE YOU WILL SEE YOUR FUTURE.

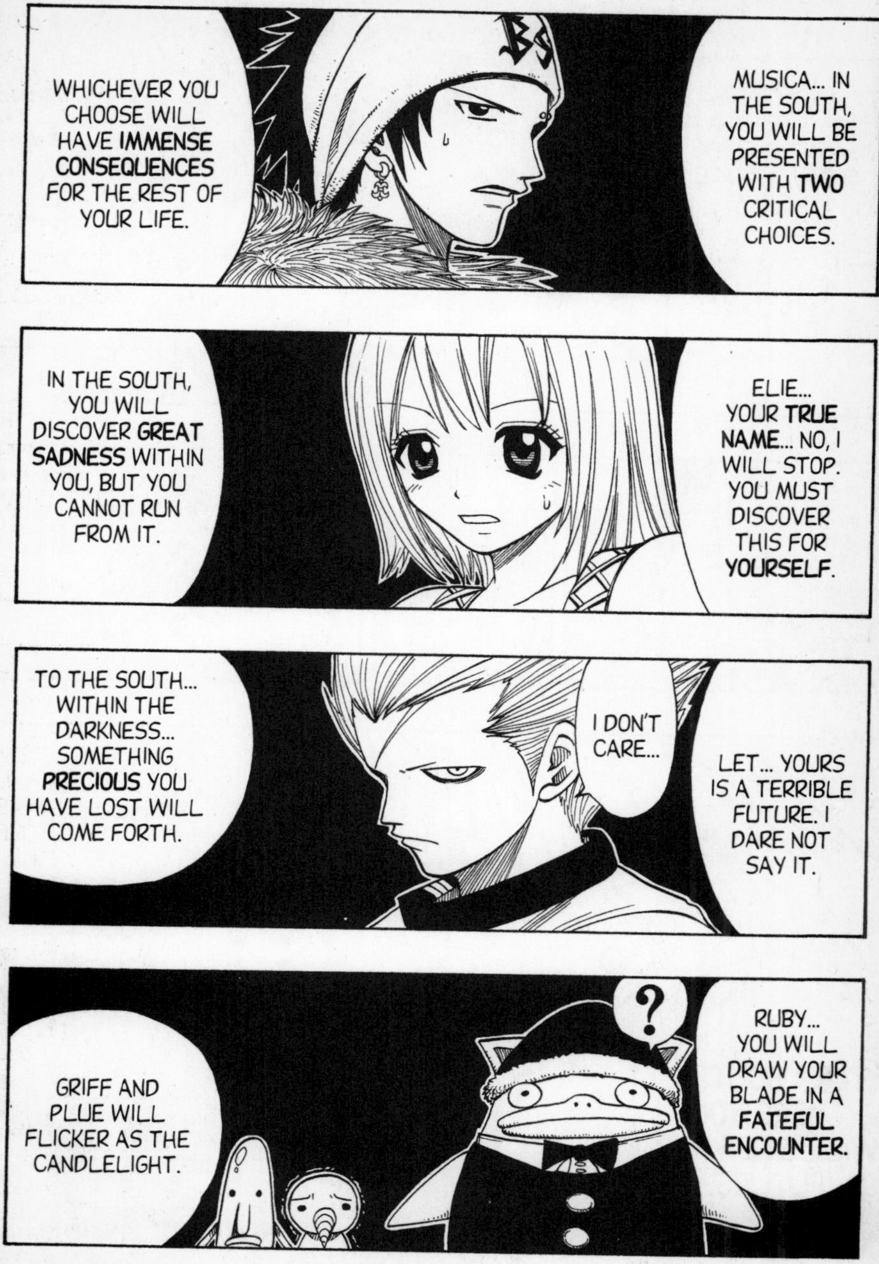
MUSICA... IN THE SOUTH, YOU WILL BE PRESENTED WITH **TWO** CRITICAL CHOICES.
WHICHEVER YOU CHOOSE WILL HAVE **IMMENSE CONSEQUENCES** FOR THE REST OF YOUR LIFE.
ELIE... YOUR **TRUE NAME**... NO, I WILL STOP. YOU MUST DISCOVER THIS FOR **YOURSELF**.
IN THE SOUTH, YOU WILL DISCOVER **GREAT SADNESS** WITHIN YOU, BUT YOU CANNOT RUN FROM IT.
LET... YOURS IS A TERRIBLE FUTURE. I DARE NOT SAY IT.
I DON'T CARE...
TO THE SOUTH... WITHIN THE DARKNESS... SOMETHING **PRECIOUS** YOU HAVE LOST WILL COME FORTH.
RUBY... YOU WILL DRAW YOUR BLADE IN A **FATEFUL ENCOUNTER**.
?
GRIFF AND PLUE WILL FLICKER AS THE CANDLELIGHT.

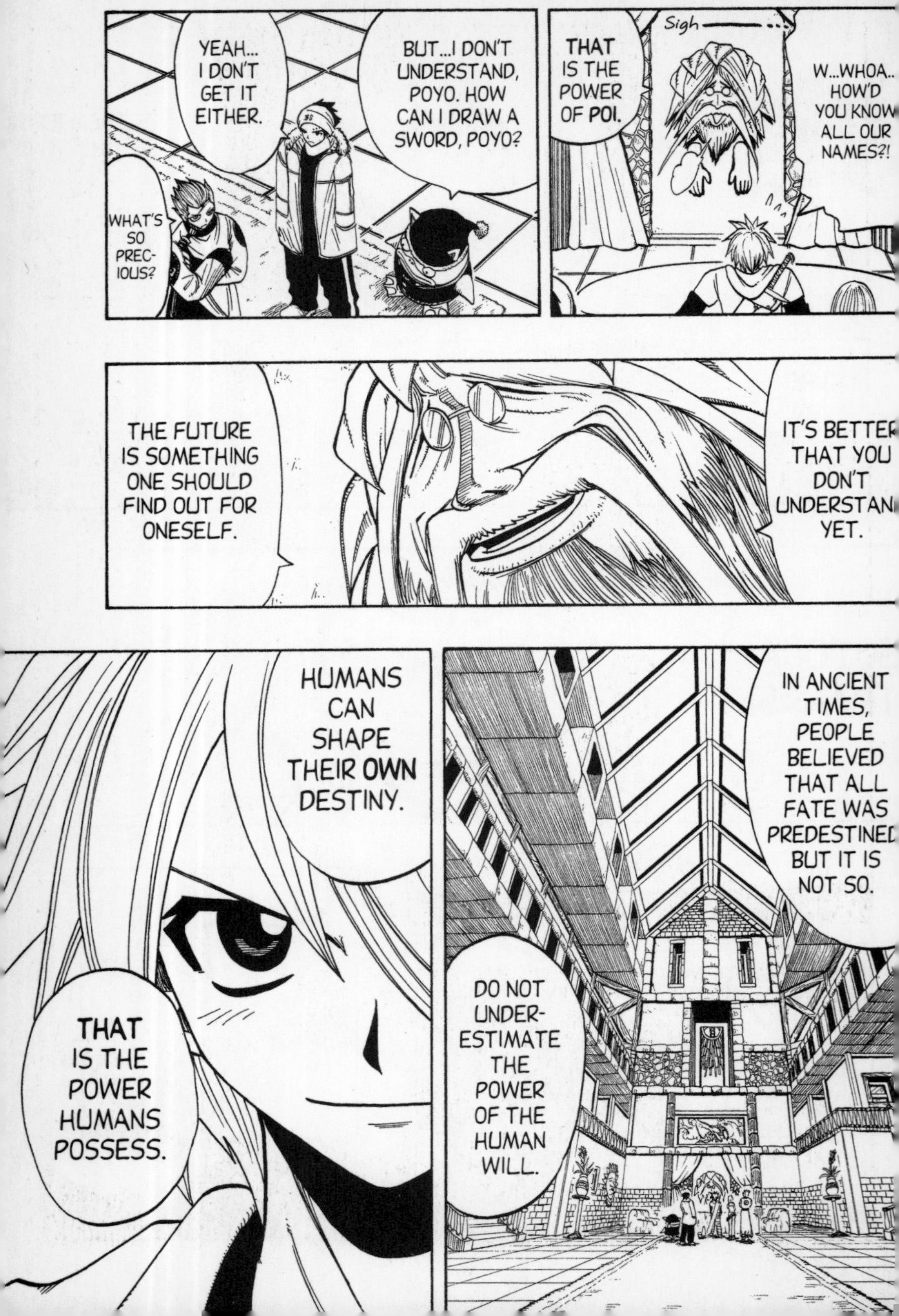
Sigh
W...WHOA.. HOW'D YOU KNOW ALL OUR NAMES?!
THAT IS THE POWER OF **POI**.
BUT...I DON'T UNDERSTAND, POYO. HOW CAN I DRAW A SWORD, POYO?
YEAH... I DON'T GET IT EITHER.
WHAT'S SO PREC-IOUS?
IT'S BETTER THAT YOU DON'T UNDERSTAN YET.
THE FUTURE IS SOMETHING ONE SHOULD FIND OUT FOR ONESELF.
IN ANCIENT TIMES, PEOPLE BELIEVED THAT ALL FATE WAS PREDESTINED BUT IT IS NOT SO.
DO NOT UNDER-ESTIMATE THE POWER OF THE HUMAN WILL.
HUMANS CAN SHAPE THEIR **OWN** DESTINY.
THAT IS THE POWER HUMANS POSSESS.

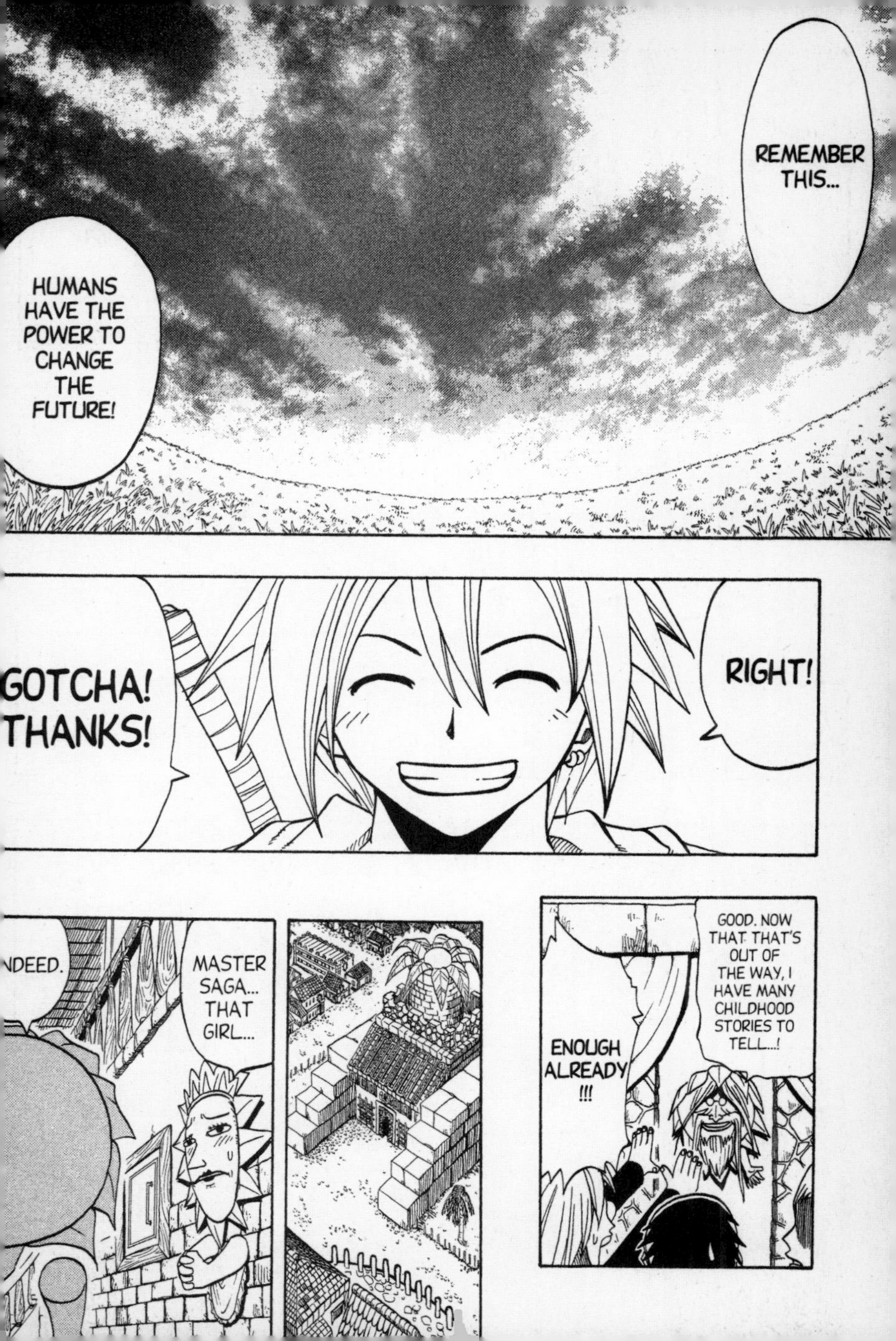
REMEMBER THIS...
HUMANS HAVE THE POWER TO CHANGE THE FUTURE!
RIGHT!
GOTCHA! THANKS!
GOOD. NOW THAT THAT'S OUT OF THE WAY, I HAVE MANY CHILDHOOD STORIES TO TELL...!
ENOUGH ALREADY!!!
MASTER SAGA... THAT GIRL...
NDEED.

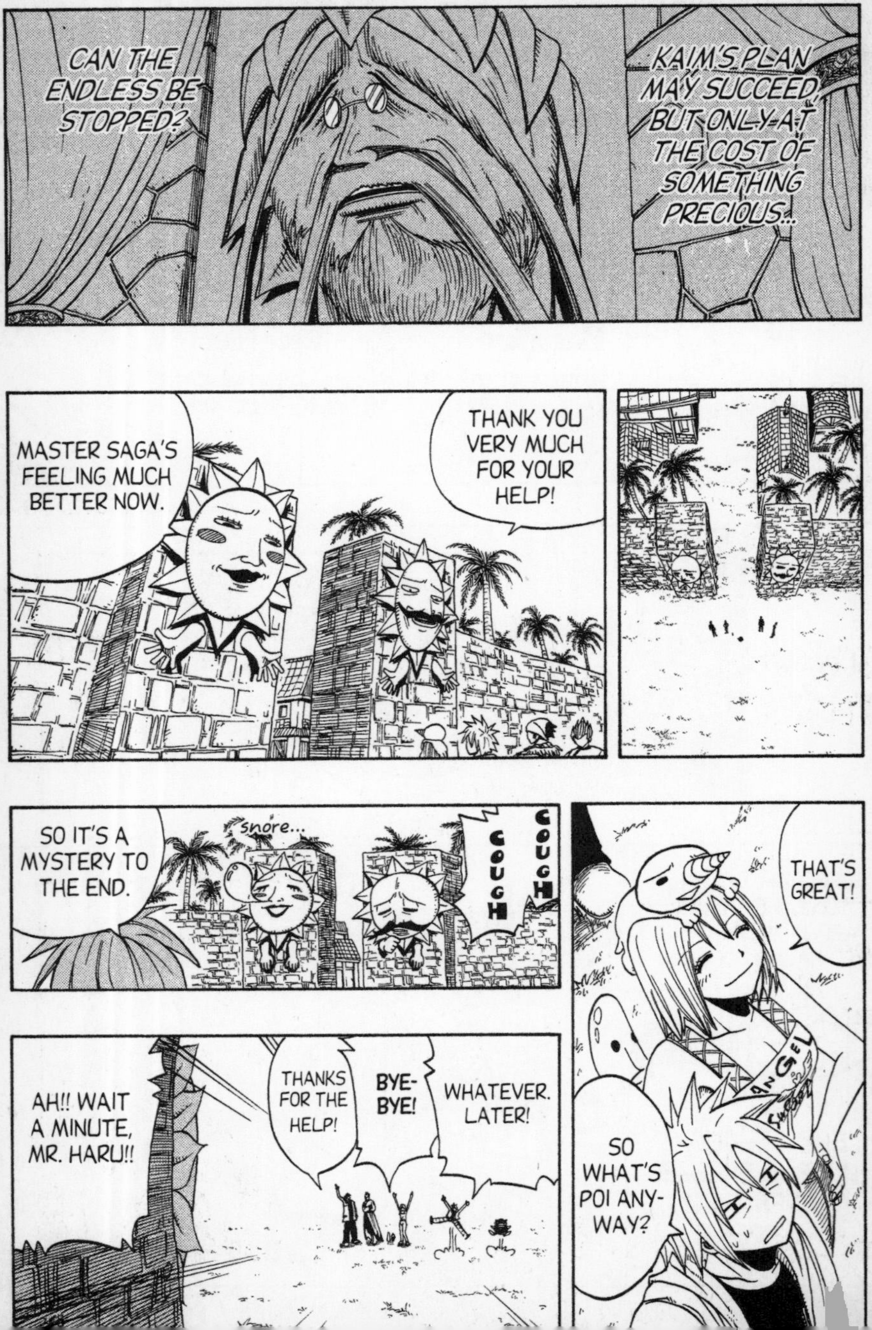
KAIM'S PLAN MAY SUCCEED, BUT ONLY AT THE COST OF SOMETHING PRECIOUS...
CAN THE ENDLESS BE STOPPED?
THANK YOU VERY MUCH FOR YOUR HELP!
MASTER SAGA'S FEELING MUCH BETTER NOW.
THAT'S GREAT!
SO WHAT'S POI ANY-WAY?
COUGH
COUGH
snore...
SO IT'S A MYSTERY TO THE END.
WHATEVER. LATER!
BYE-BYE!
THANKS FOR THE HELP!
AH!! WAIT A MINUTE, MR. HARU!!

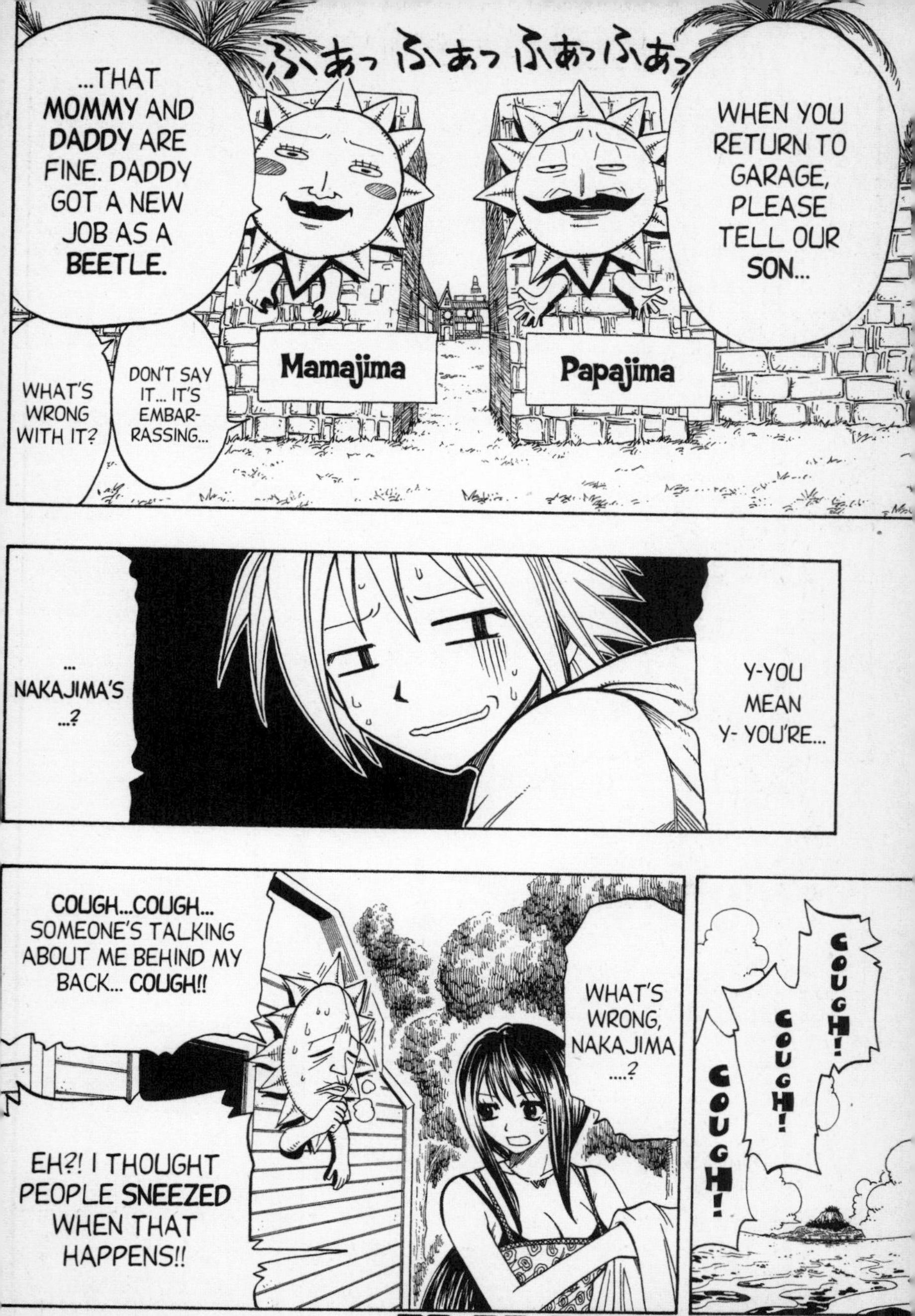

ふあっふあっふあっふあっ
WHEN YOU RETURN TO GARAGE, PLEASE TELL OUR SON...
...THAT MOMMY AND DADDY ARE FINE. DADDY GOT A NEW JOB AS A BEETLE.
Papajima
Mamajima
DON'T SAY IT... IT'S EMBAR-RASSING...
WHAT'S WRONG WITH IT?
Y-YOU MEAN Y- YOU'RE...
... NAKAJIMA'S ...?
COUGH!
COUGH!
COUGH!
WHAT'S WRONG, NAKAJIMA ....?
COUGH...COUGH... SOMEONE'S TALKING ABOUT ME BEHIND MY BACK... COUGH!!
EH?! I THOUGHT PEOPLE SNEEZED WHEN THAT HAPPENS!!

TO BE CONTINUED

Character Profiles

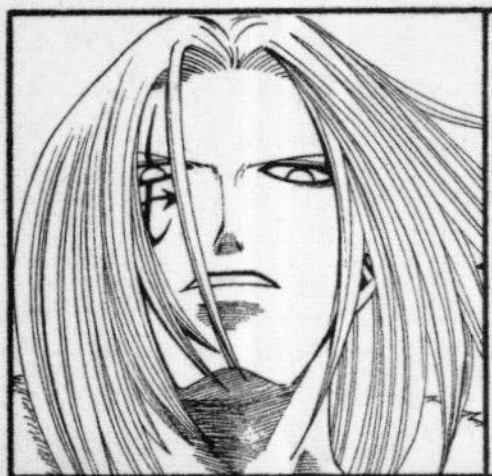

MEMBER OF THE ORACION SIX: DRAGON MASTER JEGAN

① GREAT SWORD & DB (YGDRASSIL)
② MARCH 13, 0041/26 YRS
③ 179CM/72KG/UNKNOWN
④ BRAYA VILLAGE (MYSTIC REALM)
⑤ KEEPING DRAGONS
⑥ HYPNOSIS
⑦ JULIA, DRAGONS
⑧ LET

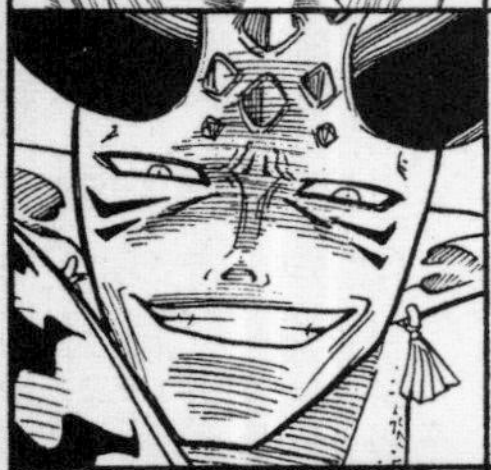

MEMBER OF THE ORACION SIX: DEMON COUNT BERIAL

① DB (THE EARTH)
② AUGUST 20, 9864/202 YRS
③ 245CM/113KG/UNKNOWN
④ MYSTIC REALM
⑤ KILLING
⑥ GEOLOGY
⑦ TERRIFYING HUMANS
⑧ ANYTHING THAT WOUNDS HIS EGO

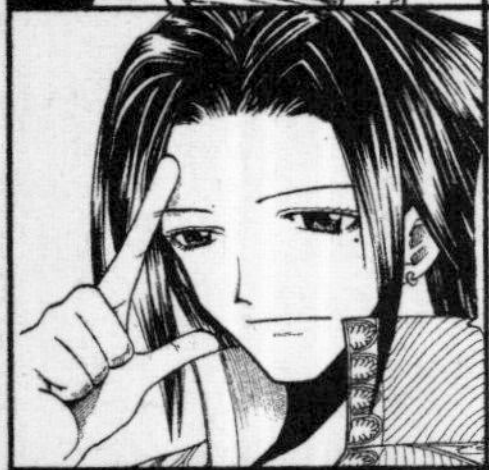

MEMBER OF THE ORACION SIX: FROST MAGIC SWORDSMAN IULIUS

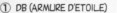

① DB (ARMURE D'ETOILE)
② SEPT. 17, 0043/23 YRS
③ 176CM/60KG/TYPE A
④ UNKNOWN
⑤ GAZING AT HIS MIRROR
⑥ PAINTING
⑦ BEAUTIFUL THINGS
⑧ UGLY THINGS

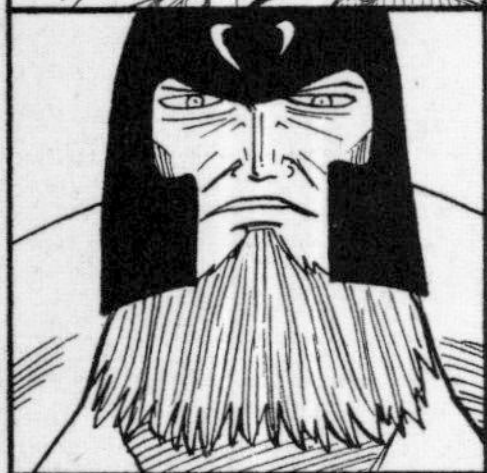

MEMBER OF THE ORACION SIX: HAJA THE INFINITE

① MAGIC & DB (?)
② UNKNOWN/UNKNOWN
③ UNKNOWN/UNKNOWN/UNKNOWN
④ UNKNOWN
⑤ UNKNOWN
⑥ INFINITE MAGICAL POWER
⑦ UNKNOWN
⑧ UNKNOWN

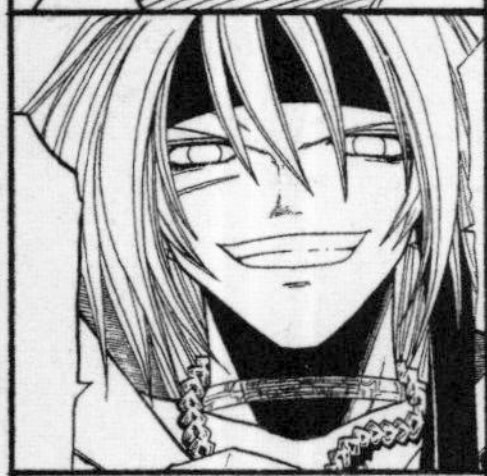

SECOND COMMANDER OF DEMON CARD: LUCIA RAREGROOVE

① SWORD & DB (DECALOGUE)
MOTHER DB (SINCLAIRE)
OTHER DB (?)
② JULY 7, 0050/16 YRS
③ 170CM/57KG/TYPE B
④ MARRY LOOSE → MEGA UNIT
⑤ FIGHTING
⑥ USING DARK BRINGS
⑦ POWER & DARKNESS
⑧ KINDNESS & LIGHT

LEGEND ▷

① WEAPON ② B-DAY/AGE ③ HEIGHT/WEIGHT/BLOOD TYPE
④ BIRTHPLACE ⑤ HOBBY ⑥ SPECIALTY ⑦ LIKES ⑧ DISLIKES

ABOUT THE CHARACTERS

JEGAN'S REALLY NOT A NICE GUY. MORE ACTION THAN WORDS. I'M SURE HE AND LET WILL SETTLE THINGS SOMEDAY. YGDRASSIL IS NAMED AFTER THE GIANT TREE OF NORSE MYTHOLOGY.

BERIAL MAY LOOK LIKE THE LOWLIEST OF THE ORACION SIX, BUT HE'S ALSO THE STRONGEST. HE MUST'VE ALWAYS BEEN A BIG GUY, EXCEPT WHEN HE WAS A BABY (^_^). HE GREW UP FAST, AT ANY RATE.

IULIUS. HE'S... PRETTY DENSE. I TRIED TO IMAGINE THE MOST DETESTABLE CHARACTER I COULD. ALL THAT "BEAUTIFUL... BEAUTIFUL" STUFF MAKES ME WANT TO HURL. NOW, HE MAY BE DENSE, BUT I REALLY ENJOYED DRAWING HIM. MAYBE THAT MAKES **ME** THE DENSE ONE. "ARMURE D'ETOILE" MEANS "STAR ARMOR" IN FRENCH.

HAJA.... NOW HERE'S AN ODD DUCK! STARTING WITH HIS NAME-- "HAJA" IS ALSO A JAPANESE WAY TO SAY "EVIL." NOT THAT I THOUGHT OF THAT AT THE TIME! HONEST! SOMETIMES EVEN AUTHORS MISS THESE KINDS OF THINGS UNTIL AFTER THE FACT. THIS TIME I GOT LUCKY.

I DON'T WANT TO WRITE TOO MUCH ABOUT LUCIA YET, BUT THERE'S A BIG SECRET ABOUT HIM BESIDES BEING KING'S SON. SOMETHING RELATING TO HARU... I WON'T WRITE ANOTHER THING ABOUT IT...YET.

EVERYTHING ABOUT LUCIA WAS DECIDED AROUND VOL. 9, CHAPT. 65. IT WASN'T EASY, EITHER!

Aw snap! Mermaid babes imprisoned?! Who would do it?! Come on, Rave Master–don't let this injustice stand!

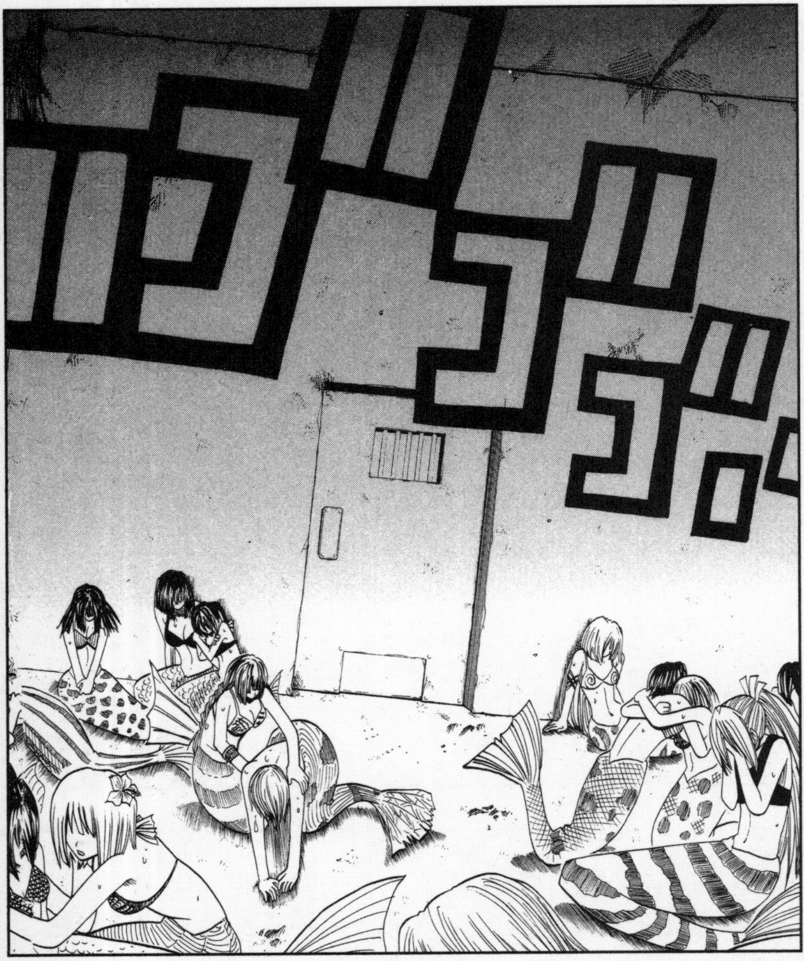

Pumpkin Doryu and his Ghost Attack Squad are at it again! It's out of the frying pan and into the fire in the next issue of Rave Master!!

Rave Master Volume 13
Available February 2005

RAVE0077
Levin Minds the House

11 - IT'S HUGE!

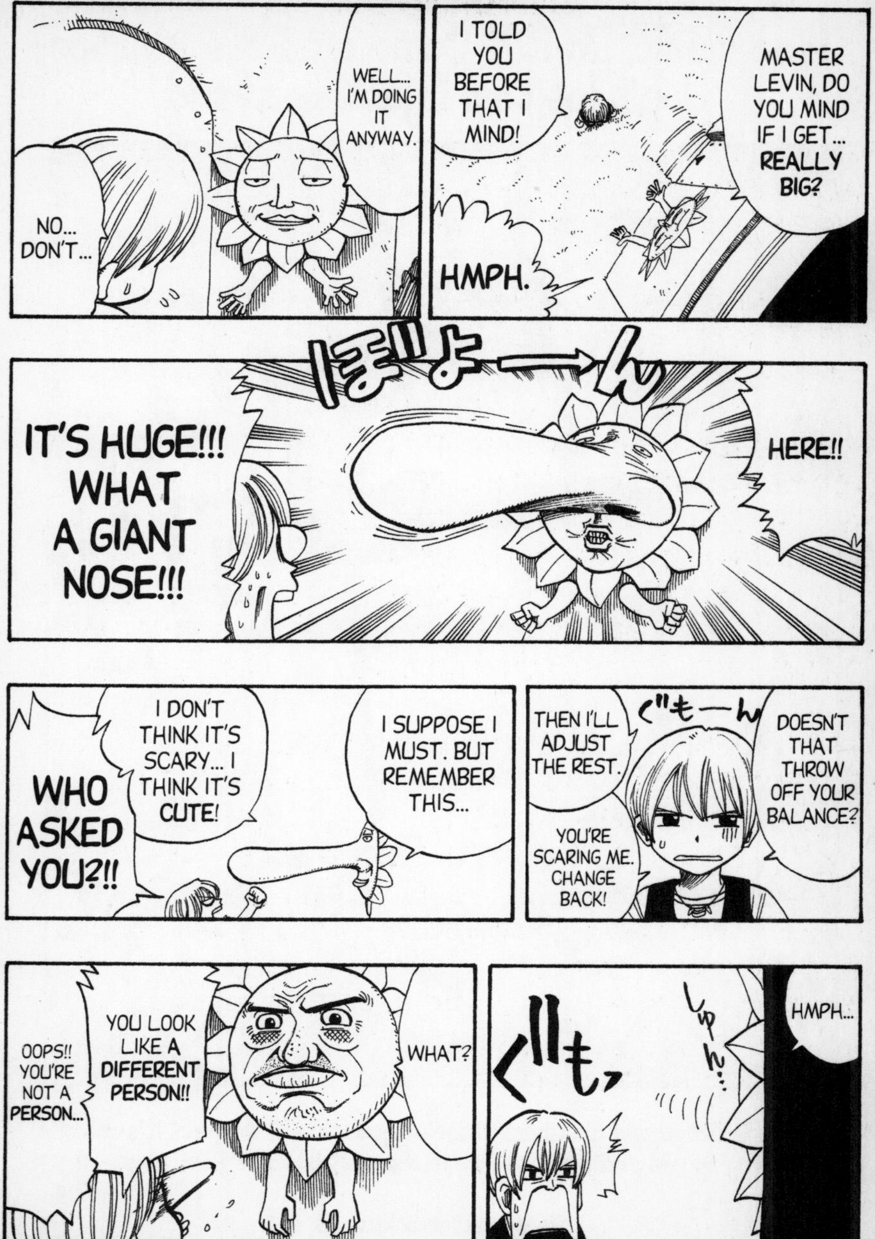

MASTER LEVIN, DO YOU MIND IF I GET... REALLY BIG?
I TOLD YOU BEFORE THAT I MIND!
HMPH.
WELL... I'M DOING IT ANYWAY.
NO... DON'T...
ぼよーん
HERE!!
IT'S HUGE!!! WHAT A GIANT NOSE!!!
DOESN'T THAT THROW OFF YOUR BALANCE?
ぐもーん
THEN I'LL ADJUST THE REST.
YOU'RE SCARING ME. CHANGE BACK!
I SUPPOSE I MUST. BUT REMEMBER THIS...
I DON'T THINK IT'S SCARY... I THINK IT'S CUTE!
WHO ASKED YOU?!!
HMPH...
しゅん...
ぐもっ
WHAT?
YOU LOOK LIKE A DIFFERENT PERSON!!
OOPS!! YOU'RE NOT A PERSON...

TO BE CONTINUED...?

"AFTERWORDS"

GINYA!! THAT'S ALL MY ONLY ASSISTANT EVER SAYS WHILE HE'S AT WORK. GINYA!! DOESN'T MATTER WHAT TIME IT IS... NO... I'LL STOP HERE. I'M NOT GOING TO MAKE A BIG DEAL OUT OF IT.

I WON'T DENY THAT IT'S WHAT GAVE BIRTH TO ALICE'S "MUNYA!"... BUT I'VE BEEN MEANING TO HAVE A CHARACTER TALK LIKE ALICE FOR A WHILE NOW. I GUESS I JUST LIKE WRITING WEIRD DIALOGUE. WELL, IT'S NOT LIKE MAKING THIS STUFF IS EASY. ROMANTIC TALK AND EXPRESSING DEEP EMOTION... THAT'S TOUGH, TOO. ALSO, WHAT PEOPLE GRUMBLE WHEN THEY'VE BEEN BEATEN... ANYWAY, AFTER ALL THE STUFF ABOUT ELIE GETTING INJURED, THEN FINDING OUT ABOUT HER PARENTS' DEATHS, I JUST HAD TO DRAW IT. (^_^) THEN THE ACAPPELLA ISLAND CHAPTER! I'VE WANTED TO DO THAT ONE FOR A WHILE. REMEMBER THAT SAGA PENDRAGON'S NAME FIRST CAME UP ON THE FIRST PAGE OF CHAPT. 57? NO? WELL, THAT'S FINE THEN.

WHEN I WAS REREADING THIS VOLUME, I REALIZED JUST HOW MUCH FORESHADOWING IT HAD IN IT. THAT BIG "CAN SHE TAKE IT ALL!?!" FEELING CAME UP MORE THAN ONCE. HEY, EVERYTHING'S A MYSTERY UNTIL THE FINAL VOLUME. OH, THAT'S RIGHT... "HOW MANY VOLUMES IS RAVE MASTER GONNA GO?" I GET ASKED THAT A LOT, BUT SORRY, IT HASN'T BEEN DECIDED YET! I WAS THINKING IT COULD GO ANYWHERE FROM 20 TO 30 VOLUMES. IT ALL DEPENDS ON IF I CAN THINK OF MORE INTERESTING STORIES. AT THIS RATE, IT COULD BE WRAPPED UP BY 15, OR GO AS LONG AS 50. WELL, WHATEVER THE CASE, STICK WITH ME UNTIL IT'S DONE, EVERYONE!!

I'M NOT DONE YET. GINYA!!

- HIRO MASHIMA

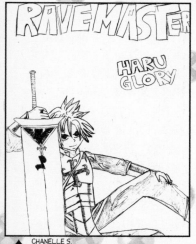

RAVE MASTER™ Fan Art

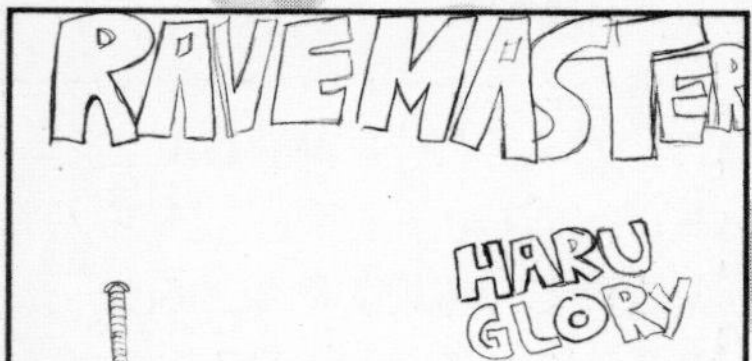
RAVEMASTER
HARU GLORY

CHANELLE S.
MARTINEZE, CA

HARU'S ALL DECKED OUT FOR BATTLE! HE LOOKS READY TO TAKE ON ANYBODY. BUT COULD HE SURVIVE ANOTHER DUEL WITH LUCIA? I GUESS WE'LL JUST HAVE TO WAIT AND SEE!

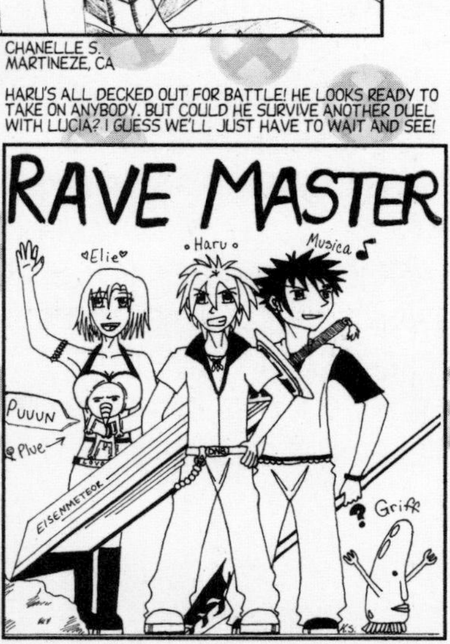
RAVE MASTER
Elie
Haru
Musica
PUUUN
Plue
EISENMETEOR
Griff
K.S.

KASEY S.
WINLOCK, WA

THE RAVE GANG! IT'S NICE TO SEE GRIFF WASN'T LEFT OUT. BUT WHY DOES PLUE HAVE EARS? OH WAIT... THOSE ARE ELIE'S–NEVER MIND...

HEY, ASPIRING MANGA ARTISTS! WANT TO SEE YOUR PICTURES IN PRINT? WELL, IF YOU THINK YOU CAN DRAW A COOL-LOOKING HARU, A SEXY ELIE OR A FUNNY PLUE, SEND 'EM THIS WAY! WE'LL PICK ONE LUCKY WINNER FROM EACH ROUND AND SEND THEM A SPECIAL PRIZE! WHAT DO HAVE TO LOSE? NOTHING!

HOW TO SUBMIT:

1) SEND YOUR WORK VIA REGULAR MAIL (NOT E-MAIL) TO:

RAVE MASTER FAN ART
C/O TOKYOPOP
5900 WILSHIRE BLVD.
SUITE 2000
LOS ANGELES, CA 90036

2) ALL WORK SUBMITTED SHOULD BE IN BLACK-AND-WHITE AND NO LARGER THAN 8.5" X 11". (AND TRY NOT TO FOLD IT TOO MANY TIMES!)

3) ANYTHING YOU SEND WILL NOT BE RETURNED. IF YOU WANT TO KEEP YOUR ORIGINAL, IT'S FINE TO SEND US A COPY.

4) PLEASE INCLUDE YOUR FULL NAME, AGE, CITY AND STATE FOR US TO PRINT WITH YOUR WORK. IF YOU'D RATHER US USE A PEN NAME, PLEASE INCLUDE THAT TOO.

5) IMPORTANT: IF YOU'RE UNDER THE AGE OF 18, YOU MUST HAVE YOUR PARENT'S PERMISSION IN ORDER FOR US TO PRINT YOUR WORK. ANY SUBMISSIONS WITHOUT A SIGNED NOTE OF PARENTAL CONSENT CANNOT BE USED.

6) FOR FULL DETAILS, PLEASE CHECK OUT HTTP://WWW.TOKYOPOP.COM/ABOUTUS/FANART.PHP

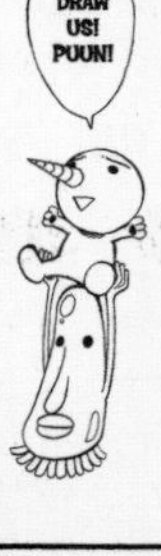
DRAW US! PUUN!

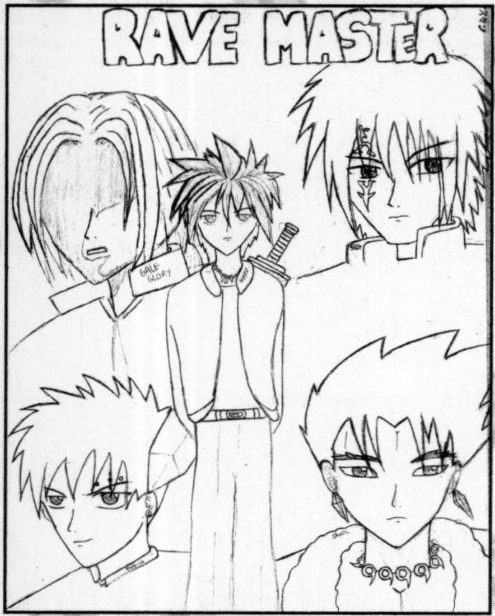
RAVE MASTER

YASMINE R.
AGE 15
SEASIDE, CA

ALL THE RAVER BOYS. GALE'S GONE FOR GOOD. WILL WE EVER SEE SHUDA AGAIN...? THANKS FOR THE COOL PIC!

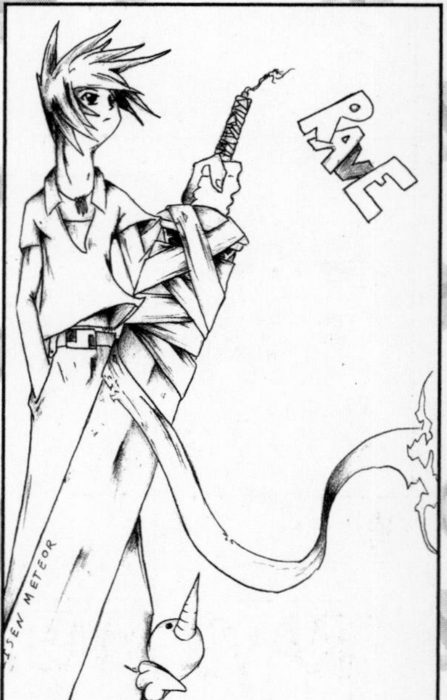
RAVE

TAYLOR Z.
WEST HAVEN, UT

WOW! COOL LOOKIN' HARU. IT ALMOST LOOKS LIKE HE'S OUT OF JING, TWILIGHT TALES. I LOVE THE WAY YOU DRAW PLUE, TOO.

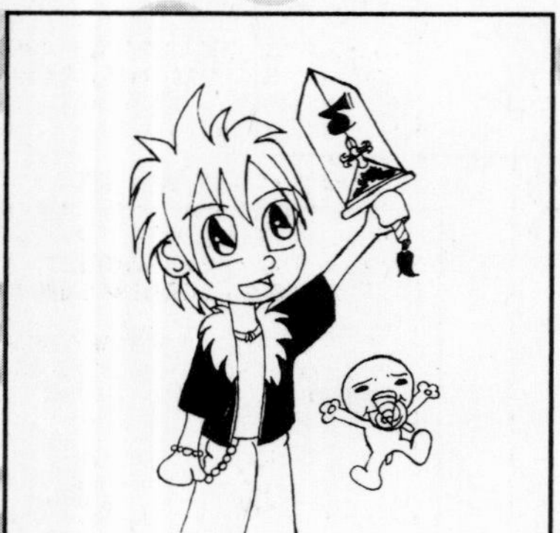

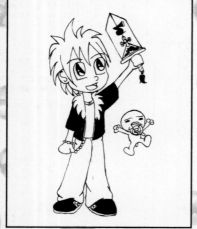

"HAFPINT"
SAN PABLO, CA

CHIBI HARU! SUCH A TINY SWORD—HOW IS HARU SUPPOSED TO SMITE THE FORCES OF DARKNESS WITH THAT?! I KNOW—HE'LL DEFEAT THEM WITH CUTENESS!

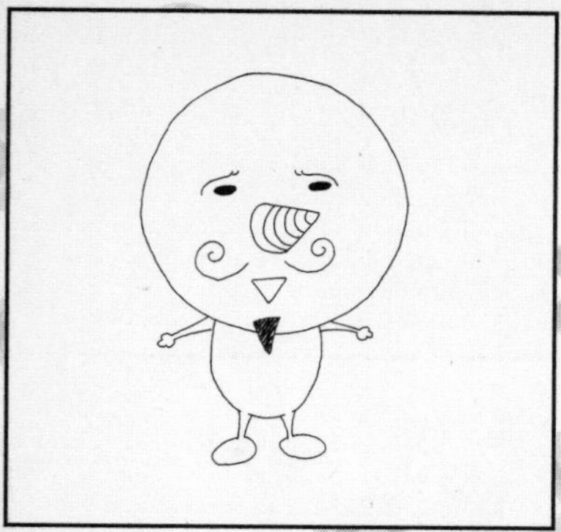

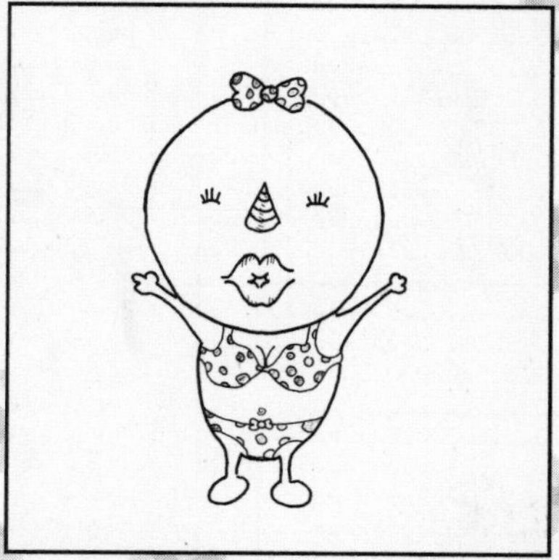

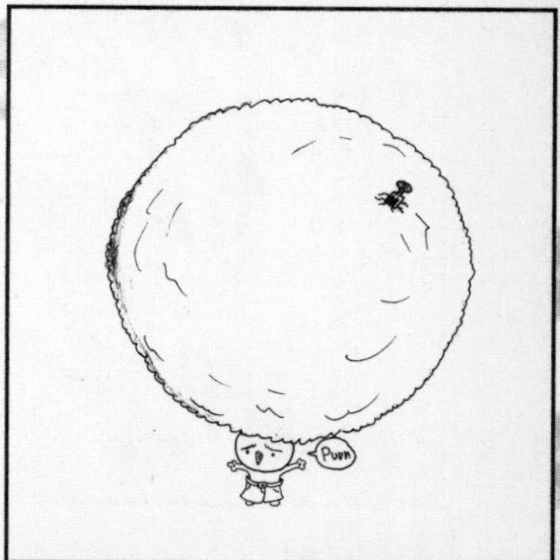
Puun

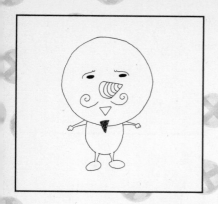

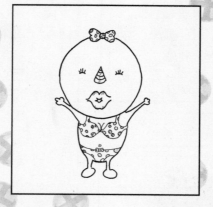

PETER M.
AGE 14
NEW WINSOR, NY

A TRIO OF TRICKED OUT PLUES! HOW CAN PLUE STAND UP WITH AN AFRO THAT BIG? AND PLUE IN A BIKINI...SCARY!!

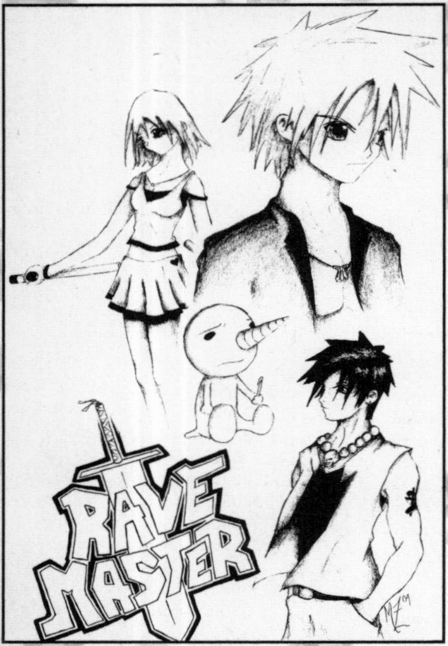
RAVE MASTER

MADISON Z.
AGE 16
WEST HAVEN, UT

GREAT STYLE. YOUR SHADING IS AMAZING! YOU EVEN MADE YOUR OWN VERSION OF THE LOGO. POOR PLUE, THOUGH—NO MORE SUCKER!

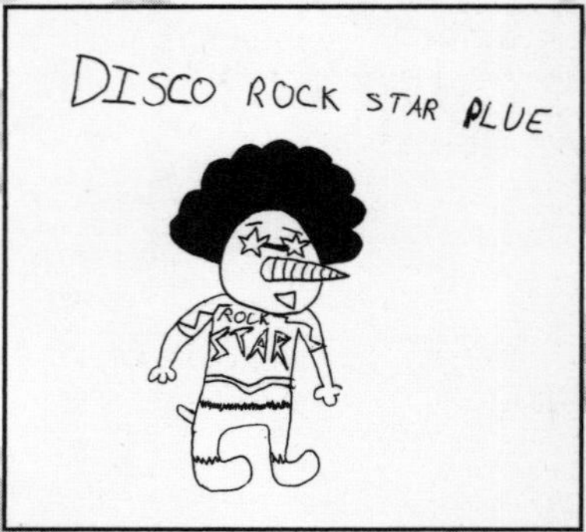
DISCO ROCK STAR PLUE
ROCK STAR

JONATHAN M.
AGE 11
POMPANO BEACH, FL

THE RAVE BEARER ALL DRESSED UP FOR A RAVE! ROCK ON, DAWG!

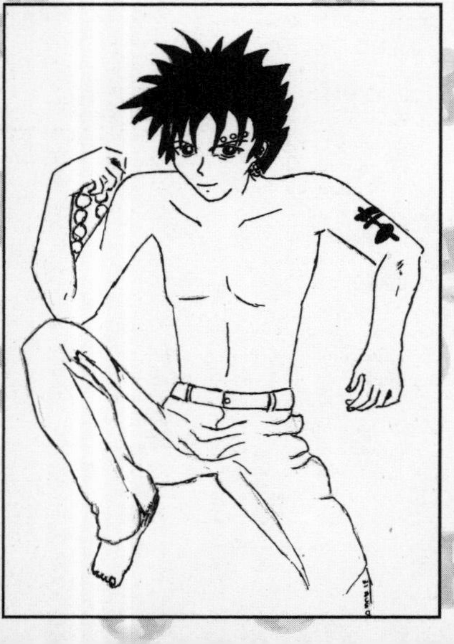

MARHEA N.
AGE 18
FALBROOK, CA

SEXY LOOKIN' MUSICA! "HEY, DUDE! PUT YOUR SHIRT ON!" OH WELL, LET THE LADIES HAVE THEIR HUNK.

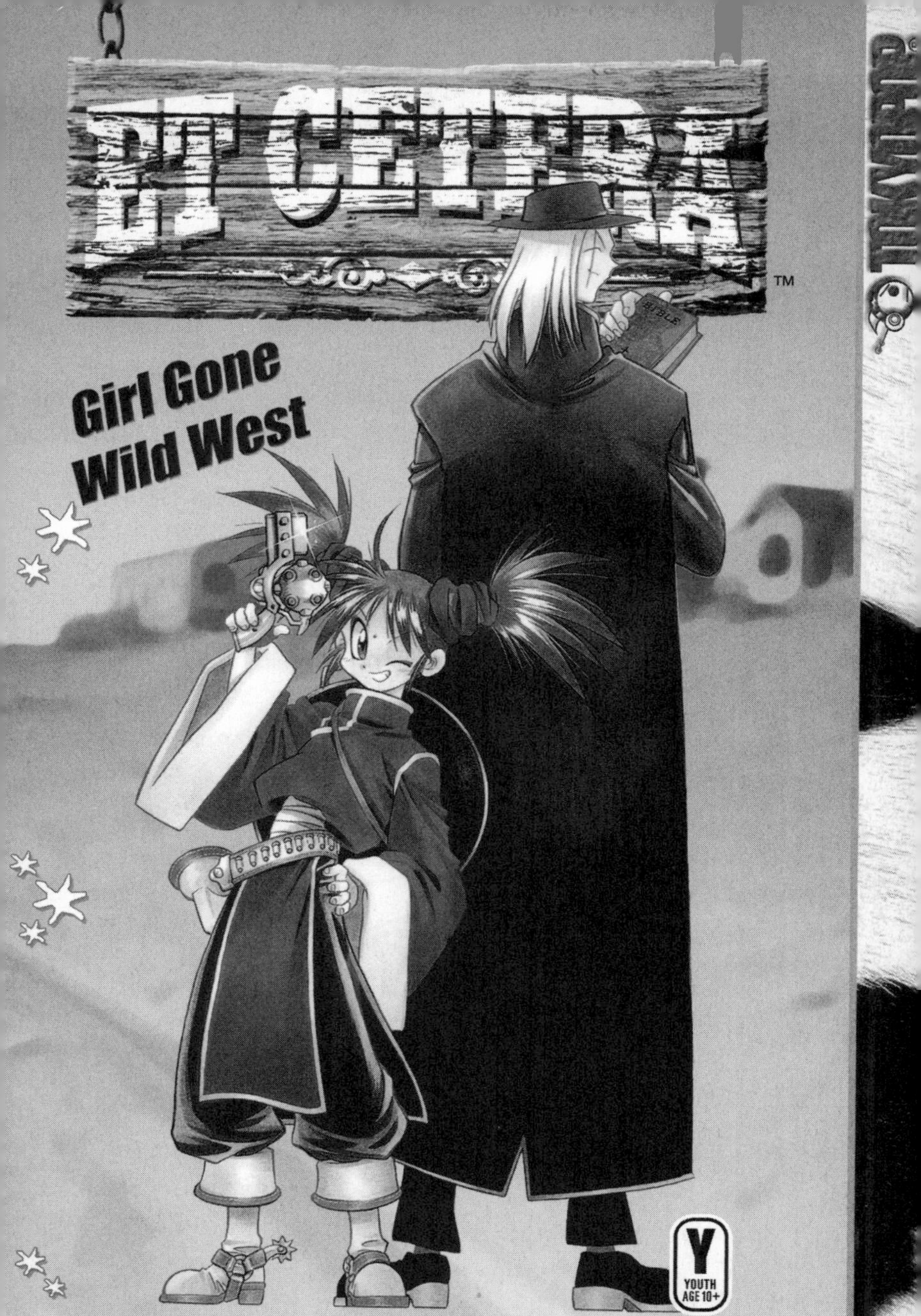
Girl Gone
Wild West
BIBLE
Y
YOUTH
AGE 10+
TOKYOPOP

www.TOKYOPOP.com

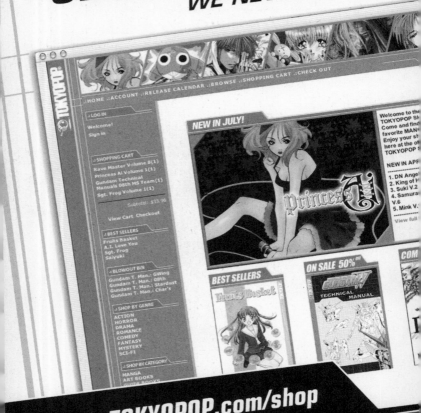

BOYS BE™

A GUY'S GUIDE TO GIRLS

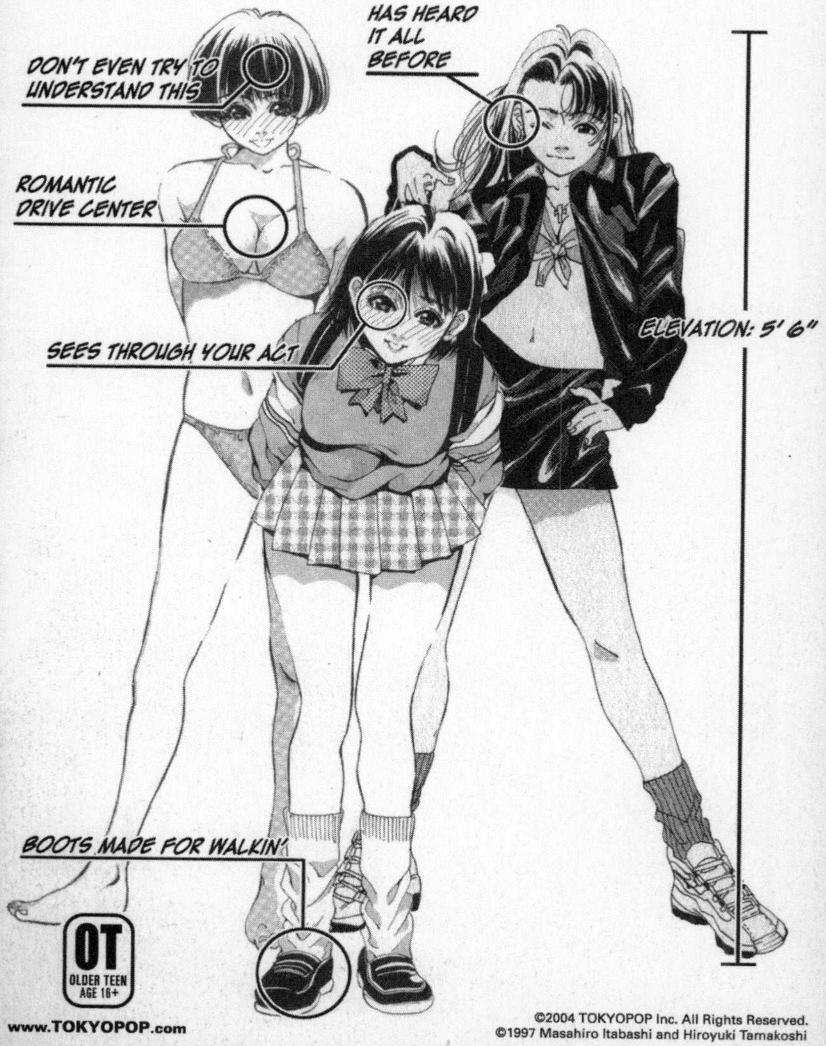
HAS HEARD IT ALL BEFORE
DON'T EVEN TRY TO UNDERSTAND THIS
ROMANTIC DRIVE CENTER
ELEVATION: 5' 6"
SEES THROUGH YOUR ACT
BOOTS MADE FOR WALKIN'
OT
OLDER TEEN
AGE 16+

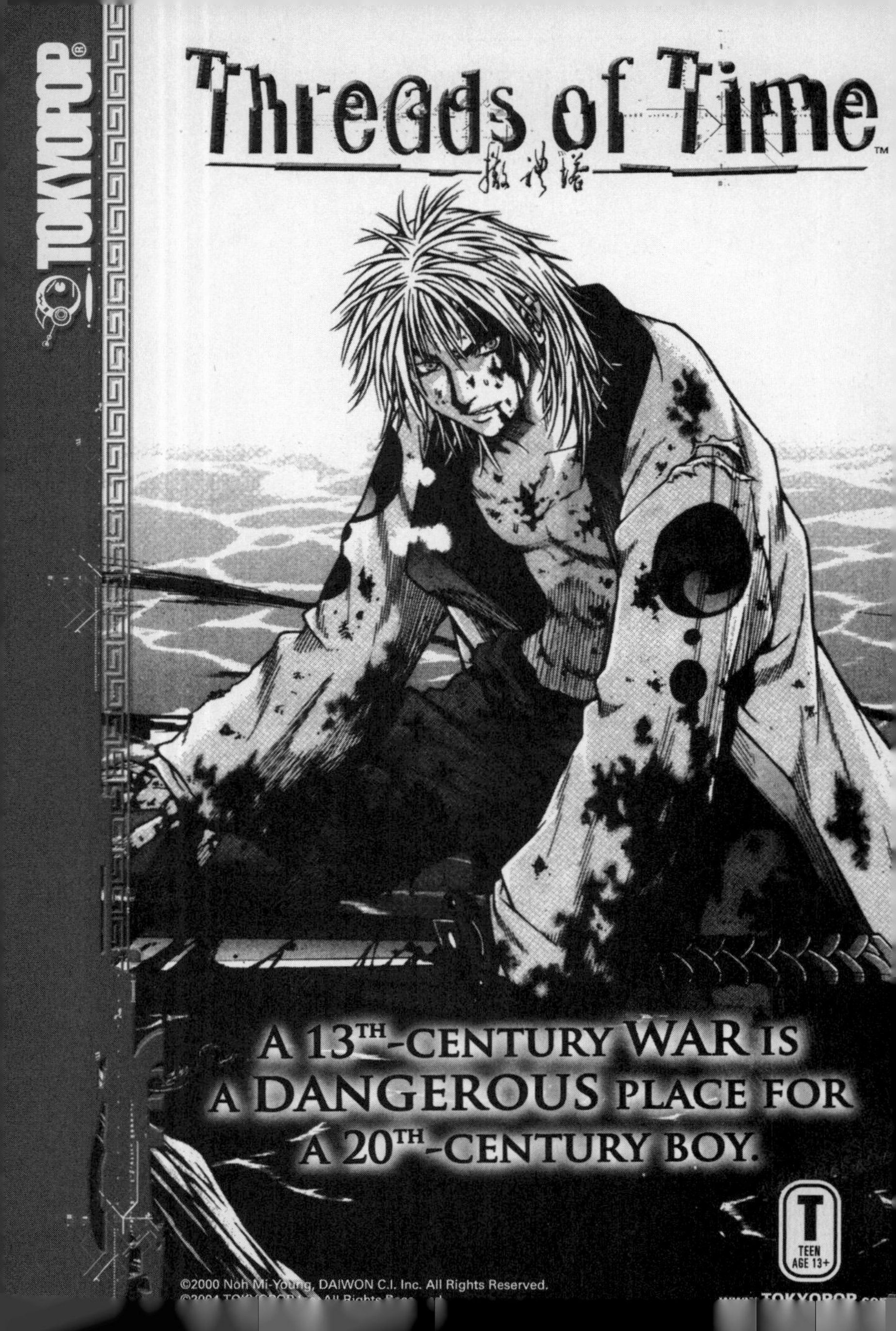
TOKYOPOP®
Threads of Time™
A 13TH-CENTURY WAR IS
A DANGEROUS PLACE FOR
A 20TH-CENTURY BOY.
T
TEEN
AGE 13+
©2000 Noh Mi-Young, DAIWON C.I. Inc. All Rights Reserved.

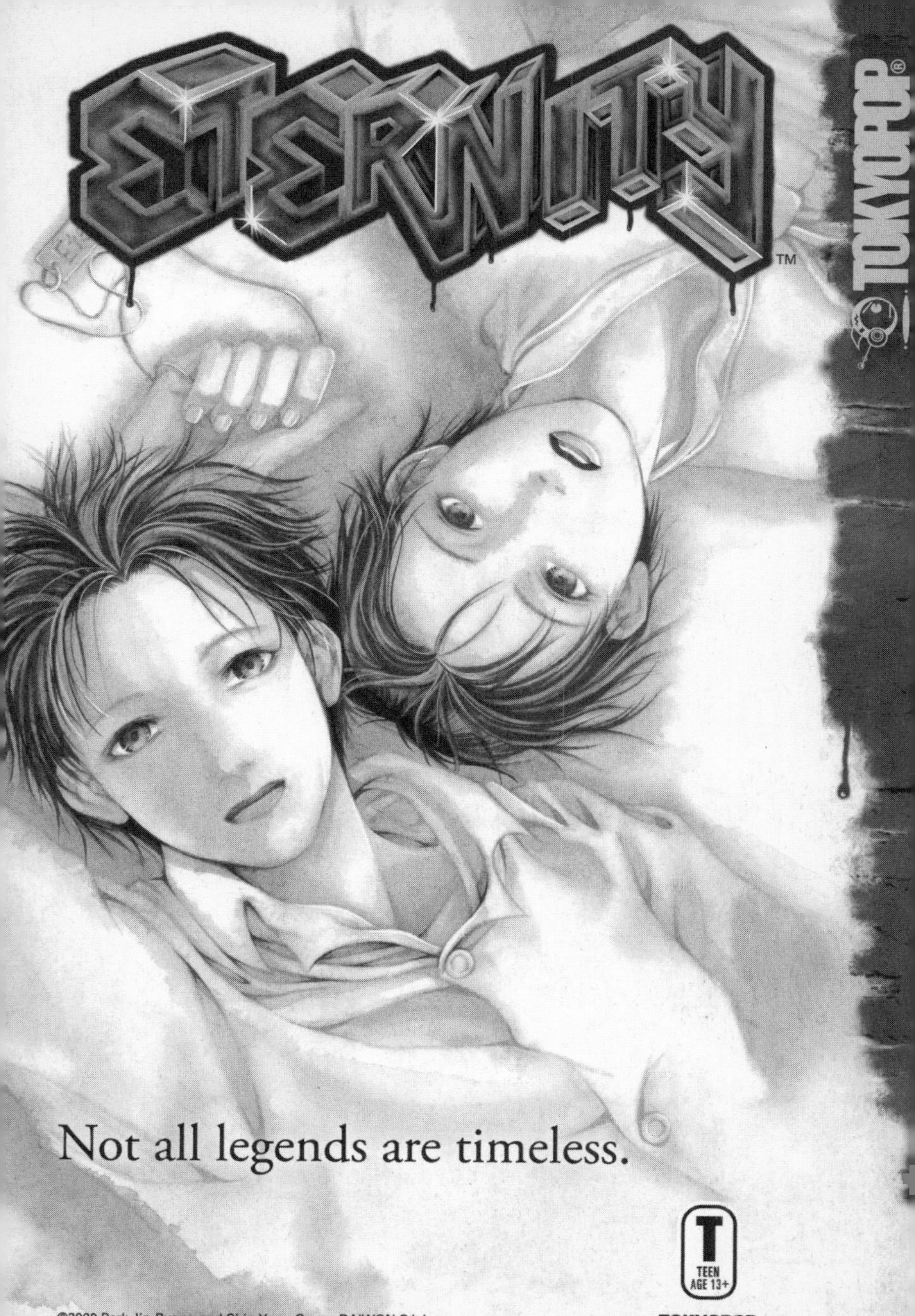
ETERNITY
TM
TOKYOPOP
Not all legends are timeless.
T
TEEN
AGE 13+

CHRONICLES OF THE
CURSED SWORD

BY YEO BEOP-RYONG

A living sword forged in darkness
A hero born outside the light
One can destroy the other
But both can save the world.

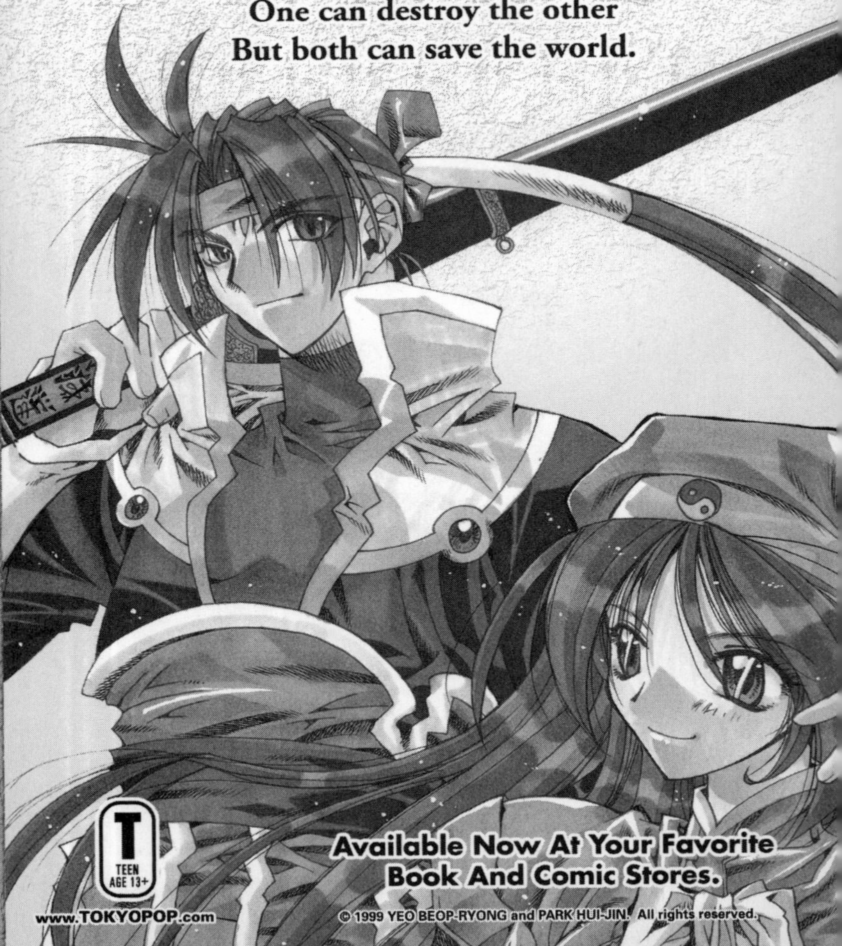

TOKYOPOP

**Available Now At Your Favorite
Book And Comic Stores.**

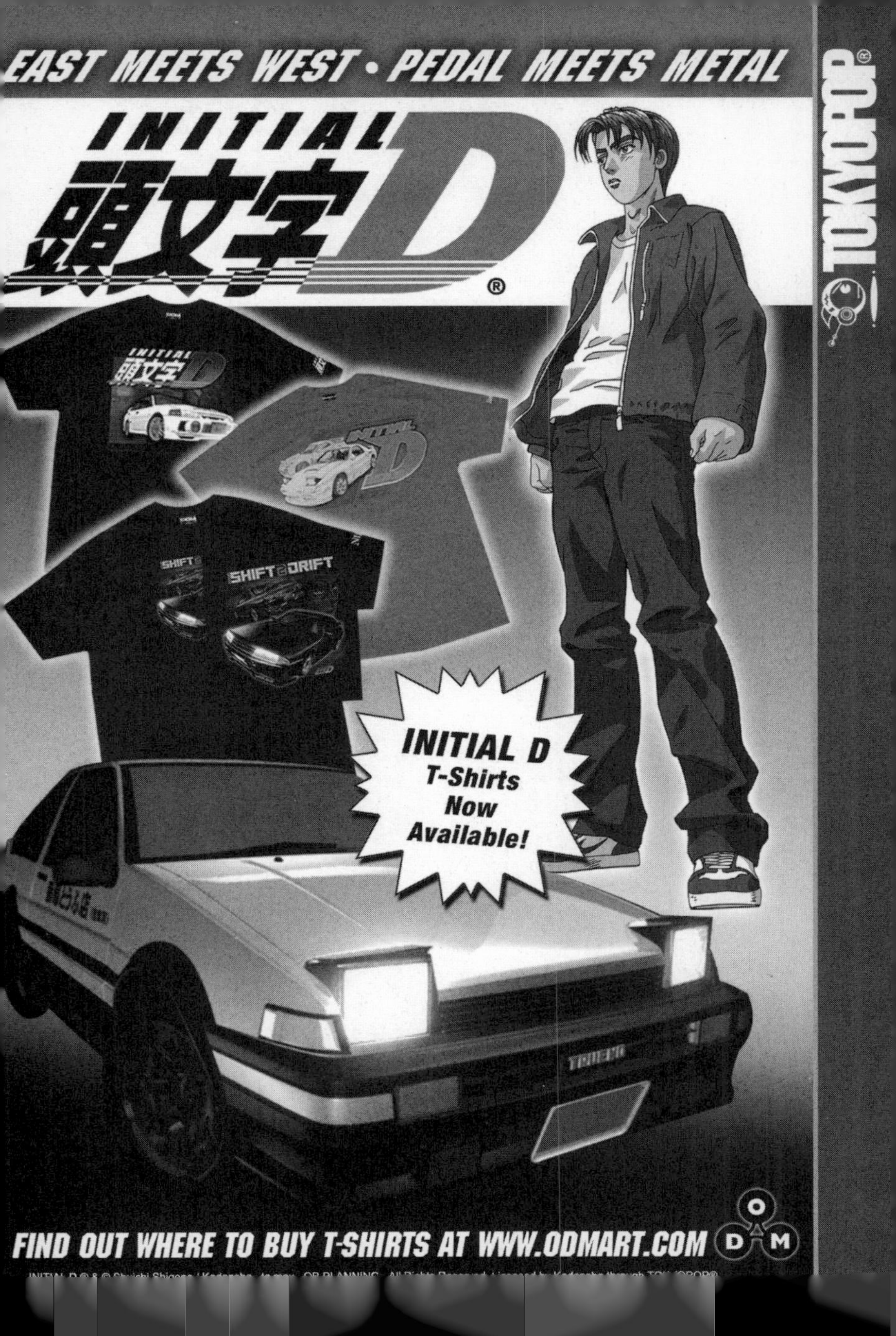
EAST MEETS WEST • PEDAL MEETS METAL
TOKYOPOP®
INITIAL
頭文字D®
INITIAL D
T-Shirts
Now
Available!
FIND OUT WHERE TO BUY T-SHIRTS AT WWW.ODMART.COM
ODM

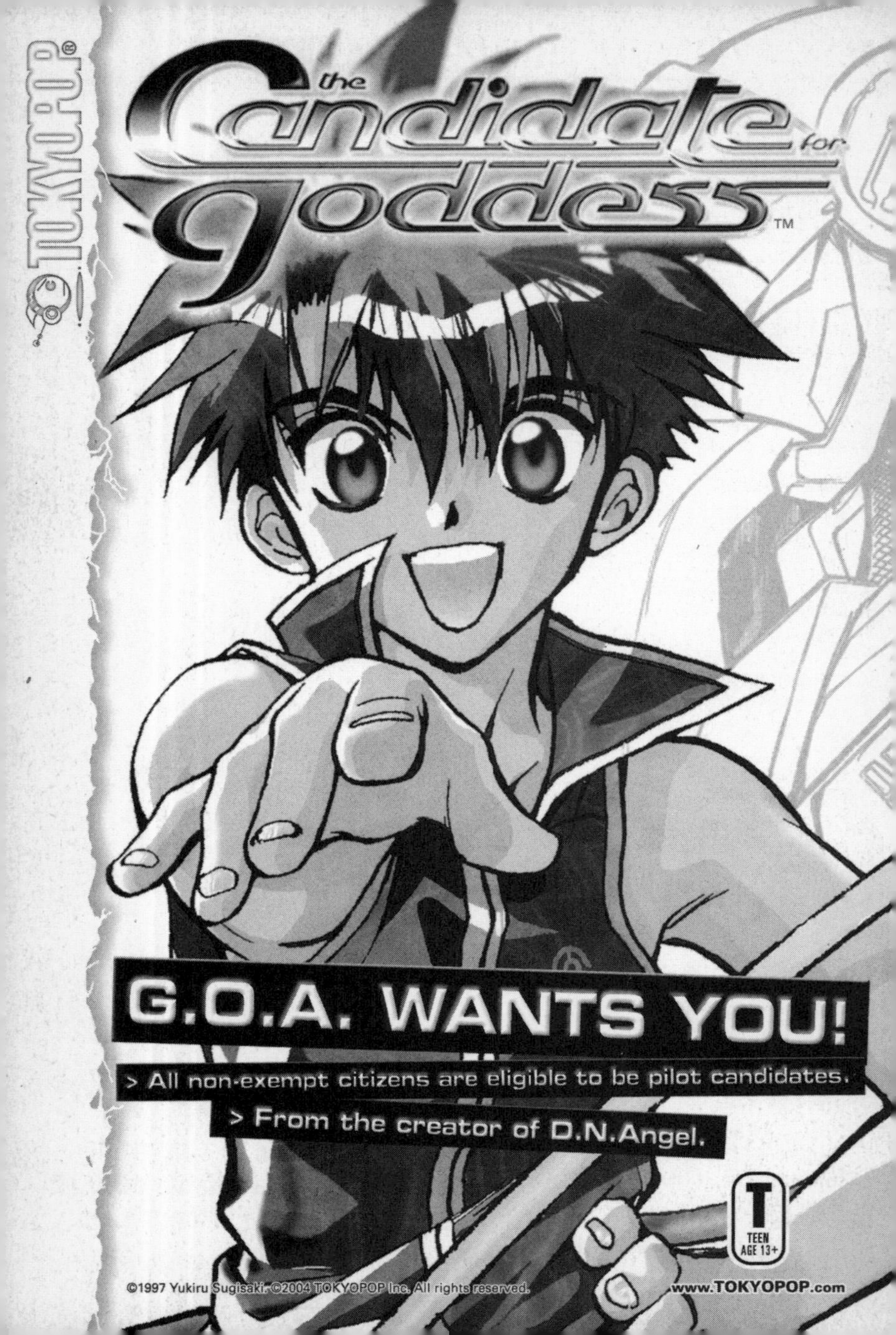

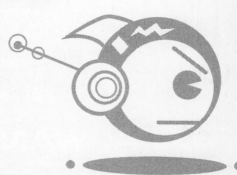

ALSO AVAILABLE FROM 🐢 TOKYOPOP®

MANGA

.HACK//LEGEND OF THE TWILIGHT
ALICHINO
ANGELIC LAYER
BABY BIRTH
BRAIN POWERED
BRIGADOON
B'TX
CANDIDATE FOR GODDESS, THE
CARDCAPTOR SAKURA
CARDCAPTOR SAKURA - MASTER OF THE CLOW
CHRONICLES OF THE CURSED SWORD
CLAMP SCHOOL DETECTIVES
CLOVER
COMIC PARTY
CORRECTOR YUI
COWBOY BEBOP
COWBOY BEBOP: SHOOTING STAR
CRESCENT MOON
CROSS
CULDCEPT
CYBORG 009
D•N•ANGEL
DEARS
DEMON DIARY
DEMON ORORON, THE
DIGIMON
DIGIMON TAMERS
DIGIMON ZERO TWO
DRAGON HUNTER
DRAGON KNIGHTS
DRAGON VOICE
DREAM SAGA
DUKLYON: CLAMP SCHOOL DEFENDERS
ET CETERA
ETERNITY
FAERIES' LANDING
FLCL
FLOWER OF THE DEEP SLEEP
FORBIDDEN DANCE
FRUITS BASKET
G GUNDAM
GATEKEEPERS
GIRL GOT GAME
GUNDAM SEED ASTRAY
GUNDAM WING
GUNDAM WING: BATTLEFIELD OF PACIFISTS
GUNDAM WING: ENDLESS WALTZ
GUNDAM WING: THE LAST OUTPOST (G-UNIT)
HANDS OFF!

HARLEM BEAT
HYPER RUNE
I.N.V.U.
INITIAL D
INSTANT TEEN: JUST ADD NUTS
JING: KING OF BANDITS
JING: KING OF BANDITS - TWILIGHT TALES
JULINE
KARE KANO
KILL ME, KISS ME
KINDAICHI CASE FILES, THE
KING OF HELL
KODOCHA: SANA'S STAGE
LEGEND OF CHUN HYANG, THE
LOVE OR MONEY
MAGIC KNIGHT RAYEARTH I
MAGIC KNIGHT RAYEARTH II
MAN OF MANY FACES
MARMALADE BOY
MARS
MARS: HORSE WITH NO NAME
MINK
MIRACLE GIRLS
MODEL
MOURYOU KIDEN: LEGEND OF THE NYMPH
NECK AND NECK
ONE
ONE I LOVE, THE
PEACH FUZZ
PEACH GIRL
PEACH GIRL: CHANGE OF HEART
PITA-TEN
PLANET LADDER
PLANETES
PRESIDENT DAD
PRINCESS AI
PSYCHIC ACADEMY
QUEEN'S KNIGHT, THE
RAGNAROK
RAVE MASTER
REALITY CHECK
REBIRTH
REBOUND
RISING STARS OF MANGA
SAILOR MOON
SAINT TAIL
SAMURAI GIRL REAL BOUT HIGH SCHOOL
SEIKAI TRILOGY, THE
SGT. FROG
SHAOLIN SISTERS

09.21.04Y

This is the back of the book.
You wouldn't want to spoil a great ending!

This book is printed "manga-style," in the authentic Japanese right-to-left format. Since none of the artwork has been flipped or altered, readers get to experience the story just as the creator intended. You've been asking for it, so TOKYOPOP® delivered: authentic, hot-off-the-press, and far more fun!

DIRECTIONS

If this is your first time reading manga-style, here's a quick guide to help you understand how it works.

It's easy... just start in the top right panel and follow the numbers. Have fun, and look for more 100% authentic manga from TOKYOPOP®!

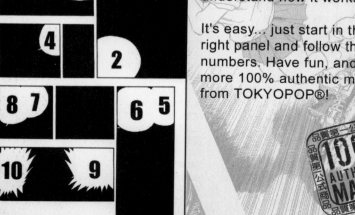

100% AUTHENTIC MANGA